Ford & the Economy

Ford & the Economy

Edited by Lester A. Sobel

Contributing editors: Joseph Fickes, Mary Elizabeth Clifford

Indexer: Grace M. Ferrara

FACTS ON FILE, INC. NEW YORK, N.Y.

Ford & the Economy

Published by Facts on File, Inc.,
119 West 57th Street, New York, N.Y. 10019.

Library of Congress Catalog Card No. 75-43356
ISBN 0-87196-277-2

9 8 7 6 5 4 3 2 1
PRINTED IN
THE UNITED STATES OF AMERICA

Contents

Introduction

WHEN GERALD R. FORD BECAME PRESIDENT of the United States August 9, 1974, the nation was already struggling with what the Congressional Budget Office later described as "the deepest recession in the American economy since the Depression of the 1930s."

The new President, expressing concern over the nation's economic plight, indicated at first that he did not consider the situation to be one of recession. The fourth post-World War II period of inflation had been pushing prices and labor costs continually higher since 1965, and Ford cited inflation, rather than recession, as America's prime economic problem. He said to economic advisers the day he took office that control of inflation was a "high and first priority of the Ford Administration."

By Dec. 2, 1974, however, Ford conceded that "recession" was one of "three serious challenges" the nation was facing. And he told members of the Business Council nine days later that "we are in a recession." After the extent of the decline in employment, "real" production and "real" income had been compared with the increases in prices and wages, Ford told Congress Feb. 5, 1975 that "the economy is in a severe recession." In April 1975, Ford submitted to Congress a manpower report asserting that "recession, inflation" and the energy problem had contributed heavily to 1974's economic woes.

Secretary of the Treasury William Simon had told the Joint Congressional Economic Committee in February that "we have an economy with a short-run problem of recession and a continuing problem of inflation. There is no doubt about the recession; it may very well turn out to be the longest and deepest decline since World

War II. There is also no doubt about the inflation. It dwarfs anything that we have experienced in our peacetime history." Simon noted that inflation had "cut deeply into the real income of consumers as prices transferred income from most consumers to growers of grain and sugar and to owners of oil both here and abroad." Commenting on the recession's effects abroad, Simon reported that "collectively, our partners in the Organization for Economic Cooperation & Development (OECD) saw their growth rate fall to 1½% last year from 6½% in 1973."

James F. Gannon reported in the *Wall Street Journal* April 25, 1975, after interviewing academic economists, business forecasters, corporate executives and other analysts, that "the root cause of this recession was rampant inflation." He explained that "inflation swelled profits and sales figures, producing a phony euphoria among businessmen; it distorted government economic statistics, making it hard to see that a recession was brewing; it bred a buy-and-stockpile psychology among businessmen even as it was eroding purchasing power and increasing the income-tax bite on consumers, producing a save-and-retrench attitude. Inflation's impact is the key thread linking all the many causes of recession, including the Federal Reserve's heavy-handed tight-money policy of 1974 that sought to stop the frightening price spiral at all costs."

The current inflationary period, already more than a decade old, was characterized initially by a high level of employment. The rate of unemployment dropped from an average of 4.5% of the U.S. labor force reported for 1965 to 3.8% in 1966-67, to 3.6% in 1968 and to 3.5% in 1969. But then the unemployment rate began to climb—to 4.9% in 1970 and 5.9% in 1971. The rate dropped to 5.6% in 1972 and to 4.9% in 1973. In 1974, when the average unemployment rate for the year amounted to 5.6%, the trend actually was sharply up—from 5.2% during most of the first half of the year to 7.2% in December. The rate for 1975 was 8.5%.

Prices advanced steadily throughout this period. The Consumer Price Index (sometimes called the "cost-of-living" index) rose from 94.5% of the 1967 average in 1965 to 97.2% in 1966. After 1967 the index increased at what soon became an accelerating rate to 104.2% in 1968, 109.8% in 1969, 116.3% in 1970, 121.3% in 1971, 125.3% in 1972, 133.1% in 1973, 147.7% in 1974 and 161.2% in 1975. The 12.2% increase in the Consumer Price Index in 1974 was the biggest yearly jump since 1947.

Wage rates were also on the way up. The average weekly earnings of production or nonsupervisory workers on nonfarm payrolls rose from $95.06 in 1965 to $98.82 in 1966, $101.84 in 1967,

$107.73 in 1968, $114.61 in 1969, $119.46 in 1970, $127.28 in 1971, $136.16 in 1972, $145.43 in 1973 and $154.45 in 1974. During this period, although their weekly earnings increased, the average number of hours worked by these employes declined steadily—from 38.8 in 1965 to 36.6 in 1974. Average hourly earnings, obviously, rose at a more precipitous rate than did average weekly earnings, increasing from $2.45 in 1965 to $4.22 in 1974.

"Real" earnings, however, rose only during some years of this period. During other years, as the increase in prices outpaced the advance in wages, "real" earnings actually dropped. Average "real" weekly earnings (expressed in 1967 dollars) of production or nonsupervisory workers on nonfarm payrolls rose from $100.59 in 1965 to $104.38 in 1969, fell to $102.72 in 1970, increased to $109.26 in 1973 and dropped to $102.59 in 1974.

Economic production was another casualty of the recession. According to a June 30, 1975 report of the Congressional Budget Office, "the events of 1973 and 1974," including increases in world food and oil prices as well as the earlier inflationary trends, "triggered a sharp and rigid decline in spending" that produced the current recession. As a result, the report noted, "output dropped 7.8% from its peak in the fourth quarter of 1973 to the first quarter of 1975, a percentage decline that was more than twice that of 1957-58 (which had been the deepest of the previous postwar recessions). . . . The recession has produced an enormous gap between current output levels and the potential productive capacity of the economy. In the first quarter of 1975 real GNP [Gross National Production] was only 86% of its potential, the lowest rate in the 23 years for which a measure of potential GNP is available. In current dollar terms, the GNP gap is about $230 billion. . . . On a per capita basis the GNP gap represents a $1,000 loss for every American."

Former Budget Director Charles Schultze, a Brookings Institution associate, told the Senate Budget Committee Dec. 19, 1974 that "the current recession is *not* a typical economic cycle, in which business spending on plant and equipment and inventories or consumer purchases of durable goods temporarily over-reach themselves, fall off, and with the aid of easy money and stimulative fiscal measures, snap back to more normal levels. There are several more pervasive influences at work that tend to make this recession deeper and more stubborn than has been typical of other postwar downturns." According to Schultze, "the first of these features has to do with *oil*. . . . George Perry has compared the sudden increase in the price of crude oil that occurred this year to a giant excise tax levied on the American consumer, siphoning off purchasing power and leading to a drop in real incomes. . . . Ultimately a large part of this diverted flow of funds will be respent—on American exports to the producing countries and on increased investment in domestic energy sources. But in 1974 and 1975 most of the 'oil excise tax' will not be respent—it is being drawn off from the income stream and effectively sterilized. . . . One does not need to invoke complex psychological theories of consumer confidence to explain why markets are weak and sales are falling—about $25 to $30 billion is being removed from the spending stream and not replaced."

Schultze charged that "the behavior of the federal budget has been exacerbating the problem. In the third quarter of 1974 total output in the American economy was 3% below late 1973 and still falling, while unemployment was racing past the 6% level. Despite the recession, however, the federal budget (on a national income accounts basis) was virtually in balance during the third quarter. While output was below a year ago, federal revenues, pushed upward by inflation, were 16% higher. In practice, even if not through intent, we are reverting to the outdated practice of trying to balance the budget in the face of a rapidly falling economy."

This book is an account of these and associated economic troubles against which the Ford Administration struggled. It chronicles the domestic and international events that affected the U.S. economy and details the steps taken by the Ford Administration, often in cooperation with other governments and international bodies, to restore economic stability. Thus, this book continues the narrative of two predecessor volumes, *Inflation & the Nixon Administration: Volume 1, 1969-71,* and *Volume 2, 1972-74*. The material in this book consists largely of the record compiled by FACTS ON FILE in its weekly reports on world events. As in all FACTS ON FILE works, there was a conscientious effort to keep this volume free of bias and to make it a balanced and accurate reference tool.

LESTER A. SOBEL

New York, N.Y.
March, 1976

Ford Takes Charge

Attack on Inflation

Richard M. Nixon was forced out of office as President of the United States Aug. 9, 1974 under pressures generated by the Watergate scandal. Gerald R. Ford, who succeeded Nixon as President, indicated during his first day as head of the U.S. government that an attack on inflation was high on his list of priorities.

Ford takes office. The oath of office as President was administered to Ford in the White House by Chief Justice Warren E. Burger shortly after noon.

After his swearing-in Aug. 9, Ford met with a bipartisan group of Congressional leaders and the Nixon Administration's top economic advisers. The latter were told that control of inflation was a "high and first priority of the Ford Administration."

In his first full day in office Aug. 10, Ford met with the government's top economic policy makers and stressed that he would pursue the budget-cutting policies devised by the Nixon Administration to curb rising prices. Unlike the Nixon approach, however, Ford indicated that he would seek close cooperation from Congress in choosing the areas slated for spending reductions at the outset of the budget-cutting process.

Ford also told his advisers he would ask Congress to sustain Nixon's final veto involving a $13.5 billion appropriations bill.

In a statement issued Aug. 12, Ford strongly rebuked General Motors Corp. for its decision to raise prices on its 1975 model cars by an average of nearly 10%.

"I was very disappointed," Ford said in a statement, "and I hope that the General Motors action will not be viewed as a signal by other auto companies or other industries. In this critical period, the President of the United States cannot call on others to sacrifice if one or more parts of the economy decides to go it alone."

Ford called on "all segments" of the economy to "exercise restraint in their wage and price actions."

In line with his plea to both business and labor for restraint, Ford coupled his admonition to General Motors with an invitation to AFL-CIO President George Meany to confer with him at the White House. The gesture was regarded as forming part of Ford's initial strategy for dealing with inflation by trying to convince the public that the government was moving vigorously to curb rising prices. The "jawboning" session with Meany was held Aug. 13 as Ford intensified his efforts to use moral suasion to offset further escalation of wages and prices. Meany, who had been sharply critical of Nixon's anti-inflation policies, had not visited the White House since June 1973. The meeting with Ford was intended to patch up the feud between government economists and labor and to cement relations between the new President and Meany.

In other actions Aug. 13 related to economic policy, Ford vetoed his first bill—minor legislation that would increase the pay of deputy U.S. marshals. Ford termed the measure "unwise and discriminatory."

Ford also met with Labor Secretary Peter J. Brennan and other department officials to discuss the implementation of programs that could deal with the expected rise in unemployment resulting from a sluggish economy.

Congress' cooperation sought. In a nationally televised address Aug. 12, President Ford urged Congress to cooperate with him in confronting the problems of the nation, citing inflation as the major issue.

"My first priority is to work with you to bring inflation under control," Ford said. "Inflation is our domestic public enemy No. 1. To restore economic confidence, the government in Washington must provide leadership. It does no good to blame the public for spending too much when the government is spending too much."

In a well-received appearance (his speech was interrupted 32 times with applause) before an evening joint session, the new President announced several opening moves on the economic front, pledged an open Administration in domestic and foreign policy and declared his belief in "the absolute necessity of a free press."

But the brunt of the speech was addressed to Congress for cooperation in an attack on inflation. "The nation needs action, not words," he said, and there was "a lot of work to do, let's get on with it." His own "motto" towards Congress, he said, was "communication, conciliation, compromise and cooperation." He was confident Congress would "be my working partner as well as my most constructive critic" and he was "not asking for conformity." "I do not want a honeymoon with you," he said, to an outburst of applause. "I want a good marriage."

Ford asked Congress to join with him "in getting this country revved up and moving. My instinctive judgment is that the state of the union was excellent. But, the state of our economy is not so good."

He said he would work with the members of the newly created budget reform committee "to bring the federal budget into balance by fiscal 1976." The committee had been created under the Congressional Budget & Impoundment Control Act of 1974, signed into law by President Nixon July 12.

While ruling out "unwarranted cuts in national defense," which he considered "nonpartisan policy," Ford suggested that Congress exercise restraint in setting appropriations levels. Instead of getting into a veto situation, he asked, "can't we do the job better by reasonable compromise?"

The President said the "first specific request by the Ford Administration" was not to Congress but the voters: "Support your candidates, congressmen and senators, Democrats or Republicans, conservative or liberal, who consistently vote for tough decisions to cut the cost of government, restrain federal spending and bring inflation under control."

Specifically, Ford said Congress should reactivate the Cost of Living Council, without reimposing controls, to monitor wages and prices "to expose abuses."

He also referred to Senate Democratic Leader Mike Mansfield's (Mont.) request to convene an economic conference of members of Congress, White House consultants "and some of the best economic brains from labor, industry and agriculture." He cited the resolution to assemble a "domestic summit meeting" to plan for stability and growth in the economy. "I accept your suggestion," Ford told Congress, "and I will personally preside."

Excerpts from Ford's speech:

Everywhere I have been as vice president, some 118,000 miles into 40 states and through 55 news conferences, the unanimous concern of Americans is inflation. For once all the polls agree. They also suggest that people blame government far more than either management or labor or the high cost of everything.

You who come from 50 states, three territories and the District of Columbia know this better than I. That is why you have created since I left here your new budget reform committee. I welcome it and will work with its members to bring the federal budget into balance by fiscal 1976. The fact is that for the past 25 years that I had the honor of serving in this body, the federal budget has been balanced in only six.

Mr. Speaker, I am a little late getting around to it, but confession is good for the soul. I have sometimes voted to spend more taxpayers' money for worthy projects in Grand Rapids, Mich., while vigorously opposing wasteful boondoggles in Oklahoma. Be that as it may, Mr. Speaker, you and I have always stood together against unwarranted cuts in national defense. This is no time to change that nonpartisan policy.

Just as escalating federal spending has been a prime cause of higher prices over the years, it may take some time to stop inflation. But we must begin now.

For a start, before your Labor Day recess, Congress should reactivate the Cost of Living Council through passage of a clean bill, without reimposing controls, that will let us monitor wages and prices to expose abuses.

Whether we like it or not, the American wage earner and the American housewife are a lot better economists than most economists care to admit. They know that a government big enough to give you everything you want, is a government big enough to take from you everything you have. If we want to restore confidence in ourselves as working politicians, the first thing we all have to do is learn how to say "no." ...

The economy of our country is critically dependent on how we interact with the economics of other countries. It is little comfort that our inflation is only part of a worldwide problem, or that American families need less of their paychecks for groceries than most of our foreign friends.

As one of the building blocks of peace, we have taken the lead in working toward a more open and equitable world economic system. A new round of international trade negotiations started last September among 105 nations in Tokyo. The others are waiting for the United States Congress to grant the necessary authority to proceed.

With modification, the trade reform bill passed by the House last year would do that. I understand good progress has been made in the Senate committee. But I am optimistic, as always, that the Senate will pass an acceptable bill quickly as a key part of our joint prosperity campaign.

I am determined to expedite other international economic plans. We will be working together with other nations to find better ways to prevent shortages of food and fuel. We must not let last winter's energy crisis happen again. I will push Project Independence for our own good and the good of others. In that, too, I will need your help....

I began to put my Administration's own economic house in order, starting last Friday.

I instructed my Cabinet officers and counsellors and my White House staff to make fiscal restraint their first order of business, and to save every taxpayer's dollar the safety and genuine welfare of the country will permit. Some economic activities will be affected more by monetary and fiscal restraints than other activities. Good government clearly requires that we tend to the economic problems facing our country in a spirit of equity to all our citizens.

Tonight is no time to threaten you with vetos. But I do have the last recourse and I am a veteran of many a veto fight in this very chamber. Can't we do the job better by reasonable compromise?

Minutes after I took the Presidential oath, the joint leadership of Congress told me at the White House that they would go more than half way to meet me. This was confirmed in your unanimous concurrent resolution of cooperation, for which I am deeply grateful. If for my part I go more than half way to meet the Congress, maybe we will find a much larger area of national agreement. ...

Congress OKs wage-price task force. The House gave final approval Aug. 20 to a Senate-passed bill establishing a new wage-price monitoring agency. The cost of living task force, originally requested by President Nixon and quickly endorsed by President Ford, would lack any enforcement powers in its efforts to monitor wages, prices, profits, dividends, interest rates, the concentration of business power and antitrust practices.

The legislation authorized creation of an eight-member Council on Wage and Price Stability made up of government officials. They would be aided by a four-member advisory group composed of persons outside government. Under the bill, the council's statutory authority would extend through Aug. 15, 1975.

The measure had overwhelming support in Congress. President Ford, who signed the bill Aug. 24, met with a bipartisan group of Congressional leaders Aug. 20 to assure them he did not intend to ask for legislation for "either standby or mandatory wage and price controls." There was unanimous agreement, Ford said in a statement issued later, that "as a practical matter, this Congress wouldn't approve such legislation." Business and labor also indicated their opposition to such a plan, Ford added. The statement was designed to head off any "anticipatory" wage or price increases planned by business or labor leaders fearful of the reimposition of controls, according to White House sources.

Ford Aug. 29 named eight people to the new Council on Wage & Price Stability: Treasury Secretary William P. Simon, Agriculture Secretary Earl L. Butz, Commerce Secretary Frederick B. Dent, Labor Secretary Peter J. Brennan, Office of Management and Budget Director Roy Ash, Virginia Knauer, White House consumer affairs assistant, and Anne Armstrong, presidential counselor.

The subject of wage and price guidelines remained a controversial issue. C. Jackson Grayson, former chairman of the Nixon Administration's Price Commission, had said Aug. 25 that the new council would do little to reduce inflation and that it actually could "do some harm." The voluntary approach toward wage and price restraint favored by Ford, Grayson said, could result in higher wages and prices because of fears that mandatory controls were the next step planned by the Administration. "Jawboning" by the council also might reduce Congressional "zeal" for cutting federal spending. Grayson, who opposed mandatory controls because they served as "ceilings" as well as "floors," said he preferred budget cuts, active enforcement of anti-trust laws and tax law changes as anti-inflation weapons.

According to Treasury Secretary Simon Aug. 27, the new monitoring agency "obviously" would have to establish "some guidelines," although he said the single 5.5% wage standard used during the Nixon Administration's Phase 1 and 2 was not what he had in mind. The council "will have to look at each industry separately—what we need is a very flexible system," Simon said.

Other anti-inflation plans under consideration, Simon added, were additional budget cuts for fiscal year 1975; a 6¢ increase in the federal excise tax for gasoline (from 4¢ per gallon to 10¢); and tax law changes providing new incentives for business investment.

In another effort to isolate the inflation problem, the Administration was conducting a comprehensive study of government policies and programs searching for those that fostered inflation by contributing to inefficient operation in the private sector of the economy, the New York Times reported Aug. 27.

Economic summit goals. In late August 1975 Ford started to narrow down the major objectives of his projected summit meeting on the nation's economy.

White House Press Secretary J. F. terHorst said Aug. 26 that Ford had finally set five goals. The broad aims of the summit meeting, according to terHorst, would be to "clarify" the nation's present economic situation; to identify the causes of inflation; to consider "new and realistic" anti-inflation policies; to develop a "consensus" on basic policies; and to define "hardship areas" requiring immediate attention. (The housing and public utilities industries were two such "distressed areas" of the economy, Treasury Secretary William P. Simon said Aug. 27. The President met that day with Housing & Urban Development Secretary James Lynn to discuss the ailing housing industry.)

White House spokesmen sought to dampen public expectation that "miracles" would result from the summit meeting, but they also emphasized that the conference would provide more than "cosmetic treatment" for the economy. The summit was not "designed to be a decision-making apparatus," William Seidman, executive director of the conference, said, but to develop recommendations for subsequent White House action.

Nine preliminary meetings were scheduled in September for representative groups in the economy. Ford would chair two of the meetings and also would preside over the final two-day conference in Washington. An estimated 600–700 persons had been invited to participate, White House spokesmen said.

(It was announced Aug. 22 that the four Congressional members of the summit meeting's steering committee would be Sen. Hubert H. Humphrey [D, Minn.], Sen. John G. Tower [R, Tex.], Rep. John J. McFall [D, Calif.] and Rep. Barber B. Conable [R, N.Y.].)

Federal Reserve Board Chairman Arthur F. Burns said Aug. 22 that consensus on two major points should come out of the summit: agreement that the government should pursue a "prudent fiscal policy" aimed at avoiding budget deficits; and agreement that labor and business leaders should begin an active "dialogue" to develop guidelines governing wage and price behavior.

Ford bars controls. At a televised press conference Aug. 28, Ford reaffirmed his intentions to cut the fiscal 1975 budget and reasserted that "wage and price controls are out, period."

Federal spending would be cut to levels of "less" than $300 billion, Ford said, adding that the effect of this action would be to "make our borrowing from the money market less, freeing more money for housing, for the utilities to borrow." This move was also intended to "convince people who have some doubt that we mean business," Ford said.

On the subject of wage and price controls, Ford said, "I foresee no circumstances under which I can see the reimposition of wage and price controls."

Ford reiterated that fighting inflation, "public enemy No. 1," remained the top priority of his Administration. "If we take care of inflation and get our economy back on the road to a healthy future, I think most of our other domestic programs or problems will be solved."

Ford's other remarks, however, on the subject of inflation and policies that the Administration would pursue to combat rising prices, were confined to generalities because his advisers were "collecting better ideas" from diverse groups on how to wage the battle against inflation.

Ford acknowledged that a public works program costing $4 billion was under consideration. If restrictive monetary and fiscal policies caused the unemployment rate to rise, Ford said, "we will approach this problem with compassion and action if there is a need for it."

He also urged wage earners to "watch every penny" in following the government's example as it "tightened its belt."

As a congressman, Ford had strongly opposed efforts to reduce the defense budget, but at his press conference, the President said, "No budget for any department is sacrosanct. And that includes the defense budget." While continuing to "insist" that "sufficient money" be made available to the armed forces "so that we are strong militarily for the purpose of deterring war or meeting any challenge by any adversary," Ford also called for elimination of "any fat" in the defense budget.

Ford was asked if the U.S. could take any action against oil exporting nations, which recently had decided to reduce production in order to maintain high prices, through cartels such as Aramco, in which a number of U.S. oil firms participated. Ford gave no direct answer, but called for acceleration of Project Independence—increased oil and natural gas drilling, expansion of geothermal and solar research, and greater efforts toward expediting the licensing of new nuclear reactors. Former President Nixon had emphasized these points many times.

The situation also required short-term action entailing international cooperation, the President continued. "High oil prices and poor investment policy" for these nations' greatly increased petrodollars could result in "adverse repercussions" for the industrial world, Ford said, and underscored the need for oil consuming industrial nations to "meet frequently and act as much as possible in concert."

Ford seeks pay increase deferral. President Ford Aug. 30 ordered a three-month delay in a 5.5% pay increase scheduled to take effect Oct. 1 for 3.5 million federal employes.

"We in government set the example, and have a special role to play in the fight against inflation," Ford said in his appeal for other groups in the economy to exercise wage and price restraint. According to Ford, the action could reduce the federal budget by $700 million.

Meany sees slide toward depression. AFL-CIO President George Meany said Aug. 29, in a pre-Labor Day interview, that "we are in a recession now, and there is every indication that we are going into a depression."

Meany said he was not optimistic that President Ford could "turn" the situation around. "I don't expect any miracles from him." "But, at least," Meany said, "I think we'll have no trouble communicating with the President. I think that he is open and frank." "Of course," he added, "his record is very much on the conservative side."

Meany expressed the labor federation's view that the government should move to help finance home building.

Interest rates had to be reduced, he said, and he was highly critical of the tight-money policies of Arthur F. Burns, chairman of the Federal Reserve Board, and of the stance that a balanced budget would solve all economic problems. Meany opposed wage guidelines, saying they were "just as bad as controls."

Meany said labor should not temper its demands despite the inflationary times. Labor had been "quite moderate" in its demands, he said, and had not caused the spiral. "Labor's got to do what they can to keep pace with it," he said.

In a Labor Day radio address Sept. 2, Meany said the basic economic problem was a crisis of confidence in government brought about by "the past five and a half years of deceit and deviousness."

Meany said one of the first things needed to be told was that "today's inflation is not caused by excessive demand" and that "budget cuts, high interest rates and tight money—which might be appropriate weapons against excessive demand inflation—simply will not work."

Jobless help planned. Labor Secretary Peter J. Brennan Sept. 1 outlined plans to launch a public service job program if the U.S. unemployment rate reached 5.5%. At the 5.5% level, Brennan said, an existing $500 million program to create some 100,000 public service jobs was to be doubled. At 6%, another $1 billion was to be pumped in for a 200,000-job level. If the jobless rate neared 7%, a $4 billion, 800,000-job level was contemplated.

The Labor Department announced Sept. 6 that the unemployment rate had gone up from 5.3% of the labor force reported for July to 5.4% in August. It then rose to 5.8% in September, 6% in October, a 13-year high of 6.5% in November and a new 13-year high of 7.2% in December.

The number of workers without jobs rose from 4,874,000 reported for August to a 26-year record 5,300,000 in September, 5,513,000 in October, 5,975,000 in November and a 34-year record 5,535,000 in December.

The December figure reflected a coal strike's impact and continued layoffs in the auto industry and related areas. Unemployment among auto workers climbed from 8.5% in November to 20% in December. (The Detroit jobless rate was 12.4% during December. For all of Michigan, the unemployment rate was 11.2%.) For construction workers, unemployment totaled 15%, its highest level since 1961. Manufacturing unemployment totaled 8.6%, up sharply from 5.4% in August.

Stock market in deep decline. Gloom settled over Wall Street during the first

Unemployment Rate

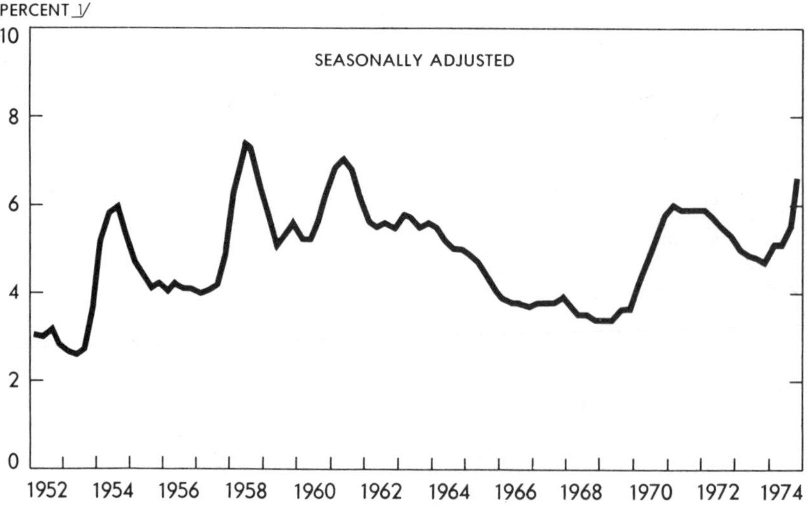

1/UNEMPLOYMENT AS PERCENT OF CIVILIAN LABOR FORCE; QUARTERLY.

SOURCE: DEPARTMENT OF LABOR.

few weeks of the Ford Administration—a mood in tangible contrast to the ebullience with which Washington greeted the new Administration. The difference in moods marked a new distinction being made between the nation's political and economic crises, issues which had been closely linked by the widespread uncertainties associated with the final months of the Nixon Administration.

While politicians experienced a large measure of relief with Nixon's resignation, financial leaders saw no respite ahead for the problem of inflation. Their fears were reflected in the Dow Jones industrial average Aug. 27 when the index dropped to a four-year low, closing at 671.54 on the New York Stock Exchange. Since Aug. 8, the day President Nixon announced his intention to resign, the Dow had dropped 126.02 points. During this period only two sessions posted gains, one of them Aug. 20 when Ford announced his intention to nominate Nelson Rockefeller as vice president. (The index rose 5.01 points.)

The Dow dipped below the 700 level in trading Aug. 22, although it closed at 704.63. The steep plunge continued Aug. 23 when the index fell 17.83 points to close at 686.8. There was a technical rally Aug. 26, but the retreat resumed Aug. 27 when the Dow lost 16.59 points.

Ford scores no-growth approach. In his first environmental policy message, President Ford said Aug. 15 that the "zero economic growth" approach to conserving natural resources "flies in the face of human nature" and must be compromised to meet economic and energy needs.

Ford's message was delivered at the Expo '74 fair in Spokane, Wash. by Interior Secretary Rogers C. B. Morton.

Ford said the previous winter's energy crisis had demonstrated the need for more coal mining, offshore oil exploration, oil shale development and nuclear power plant construction.

Rejecting the zero-growth argument that economic expansion and a clean environment were inconsistent, Ford said expansion was necessary to rebuild cities, improve transportation systems, generate employment and fund important environmental programs already under way.

Ford contended that meeting energy needs did not mean "that we are changing our unalterable course to improve the environment, and it doesn't mean that we are retreating or giving up the fight." He added, however, that "it does mean stretching the timetable in some cases," adjusting some long-range goals "to accommodate the needs of the immediate present," and some "trade-offs."

Ford noted that in the last five years the U.S. had launched "the greatest environmental clean-up in history," but that the energy situation had added a "critical new element in the environmental equation." Full energy production would "entail environmental costs or risks of one kind or another," Ford said, "but we must all be prepared to bear those costs."

U.S. citizens may own gold. President Ford signed legislation Aug. 14 ending a 40-year ban on the sale and purchase of gold by private citizens. The bill had been cleared by the House July 31 after it accepted a Senate amendment providing that no existing law could conflict with the new measure.

Omnibus aid bill approved. President Ford Aug. 22 signed an $11.1 billion housing and community development bill containing broad revisions in the formulas for distribution of federal aid. The House had approved the conference committee version of the bill Aug. 15 by a vote of 377–21. The Senate had accepted the measure, 84–0, Aug. 13.

Most of the money ($8.6 billion over three years), as well as the major departure from previous programs, lay in provisions authorizing locally-administered block grants for community development to replace categorical aid plans such as Model Cities and urban renewal.

The funds would be allocated on the basis of population, degree of overcrowding and poverty (weighted double in the formula). During the three-year period, no community would receive less than the total previously granted under the categorical programs.

A separate provision established a $1.23 billion rent subsidy program for low-income families under which tenants would pay 15%–25% of gross income towards local fair market rentals, with the difference subsidized.

The bill also extended through fiscal 1976 two home ownership and rental assistance programs suspended in 1973, but with authorizations of only $75 million in new funds.

Among other features of the bill:

- The final version included a scaled-down House amendment authorizing $800 million in loan subsidies for developers of housing for the aged and handicapped.
- The Federal Housing Administration mortgage ceiling for single-family homes was increased from $33,000 to $45,000, and down payment requirements were reduced.
- Rules governing real estate loans by savings and loan associations were eased, and the mortgage ceiling was raised from $45,000 to $55,000.
- Annual funding of $40 million was authorized for the experimental program of cash housing allowances for the poor.
- The conference version included a Senate-passed provision extending as a separate program the low-interest loans for private rehabilitation of urban property.
- The bill established minimum rent for public housing units at 5% of gross income, and specified that at least 20% of new public housing be reserved for families with incomes below 50% of the median income for an area.

Congress approves 1975 defense funds. Congress approved, and sent to President Ford for his signature, legislation appropriating $82.6 billion for the Defense Department for fiscal 1975 (July 1, 1974 to June 30, 1975). Passed by voice vote in the Senate Sept. 24 and by a 293–59 margin in the House Sept. 23, the bill provided $4.5 billion less than the original Pentagon request of $87.1 billion.

House-Senate conferees had settled on the compromise total of $82.576 billion despite a warning by Ford Sept. 12 that it would be "extremely unwise" to cut funding levels below the $83.393 billion approved by the House Aug. 6. But Rep. George Mahon (D, Tex.), chairman of the House Appropriations Committee, told the House Sept. 23 that given the existence of double-digit inflation, the compromise was "regarded by the conferees as the best that can be reasonably done at this time for national defense."

The bill still ran into opposition on the House floor among members who saw it as excessively large and inflationary, and among those opposing sections of the bill containing concealed appropriations for the Central Intelligence Agency and $205 million for the F-111, aircraft not requested by the Air Force.

Pre-Summit Conferees Ponder Problems & Solutions

President Ford's summit conference on the nation's economic predicament took place Sept. 27–28, 1974. It was preceded by a series of pre-summit meetings at which representatives of various sectors of the economy, economists and government officials presented their views on the situation.

Ford meets with economists. President Ford presided over the first of several pre-summit meetings Sept. 5 when 28 economists gathered at the White House for a seven-hour televised conference to devise anti-inflation policies for the new Administration. Ford opened the meeting with an appeal for a "battle plan" providing "action that is practical, possible and as rapid in its effects as we can reasonably expect." However, Ford also reiterated his belief that "there is no quick fix for what ails our economy."

The Administration had set as one of its principal goals for these series of 12 meetings the development of consensus over economic policies that were potentially divisive as well as being partisan. Ford emphasized these views at the conference, which featured a number of prominent Democrats and was also attended by a bipartisan group of Congressional leaders. "The American people fall in the middle and they want us to take those actions that fall in the middle," he said.

The conference, Ford said, "unites Republicans and independents and Democrats in an election year against an enemy that doesn't recognize one political party from another."

"The President cannot lick inflation," Ford continued. "The Congress cannot lick inflation. Business, labor, agriculture and other segments of America cannot lick inflation. Separately we can only make it worse, but together we can beat it to its knees."

"The people understand economics very very well and they are sick and tired of having politics played with their pocketbooks," Ford said.

As Ford sought to defuse inflation's political impact, Senate Democrats were caucusing and decided to stay in session for the remainder of the year if necessary to act on Administration proposals to treat inflation.

Ford was present for the beginning and end of the day long meeting with economists. Cabinet members, White House aides, congressmen and others also heard the economists present their individual views. The diverse group voiced agreement on the nature of the nation's economic ills but exhibited less unanimity on how to deal with those problems. Participants, representing a wide range of views from business, labor and academia, predicted continued "stagflation" combining the basic features of a recession—stagnant economic growth and unemployment possibly rising to 6.5% by mid-1975, and inflation—rising prices. Several speakers, however, voiced confidence that the inflation rate would subside slightly from the current double digit rates to just below 10% at an annual rate. There was little prospect that the nation would slip into a depression, according to the experts.

There was broad agreement from economists of widely differing views that the Federal Reserve should ease its current policy of strict monetary restraint in order to lower interest rates and prevent a precipitous slowdown in the economy. Those who dissented from this view—Andrew Brimmer, formerly of the Federal Reserve, John Kenneth Galbraith of Harvard University and Milton Friedman of the University of Chicago—favored the tight money approach which aimed at curbing spending and making borrowing more difficult.

The economists generally endorsed the Administration's efforts to couple monetary restraint with fiscal restraint, but there were few suggestions on how much should be cut from the federal budget or which programs should be reduced.

There was little support for reimposition of wage and price controls, although Galbraith advocated a return to mandatory controls. Some favored continued "jawboning" in an effort to achieve voluntary limits on wage and price increases, but others, such as former Treasury Secretary George P. Shultz and former Price Commission Chairman C. Jackson Grayson Jr., opposed even that action. They feared that business and labor might raise prices and wages in "anticipation" that jawboning augured a return to mandatory controls.

Many economists asked for an overhaul of federal regulations governing transportation, banking, agriculture and other areas that they said acted as structural impediments to anti-inflation efforts by supporting high prices, limiting competition or creating business or labor monopolies. Some proposed stiffer antitrust enforcement and Hendrick Houthakker of Harvard suggested a "restructuring" of the auto industry to increase price competition.

There was general agreement that efforts must be made to defuse the expected demand for higher wages by organized labor. Several economists favored the use of tax cuts for lower income groups to take the pressure off wage demands. Richard Cooper of Yale University, whose call for a $10 billion-$15 billion tax cut for the poor was one of the most radical proposals put forth at the meeting, said the nation could afford the loss of tax revenues because of the huge flow of investment funds to the U.S. that was anticipated from the oil-producing nations. Galbraith urged the Administration to increase taxes paid by corporations and individuals earning more than $15,000 annually.

The White House made it known Sept. 17 that President Ford had asked

Paul W. McCracken, a University of Michigan economist and former chairman of the Council of Economic Advisers, to prepare policy proposals. He was also named to serve as special consultant at the economic summit meeting.

Democrats offer to stay in session—A Sept. 5 caucus of Senate Democrats unanimously approved a resolution offering to remain in Congressional session throughout the year if necessary to enact legislation in cooperation with President Ford to combat inflation. The resolution urged the upcoming White House economic summit conference to consider "every alternative."

The caucus assigned to its policy unit the task of devising specific anti-inflation proposals.

Senate Majority Leader Mike Mansfield (D, Mont.), an advocate of wage and price controls, sponsored the resolution to extend the session. Senate Majority Whip Robert C. Byrd (D, W. Va.) strongly urged "action now." "The country cannot afford to wait until next year," he said. "We want to debunk the idea that Congress is ready to wrap up and go home" while the nation faced severe economic problems.

The resolution arose in part from the Democrats' concern over public reaction to a Democratic-led Congress not being in session to cope with what President Ford had designated the nation's No. 1 problem.

Tight-money policies debated—Although economists of widely divergent views urged the Federal Reserve to relax its tight money policies, two top economic advisers to President Ford quickly opposed suggestions that the nation's money supply be expanded and credit eased.

In his first news conference as chairman of the Council of Economic Advisers, Alan Greenspan said Sept. 6 that any significant easing of monetary policies would "serve no useful purpose" and would "almost certainly put us back into the situation we find ourselves in—and perhaps worse" because people would be lulled into a false belief that the nation's economic difficulties had been solved.

In a speech given in Texas Sept. 6, Treasury Secretary William P. Simon said fiscal and monetary restraint "must be exercised patiently and consistently for a sustained period of time." Restraint, Simon said, was the only alternative to economic controls, which he labeled the "enemy of the markets."

Despite the resistance to proposals for an easing of tight money policies expressed by Administration policy makers, unidentified officials of the Federal Reserve were reported Aug. 31 and Sept. 8 to have emphasized that a relaxation of monetary policies had already taken place, although they warned that no "substantial" further easing should be expected.

An indication of a move toward lower interest rates was seen in the downward movement of interest rates on federal funds—short term loans within the banking network. In the week ending July 3, the rate peaked at 13.55%, but by the week ending Sept. 6, interest had fallen to 11.5%.

Another sign of the eased monetary policy was seen in technical changes made by the Federal Reserve in bank reserve requirements on large certificates of deposit. It was announced Sept. 4 that the bank reserve requirements on certificates of $100,000 or more left on deposit for at least four months at a set rate of interest was being reduced from 8% to 5%, increasing the availability of bank credit.

Several reasons were cited prompting the policy change toward lower interest rates and expanded money supply, chief among them the recent decline in stock prices. Between Aug. 8 and Sept. 9, the Dow Jones industrial average had fallen 154.82 points on the New York Stock Exchange, closing at 656.84 Aug. 29—the lowest level since May 1970.

The market rallied Aug. 30, gaining 21.74 points to close at 678.58, but the recovery was short-lived. The Dow lost 15.25 points Sept. 3 and 15.33 points Sept. 4 when it closed at 648. There was another sharp upturn Sept. 5 when the index advanced 22.76 points, but selling resumed Sept. 9, when the index lost 14.94 points.

The Dow lost 12.98 points Sept. 12 to close at 641.74, another four-year low.

(One reflection of the troubles on Wall Street was the drop in price of a seat on the New York Stock Exchange. Membership sold for $65,000 Sept. 12—a 20-

year low and sharp drop from the high set in 1969 when a seat sold for $515,000.)

Another reason given for the easing of monetary restrictions was a belief that the Federal Reserve had succeeded in slowing the annual rate of growth in the money supply to 4%–5% on a month-to-month basis.

No letup in inflation rate seen. President Ford's economic advisers indicated Sept. 13 that they did not expect the nation's inflation rate to ease during the final months of 1974 despite earlier predictions made during the Nixon Administration that the current rise in prices would abate.

Treasury Secretary William Simon said he expected prices to continue to rise by 9% or more. White House economic adviser Kenneth Rush foresaw an inflation rate possibly exceeding 10% at the end of the year.

Alan Greenspan, chairman of the Council of Economic Advisers, said Sept. 12, after release of the August Wholesale Price Index report showing a 17.8% rise in prices over 12 months, "it does not appear as though the inflation rate is turning down."

The Federal Reserve Bank of New York concurred in those assessments, noting Sept. 7 that the price situation remained "unrelentingly dismal."

According to a survey by the National Association of Purchasing Management reported Sept. 9, economic indicators for August pointed to a worsening recession, including deteriorating business activity, a slowdown in new orders and production and rising unemployment.

Ford, labor leaders confer. President Ford met with 29 union officials at the White House Sept. 11 in the second of the pre-summit meetings.

Ford, who presided over the morning session of the day-long meeting, repeated his call for "self-imposed" restraint on wage and price demands and restated his flat opposition to reimposition of economic controls—a view that was widely shared by union officials and expressed at the meeting by AFL-CIO President George Meany.

The subject of wages and wage contracts was not emphasized at the meeting, although union officials defended their efforts to keep up with rising prices by seeking higher wages. Wages were not responsible for the current inflationary spiral, the labor leaders declared. Alan Greenspan, chairman of the Council of Economic Advisers, supported their position, displaying a chart showing that the inflation rate exceeded wage costs. "I find it hard to believe that anyone seeing that could believe that wages are responsible for inflation," Greenspan said.

Most of the discussion focused on the problem of rising unemployment. "All America agrees with your announced objective of breaking the back of inflation," Meany told Ford. "But we're also worried about recession—the forgotten twin of America's economic woes." Workers, whose only "hedge against inflation is their job," were fearful of a worsening recession, Meany said, adding, "We look to our government for protection."

Ford responded that he had ordered the Labor Department to speed up the spending of $350 million allocated under the Comprehensive Employment and Training Act, which would finance 85,000 public sector jobs. Another $65 million in discretionary funds would be dispersed "immediately" to communities "in which unemployment is highest" by Labor Secretary Peter J. Brennan, Ford said. Although the accelerated spending represented no commitment of new funds, Ford said that use of these existing programs would provide about $1 billion for "170,000 public service jobs this coming winter."

Labor officials also suggested that new jobs could be generated with federal aid programs for the housing industry, for public utilities whose projects had been postponed because of the lack of cash, and for the rebuilding of railroad tracks.

Labor leaders were unanimous in their criticism of the tight-money policy the Federal Reserve had followed. Lane Kirkland, secretary-treasurer of the AFL-CIO, said a restrictive credit policy "enshrines what not too long ago used to be regarded as usury as an instrument of national politics. It sanctifies loan sharks." Tight money policies were "equivalent to treating a fever with a dose of arsenic," Kirkland declared.

Tight money, Meany said, "only chokes an economy that needs to grow." "It would be bad government, in our view, to fight inflation by making recession worse," he continued. The current inflation was not caused by excessive demand—the classic cause of rising prices, Meany said. Therefore, classic antidotes such as "budget cuts, high interest rates and tight money" will not work, according to Meany.

Roy Ash, director of the Office of Management and Budget, discussed the Administration's budget cutting proposals during the afternoon session. He encountered strong opposition from union officials to any plans to reduce federal expenditures for social programs.

Murray H. Finley, president of the Amalgamated Clothing Workers, said in response to Ash's presentation documenting rising federal expenditures for social programs and declining defense spending, "It's not charts, it's not numbers, it's the kid who doesn't have enough nutrition when he goes to school." "If the problem is balancing the budget," Finley said "why not look at who pays our taxes" and raise taxes paid by corporations and the rich.

Jerry Wurf, president of the American Federation of State, County and Municipal Employes, charged that corporate profits "are going up into triple digits." Tax loopholes were "letting corporations get away with blue murder" while the "load falls heavier and heavier" on the poor.

At the outset of the meeting, Ford said he welcomed "unvarnished truth." Much of the give and take between labor leaders and Administration officials was blunt. Meany told the President that he hoped the "American people will be spared the optimistic rhetoric so often used by the past Administration." George Hardy, president of the Service Employes Union, added, "The track record you inherited from the last Administration stinks."

Controversy over controls policy—There was some dispute during the pre-summit meetings over Ford Administration policy.

A remark by President Ford's White House aide, Robert Hartmann, prompted a minor economic controversy Sept. 17. While disavowing any expertise in the field of economics, Hartmann told a Washington group that Ford's statements opposing reinstatement of wage-price controls should "not be written in stone."

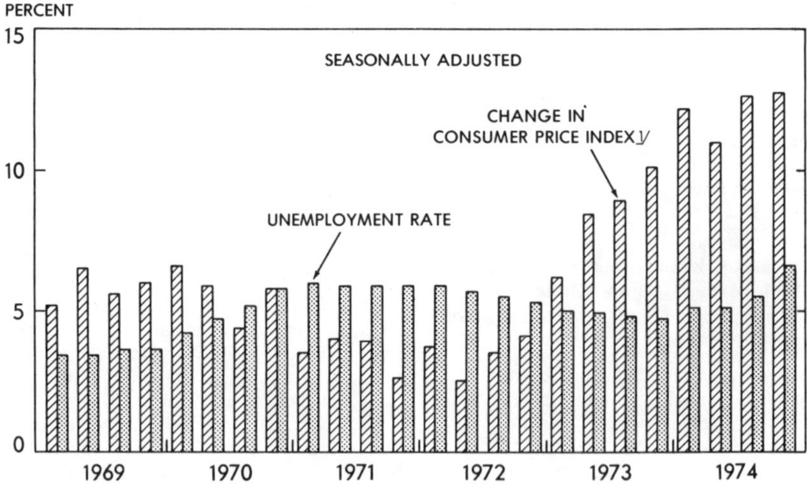

Another White House aide, L. William Seidman, tried to calm fears that the Administration might seek the use of economic controls. Asked Sept. 24 what circumstances in the near future might prompt the Administration to consider controls, Seidman replied, "None." He added, however, "Basically, you try what you think is the proper program and see if you're making any progress. If you've tried that and it hasn't succeeded, then you have to try something else."

The New York Times reported Sept. 25 that a number of leading economic consultants were advising their corporate clients to plan for controls. Some economists believed that the recent sharp jumps in consumer and wholesale prices reflected precautionary price increases undertaken by business as a means of offsetting the expected controls.

Housing industry meeting. James T. Lynn, secretary of housing and urban development, met in Atlanta Sept. 12 with housing and construction industry representatives, who warned that the industry had become both the "victim of inflation" and the "scapegoat" of the Administration's anti-inflation policies aimed at monetary and fiscal restraint. Rising materials prices were reflected in the cost of home buying; tight credit policies and high interest rates were reducing the amount of mortgage money and raising rates on the funds available to purchasers to "intolerable" levels, they said.

"The housing industry needs relief if it is going to survive," Lewis Cenker, president of the National Association of Home Builders, told the conference. Alan Greenspan, chairman of the Council of Economic Advisers, responded that there was little the Administration could do to aid the housing industry until inflation eased. He warned against "palliative" measures that might cause conditions to worsen. Greenspan said he anticipated an "exceptionally sluggish, dull economy—one that isn't likely to pick up in any meaningful way at least until the spring of 1974." A recovery in housing starts, which had dropped to a level 38% below the previous year, "will continued to be thwarted until the rate of inflation has been reduced by several percentage points," Greenspan said.

Conference delegates, who included representatives of construction unions, builders, construction suppliers and thrift institutions, agreed that little upturn in the housing industry could be expected before early 1975. To spur that recovery, they sought an easing of the Federal Reserve's tight money policies, expanded use of government funds to provide mortgage money at below-market levels, and tax breaks on savings to encourage increased deposits at savings institutions, which were the chief sources of mortgage funds.

Advance Mortgage Corp. of Detroit, a subsidiary of Citicorp, holding company of the U.S.' second largest bank, had said Aug. 23 that the housing market was experiencing its worst slump since World War II, and warned that prospects could worsen.

The housing industry slump deepened as 1974 advanced. The number of housing starts declined from a seasonally adjusted rate of 1,126,000 units in August to an eight-year low of 868,000 in December. The total for the year was at a seven-year low of 1,340,000, down 35% from the 1973 level. The year's decline was the steepest since 1943.

The number of building permits issued during December was 9.9% higher than the November total, which was a record low. Although the increase marked the first improvement in building permits since March 1974, the December pace was 38% below the year-earlier level.

(Housing industry representatives met with Ford at the White House Dec. 13 and asked that he consider three proposals to give consumers "quick purchasing power." Ford was asked to lift a freeze imposed in 1972 on federal aid to low and middle income families seeking to buy housing, to implement an unused federal law allowing federal aid for mortgages on houses built without Federal Housing Administration help, and to ease monetary policy in order to make more money available for mortgages.)

Food-industry conference. The impact of inflation on the agriculture and food industry dominated discussions held Sept. 12 when Agriculture Secretary Earl L. Butz met in Chicago with 58 delegates to the pre-summit conference representing farmers, food processors, trade associations, labor and consumers.

Strong support was voiced for the Administration's plan to cut federal spending and most of the delegates opposed reinstatement of wage and price controls. "One significant contributing cause [of inflation] has been federal budgetary deficits totaling $95.2 billion since 1968 which have been financed through expansionary monetary policies," a representative of Jewel Food Stores Inc. told the conference. She also warned that "productivity increases, at all stages of food distribution other than at the farm, have not kept pace with wage increases" and had caused inflation to worsen. Many of the delegates attacked environmental, occupational health and safety standards, union rules, and federal transportation regulations, claiming they reduced the industry's efficiency.

"This conference has given me a new determination to balance the budget," Butz told the group. He also revealed that anti-inflationary steps planned by the Administration did not include new incentives to farmers for expanded food supply. Butz said he would not seek an increase in milk price supports and would not set higher target prices for key crops during 1975 or raise the rates on price-supported loans for those crops.

Butz and most of the delegates at the conference attributed the rise in food prices to the widening spread between prices received at the farm level and prices paid by the consumer.

Although Butz revised upward by 1% department price forecasts issued only Aug. 23 (now expected to show a 12-month increase of 16% by the end of the year) he also predicted that the "bulk" of the price increases "are behind us."

There was nearly unanimous opposition at the conference to any type of federal controls imposed on the export of U.S. grains. Such a step would reduce the price of grain received by the farmer and widen the already large gap between farm costs (soaring because of the rising price for fertilizers, gasoline and other farm supplies) and farm income. Although export controls would reduce grain prices in the short run, delegates agreed, controls in the long run would result in a curtailment of crop production and higher prices for grain and grain fed livestock.

Business leaders' meeting. Forty of the nation's top business leaders met in Pittsburgh Sept. 16 with Commerce Secretary Frederick Dent, White House aides and Congressional leaders. The group expressed strong support for budget cutting proposals planned by the Ford Administration and other policies of fiscal restraint, but they were emphatic in their opposition to a continuation of tight money policies. They voiced concern, evident at other pre-summit meetings held by the White House for representative groups in the economy, that the economy was weakening while financial strains were worsening.

The group unanimously agreed that the federal budget should be held to $300 billion or less for fiscal 1975 (which began July 1). Many also favored a balanced budget for the current year and efforts to create a fiscal surplus for fiscal 1976 (beginning July 1, 1975). (The use of renewed wage and price controls as an anti-inflation weapon was widely rejected.)

Most participants called on the Federal Reserve to make small adjustments in its tight money policy "to stop the developing liquidity problem." Reginald Jones, chairman of General Electric Co., suggested that the Federal Reserve allow the money supply to expand at a rate 2%–3% below the prevailing inflation rate, significantly easing credit curbs but also slowing the growth of the money supply as inflation abated.

There was a strong support for government use of tax incentives to spur investment that could be used in capital expansion. Among the proposals were "substantial increases in the investment tax credit," reduced capital gains taxes, a "rollover" provision allowing deferral of tax payments on capital gains if the money were reinvested, tax credits on savings account interest and stock dividends, a temporary tax surcharge on incomes above $15,000 with the revenue earmarked for reducing the federal debt, "tax relief for low income people," and as an added incentive to increase industrial capacity, easing of antipollution standards and occupational health and safety regulations.

Natural resources conference. Interior Secretary Rogers C. B. Morton and other

Administration officials discussed the inflationary impact of terminating oil price controls during a meeting in Dallas Sept. 16 with 45 representatives of the oil, natural gas, coal, metals mining and electric power industries.

Although most industry executives charged that federal price controls caused shortages and aggravated inflation, Morton warned that phasing out controls might take "two years or more" to prevent an international oil cartel from driving up the unregulated price of fuel and adding to the nation's inflationary problems.

(The price of "old" oil, that which was produced at pre-1972 output levels, was subject to a federal price ceiling of $5.25 a barrel. The remaining "new" oil sold at free market prices. According to the Wall Street Journal Sept. 17, new oil was selling for about $10 a barrel, while imported oil cost an average $9.50 a barrel.)

(Morton and Treasury Secretary William P. Simon had earlier indicated strong backing for an end to oil price controls although neither proposed a timetable for the decontrol action. Their remarks were made before a Sept. 10 meeting of the National Petroleum Council, an industry group that advised the Interior Department.)

Consumer representatives at the Dallas meeting called for a rollback in the price of crude oil. As an alternative to price decontrol, Rep. John Anderson (R, Ill.) urged enactment of a bill pending in Congress imposing a temporary windfall profits tax on oil producers. Anderson similarly called for the repeal of the oil depletion allowance to reduce inflationary pressures. Anderson challenged charges by industry spokesmen that environmental and health safeguards spurred inflation by increasing the costs of energy production. The short-term costs of these regulations should be viewed against their long-term benefits, Anderson said. It was also suggested that investment in energy conservation, as opposed to investments in new supplies, should be emphasized to alleviate shortages.

There was also support for a change in U.S. foreign policy that aimed at confronting the oil producing nations to force a reduction in oil prices.

Sen. Floyd K. Haskell (D, Colo.), who attended the Dallas meeting, and Sen. Henry M. Jackson (D, Wash.) Sept. 16 attacked the Administration's energy policies, which they said "had not focused" on alternatives to the two-tiered price system for old and new oil. The legislators, both members of the Senate Interior Committee, charged that new oil could be brought under federal price control, at a savings of $5–$10 billion in consumers' costs without significantly hurting industry incentives for domestic oil production.

Project Independence, they said, would be "massively inflationary, bidding up the prices of those commodities, services and capital goods that are in the shortest supply," in an effort to make the nation self-sufficient in energy supplies.

Industrialists meet in Detroit. There was sharp debate Sept. 19 over suggestions by a group of the nation's major industrialists that slashes in the federal budget be coupled with grants of tax incentives to industry. A bipartisan group of Congressional leaders who attended the conference, presided over by Commerce Secretary Frederick B. Dent, criticized the proposals.

Rep. Barber B. Conable (R, N.Y.), who said it was a "very frustrating thing" to trim the federal budget, asked how tax incentives for one group could be set against spending cuts for others. Rep. William D. Ford (D, Mich.) warned that states might act to offset their revenue losses resulting from cuts in the federal budget's social welfare payments by raising business taxes.

In another controversial proposal, General Motors Corp. Chairman Richard C. Gerstenberg asked the Administration to impose a "three-year freeze" on new federal environmental and safety standards, a request that was echoed by Ford Motor Co. Chairman Henry Ford 2nd, who urged a deferral of "at least five years," beginning January 1975, on "all but the most urgently needed new standards." Chrysler Corp. President John Riccardo asked for a postponement in enactment of new rules until 1980.

The federal regulations were too costly, had accomplished little, and had reduced industrial productivity, according to most of the conference delegates. "This is no time for an overzealous attitude by the Environmental Protection Agency," Philip O. Geier, president of a large machine tool firm, said. David Lewis, chairman of General Dynamics Corp., charged, "Costs were brushed aside when Congress made these [environmental] laws. What we have to do now is to de-zeal the environmental zealots for a few years and give industry a chance to catch up."

The remarks prompted an angry reply from Russell W. Peterson, chairman of the President's Council on Environmental Quality. Federal pollution control and safety standards for cars had contributed "only .5% to our current rate of inflation," Peterson said. "There are some things besides goods that people are interested in."

In other respects, suggestions at the industrialists' meeting resembled those that came out of the earlier pre-summit conference for business leaders. Most participants favored a slight easing of monetary policies, further tax incentives to spur productivity, and efforts to balance the federal budget. There was widespread, but not unanimous, opposition to reinstatement of wage-price controls.

Social services meeting. Representatives of the poor, the aged, the handicapped, the young, minority groups, and consumers met in Washington Sept. 19–20 with Administration officials and Congressional leaders to discuss ways to curb inflation in the fields of social welfare, health, and education.

Controversy quickly dominated the proceedings. Delegates to the conference charged Sept. 19 that the Administration planned to implement one of its principal anti-inflation policies—fiscal restraint—by making major budgetary cutbacks in the Health, Education & Welfare Department's social services programs.

Asked why the poor should be expected to make the greatest sacrifices in the fight against inflation, Alan Greenspan, chairman of the Council of Economic Advisers, remarked, "Everybody is hurt by inflation. If you really want to examine percentage-wise who was hurt most in their income, it was Wall Street brokers." Catcalls drowned out the rest of his remarks.

Greenspan's comment had been prompted by statements from Clarence Mitchell, representing the National Association for the Advancement of Colored People, and Jerry Wurf, president of the American Federation of State, County and Municipal Employes. Mitchell, noting that the jobless rate among blacks and other minorities in August was 9.2% or almost double the national average, said unemployment for large numbers of persons was at "intolerable" limits.

Administration policies, Wurf said, were hurting the poor and middle income Americans while encouraging big profits for businessmen. "You are saying, 'Let those who are suffering suffer a little more.' "

Greenspan denied charges that Administration policies were aimed at aiding big business. In an effort to dull the controversy, Greenspan continued, "To single out groups who are suffering is wrong. Everyone is suffering. We all suffer. What concerns me is the creation of social divisiveness."

Wurf cited statistics on the income of hospital workers. With the exception of the "outrageous incomes" of physicians, he said, hospital workers earned an average $6,100 a year. "They are suffering a hell of a lot worse from high prices than Wall Street brokers."

Citing the impact of inflation on social services, Sen. Edward Kennedy (D, Mass.) quoted from an HEW position paper prepared for the conference showing that $2 billion–$3 billion in the total $43 billion increase in Medicaid and Medicare appropriations was caused by rising prices.

(According to the HEW paper, "direct out-of-pocket payments by consumers for medical care fell from 68% to 35% of personal health care expenditures" between 1950–1973. "However, due to inflation, population growth and expanded use of services, out-of-pocket expenditures actually increased by almost $21 billion during the same period" to total $28 billion.)

The problem of rising health costs was also discussed Sept. 20, when the Consumer Price Index for August was released showing that the 1.5% monthly increase in the cost of health care outpaced the average inflation rate, which was 1.3%.

In the four months since wage and price controls had been lifted, the medical component of the index had increased at an annual rate of 17.6%, compared with a 13.5% increase for the index as a whole.

A statement endorsed by 16 major national groups and signed by 69 participants to the conference was issued Sept. 20 as a counter-position paper to protest possible budget cuts by the Administration.

"No evidence was presented at the conference that federal spending levels have been one of the major causes of high inflation of the past 18 months," the paper declared. "Rather, the inadequacy of federal health, education and welfare expenditures have resulted in a deterioration of services to the poor and low income groups, which is unjustified at any time and particularly undesirable during a period of rapid inflation. Any increases in the already too-high unemployment rate is a completely unacceptable approach to meeting the current inflationary period."

"Major tax reform" and "tax increases based on the ability to pay" would prove more effective anti-inflation weapons than budget cuts penalizing the poor, the statement said.

Signers of the statement included nearly all of the meeting's participants who represented the poor, the aged, the handicapped, minority groups and consumers. (The balance of the delegates—about 150—represented professional groups in the health and education fields.) Among the wide-ranging groups which endorsed the statement were the AFL-CIO, the League of Women Voters, the National Council of Churches, the National Urban League, and the National Conference of Catholic Charities. Wilbur J. Cohen, a former HEW secretary and developer of Medicaid and Medicare, was a chief backer of the consensus statement.

At a news conference following the tumultuous two-day meeting, HEW Secretary Caspar Weinberger justified cutbacks in the federal budget, saying that many persons regarded federal spending as a major cause of inflation and therefore, attempts to reduce expenditures would be perceived as progressive steps in the inflation fight.

"The Administration will not base its anti-inflationary effort on increasing the burdens of our less advantaged citizens," Weinberger said. "Our efforts will be to deliver more benefits at less cost to those who are most in need. Such sacrifices as are required will be borne by all our citizens."

Finance & banking conference. Arthur Burns, chairman of the Federal Reserve Board, indirectly confirmed reports that tight money policies were being eased and said "there will be no credit crunch in our country." But he also warned that "in view of the intensity of inflation, a policy of moderate monetary restraint remains appropriate." Burns' remarks were made Sept. 20 before a pre-summit conference in Washington attended by representatives of banking and savings institutions and the securities industry, which had been among the first groups to feel the effects of high interest rates and a shortage of capital.

The meeting resulted in nearly unanimous agreement that the Administration should attempt to balance the federal budget. There was also support for tax incentives to spur investment and savings and for removal of government regulations on business—three major themes voiced at most other pre-summit conferences. Like other groups, finance leaders also opposed reimposition of wage and price controls. There was also wide backing for special federal help for the unemployed and other victims of inflation.

Burns, whose tight money policies had been criticized by a wide range of participants in the pre-summit meeting series, coupled his endorsement of a slight relaxation in restrictive money policies with a plea for fiscal restraint. "If fiscal policy is tilted toward surplus instead of deficits, it can make an enormous contribution to curbing inflation and lowering interest rates," he said.

One of the tax proposals with broad support from participants at the conference was offered by savings and loan institution executives. They suggested an income tax exemption on the first $1,000 in interest paid on a depositors' savings account, an action that officials said could generate $24 billion in additional deposits annually for the industry. (It was also acknowledged that such a step would cost the Treasury about $2 billion annually in lost revenue.)

Transportation industries conference. Representatives of transportation industries and unions met Sept. 20 in Los Angeles with Congressional leaders and Administration officials, headed by Transportation Secretary Claude Brinegar. Although one of the chief purposes of the meeting was to explore ways to hold prices down, most of the anti-inflation proposals offered by transportation executives were aimed at aiding their own special interests. The conference also produced agreement that federal spending should be curbed, but there were few specific suggestions on areas to be cut back.

Among the proposals advanced at the meeting, two were immediately rejected by Brinegar. He said he would not support an increase in the gasoline tax, favored by spokesmen for mass transit systems, and he opposed calls by the trucking industry to permit speed limits higher than the 55 m.p.h. limit mandated during the energy crisis.

Brinegar generally supported two other proposals: he agreed that "tradeoffs" between environmental and consumer safety laws and inflation considerations were necessary; and he endorsed some easing of government regulations over the transportation industries.

Many industry officials charged that federal environmental, health, and safety rules contributed to inflation by spurring inefficiency. Suggestions were made that the government require submission of an "inflation impact" statement, similar to the already required environmental impact reports, for every new federal regulation to assess the rule's costs.

Government regulations also resulted in reduced productivity, the business officials charged, citing Interstate Commerce Commission (ICC) trucking restrictions and freight rate policies. ICC Chairman George M. Stafford responded angrily that he could not understand how anyone could argue that deregulation could reduce transportation rates.

Inflationary problems of the airlines industry were also taken up at the meeting. Edward J. Driscoll, president of the National Air Carriers' Association, a charter airline trade group, said charter fares could be expected to rise 30%–35% during 1975. (Fares already had been increased 20%–30% during 1974, according to the Wall Street Journal Sept. 23.)

Other developments included calls by road builders for more federal highway and bridge construction, calls by an environmental group for reduced interstate highway construction, pleas by charter airline groups for liberalized Civil Aeronautics Board flight policies, and calls by truckers, shippers and others for bigger and faster freight-rate and passenger rate increases.

The president of Greyhound Lines Inc., James L. Kerrigan, sought cuts in transportation subsidies for the federally funded railroad system Amtrak, and Richard V. Gallagher, director of the International Taxi Cab Association, asked the government not to aid other transit systems that competed with taxis.

State & local government conference. State and local government officials cautioned Sept. 23 that Administration efforts to curb inflation by reducing domestic expenditures could prove counter-productive by forcing local governments to pay for the social and public service programs affected by federal budget cutbacks.

The warning was aimed at James T. Lynn, secretary of housing and urban development, and other Administration officials who convened the pre-summit meeting of more than 60 governors, mayors, county officials, public employe labor union leaders and consumer advocates.

Mayor Joseph Alioto of San Francisco (D), president of the U.S. Conference of Mayors, told the group, "Too often, cutting the budget transfers rising expenditures to local governments" without reducing overall government spending.

"We cannot sanction the concept of bleeding our cities in hopes of achieving national economic health," New York Mayor Abraham Beame (D) said. State and local government officials were particularly concerned about federal efforts to shift the burden of paying for domestic programs because aggregate state budgets showed an $11 billion surplus during fiscal 1973. (According to Commerce Clearing House Sept. 18, revenues of state governments from all sources totaled $129.8 billion in fiscal 1973, up 15.6% from 1972, and total state expenditures were $118.8 billion, up 8.8%. The aggregate state surplus had totaled only $3.1 billion in fiscal 1972 and $1.6 billion in fiscal 1971.).

Participants at the conference supported the concept of a balanced budget, but proposed alternative cuts in the areas of defense, foreign aid and the space program.

Other anti-inflation weapons favored by state and local government leaders included renewal of general revenue sharing; strict enforcement of antitrust laws; tax reforms in the areas of corporate and individual tax loopholes, excess profits, and luxury levies; creation of a large public works program keyed to local unemployment rates; easing of restrictions on categorical grants to free the use of federal money received by localities; easing of credit restrictions; and curbs on the oil industry.

Mayor Kathryn Kirschbaum (D) of Davenport, Iowa charged that there was "insufficient competition" in the oil industry and cited price rises in petroleum products that her city had been forced to pay in the last year: diesel fuel, up 136%; gasoline, up 248%; road oil, up 134%; chemicals, up 150%; antifreeze, up 450%.

Economists confer again. One of the final pre-summit meetings produced more disagreement than consensus. Twenty-eight of the nation's leading economists met in New York Sept. 22 and agreed that the nation faced serious economic problems, but they were unable to reach agreement on how to fight inflation.

Wide support for an easing of the Federal Reserve Board's tight money policies, expressed at the first pre-summit meeting when a larger group of economists met with President Ford, dissipated at the New York meeting. Debate centered on the target rate of growth in the money supply that should be permitted by the Federal Reserve.

Disagreement also surfaced in another area where there had been earlier broad agreement—the reform of some government regulations deemed counterproductive and contributing to inflation. Thomas Moore of the Hoover Institution, Stanford, Calif., proposed that 22 barriers to competition, such as certain import quotas, antitrust law exemptions and price supports, be eliminated, but others dismissed the suggestions as "conventional pieties" and a "hodgepodge that is largely, if not entirely, irrelevant" to fighting inflation. The group was unable even to devise a statement that all participants would sign backing the elimination of barriers to competition in government and the private sector.

None of the participants supported "massive fiscal expansion," Alan Greenspan said later, but there also was little agreement on specific areas of spending cuts and tax reform.

Otto Eckstein of Harvard University and David L. Grove of International Business Machines Corp. agreed that reductions in the federal budget of up to $10 billion could still leave the nation with nearly double digit inflation and high unemployment.

Arthur Okun, a Brookings Institution economist who was formerly chairman of the Council of Economic Advisers, proposed a "social compact" allowing workers to offset the effects of inflation through tax breaks rather than wage increases.

Economists also disagreed on how to curb rising energy prices. Walter Levy, an oil industry consultant, proposed that the U.S. limit the amount of petro-dollars invested by oil exporting nations if they refused to finance a new international credit agency designed to aid nations unable to pay for petroleum exports. Others criticized the government's "complacency" considering threats to international economic and financial stability posed by rising oil prices. Milton Friedman was less concerned, predicting that the international oil cartel would "break up as every other cartel has broken up."

Black economic summit meeting held. Representatives of more than 50 black professional, business, religious, civil rights and community organizations met Sept. 22–23 for the first national black economic conference, urging the Administration to establish a public service work program that would provide a million jobs as a means of easing the "depression" that inflation had produced among blacks.

In a position paper issued at the close of the two-day meeting in Washington, the group also called for sharp tax increases on excess profits, a surtax on upper income persons, direct tax relief for the poor, substitution of cash for federal food stamps, and direct price controls.

The group opposed Administration plans to cut domestic spending levels. "Social programs have traditionally enhanced the participation of blacks in America's economy. It is imperative that these programs not be cut," the paper stated.

Congressional panel urges action. The Joint Economic Committee of Congress Sept. 21 urged the federal government to take remedial action soon on the deteriorating state of the economy and presented its own list of recommendations. In a report supported by a majority of its members, the committee termed the economic status "grave" because of escalating prices and stagnant or falling production. It was vital, it said, that the White House-sponsored economic summit meeting "be followed by action."

The panel said the current high rate of inflation was not the result of excess demand or inflationary wages. Other factors were contributory, such as the oil-price increase, crop failures and dollar devaluations, it said, but "increasingly a significant part of the current inflation can be understood only in the context of administered prices in concentrated industries which typically increase despite falling demand." It cited the price rises in metals, chemicals, autos and other basic industries.

The committee unanimously supported President Ford's goal to hold federal spending in the current fiscal year to $300 billion and urged a "strenuous effort" to restrain the growth of federal spending in the next fiscal year. If these were done, it said, "there should now be a shift toward less restrictive monetary policy." The panel cautioned against "severe fiscal and monetary restraint" because of the danger of contributing to a rising unemployment rate.

It said the shift toward less restrictive monetary policy should be "moderate," and proposed a channeling of credit to areas "most strapped by monetary restraint," such as housing, utilities and small business.

A major recommendation of the committee was promulgation of pay and price guidelines. The new Council on Wage and Price Stability, it said, should "recommend appropriate non-inflationary behavior for prices, wages and executive compensation on a specific industry-by-industry basis." If this did not work, it said, Congress should consider giving the council authority to defer or rescind "clearly unjustified price increases."

Another major proposal was for tax revision to "provide immediate relief to low and middle income workers" and to offset the revenue loss by "elimination of unjustified tax subsidies, an increase in the minimum tax on those in the highest income brackets and the introduction of new taxes designed to encourage the conservation of energy."

The report opposed new tax incentives for business investment.

A third major proposal of the panel was for a public service employment program to be effected when the jobless rate reached 5.5% and expanded at a 6% rate.

Improvement of the unemployment compensation program and increased benefits for the elderly poor were also recommended.

The panel objected to "structural distortions" built into the economy and recommended creation of a commission to "break up private market power" and reduce government interference with markets. As areas for review, it cited federal subsidies, price supports, import quotas, regulatory practices and antitrust procedure.

Economic Summit Conference

The economic summit conference was held in Washington Sept. 27–28, 1974, with President Ford presiding and about 800 delegates participating.

Policy alternatives offered. President Ford Sept. 27 opened the conference, which was held at the Washington Hilton Hotel, with a renewed appeal for bipartisan cooperation on economic policy, but leading Democratic spokesmen quickly attacked Administration policies and offered alternative programs.

"The inflationary problem," Ford told the meeting, "transcends America's special interest—whether Republican or Democratic, labor or business, urban or rural."

Speaker of the House Carl Albert (D, Okla.) replied, "There is a divergence of views, generally and specifically, between the Republican Administration and the Democratic majority in Congress with regard to economic policy." Albert also noted that the summit meeting itself had been "managed by the executive branch" of government "and that Congressional input has been limited." (Ford had referred to the conference as a "joint executive-legislative undertaking in response to a bipartisan recommendation of the Congress.")

Albert also criticized the Administration's reliance on familiar and conservative inflation fighting weapons, "tight money and fiscal stringency coupled with tax incentives for business and cutbacks in social programs" policies that had been referred to as "old time religion" by Nixon and Ford Administration officials.

These policies alone, Albert said, would not solve the nation's economic problems. "We must recognize from the outset that several major factors in our current price inflation lie beyond our immediate control," he said, such as poor harvests throughout the world and bad weather in the U.S. which were affecting the nation's food prices, and the oil exporting nations' decision to curtail oil production.

"Other factors we can readily control, such as federal spending," Albert said, but they have "had little role in causing price increases." The Joint Economic Committee of Congress, Albert noted, had concluded that "massive reductions in federal spending would do little to forestall inflation while such reductions might in fact trigger a major inflation," a conclusion that he termed a "major breakthrough in economic thinking."

Albert listed three policies that Congressional Democrats favored "to counteract the many and varied elements" contributing to the inflation problem: an expanded public service jobs program, that would provide immediately for creation of 500,000 new jobs; a reduction in interest rates "through channeling credit" to areas in the economy especially hard hit such as the housing industry and utilities; and a balanced tax reform package including measures to offset the harm done by inflation to the purchasing power of lower and middle income families."

Senate Majority Leader Mike Mansfield (D, Mont.) offered a specific, seven-point economic program developed by Senate Democrats to deal with what he termed an "economic emergency." "The need is for a new action—equitable action—by this Administration in cooperation with the Congress. It exists not only with regard to petroleum but in many other matters," Mansfield said. "Integrated action in seven fields is needed to curb inflation to halt the recession. These fields are: budget reductions; wage, prices and profit controls; selective monetary credit easement; tax adjustments; positive action to deal with shortages and supplies; development of new employment; and readjustment of international policies."

Mansfield said he was "not too optimistic about the results" of the summit conference because economists in pre-summit talks had spent a great deal of time in academic discourse, about which "the public knows nothing." "Of inflation, the public knows a greal deal. Of recession, the public is learning more and more each day. The public knows, too, that little has been done to stem the inflation or to halt the march of recession, anywhere by anyone."

"The time for words is at an end. Words will no longer satisfy the nation. Inflation is social dynamite. Recession is social dynamite. The divisions among people, among societies, among nations, are on the rise. They will not wait for the 'self-adjusting mechanisms' of the economy to self-adjust," Mansfield warned.

"It is said, too, the fault lies with the American consumer," he continued. "Tell that to the grocery-shopper who feeds a family on inflation-eroded wages or a fixed income. Tell it to the home-owner who uses oil to keep out the cold and the worker who uses gasoline to get to work. The fact is that the laissez-faire application of the laws of demand and supply no longer correct the economic ills of a society already bound in by a massive complex of intervention built up over decades. The clock cannot be turned back to Adam Smith's eighteenth century England."

Mansfield offered his own nine-point program of federal action:

1. Establishing, as needed, mandatory wage, price, rent and profit controls;
2. Reviving the Reconstruction Finance Corporation to deal with the credit needs of ailing businesses such as Penn Central, Lockheed and Grumman, Pan American, TWA and many more headed in the same direction; Congress is not the proper forum for specific decisions involving government bail-outs;
3. Restoring Regulation W to require larger down payments on credit purchases and shorter periods for repayment and allocating credit on a priority basis in the light of the nation's critical needs;
4. Beginning an equitable rationing system for energy and other scarce materials to the end that dependency on foreign sources of petroleum can be reduced and beginning, too, a stringent conservation system including measures to enforce the speed limit and to bring about a reduction of wastage in the utility and other industrial fields;
5. Developing a broader system of indexing to the end that the real incomes of wage earners can be tied to real living costs:
6. Without delay, to establish a commission on supplies and shortages, legislation for which has already passed the Congress.
7. Curbing excessive profits and controlling the flow of investments abroad through the taxing power while conversely cutting taxes on Americans hardest hit by inflation, those in low and moderate income categories and those on moderate fixed incomes.
8. Creating without delay, a jobs program which puts people to work in public services and elsewhere as necessary to keep down the level of unemployment.
9. Working with all nations prepared to work with us to deal with cartel-created shortages in petroleum or other commodities, and there are other commodities, recognizing that petroleum is only one aspect of the larger question of the interrelationship of the economic well-being of all nations and the stability of the world.

The summit recommendations offered the President were generally similar to proposals originating in the preliminary economic conferences. Rather than focusing on root causes of inflation in their areas, most of the different special interests represented depicted themselves as victims of "stagflation" and sought federal help in overcoming their special economic problems.

Labor leaders, led by AFL-CIO President George Meany, warned that inflation cures could lead to a worsening recession and high rates of unemployment. Organized labor was especially critical of Arthur Burns and the Federal Reserve's tight money policy. Meany and others urged Ford to replace White House economic advisers who were holdovers from the Nixon Administration, and they called for a reduction in interest rates, an expanded public service jobs program, credit allocation for the housing industry, tax breaks for the poor, and an end to tax loopholes for the wealthy. Labor opposed reductions in federal spending for social programs.

Banking and finance leaders supported some form of tax relief for lower income persons and tax changes to encourage savings (a proposal also backed by the housing industry). They also agreed with spokesmen for the natural resources industry that a massive energy conservation campaign should be waged. Consumer groups represented at the conference supported vigorous enforcement of antitrust laws, a rollback in oil prices and an excess profits tax on energy companies.

Business and manufacturing groups urged tax incentives to spur capital investment and sought a slowdown in enactment of new environmental and plant safety regulations. Like representatives of labor and banking and finance, they also opposed a return to wage and price controls.

There was wide support for cuts in the federal budget, but spokesmen for those benefitting from social welfare programs urged the government to increase federal spending in their area. They also favored tax increases for nearly every social group except the poor.

Agriculture and housing representatives asked for special consideration in the form of farm production incentives, higher federal food subsidy prices, credit allocation favorable to farmers, builders and building financers, eased federal credit restrictions and a special construction industry advisory panel within the Council on Wage and Price Stability. Representatives of the transportation industries also sought tax breaks, freight rate increases, relaxation of Interstate

Commerce Commission regulations and the enactment of a "cost impact statement" to accompany any new government programs.

Ford promises swift action. President Ford promised at the conclusion of the conference that he would move quickly to produce a "coherent and consistent" policy to fight inflation and recession.

Ford told the group in his closing address Sept. 28, "You have discussed many ideas. You have spoken candidly and as a result, I, along with other Americans, have gained a far better understanding of our economic problems. Perhaps we have caught glimpses of the political problems and we understand those. But even in our controversies, we have all developed a surer sense of direction."

He also announced major changes in his economic policy-making team. Treasury Secretary William E. Simon was appointed to head a 14-member Economic Policy Board set up to formulate and coordinate domestic and international economic policy decisions. Simon was also named the Administration's "principal spokesman on matters of economic policy." Ford also established a White House Labor-Management Committee and named Albert Rees, a Princeton University economist, to direct the newly established Council on Wage and Price Stability.

In his closing address, Ford renewed his commitment to fight "stagflation" with policies of fiscal and monetary restraint, but he also promised federal aid for the unemployed if anti-inflationary policies resulted in higher jobless rates.

"Inflation strikes society unevenly," Ford said. "Government must concern itself with those on whom this burden falls excessively." In addition to aid for the unemployed, Ford gave support to tax-law changes that would "encourage savings, stimulate productivity, discourage excessive debt, and . . . correct inflation-caused inequities."

Ford repeated his pledge to keep "federal outlays for fiscal year 1975 at or under $300 billion." "Every dollar the federal treasury must borrow is a dollar not available to the homebuyer or to the businessman trying to expand or to other citizens who are borrowers," the President said.

Ford paired his call for "disciplined management" of fiscal and monetary affairs with a call for "more prudent use of available energy" supplies. "A coherent national policy on energy is essential for economic stability," Ford said, adding that the Administration would soon propose a national energy program.

Ford appealed to citizens to "become inflation fighters and energy savers," and asked that they draw up lists of 10 ways to fight rising prices and conserve energy.

Ford made two references to the international aspects of the ioint inflation and energy problems. While the summit meeting was in progress, Ford noted, Secretary of State Henry Kissinger and Treasury Secretary Simon were meeting with the representatives of Great Britain, West Germany, France and Japan to devise a "coordinated plan to cope with the world energy crisis and economic distortions."

At the close of his address, Ford told foreign observers present that the U.S. "is seeking honest solutions that will help, not hinder, other nations' efforts to advance or restore their economic health." He promised "extensive consultations" with other world leaders "aimed at strengthening international institutions" and preventing future "interacting inflations and deflations."

Economic Policy Board members—Ford named L. William Seidman his assistant "for the coordination and implementation of economic affairs as well as executive director" of the Economic Policy Board. Others on the panel were Secretary of State Henry Kissinger; Interior Secretary Rogers C. B. Morton; Agriculture Secretary Earl L. Butz; Commerce Secretary Frederick Dent; Labor Secretary Peter J. Brennan; Health, Education & Welfare Secretary Caspar Weinberger; Housing & Urban Development Secretary James T. Lynn; Transportation Secretary Claude S. Brinegar; Office of Management and Budget Director Roy Ash; Council of Economic Advisers Chairman Alan Greenspan; and William D. Eberle, executive director of the Council on International Economic Policy. Arthur Burns, chairman of the Federal Reserve Board, would attend board meetings, Ford said. (A small six-member executive committee would meet daily.)

White House Labor-Management Committee members—John T. Dunlop, a Harvard University economist and former director of the Cost of Living Council, was named committee coordinator. Eight business leaders and eight union officials were also appointed: John D. Harper of the Aluminum Co. of America (Alcoa); Reginald H. Jones of General Electric Corp.; Stephen D. Bechtel Jr. of the Bechtel Group; Richard C. Gerstenberg of General Motors Corp.; Rawleigh Warner Jr. of Mobil Oil Corp.; Walter B. Wriston of First National City Corp.; Arthur Wood of Sears, Roebuck and Co.; R. Heath Larry of U.S. Steel Corp.; George Meany, AFL-CIO president; Lane Kirkland, AFL-CIO secretary-treasurer; I. W. Abel, president of the United Steelworkers of America; Murray H. Finley, president of the Amalgamated Clothing Workers; Paul Hall, president of the Seafarers International Union; Frank E. Fitzsimmons, president of the International Brotherhood of Teamsters; Leonard Woodcock, president of the United Auto Workers; and Arnold Miller, president of the United Mine Workers.

The group would serve as presidential advisers and "help assure effective collective bargaining, promote sound wage and price policies, develop higher standards of living, boost productivity and establish more effective manpower policies," Ford said.

Other appointments—In addition to Rees' appointment as executive director of the new inflation monitoring panel, Ford named Simon to replace Kenneth Rush as chairman. Seidman became deputy chairman. Popular financial writer Sylvia Porter was named to coordinate consumer action in curbing inflation and conserving energy supplies.

No quick inflation relief seen. Participants at the summit meeting privately were fearful that the public might expect immediate economic miracles to result from the conference. Alan Greenspan, chairman of the Council of Economic Advisers, tried to deflate those expectations Sept. 26 when he testified before the Joint Economic Committee of Congress, warning that there would be no quick, easy cures for inflation and recession.

"I don't know of any reputable economist at this point who has a [short term] program" to reduce inflation and restore economic growth, Greenspan said.

Committee members were not pleased with his testimony. Democrats accused Greenspan of advocating a "do nothing" approach to the economy over the short run, and Republicans said he should substitute positive thinking for his negative remarks. Greenspan replied, "What we need more than positive statements is to tell it like it is. I'd like very much to sit here and say things are improving and our problems are simmering down, but, unfortunately, those aren't the facts."

Greenspan conceded that budget cuts planned by the Administration would have little immediate effect in curbing inflation, but he added, that if the effort also contributed to slower spending in the future and reduced government borrowing, "there is a good chance interest rates would fall."

White House Press Secretary Ron Nessen said Sept. 26 that White House economic advisers had concluded it would take up to three years to make a major impact on inflation. Little significant relief from inflation was expected for 18 months, Nessen said.

Ford's Anti-Inflation Plan

'Total mobilization' urged. President Ford presented his anti-inflation program Oct. 8, 1974 in a televised address before a joint session of Congress.

Included were creation of a board to develop a national energy policy, a proposed cut in foreign oil imports by 1 million barrels a day, a 5% surtax on families earnings more than $15,000 annually and corporations, and measures to help the depressed housing industry.

Ford called on the nation to "enlist" in the fight against inflation. "I concede," he said, "that there will be no sudden Pearl Harbor to shock us into unity and to sacrifice, but I think we've had enough early warning. The time to intercept is right now. The time to intercept is almost gone."

"Inflation, our public enemy number one, will, unless whipped, destroy our country, our homes, our liberty, our property and finally our national pride as surely as any well-armed wartime enemy," Ford said.

(At a news conference Oct. 9, the President expressed confidence that his program would reduce inflation by early 1975.)

His economic package contained few mandatory features, relying instead on renewed appeals for the "total mobilization" of persons motivated by "self-discipline" and exhibiting "voluntary restraint."

Most of Ford's proposals required the concurrence of Congress, but in a special message to citizens, the President asked for specific individual efforts to conserve food and fuel.

"To help increase food and lower prices, grow more, waste less," Ford said. "If you can't spare a penny from your food budget, surely you can cut the food you waste by 5%."

"To help save scarce fuel in the energy crisis, drive less, heat less. If we all drive at least 5% fewer miles we can save 250–300 thousand barrels of foreign oil per day," the President said.

"One final thing that all Americans can do," Ford said, is "share burdens as well as blessings. It will strengthen our spirits as well as our economy."

Ford's "grand design" included many proposals which had been discussed at the White House-sponsored economic summit conference and preliminary meetings preceding it.

Ford continued to emphasize the need for a bipartisan approach to economic policy. Noting all the disagreements which had surfaced at the summit meeting, Ford said, "there is only one point on which all advisers have agreed. We must whip inflation now."

Ford's battle plan reflected his efforts to seek consensus and compromise over economic issues that had political ramifications, especially in an election year. In presenting Administration policies to the Congress, Ford "identified" 10 areas that he said required "joint action"

Changes in GNP Implicit Price Deflator & Consumer Price Index (1930–74)

Year	Percent change from preceding year		Year	Percent change from preceding year	
	GNP implicit price deflator	Consumer price index		GNP implicit price deflator	Consumer price index
1930	−2.7	−2.5	1955	1.4	−.4
1931	−9.1	−8.8	1956	3.4	1.5
1932	−10.1	−10.3	1957	3.7	3.6
1933	−2.4	−5.1	1958	2.5	2.7
1934	7.3	3.4	1959	1.7	.8
1935	1.1	2.5	1960	1.6	1.6
1936	.3	1.0	1961	1.3	1.0
1937	4.1	3.6	1962	1.1	1.1
1938	−1.4	−1.9	1963	1.3	1.2
1939	−1.5	−1.4	1964	1.6	1.3
1940	1.5	1.0	1965	1.8	1.7
1941	7.7	5.0	1966	2.8	2.9
1942	12.3	10.7	1967	3.2	2.9
1943	7.2	6.1	1968	4.0	4.2
1944	2.3	1.7	1969	4.8	5.4
1945	2.6	2.3	1970	5.5	5.9
1946	11.8	8.5	1971	4.5	4.3
1947	11.9	14.4	1972	3.4	3.3
1948	6.6	7.8	1973	5.6	6.2
1949	−.6	−1.0	1974	10.2	11.0
1950	1.3	1.0			
1951	6.8	7.9			
1952	2.1	2.2			
1953	1.0	.8			
1954	1.5	.5			

Sources: Department of Commerce (Bureau of Economic Analysis) and Department of Labor (Bureau of Labor Statistics)

by the executive branches of government: food, energy, restrictive practices, increased capital supply, aid for inflation victims, housing, thrift institutions, international interdependency, federal taxes, spending.

The 10 areas covered by Ford:

Food—Ford said efforts would be made to reduce prices by increasing supplies. Congress would be asked to remove all remaining acreage limits on rice, peanuts and cotton. Farmers were promised all the fuel allocations required to produce at full capacity. Ford said he would ask for authority to allocate the needed fertilizer supplies. "Agricultural marketing orders and other federal regulations are being reviewed to eliminate or modify those responsible for inflation prices," Ford said.

He also directed the Council on Wage and Price Stability to "find and expose all restrictive practices, public or private, which raise food prices." The Administration also would "monitor" food production, margins, pricing and exports.

In a reference to the voluntary monitoring program for grain exports, Ford said the newly created Economic Policy Board would determine policy for that program. Ford also requested that Congress provide him with the authority to "waive certain of the restrictions on [food] shipments based on national interest or humanitarian grounds."

Energy—"We have a real energy problem," Ford said. "One third of our oil, 17% of America's total energy, now comes from foreign sources we cannot control—at high cartel prices costing you and me $16 billion more than just a year ago. The primary solution has to be at home."

Ford named Interior Secretary Rogers C.B. Morton to head a newly established National Energy Board charged with developing a national energy policy. "His marching orders are to reduce imports of foreign oil by 1 million barrels per day by the end of 1975, whether by savings here at home or by increasing our own sources," Ford said. Morton was also directed to increase domestic energy supplies by "promptly utilizing coal resources and expanding the recovery of domestic oil still in the ground in old wells," the President added.

In his legislative requests, Ford asked Congress to give priority to four areas involving the deregulation of natural gas, increased use of the naval oil reserves in California and Alaska, amendments to the Clean Air Act, and passage of strip mine legislation that would "insure adequate supply with common sense environmental protection."

Ford also said he would seek new legislation requiring the use of cleaner coal processes and nuclear fuel in new electric plants and "the quick conversion of existing oil plants." Ford proposed setting a target date of 1980 for "eliminating oil-fired plants from the nation's base loaded electrical capacity."

The President said he would use the existing Defense Production Act to allocate scarce materials, but amendments to the law might be required. He also promised to meet with automobile industry officials "to assure, either by agreement or by law," a program that could achieve a 40% increase in gasoline mileage within a four-year development deadline.

The development of coal gasification programs and efforts to make new use of nonfossil fuels were long-term programs needed to increase domestic energy supplies, Ford said.

Restrictive practices—Ford called for an end to restrictive practices, "whether instituted by government, industry, labor or others." The President sought such a change as a method of increasing productivity and containing prices. He promised a "vigorous enforcement of antitrust laws," especially in areas of price fixing and bid rigging. ("Non-competitive professional fee schedules and real estate settlement fees" were cited as practices that must be eliminated.) He also asked Congress for authority to increase maximum penalities for antitrust violations from $50,000 to $1 million for corporations and from $50,000 to $100,000 for individual violators.

Ford introduced a four-point program to overhaul government regulations: the Council on Wage and Price Stabilty was given watchdog authority to examine the inflationary costs of all governmental actions; Congress was asked to create a National Commission on Regulatory Reform to examine rules promulgated by independent government agencies; legislative proposals and regulations emanating from the executive branch, Ford said, would be accompanied by "inflationary impact statements" and he asked Congress to provide the same impact statements for its legislative initiatives; state and local governments were asked to "undertake similar programs to reduce inflationary effects of their regulatory activities."

The President restated his opposition to reimposition of wage and price controls, but emphasized that the Council on Wage and Price Stability was empowered to monitor wage and price practices in the private economy. The National Council on Productivity, recently revitalized by Congress, would also be used to develop labor-management cooperation, "particularly in the construction and health care industries," Ford said.

Capital—"Today our capital markets are in disarray," Ford declared. "Prudent monetary restraint is essential ... to restore their vitality." Although Ford said he had received the personal assurances of Federal Reserve Chairman Arthur Burns that the money supply would expand sufficiently to avert a "credit crunch," the President recommended enactment of a "liberalized 10% investment tax credit" to meet the needs of "capital-intensive industries, such as primary metals and public utilities where shortages have developed."

Ford sought Congressional approval for tax legislation to provide that "all dividends on preferred stocks issued for cash be fully deductible by the issuing company," thereby increasing revenue, especially for the hard pressed energy-producing utilities, and also helping "other industries shift from debt to equity, providing sounder capital structure."

Ford also endorsed several features of a bill pending before the House Ways and Means Committee. The tax reform measure, which had not been reported out of committee, closed several tax loopholes, liberalized capital gains taxation, provided $1.5 billion in tax relief for low and middle income groups, and imposed a windfall profits tax on oil producers. All of these proposals were endorsed by Ford in his economic address.

Aid to victims of inflation—Ford proposed a two-step program to augment actions already taken by the Administration to aid the casualties of inflation and anti-inflation actions. Unemployment insurance would be extended for 13 weeks to those who had already exhausted their benefits; those qualifying but not currently covered by unemployment insurance would be able to receive 26 weeks of jobless benefits. Funding would be provided from the general treasury, not from employers' taxes. Ford also asked Congress to create a Community Improvement Corps, providing work for the unemployed on short-term projects to "improve, beautify and enhance the environment." The program would be activated when the national unemployment rate exceeded 6% (and be terminated when the rate dropped below 6%).

Localities could qualify for grants when their jobless rate exceeded 6.5%. The one year program would be supervised by state and local government contractors, who could hire only those who had exhausted their unemployment benefits.

Stimulating housing—For the ailing housing and construction industries, Ford asked Congress to give its approval before recess to legislation making "most home mortgages eligible for purchase by an agency of the federal government." Currently only 20% of home mortgages, those guaranteed by the Federal Housing Administration or insured by the Veterans Administration, were covered by such legislation, the President said. Ford also endorsed legislation before the Senate that he said would immediately free $3 billion for mortgage purchases, enough to finance about 100,000 homes.

Immediate action was required on these credit proposals, Ford said, because the nation currently was "suffering the longest and most severe housing recession since the end of World War II" while unemployment among construction workers was about twice the national average.

Thrift institutions—Problems faced by the housing industry and thrift institutions were closely related. Both were affected by high interest rates, with savings and loan institutions and other similar groups unable to attract adequate deposits, Ford said. For the third time in eight years, according to the President, thrift institutions were encountering "another period of serious mortgage credit scarcity." He urged passage of the pending financial institutions bill and promised cooperation with the Congress in developing additional assistance programs for thrift institutions to meet the mortgage credit crisis.

International interdependency—The U.S., Ford declared, had a "responsibility not only to maintain a healthy economy at home but also to seek policies which complement, rather than disrupt, the constructive efforts of others." Administration officials had just left to brief Canadian, European and Japanese governments on the U.S. economic proposals, Ford said, but he emphasized that Congressional passage of "an acceptable" trade reform bill was "essential" to U.S. efforts "to resolve common [international] economic problems."

Taxation—Ford asked Congress to approve a "temporary surcharge of 5% on corporate and upper level individual incomes," generally affecting families with gross incomes of $15,000 or more, and individuals earning $7,500. The estimated $5 billion raised from the added taxes would pay for all the new programs mentioned in the Administration anti-inflation package, according to the President.

Ford said he was aware that any request for new taxes made just prior to a Congressional election was "considered politically unwise," but he declared, "I will not play politics with America's future. Our present inflation to a considerable degree comes from many years of enacting expensive programs without raising enough new revenues to pay for them. Nineteen out of the 25 years I served in this [House] chamber the federal government ended up with federal deficits," Ford told the Congress.

Federal spending—The taxation proposal was linked to new austerity measures planned for the federal budget. Ford asked Congress to move quickly before its recess to set a "target spending limit of $300 billion for the federal 1975 budget." If agreement were reached on this ceiling level, Ford said, he would submit a number of "budget deferrals and recissions" to keep expenditures within the new limit. Budget reductions would require "hard choices," Ford said, but he promised that "no federal agency, including the Defense Department, will be untouchable."

Reiterating a constant theme, Ford said "Fiscal discipline is a necessary weapon in any fight against inflation. We cannot ask the American people to tighten their belts if Uncle Sam is unwilling to first tighten his."

Reaction to Ford's proposals. Widespread opposition to several of Ford's economic proposals quickly developed in Congress. Two features of the Administration's anti-inflation plan—the surtax and jobless aid—were attacked by members of both parties during Congressional hearings.

Other elements of the plan, such as the $300 billion spending limit for fiscal 1975 and tax reform measures, were generally endorsed by Democrats and Republicans.

There was no support for the tax surcharge Oct. 9 in the House Ways and Means Committee. Opposition centered on the proposed income cutoffs of $15,000 for a family and $7,500 for an individual—floors that many members of Congress regarded as too low.

House and Senate labor subcommittees held a joint session Oct. 9 to hear Labor Secretary Peter J. Brennan expand on the President's unemployment aid proposals. Most members said they regarded the Community Improvement Corps plan as "cumbersome." The 6% national unemployment rate that would trigger the program was too low, the one-year duration too short and the planned spending figures too small, critics charged. Several suggestions were made that the Administration abandon its new program and seek supplemental funds for the existing public service jobs program.

Reaction in the business and financial communities was generally mixed, although prices on the New York Stock Exchange rebounded from steep losses in anticipation of the President's program. The Dow Jones industrial average gained 23 points Oct. 7 and closed up 28.39 points at 631.02 Oct. 9. It closed up 17.21 points at 648.23 Oct. 10. Analysts attributed the increases to a lowering of interest rates and removal of the uncertainty that had surrounded the Administration's plans.

In interviews conducted Oct. 8 and 9 by the Wall Street Journal and the New York Times, business leaders expressed restrained approval for Ford's program but doubts were voiced that the moderate proposals would prove strong enough to make a real impact on inflation.

Many labor leaders and environmentalists denounced the speech. There were mixed comments from economists. Walter W. Heller, former chairman of the Council of Economic Advisers, said Oct. 8 that he felt a "considerable sense of letdown." "It was a tiny step in the in the right direction."

Mansfield responds to Ford plan—Senate Majority Leader Mike Mansfield (Mont.) delivered the Democratic response to President Ford's economic program in a nationally televised address Oct. 15. Mansfield rejected the Ford program as one that "bears too close a resemblance to the fiscal and monetary policies of the previous Administration—policies which have long since proved to be inadequate to meet the emergency."

Mansfield called for fuel rationing, controls on wages, prices and profits, credit allocation, and a tax break for the poor—proposals which he had detailed during the White House sponsored economic summit meeting.

News conference. At a news conference Oct. 9, Ford expressed confidence that his new economic program would work, was adequate and would reduce inflation by early 1975.

On the economy, the President made these remarks:

He was confident, concerning his economic program, "if the Congress responds, if the American people respond in a voluntary way, that we can have, hopefully early in 1975, some meaningful reduction in the rate of inflation."

There were problems, he said, and it was "a very mixed situation." Care would have to be exercised "that we don't tighten the screws too tightly" and at the same time programs would have to be forthcoming to combat inflation.

Ford did not believe his proposed surtax would have to be extended beyond a year. "We're in a temporary situation," he said, and the tax would provide sufficient income to meet the additional cost of his community improvement program and at the same time help dampen inflation "by reducing the amount of money of 28% of the taxpayers."

(In a correction issued Oct. 11, the White House said that the proposed 5% surtax would affect about 28% of all personal tax returns, including joint returns, but not 28% of all taxpayers.)

What other measures did he have in mind if his program was not successful? Ford was "very confident" that if all 31 of his recommendations were implemented "the program will work. And we're going to concentrate on making it work. And I therefore don't think we should speculate about something that I don't think will take place."

Was there anything in his program to persuade business to lower prices or labor to moderate wage demands? Some of his proposals would increase supply, Ford said, which was "a very important ingredient," and some would remove restrictive practices of government, private industry and labor and, if this were done, prices would come down in the private and government sectors of the economy.

Why had he not proposed mandatory gasoline taxes or rationing to conserve fuel? Ford said this had been considered but found to be potentially "harmful to people," especially those "less able to pay." As for rationing, "we believe," he said, "that the American people will respond to our volunteer program," which was "far preferable and more in the traditions of the American system."

Ford expressed disappointment that more had not been done on Project Independence to make the U.S. self-sufficient in energy. "This concerns me," he said, and was one of the reasons he was launching the new energy council. He said Congress "has to share some of the blame with the executive branch" on the matter. He thought the situation would improve and was confident of public cooperation.

Asked whether it was his view that the oil depletion allowance should be phased out, Ford responded, "The answer is yes."

The next day, White House Press Secretary Ron Nesson issued a clarification of Ford's answer, which was said to be "perhaps imprecise." The clarification: "As long as the price of oil continues to be controlled, the President believes that the elimination of the percentage depletion on domestic oil production would be a mistake. The President believes that oil should be sold on a free market basis and he thinks that many oil producers would be glad to trade the percentage depletion in order to achieve the important result of a free market for oil. As for the foreign oil depletion allowance, the President believes that should be phased out immediately and finally."

Burns sees U.S. in a recession—Federal Reserve Chairman Arthur Burns disagreed Oct. 10 with President Ford's press-conference assertion that the U.S. was not in a recession.

In testimony before the Joint Economic Committee of Congress, Burns said he believed that the nation was experiencing a "most unusual recession" with "no precedent in history." It was characterized by runaway inflation and booming capital spending by business. Burns also said he disagreed with those who forecast a deepening recession.

The Federal Reserve intended to pursue its "basic policy of restraining the expansion of money and credit in the present inflationary environment," Burns said, but he also conceded that the current rate of growth in the money supply (1.3% at an annual rate) was too small and that tight money policies should be eased.

Burns generally supported Ford's economic program, endorsing it as "useful beginning toward a rebuilding of confidence" in the government's handling of the economy, but he also expressed reservations about portions of the program. Burns said he favored a larger public service jobs program, and that only "reluctantly" did he support a general increase in the investment tax credit. The "concept" of the surtax was "appropriate," Burns said, but he added, "whether the specific numbers are ideally chosen or not, I don't know."

Burns was strongly critical of attacking the petrodollars problem by "recycling" oil revenues to oil importing nations. "What recycling really means is piling debt upon debt, and more realistically, bad debt on top of good debt. All the talk about recycling is an escape from reality," Burns declared. The only solution to the oil-money crisis, he said, was a reduction in oil prices, a cut in consumption and the development of a "common policy" by oil importing nations.

McCracken sees recession—White House economic adviser Paul McCracken joined Federal Reserve Chairman Arthur Burns in characterizing the nation's current economic downturn as a recession. In a Los Angeles speech Oct. 23, McCracken said President Ford, who had rejected use of the term in his press conference, was "ill-advised" not to "call a spade a spade" and admit that the economy was undergoing a recession.

McCracken said he expected the current recession to be "V-shaped," with production declining sharply and then rebounding sharply. He predicted that the slump would continue until mid-1975, with the "real" Gross National Product dropping 4% from mid-1974 to July 1975; unemployment was expected to peak at about 7%; and wage increases were expected to average 11% in 1975.

According to McCracken, inflationary pressures were "abating every day." By mid-1975, McCracken said, the price rise would slow to about 7% (at an annual rate) and inflation would continue to decline. On food prices, however, McCracken was not "quite as optimistic," saying he did not foresee "any real good news in terms of decline."

Treasury Secretary William Simon voiced fears Oct. 24 that the debate about recession was jeopardizing the Administration's emphasis on combating inflation. "The slowing of the economy is far less threatening to us than inflation," Simon said in a New York speech, adding that the temptation to deal with recession by abandoning restrictive fiscal and monetary policies "is a temptation that must be stoutly resisted." Attempts to stimulate economic activity could result in "another round of rapid inflation [that] would create almost irresistible pressures to establish a new system of mandatory wage and price controls," Simon warned.

Economic forecasts are gloomy. The Business Council, a group representing the nation's major businessmen and industrialists, Oct. 13 issued a gloomy economic forecast for 1975. According to the report, output was expected to remain "fairly flat" until the second half of the year when a 4% growth rate was foreseen, inflation would remain at high levels for all of 1975 and unemployment would climb to 6.5% by September 1975.

Commerce Secretary Frederick Dent told the group Oct. 14 that the nation's 1974 trade deficit could total $5 billion. Treasury Secretary William Simon agreed with that figure Oct. 16 and warned that the 1975 deficit could be more severe.

These pessimistic economic assessments were also shared by the public. According to a Gallup Poll released Oct. 16, 51% of those surveyed believed the U.S. faced a major depression; 70% said they expected economic problems to worsen over the next six months.

In a survey published Oct. 14, the University of Michigan Survey Research Center reported that consumer confidence was at its lowest point in the 28

Measures of Price & Wage Change During & After Economic Stabilization Program

[Percent change; seasonally adjusted annual rate]

Price or wage measure	Freeze and Phase II Aug. 1971 to Jan. 1973	Phase III Jan. 1973 to June 1973	Second freeze and Phase IV June 1973 to Apr. 1974	Phase IV Dec 1973 to Apr. 1974	1974	
					Apr. to Aug.	Aug. to Dec.
PRICES						
Consumer price index:						
All items	3.4	8.3	10.7	12.2	12.7	11.8
Food	5.9	20.2	16.2	12.8	7.0	17.0
All items less food	2.7	5.0	8.7	11.8	15.3	9.7
Commodities less food	2.2	4.8	9.2	14.9	16.4	8.6
Services [1]	3.5	4.3	8.6	8.8	13.3	11.7
Personal consumption expenditures deflator [2]	2.8	6.7	10.8	13.9	11.8	11.4
Wholesale price index: [3]						
All commodities	5.9	22.2	15.2	21.9	31.8	10.2
Farm products and processed foods and feeds	13.4	48.9	6.3	.4	24.5	9.5
Industrial commodities [4]	2.9	12.3	19.6	33.9	35.5	9.4
Finished goods, consumer and producer [5]	1.9	7.2	13.4	23.4	25.8	14.6
Crude and intermediate materials [5]	3.6	15.1	23.3	39.1	40.9	7.1
WAGES [6]						
Average hourly earnings, private nonfarm economy: [7]						
Monthly series	6.2	6.3	6.9	6.5	11.9	9.3
Quarterly series [2]	6.4	5.9	7.0	6.3	10.3	9.7
Average hourly compensation:						
Total private economy [2]	5.8	8.9	7.0	7.0	11.2	9.0
Nonfarm [2]	5.9	8.8	7.5	7.9	10.7	9.3

1 Not seasonally adjusted.
2 Percent changes based on quarterly data: 1971–III to 1972–IV (col. 1), 1972–IV to 1973–II (col. 2), 1973–II to 1974–I (col. 3), 1973–IV to 1974–I (col. 4), 1974–I to 1974–III (col. 5), 1974–III to 1974–IV (col. 6).
3 Seasonally adjusted percentage changes in components of the WPI do not necessarily average to the seasonally adjusted percentage change in the total index because adjustment of the components and the total are calculated separately.
4 Includes a small number of items not shown separately.
5 Excludes foods but includes a small number of items not in the industrial commodity index.
6 Average hourly earnings are for production workers or nonsupervisory employees and average hourly compensation for all employees.
7 Adjusted for overtime (in manufacturing only) and interindustry shifts.

Sources: Department of Commerce (Bureau of Economic Analysis) and Department of Labor (Bureau of Labor Statistics).

years since consumer attitudes were first examined.

Ford seeks citizens' aid. President Ford, in a nationally televised address Oct. 15 before a national convention of the Future Farmers of America, renewed his appeal for a "great citizens mobilization" in the fight against inflation. All of his proposals involved voluntary individual measures designed to help save energy and slow inflation. Many of the suggestions originated from the 22-member Citizen's Action Committee to Fight Inflation, headed by columnist Sylvia Porter, but others were from citizens who had responded to Ford's request that families draw up their own anti-inflation plans and send them to the White House.

Ford also responded to critics who had charged that his program was not tough enough. He accused Congress of failing to support his efforts to delay a pay increase for federal employes, a postponement that could have "saved $700 million taxpayers dollars." "Congress wouldn't even chew that marshmallow," Ford said, alluding to charges that instead of asking the nation to bite the bullet against inflation, he had offered a marshmallow.

Ford promised stronger measures if Congress did not act on his economic proposals, but in a warning, added "We will not be out of the economic trenches by Christmas." Ford invoked the wartime rhetoric and weapons of a home-front mobilization throughout his speech. He urged families to plant WIN gardens to save money on food, and said he was investigating the possibility of issuing special WIN savings bonds carrying a high rate of interest to attract savers. (WIN, an acronym for Whip Inflation Now, was the slogan Ford had adopted for his economic program.)

In other inflation fighting suggestions, Ford urged citizens to balance budgets, use credit wisely, conserve energy and drive at 55 m.p.h., increase savings, shop for bargains, increase productivity, and assist in recycling programs. Ford asked communities to establish local citizen action committees to monitor wages and prices and he called on governors to form WIN committees. He also asked people to cut down on waste and to guard their health in order to reduce sickdays and increase productivity.

The only controversial element in Ford's speech was his request for live television coverage. When informed of Ford's intention to address the Future Farmers of America, each network decided that the speech did not require live coverage. The decision was reversed when the White House "formally requested" coverage. Such requests by the President were automatically granted.

Democratic response—Sen. Edmund S. Muskie (D, Me.) Oct. 22 delivered the Democratic Party's response to Ford's Oct. 15 speech. Ford's proposals were not enough, Muskie said. If voluntarism failed, he warned, mandatory wage-price controls and gasoline rationing might be required. He also favored a minimum tax on the wealthy, charging that the Ford surtax plan weighed too heavily on low and middle income wage earners.

The Democrats had requested free air time from the networks, arguing that Ford had obtained broadcast coverage. Two of the networks rejected the request, which was honored by the National Broadcasting Co.

Chrysler head criticizes Ford appeal—Chrysler Corp. Chairman Lynn Townsend charged Oct. 23 that President Ford's appeal to consumers to exert greater purchasing restraint was hurting the auto industry. Noting that the industry's new car sales were down 28% in mid-October from the previous year's level, Townsend said, "We're seeing a direct reflection of the Administration's no-buy policy. The public has been asked not to buy and they aren't. They're behaving as the President asked."

If consumer confidence in the economy was not restored, Townsend warned, the automotive and housing industries would "go into a deep recession." The Administration "should be directing its efforts to stimulation of purchases, not discouragement of them," Townsend said.

Despite slumping sales, Townsend said that Chrysler planned a second round of price increases for 1975 model cars and trucks in the "very near" future.

Townsend also revealed that as part of its sweeping cost cutting plan, Chrysler was reducing its 1975 capital spending by nearly 10% to $475 million.

Townsend's remarks were made one day after Chrysler had reported an $8 million loss for the third quarter.

Ford defends economic program. President Ford defended his economic proposals to Congress as a "finely tuned, constructive program" able to "meet the challenge of inflation and any deterioration in the economy." His remarks were made at a press conference Oct. 29.

Ford was asked whether, in light of worsening economic statistics, he would agree with economist Paul McCracken, an adviser to Ford in developing the Administration's anti-inflation plans, that the economy was currently in a recession. Ford replied that "whether it is a recession or not a recession is immaterial. We have problems. The plan I submitted is aimed at solving these problems and therefore I really do not care what the name is."

Ford was asked to provide specific examples of areas in the fiscal 1975 budget where spending cuts could be made, but he said no "final determination" had been made on a "long shopping list" of proposed budget cuts. "If all of them were put into effect, . . . I think the anticipated saving in fiscal year 1975 would be around $7.5 billion," Ford said. "We are going to make a maximum effort to cut at least $5.4 billion."

(Ford instructed his Cabinet Oct. 30 to "carry the ball" in taking responsibility for making budget cuts in their areas, White House Press Secretary Ron Nessen said. Amid reports that the President planned a Cabinet shakeup, Ford told the secretaries, "You must carry the ball and if you don't score, it's your fault.")

In another question dealing with the economy, Ford was asked about a survey prepared by the House Democratic Study Group showing that while he served as House minority leader from 1971 through 1973, he supported 86% of the measures that exceeded Nixon Administration spending requests. Ford was asked, "How do you square that with your campaign argument that the Democrats are the big spenders?" Ford replied, "Their own document showed that the Democrats were much bigger spenders than I was and that I was a much better saver than they were."

According to the report published Oct. 28, the Democratic-controlled Congress had increased spending by less than .1% above the requests submitted by the Nixon Administration over the last four years. "President Nixon's spending requests ran up a deficit . . . of over $50 billion, of which only 12% can be attributed to Congressional action," the report stated. The increases were supported on average by 90% of the Republican legislators.

According to the report, Ford's record of support for 86% of the spending increases compared with a 93% record of support from Congressional Democrats.

Home mortgage aid. A Home Purchase Assistance Act to authorize an infusion of $7.75 billion in federal money into the home mortgage market was cleared by Congress Oct. 15 and sent to President Ford, who had requested such legislation Oct. 8. Ford had said then he planned to release $3 billion of the financing immediately.

The President signed the bill Oct. 18, although he objected to its "rigid, illogical interest ceiling" as inadequate to offset borrowing costs.

An interest rate ceiling was set by the bill of one-half percentage point above the average yield on Treasury bonds, or 8.25% at the time of enactment. The Secretary of housing and urban development would set the rates, within the ceiling, at which the Government National Mortgage Association (Ginnie Mae) would buy mortgages made to home buyers, using Treasury borrowings. The individual mortgages purchased in the new program were not to exceed $42,000, and 75% of the mortgages were to be on new homes.

A major feature of the legislation was extension of Ginnie Mae's authority to purchase conventional mortgages (those not backed by any government agency, such as the Veterans Administration [VA] and the Federal Housing Administration [FHA]). The latter comprised less than 20% of the mortgage market.

The Administration had favored a higher interest rate ceiling of 9.5%. The lower ceiling was attached to the bill by a 48–27 vote Oct. 10 by the Senate, which approved the bill 77–0 later that day. The House cleared the bill by voice vote Oct. 15.

Post-Election Developments

Republicans lost heavily in the 1974 midterm elections in what was interpreted as reaction to the Watergate scandals and the nation's growing economic woes.

Ford assesses policies. President Ford said Nov. 14 that he saw "no justification" for making "any major revision" in his economic proposals to Congress, despite the repudiation of many Republicans in the Nov. 5 elections when the economy appeared to be a significant voter issue. Ford, at a Sigma Delta Chi convention in Phoenix, urged Congress to pass the 5% surtax and reaffirmed his opposition to price and wage controls.

Earlier in the day, he had addressed a Las Vegas convention of the National Association of Realtors, and announced that the government would free $300 million for mortgages on existing homes in order to bolster the sagging housing industry.

The action marked the first time that the government had provided mortgage subsidy assistance for existing single-family houses purchased with conventional financing. The plan was modest in scope, however; an estimated 12,000 houses would be affected.

Authorization for the program came from the new law providing up to $7.75 billion a year in aid to the home mortgage industry. Part of this money, $3 billion, was allocated for use in new single family homes, and 10% of that was being diverted for existing housing.

Prompted by criticism from auto makers, Ford tried to clarify remarks he had made. "Somehow, the word has gone out that the best way to defeat inflation and revitalize the economy is to curtail buying. Nothing is further from the truth, and I strongly oppose that point of view," Ford said. "I believe a free society means precisely that—a free market. And sales are the heartbeat of a free market. Instead of curtailing purchases, I say to consumers: buy wisely, shop smarter."

In another revision of Administration sentiment, President Ford's press secretary, Ron Nessen, admitted Nov. 12 that the nation was "moving into a recession."

Ford had resisted use of the word, although his top economic advisers, Treasury Secretary William Simon, and Alan Greenspan, chairman of the Council on Economic Advisers, had conceded earlier in the week that the U.S. was undergoing a recession.

Nessen denied that the shift in viewpoint had anything to do with the end of political campaigns with the election Nov. 5.

In contrast to the White House view, the AFL-CIO executive council met Nov. 7 and adopted a statement warning that "the American economy is dangerously close to disaster."

Ford offers agenda. President Ford sent Congress a message Nov. 18 setting forth a "streamlined action program for the nation" in the final weeks of the 93rd Congress. Congress reconvened that day after recessing for the Nov. 5 elections to determine the composition of the 94th Congress to be seated in 1975.

The President urged a "moratorium on partisanship" for action on a number of key issues. Top priority was assigned to the President's 31-point economic program and to confirmation of Nelson Rockefeller as vice president.

Other priorities on the President's list were revision of unemployment benefits, trade reform, strip mining regulation, windfall-profits tax on U.S. oil producers, deregulation of natural gas, a permanent 55-m.p.h. speed limit and foreign aid. Other requests included urban mass transit aid and making it a crime to hire an illegal alien.

Ford criticized Congress for failing to act on his economic proposals or come up with a specific alternative program. "Time is passing," he said, and "we can't wait" until the spring of 1975 "for needed action."

He also objected to several specific bills cleared for his signature. Ford said he had serious reservations about "problems" in a bill requiring more assignment of imported oil shipments to U.S.-flag vessels. The President wanted a waiver from the restriction for economic or foreign policy considerations.

The President said he would veto as inflationary a bill to raise veterans' education aid by 22.7%, retroactive to Sept. 1. He requested the increase be scaled back to 18.2%, effective Jan. 1, 1975. The legislation had been cleared by Congress Oct. 10 but was not sent to the White House until Nov. 18 to avoid the possibility of a pocket veto during the Congressional recess.

Rail pension veto overridden. Congress already had overridden a Ford veto Oct. 16. This took place in passing a bill revising the railroad retirement system and refinancing it with an annual infusion of $285 million through the year 2000. The system currently was in arrears by $4.5 billion, largely because of a decline in the number of workers paying into the retirement fund and a dual-benefit practice permitting rail workers to receive both railroad retirement and Social Security benefits. About 40% of the one million rail workers in the country had worked other jobs long enough to qualify for Social Security as well as railroad retirement.

As cleared by Congress Sept. 30, after overwhelming votes of approval in both houses, the legislation would have phased out the dual-benefit system and replaced it with coverage for all working years, railroad and non-railroad, under Social Security and supplemental benefits for rail service, financed by the industry and managed by the federal government, to raise the benefits to the higher level of the railroad system.

President Ford vetoed the bill Oct. 12, objecting to funding the deficit with money from the Treasury. He preferred reduction of benefits or the industry financing the deficit, he said. "In return for his $7 billion contribution," Ford said, "the general taxpayer would earn no entitlement to benefits and would receive no return on his investment."

But the bill, the focus of a strong lobbying effort by rail labor and management, had enough support in both houses to provide the two-thirds majority required for enactment by overriding. The House voted to override by a 360–12 vote Oct. 15. The Senate overrode the next day 72–1.

Veterans bill veto overridden. A bill increasing educational benefits for veterans became law Dec. 3 when Congress voted to override a veto by Ford. The vote was 394–10 in the House, 90–1 in the Senate.

The bill increased benefits by 22.7%, or to the approximate level of those received by veterans of World War II and the Korean War. The beneficiaries would be the 11 million veterans of the Vietnam War and the period between the Korean and Vietnam Wars.

Ford had vetoed the measure on the ground that the increase beyond the 18.2% boost projected in the federal budget was inflationary. After the override, White House Press Secretary Ron Nessen said the President would send Congress a request for an $814 million supplemental appropriation to cover the budgetary excess in the current fiscal year.

Long-term mass transit aid enacted. A six-year, $11.8 billion mass transit program was cleared by Congress Nov. 21 and sent to President Ford for signature. The President had urged passage of the bill during the concluding House debate Nov. 21. In a telegram, Ford said the bill "represents a responsible step in our efforts to reduce energy consumption and control inflation."

The House approved the bill Nov. 21 by a 288–109 vote. The Senate vote Nov. 19 was 64–17.

A large part of the bill's funds—$7.8 billion—was allotted to capital improvements, such as purchase of new buses and subway cars. The remainder was to be distributed according to local choice, either for additional capital improvements or for operating expenses.

In the House, the measure had been enmeshed for a long time in a jurisdictional dispute between two committees. Because of it, the House Rules Committee, following a tie vote Oct. 8 denying clearance, had declined to send the bill to the floor prior to the election recess.

The long-term $11.8 billion version had been devised in a House-Senate conference committee with the strong support of President Ford and big-city mayors.

Ford had warned through his House leadership that he would veto, in pursuit of his anti-inflation policy, anything higher than an $11.6 billion funding level.

The bill would allow for the first time funding from the federal government for transit operating subsidies.

The President signed the bill Nov. 26.

Anti-inflation panel sets program. The Citizen's Action Committee to Fight Inflation established by President Ford unveiled its voluntary action program Nov. 11 and warned that mandatory wage and price controls would "almost inevitably" follow unless everyone cooperated in the joint effort.

The program called on business people, consumers and workers to sign pledges that they would fight inflation and save energy.

According to plans announced by committee chairwoman Sylvia Porter, state and local groups would be set up to enlist citizens in the Administration's plan to Whip Inflation Now (WIN). The voluntary program hit an immediate snag, however, when Arch Booth, president of the U.S. Chamber of Commerce and a committee member, objected to the pledge suggested for business people because it called on them to promise to "hold or reduce prices." Booth said labor groups were not asked to limit their pay demands.

The pledges proposed by the committee:

For business people: I pledge to my customers that to the very best of my ability I will hold or reduce prices and will buy whenever possible from those who have pledged to do the same. I also pledge to be an energy saver. This signed pledge is evidence of my participation in, and support of, the WIN program.

For consumers: I pledge to my fellow citizens that I will buy, when possible, only those products and services priced at or below present levels. I also promise to conserve energy and I urge others to sign the pledge.

For workers: I pledge that I—through my union—will join with my fellow workers and my employer in seeking ways to conserve energy and eliminate waste on the job. I also promise to urge others to sign this pledge.

Budget-cutting plans scaled down. President Ford revised his budget-cutting plans in the face of the worsening recession in late 1974. Abandoning the goal of a $300 billion budget ceiling, he sent Congress a message Nov. 26 setting a new goal of $302.2 billion for the current fiscal year ending June 30, 1975. This required $4.6 billion worth of spending reductions, which he proposed. To attain $3.6 billion of it, Congress would be required to take 135 separate actions, including enactment of new laws. Another $979 million in savings were to be achieved through 11 actions by executive authority.

The revised budget figures projected a $9.2 billion deficit from receipts of $293 billion and spending of $302.2 billion, both less than recent estimates. The deficit amount was predicated on the $4.6 billion of reductions being proposed, some $3 billion in potential revenues from federal offshore oil leases and $1 billion in revenues from the President's previous proposal for a 5% income surtax. Another underlying assumption for the new figures was that the unemployment rate would not rise above a 6.5%-to-6.7% range. In estimating the unemployment figures, Roy Ash, director of the White House Office of Management and Budget, conceded that "the conditions of the economy are changing faster than we can change the budget." Ash indicated that the deficit could double to the $18 billion level if these basic assumptions for the new figures proved incorrect.

The requested spending cuts of $4.6 billion were drawn largely from health, education and welfare programs ($1.7 billion), veterans' benefits ($1.1 billion) and agricultural programs ($600 million). Defense spending, which Congress already had reduced by $2.2 billion to an $83.6 billion total, would be cut by $381 million more in the Administration revision.

Among the changes proposed were an increase in Medicare costs to the patient, a decrease in the federal share of Medicaid funding, less funds for dental care for the poor and in the amount of money that working welfare mothers could earn without losing benefits.

Congressional leaders briefed—Congressional leaders went to the White House Nov. 26 for a meeting with the President and Ash. Ash told them the budget reductions were an exercise in "dividing up the misery," White House Press Secretary Ron Nessen reported.

Ford told the congressmen he was vetoing, on economic grounds, the bill to increase veterans' educational benefits.

Pentagon closes bases, cuts jobs—The Defense Department Nov. 22 had announced plans for consolidation of 111 domestic military installations that would result in elimination of 11,600 civilian jobs and transfer of 11,500 military personnel to other jobs. The realignment of military bases and headquarters, scheduled to begin in 1977, would result in annual savings of $300 million, which would be rechanneled into "more combat capability and effectiveness," a Pentagon spokesman said.

Pentagon officials conceded that the realignment would not result in a nét saving for taxpayers, but they pointed out that Defense Department buying power had been severely eroded by inflation. One spokesman added that the Pentagon had taken into account the depressed state of the U.S. economy, but had concluded that the elimination of 11,600 jobs would have a minimal impact because the reductions were scheduled over a 2½ year period.

Inflation impact reports sought. President Ford Nov. 27 ordered federal officials to provide inflation impact statements with all major legislation and rules. The reports, patterned after environmental impact statements, would assess the projected costs of government proposals on consumers, businesses, markets and all levels of government; the productivity of wage earners, business or government; the effect on competition, and the effect on supplies of important products or services.

Democrats adopt charter. The Democratic Party adopted a charter Dec. 7, the first such action by a major U.S. political party. The action was taken at the first non-presidential convention in U.S. politics. Some 1,900 delegates attended the mid-term "mini-convention" in Kansas City, Mo. Dec. 6–8. While the major business of the convention was the charter, an "economic recovery" program was espoused by the delegates Dec. 6 as an alternative to the "callous economic nonsense" of the Ford Administration.

In its economic proposal, adopted by voice vote Dec. 6, the convention called for across-the-board controls, a jobs program, tax reform and mandatory energy conservation measures. The statement said "the Republican Administration refuses to take the strong remedial steps that are urgently needed and that Americans are ready to support," although the country was undergoing the "worst recession since the Great Depression and the most serious inflation ever experienced in peacetime."

The controls recommended would be placed on prices, wages, executive compensation, profits and rents, with provision made for wage catch-ups and price rollbacks in particular instances.

The recommended jobs program was an expansion of the public service job program without the restrictions President Ford requested on eligibility of laid-off workers.

On tax reform, the Democrats recommended a package of reductions for low- and middle-income families and increases on high-income families and corporations by closing "tax privileges and shelters," taxing windfall profits and curbing multinational corporations.

Another point in the Democratic program was a call for higher appropriations to finance a much stronger federal antitrust effort and for revision of regulatory statutes protecting industry from competition. Congress, it said, should "explore ways of attacking the growing problem of administered prices."

To aid industry, the Democrats proposed revival of the Reconstruction Finance Corporation as a way to meet "legitimate credit needs in the private sector." The federal agencies also must develop "more selective methods of allocating credit to productive enterprises," the Democrats said, citing examples of housing, utilities, municipal borrowers, food production and small businesses as those who "should receive preference over highly speculative, nonproductive ventures."

The mandatory energy conservation proposal was coupled with a call for accelerated development of alternative sources of energy. The Congressional leadership of the Democratic Party gave its general endorsement to the program and pledged action in the Democratic-controlled Congress. House Speaker Carl Albert (Okla.), Senate Whip Robert C. Byrd (W.Va.) and House Democratic

Changes in GNP, Real GNP, GNP Price Deflator, and the Unemployment Rate

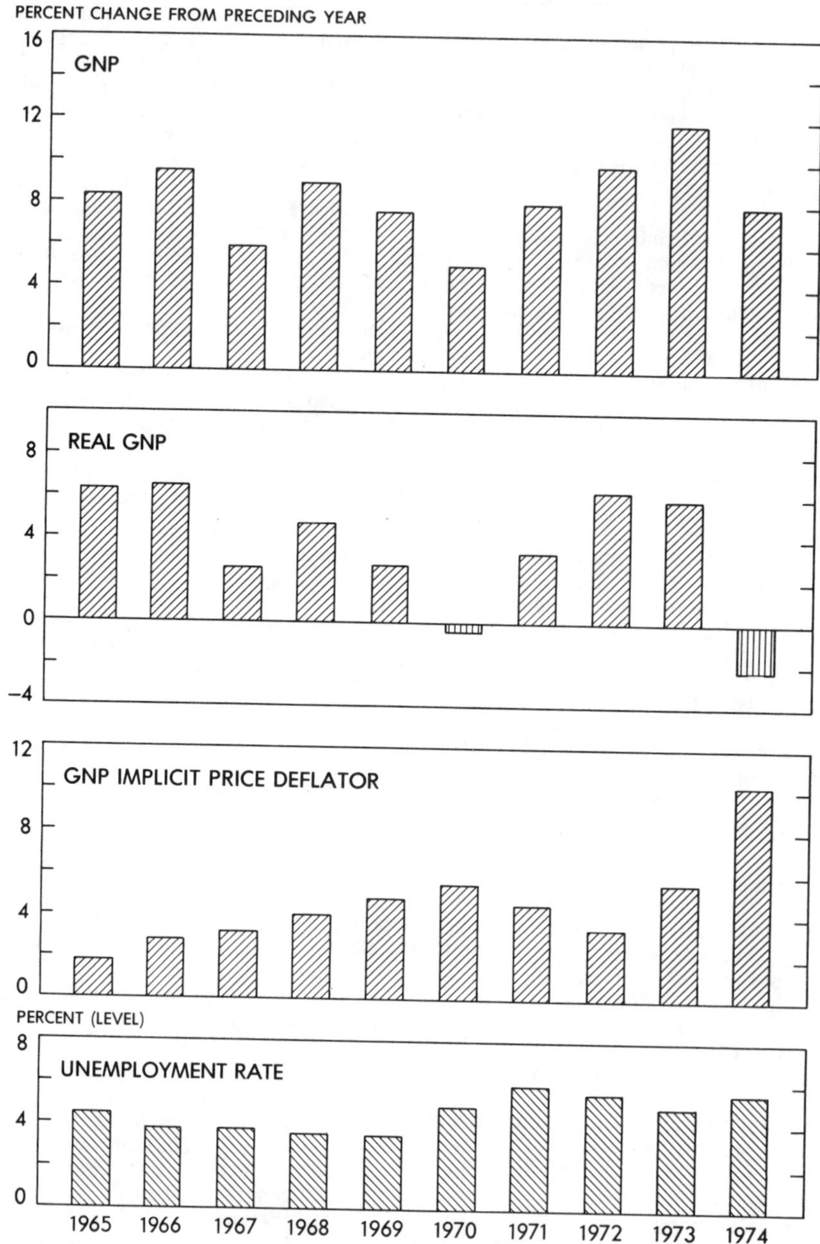

SOURCES: DEPARTMENT OF COMMERCE AND DEPARTMENT OF LABOR.

Leader Thomas P. O'Neill Jr. (Mass.), in addressing the convention Dec. 6, also criticized the Ford Administration. Albert said the Democrats would come up with alternatives to the "timorous, ineffectual, on-again, off-again policies of the Nixon and Ford administrations." O'Neill deplored what he called Ford's "faltering" leadership and promised that "Congress will generate economic recovery legislation of its own." Byrd criticized "meaningless economic summits, exhortations on looking for bargains and planting gardens and WIN-button sloganeering."

Anti-Recession Moves

Ford seeks action. At a televised news conference Dec. 2, 1974, Ford said the nation was "facing three serious challenges, all at the same time—inflation, recession and energy." He called it imperative "to fight both inflation and recession at the same time."

In a reference to the Great Depression, Ford said: "Times are nowhere near desperate enough to paraphrase President F. D. Roosevelt's great rallying cry that the only thing we have to fear is fear itself. Still, it is a good thing to remember." "We are going to take some lumps and . . . bumps," he said, but with the help of Congress and the public "we are perfectly able to cope with our present and foreseeable economic problems."

The "greatest danger," Ford stressed, was "to fall victim to the more exaggerated alarms that are being generated about the underlying health and strength of our economy."

He urged Congress to act on his pending proposals for economic legislation. "Action is more helpful than criticism," Ford said, "and every week that the Congress delays makes the prospects a little bleaker."

(White House Press Secretary Ron Nessen reported Dec. 3 "a growing sense of frustration here at the White House" because of Congressional inaction on the President's economic program given Congress in October. Objecting to complaints of presidential inaction, Nessen said "the business of dealing with inflation and recession is now up to Congress" and unless it acted, the Congress and the economy could "get into a deeper mess." Sen. Barry Goldwater [R, Ariz.] had remarked Dec. 2 that Ford should put the presidential plane away for eight months and focus on domestic problems.)

The President also said he believed Congress had time and the obligation to finish action on "several vital energy proposals before adjourning."

His spending-cut proposals were "a fairly well-balanced program," he said, and his call for a $400–$500 million cut in the defense budget should be viewed along with Congress' cut of $2.6 million in his original defense budget proposals.

He urged Congress "not to add any more spending" to his proposals.

In talking of his jobless proposals, Ford said it "would be irresponsible" for Congress to enact them without offsetting revenue measures.

The President asserted that he did not foresee any gas rationing, "serious shortage" or price rise to a dollar a gallon. There was more gas in storage than a year ago and "less than the anticipated growth" in use, he said. However, "we have to keep the pressure on the savings of energy," he said, "including a hold-down on gasoline consumption."

Asked if he would reconsider his objection to a gasoline tax increase, Ford said: "I have not been persuaded that a 20% increase in the gas tax is the right answer." "There must be a better way" to cut down on consumption than that, he said. Citing a poll to the effect that 81% of the people agreed with his position, he doubted Congress would approve a gas tax rise even if he did submit it.

Ford moves to fight recession. President Ford told members of the Business Council Dec. 11 that the "economy is in difficult straits" and indicated that his Administration was shifting its economic policies to focus on the new threat of recession after emphasizing the fight against inflation.

Ford promised no drastic "pump-priming" remedies for the economy. There would be no "180 degree turn" with recession replacing inflation as "public enemy number one," he said in his New

York speech. But, signaling a shift in economic priorities, Ford said the Administration would seek a "balanced program" aimed at combating the nation's three domestic "devils," inflation, recession and energy.

The new flexibility in Ford's economic program, evident in his message to the corporate executives, was in sharp contrast to his recent views on the economic and his Administration's remedies for the worsening situation. Most observers agreed that the big increase in unemployment during November was a major factor in forcing the White House to reassess its position and update its anti-inflation policies to reflect the changed conditions.

Ford had declined to characterize the current economic downturn as a recession, even after his chief economic advisers had done so. But in his New York address, Ford said flatly, "We are in a recession. Production is declining and unemployment unfortunately is rising."

Presidential advisers were openly discussing the possibility of asking Congress to enact a tax cut in an effort to stimulate the economy. That, too, signaled a fundamental change in White House strategy because the linchpin in Ford's economic proposals submitted to Congress in October was a tax surcharge.

In his speech to the businessmen, Ford claimed some success in reducing price pressures, and added, "I expect inflation will move steadily down from the intolerable double-digit level." He said that "the programs and policies of the federal government will be responsive to changed circumstances and our best available economic forecasts."

8% jobless rate seen by mid-1975. Arthur Okun, former chairman of the Council of Economic Advisers under President Lyndon Johnson, predicted Dec. 2 that the nation's unemployment rate could reach 8% by the summer of 1975 if total output continued to decline during the first half of 1975.

The nation's Gross National Product rate, adjusted to reflect inflation, had fallen for three consecutive quarters, and the current unemployment rate had reached a level of 6% of the U.S. work force. Okun warned that even if the recession leveled off, rather than deepened, unemployment would total at least 7% by mid-1975. The nation's highest post World War II rate of unemployment had occurred in October 1949, when 7.9% of the work force was jobless. (Alan Greenspan, chairman of President Ford's Council of Economic Advisers, said Dec. 4 that he believed the jobless rate would peak at "something over 7%" around the third quarter of 1975.)

Another economist, Michael Wachter, who, like Okun, was a fellow of the Brookings Institution, warned Dec. 2 that labor costs would continue to rise during 1975 and would "prevent a rapid descent" in the rate of inflation. "The outlook for wage inflation for the remainder of 1974 and 1975 appears grim," Wachter said, because wage gains were expected to average 10%–12% regardless of the trend in consumer prices or the unemployment rate.

Energy Policy

Project Independence blueprint. The Federal Energy Administration formally presented its 800-page "Blueprint for Project Independence" to the interagency Energy Resources Council Nov. 13, 1974. The study, in preparation for seven months at a cost of $5 million, originally had been intended to serve as a master plan for the nation's energy policy, but differences within the Nixon and Ford Administrations over energy affairs had resulted in a lack of continuity on policy matters and had diluted the report's impact as a policy setting document.

The plan was presented by Federal Energy Administrator John Sawhill, who had been dismissed by President Ford because of differences over the fuel conservation issue. Sawhill's assistant at the FEA, Eric R. Zausner, was the principal author of the report.

Although President Nixon had set national self-sufficiency in energy needs as the major goal of Project Independence when it was announced in November 1973, designers of the FEA blueprint rejected the idea, opting instead for a goal of independence from "insecure" foreign oil by 1985 and emphasis on strict conservation measures to reduce the volume of energy imports. "If we want to reduce our dependence on imports, we must reduce our energy demands. This is an inescapable conclusion," Sawhill declared.

Highlights of the FEA report:

Conservation—Adoption of a 15¢ a gallon federal tax on gasoline; a mandatory fuel economy standard requiring that cars get at least 20 miles to the gallon; a 25% tax credit for insulating existing housing and a 15% tax credit for improving the energy efficiency of commercial buildings; national heating, cooling and lighting standards for all commercial buildings; efficiency standards for electrical appliances. Greater use of public transportation and redesign of electricity rates could reduce national energy growth by more than half to 2% a year by 1985.

There were two alternatives to strict conservation programs, according to the study. One was intensive exploration and drilling for oil and natural gas, but the FEA noted that environmental hazards, as well as the social and financial costs of the operation, posed strong drawbacks to this approach.

Another choice was establishment of a 1 billion barrel stockpile of oil in underground salt caverns. Maintenance costs for the stockpile were estimated at $1.4 billion a year.

Regarding development of U.S. energy sources:

Oil—Domestic production peaked in 1970 and would continue to decline for several years, despite price increases awarded oil producers as incentives, because the development of new fields required several years. By 1985, domestic production was estimated at 12–20 million barrels a day, with output rising as government-set prices were raised. "Of the estimated 200–400 billion barrels of undiscovered oil in the U.S., one third is in offshore regions."

Natural gas—Reserves had been falling since 1967 and consumption currently was 2–3 times greater than annual discoveries of new supplies. "The outlook for increased gas supplies is not promising" if prices remained at their current, federally-regulated level. Higher prices could stimulate recovery from offshore areas and Alaska.

Coal—Coal, which had provided 90% of the nation's energy supply in 1900, now comprised 17% of all energy consumption; two-thirds of the current use was in electric utility consumption. At the 1974 production rate of 599 million tons, the U.S. had another 800 years' reserves of coal, most of it high in sulfur. Water shortages were possible consequences of some coal gasification plans.

Electricity—Nuclear power plants, which had fallen behind schedule for becoming operational, nonetheless were expected to provide 30% of all electricity by 1985. Rate redesigns could diminish peak power loads and reduce the need for new generating capacity.

Oil shale—Production could reach 250,000 barrels a day by 1985 at $11 a barrel, but a strong push to recover oil shale from the Colorado Rockies could result in a severe water shortage in the area. Development also might require federal price support.

Solar and geothermal energy—Solar energy would become a significant energy source after 1985 because of technological advances and the high recovery and storage costs of fossil fuels. Geothermal energy development had been hampered by delays in awarding federal leases on Western lands under 1970 legislation, but it might prove a significant energy source by 2000, with relatively small environmental costs.

Report calls for stress on conservation. The Ford Foundation's Energy Policy Project concluded after a three-year study that too much stress was being placed on increasing national energy supplies and not enough attention was being focused on conservation efforts.

According to the project report issued Oct. 17, the nation's energy consumption growth rate could be cut by more than half without harming the economy, allowing "massive new commitments" to offshore oil drilling, oil imports, nuclear power and development of coal and shale deposits to be postponed for 10 years.

The Ford study concluded that national energy consumption, which had been expanding at an average annual rate of 4.5% from 1965 through 1973, could be cut to 2% without affecting the U.S. standard of living. "Energy growth and economic growth can be uncoupled," project director S. David Freeman said.

However, that view was not unanimously held. Eight of the project's 21 advisory board members said in a separate statement that "even the most austere self-discipline will fail to resolve the real and ultimate problem of [energy] supply." A ninth member, Mobil Oil Corp. President William P. Tavoulareas, characterized the majority's report as a "formula for economic stagnation" and one that would intensify "government interference in the lives of the American people."

Among the project's recommendations for government imposed conservation rules: higher energy prices, elimination of the oil depletion allowance, enactment of pollution taxes, charging consumers for the cost of stockpiling oil, federal assistance (perhaps as energy stamps) to low income families hard hit by energy shortages or price increases, immediate gasoline rationing and enactment of minimum gasoline economy standards for cars in order to raise average fuel economy to 20 miles a gallon by 1980, federal loans for installation of better building insulation and upgrading construction codes to require improved insulation, and redesign of electricity rates "to eliminate promotional discounts and to reflect peak load costs."

The project also called for the immediate termination of the government's commitment to build a nuclear breeder reactor (one that makes more fuel than it uses), reassessment of federal plans to increase offshore oil leases, and increased research spending on energy derived from unconventional sources, such as solar, and solid and organic wastes.

The report also called for regulation of electric power rates by regional commissions to "assure that utility expansion plans were integrated into regional grids."

Burns asks austerity policy. Arthur Burns, chairman of the Federal Reserve Board, Nov. 27 criticized President Ford's fuel saving program, which relied on voluntary measures, and urged the Administration to adopt an "austerity policy" on energy conservation.

"I hope we won't waste precious time if the voluntary program proves to be inadequate, as many people, including myself, believe it will," Burns told the Joint Economic Committee of Congress. If stronger fuel saving measures were not adopted, he warned, the "alternative drift may lead to a permanent decline in our nation's economic and political power in a very troubled world."

Among the mandatory conservation efforts Burns supported was a "sizable" gasoline tax increase. "We have been lecturing the rest of the world [on cutting fuel consumption] while our own practices leave much to be desired," Burns said. He noted that although Britain, Italy, France, Japan, West Germany and other nations had raised gasoline taxes, "we haven't touched the tax on gasoline."

Burns also said he favored a tax on imported oil and a tax on autos based on horsepower or weight. He called for faster development of domestic energy sources and an increase in U.S. oil storage capacity to mitigate the impact of any new embargo on oil supplies.

Burns called on the U.S. to exert leadership in devising a strategy that would lead to a reduction in oil prices and a diminution of the power of the oil producing nations' cartel.

Price equalization plan adopted. Regulations that would equalize the cost of crude oil among refiners and the cost of fuel oil among distributors were adopted by the Federal Energy Administration (FEA) Dec. 2, 1974. The rules would allocate low-priced domestic oil proportionately among all refiners with the aim of eliminating the price disparities that existed between refiners with greater access to cheaper domestic oil and those which depended on the higher-priced domestic oil and imported supplies.

Although the rules were not expected to cause any net change in the nationwide price of oil, areas of the East, which relied heavily on imported supplies, were expected to benefit from the rules because the burden of using high price oil would be shared by all parts of the nation.

Savings to New England consumers could total $360 million annually, FEA officials said. In other areas, which had easy access to cheaper domestic fuel, prices were expected to rise slightly.

The new regulations, which would take effect gradually over the next two months, were designed to replace the two-tiered price control system for domestic "old" and "new" oil.*

Under the new system, refiners with access to the cheaper old oil were required to sell the rights to that oil to other refiners, reducing their competitive edge and equalizing the cost of oil production. Distributors of home heating oil and residual fuel oil would also be assigned rights to old domestic crude in order to equalize their production costs. (This feature had not been part of the original equalization program proposed in August. The measure was added after Interior Secretary Rogers C. B. Morton yielded to Congressional pressure from representatives of east coast states.)

The new rules were aimed at protecting independent refiners and distributors who had relied on major oil companies for their supplies.

According to officials, the agency's controversial crude oil sharing program, which was also designed to protect independent refiners, would remain in effect, but they added that it probably would be used only in emergencies when adequate supplies of crude were not available through ordinary market channels.

Court rejects Nader suit. Judge Gerhard Gesell of U.S. district court in Washington Dec. 13 rejected a suit brought by consumer advocate Ralph Nader seeking to roll back a $1 a barrel increase in the federally controlled price of "old" oil.

There was "clearly a rational basis" for the Cost of Living Council's decision in December 1973 authorizing the increase, Gesell ruled, adding that the emergency resulting from the Arab oil embargo was justification for the lack of public hearings and comment on the council's action.

15 oil firms roll back prices. Fifteen oil companies agreed to price rollbacks totaling about $77 million to correct alleged overcharges to customers, the Federal Energy Administration (FEA) announced Dec. 17. The FEA also disallowed about $375 million in "banked" costs claimed under a controversial agency ruling, since revised, permitting the oil industry to make a double recovery on costs. These expenses could have been passed on to consumers.

The FEA ordered price rollbacks of $10 million from Standard Oil Co. (Ohio), $6.9 million from Exxon Corp. and $600,000 from Mobil Oil Corp.

The remaining adjustments were settled voluntarily or through consent agreements:

Kerr-McGee Corp., $12.8 million in rollbacks, $2.9 million in cost reductions; Skelly Oil Co., $6.2 million cost reductions; Murphy Oil Corp., $1.4 million cost reductions; Phillips Petroleum Co., $31.7 million cost reductions, $215,000 rollbacks; Amerada-Hess Corp., $6.7 million cost reductions; Texaco Inc., $25.5 million cost reductions; Delta Refining Co., $157,000 cost reductions; Sun Oil Co., $700,000 refund to identifiable customers; Getty Oil Co., $300,000 rollbacks and $940,000 cost reductions; Shell Oil Co., $1 million cost reductions; Charter Oil Co., $4 million rollbacks; and Atlantic-Richfield Co., $1.5 million rollbacks and $8.1 million cost reductions.

The FEA revised its price regulations Nov. 6 to limit the amount of "banked" costs that oil companies could pass on to consumers in any single month to 10% of the total costs that they had delayed passing through by Oct. 31. The action was designed to protect the public from sudden large price increases in any one month. For competitive reasons, oil companies had been accumulating banked costs and postponing recovery of these expenses.

FPC raises gas price ceiling. The Federal Power Commission (FPC) Dec. 4 raised its recently adopted uniform price for natural gas to 50¢ per 1,000 cubic feet, an 8¢ increase over the previous national ceiling price of 42¢.

The new rate, which was made retroactive to June 21, applied to gas sold on an interstate basis to pipeline companies by producers from "new" wells

*Oil production from a given well for each month of 1972 formed the base level. "New" oil was the volume of domestic crude that exceeded the base level for any given month. "Old" oil was the base level minus an amount of released oil equal to new production from the well.

Released oil, which was not subject to federal price controls, provided an incentive that allowed producers to double the amount of oil production at decontrolled prices. The prices of new oil and oil from stripper wells producing less than 10 barrels a day also were uncontrolled. The price of old oil was set by Congress at $5.25 a barrel.

that began operations after Jan. 1, 1973, or that were switched from the intrastate market after that date.

The FPC conceded that the new rate could result in up to a 16% rate increase for consumers, but argued that the rate increase was "more than counterbalanced by a more probable assurance of continued service." (A severe natural gas shortage was expected during the winter months.)

In justifying its action, the FPC said the new rate would enable producers to recover all costs and make a 15% return on investment, thus stimulating exploration and development of the nation's gas supplies.

One commissioner, Rush Moody Jr., argued that the rate still was not high enough and he dissented from the FPC decision. (The FPC also modified another part of its June ruling and increased the gathering allowance for gas that was expensive to produce from 1¢ per 1,000 cubic feet to 1.5¢.)

FPC Chairman John Nassikas joined Interior Secretary Rogers C. B. Morton Dec. 4 in urging Congress to decontrol all "new" natural gas supplies to spur increased production. They coupled that proposal with a call for a tax on the gas industry's excess profits.

Court reverses FPC order—A federal appeals court in New Orleans Nov. 10 ordered the FPC to allow the delivery of greater amounts of cheap natural gas to public utilities. The FPC earlier had ruled that United Gas Pipe Line Co. must reduce its deliveries to utilities, forcing them to switch to more expensive fuels, and thereby conserving gas for use by home owners. The court ruled that the FPC exceeded its statutory authority.

Banking & Finance

Burns concerned over banking trends. Federal Reserve Chairman Arthur Burns expressed concern over the "disturbing trends in modern banking" and the fact that for the first time since the depression, public confidence was faltering in the nation's banking system and in banks throughout the world. Burns' remarks were made Oct. 21, 1974 at a meeting of the American Bankers Association.

He pronounced the U.S. system "strong and sound," but said rapid expansion, diversification and "some carelessness" had made some banks vulnerable to financial trouble. Burns said he was especially worried about the adequacy of bank capital. "The enormous upsurge in banking assets has far outstripped the growth of bank capital," Burns declared.

"At the end of 1960," Burns said, "equity capital plus loan loss and valuation reserves amounted to almost 9% of total bank assets. By the end of 1973, this equity capital ratio had fallen to about 6.5%. Furthermore, the equity capital of banks has been leveraged in some cases at the holding company level, as parent holding companies have increased their equity investments in subsidiary banks by using funds raised in the debt markets. Thus, the capital cushion that plays such a large role in maintaining confidence in banks has become thinner, particularly in some of our largest banking organizations." (Leveraging involved the use of a bank's capital base to expand the holding company's diversification capabilities.)

Burns also criticized banks' increasing reliance on "volatile" funds such as short-term certificates of deposit, potentially excessive loan commitments, deterioration in the quality of some bank-held assets, and "increased exposure of the larger banks to risks entailed in foreign-exchange transactions and other foreign operations."

These "stresses and doubts" within the banking system had brought "sharply in focus the essential role of regulation and supervision in maintaining a sound banking system," Burns said.

Asserting that the federal regulatory system had "failed to keep pace" with changes in the banking system, Burns called for a sweeping overhaul and strengthening of the roles played by the Federal Reserve, the comptroller of the currency and the Federal Deposit Insurance Corp.

Their "parallel and sometimes overlapping regulatory powers is indeed a jurisdictional tangle that boggles the mind," Burns declared. "Even viewed in the most favorable light, the present system is conducive to subtle competition among the regulatory authorities, sometimes to relax constraints, sometimes to delay corrective measures," Burns said. Acknowledging that regulators sometimes were "played off against one another," Burns said banks should not "continue to be free to choose their regulators."

Interest rates decline. The prime interest rate charged by banks on loans to major corporate borrowers registered its first significant decline since March when Morgan Guaranty Trust Co., the nation's fifth largest bank, lowered its base lending rate a quarter point to 11.75% Sept. 25. A prime rate of 12% had generally prevailed throughout the banking industry since July.

The move toward lower rates did not spread quickly, however. The nation's two largest banks, Bank of America and First National City, which announced cutbacks to 11.75% Oct. 4, waited until the Federal Reserve had reported Oct. 3 that most money market interest rates were continuing to decline. Although the demand for business loans rose sharply by $496 million in the week ending Oct. 2 (after showing moderation in recent months from the peak borrowing record set during the first half of 1974), the Federal Reserve also reported a strong slowdown in the growth of the nation's money supply. The money supply (total demand deposits plus cash in public hands) expanded at an annual rate of 1.3% in the quarter ending Sept. 25, compared with a 6% growth rate posted during the first half of 1974. (Growth slowed to 1% at an annual rate in the three months ending Oct. 2.)

There were further indications that money market rates were continuing to fall. (The rate for federal funds, uncommitted reserves that banks lent each other, was down sharply from 12% in August to 10%–10.5% on Oct. 9.) First National City announced Oct. 11 that its prime had been cut to 11.5%. Citibank based its calculations on a floating rate formula which was pegged to money market rates.

Several major banks reduced their prime rates to 11.25% Oct. 18, and First National City led a series of further cuts as it reduced the rate to 11% Oct. 27, 10.75% Nov. 1, 10.5% Nov. 8, 10.25% Nov. 15 and 10% Nov. 22.

Few other major banks followed suit, but the 10.5% prime rate was adopted throughout the industry by Nov. 22.

Analysts attributed the drop to a slowdown in corporate demand for funds and a relaxation of the Federal Reserve's tight money policy.

In a further effort to ease money conditions, the Federal Reserve announced Nov. 13 that it was restructuring its bank reserve requirements, effective Nov. 28. The effect of the changes would be to free $760 million in idle bank funds. The move was also intended to encourage banks to seek more long-term certificates of deposit, rather than rely on the more volatile short-term liabilities to meet liquidity problems.

Changes made by the Federal Reserve: reserve requirements on all time deposits that matured in four months or longer were reduced from 5% to 3%; reserve requirements on time deposits maturing in less than four months were increased from 5% to 6%; reserve requirements on net demand deposits over $400 million were lowered from 18% to 17.5%; the 3% additional reserve requirement on certificates of $100,000 or more left with banks for four months or less was removed.

The Federal Reserve bank requirements were revised again Nov. 18, however, when the Federal Reserve realized that it had "significantly underestimated" the money that would have been injected in the banking system because of the revisions. The new reserve requirement was raised from 5% to 6% on all deposits maturing in less than six months and reduced to 3% on large deposits that matured in six months or more.

The Federal Reserve Dec. 6 signaled its intention to ease its tight-money policy further when officials announced that the discount rate charged on loans to members banks in two regions had been reduced from 8% to 7.75%.

The action was taken hours after the government announced a sharp increase in the nation's unemployment rate to 6.5%.

The Department of Housing & Urban Development (HUD) had announced Nov. 22 that the interest rate on home mortgages insured by the Federal Housing Ad-

Interest Rates

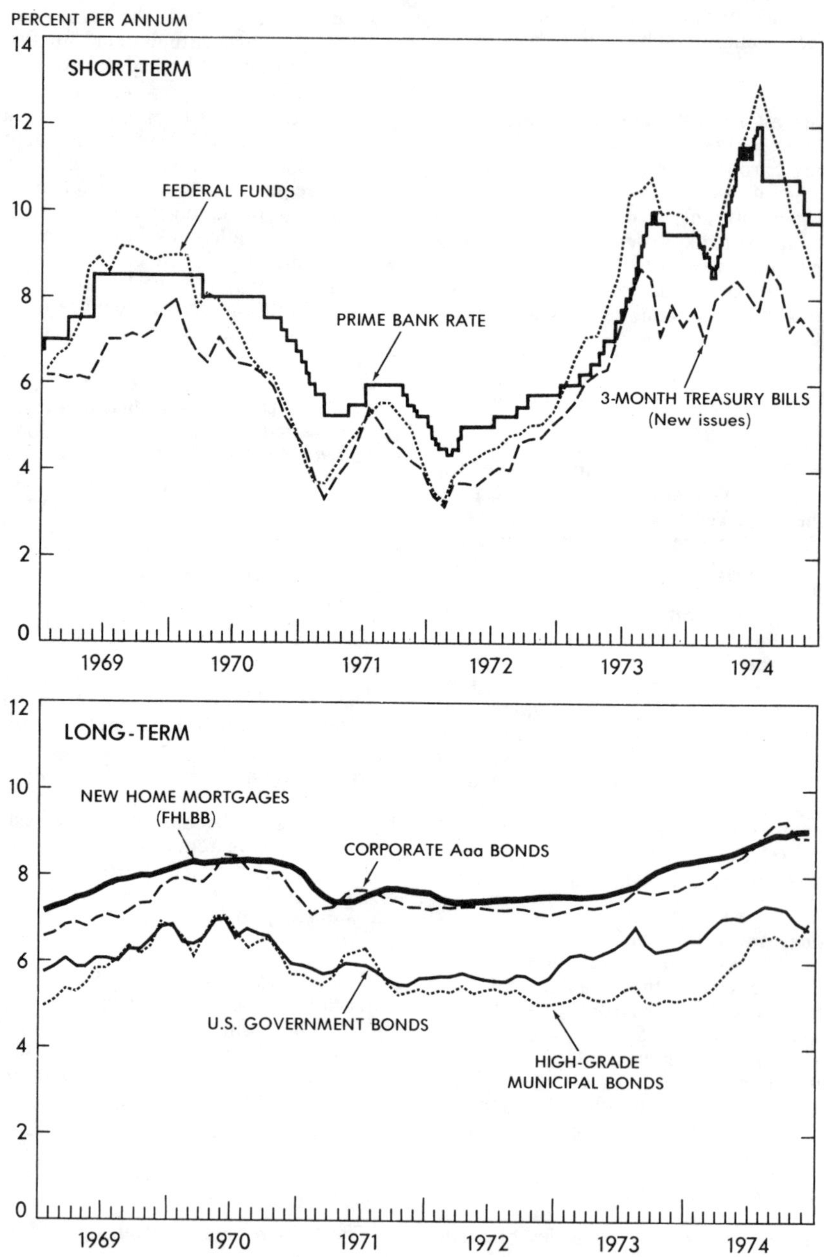

SOURCES: DEPARTMENT OF THE TREASURY, BOARD OF GOVERNORS OF THE FEDERAL RESERVE SYSTEM, FEDERAL HOME LOAN BANK BOARD, MOODY'S INVESTORS SERVICE, AND STANDARD & POOR'S CORPORATION.

ministration and guaranteed by the Veterans Administration had been reduced from 9.5% to 9%. The reduction, the first since January, reflected recent declines in short-term money market rates and the general easing of tight money conditions.

The effective interest rate for home buyers ineligible for FHA or VA mortgages was reduced from 9.92% to 8.895% under the government's conventional mortgage plan, HUD officials announced Dec. 2.

Franklin Bank declared insolvent. Franklin National Bank of New York was declared insolvent Oct. 8 by James Smith, comptroller of the currency, who named the Federal Deposit Insurance Corp. (FDIC) receiver to arrange a take-over of Franklin's assets and liabilities. The FDIC had accepted secret bids that morning from four major New York banks. After the close of banking hours, when Franklin's insolvency was declared, the FDIC named European-American Bank & Trust Co. as the winner in the take-over bidding.

European-American was a federally insured bank, chartered in New York State and owned by six of Europe's largest banks—Amsterdam-Rotterdam Bank N.V., the Netherland's largest bank; Creditanstalt Bankverein, Austria's largest; Deutsche Bank A.G., West Germany's largest; Midland Bank Ltd., a major London clearing bank; Societe Generale de Banque S.A., Belgium's largest bank; and Societe Generale, one of the largest banks in France.

European-American, which prior to the take-over had only three New York offices and deposits of $480 million, paid $125 million for Franklin and promised to assume its $1.7 billion in liabilities. Under arrangements made with the FDIC, all of Franklin's deposits were fully protected and automatically transferred to European-American, which also pledged to operate all of Franklin's 104 branch offices.

European-American, which had been the 190th largest bank in terms of deposits, advanced to 48th rank after the take-over. Franklin, which had ranked 20th among the 14,000 federally insured banks, was the largest bank ever to fail in U.S. history.

FDIC Chairman Frank Wille said Oct. 8 that in its "corporate capacity and not as receiver," the FDIC would purchase $2.08 billion of Franklin's assets. Also in its corporate capacity, Wille said, the FDIC had assumed Franklin's $1.75 billion debt to the Federal Reserve.

The FDIC also announced that Bradford Trust Co., an insured trust company, had acquired Franklin's trust business.

Prior to the take-over, the Federal Reserve announced that it had assumed responsibility for Franklin's $800 million portfolio of foreign exchange commitments. According to a government spokesman Sept. 26, the move was intended to restore confidence in the foreign exchange market, which had been badly shaken by Franklin's huge losses in currency trading and the recent collapse of a major West German bank.

According to Franklin officials, other banks were refusing to sell it foreign currency (because of Franklin's earlier losses on such transactions), thereby preventing the bank from meeting contracts for future deliveries of the currencies.

The Federal Reserve had played a crucial role in Franklin's five-month struggle to recover from the staggering losses reported in May. Depositors had withdrawn more than $1.7 billion—53% of total deposits since May. In a report made public July 21, the bank had revealed that its assets had declined by $845 million to $4.15 billion during the first six months of 1974 and that its net worth had dropped by $62 million to $171 million. Liabilities had risen from $41 million to $1.27 billion over the six-month period.

The Federal Reserve had come under criticism for providing what its chairman, Arthur Burns, described as "gigantic and unprecedented" sums for Franklin. In testimony Oct. 10 before the Joint Economic Committee of Congress, Burns said taxpayers would "not lose one dollar" of that money loaned to Franklin because the FDIC had agreed to assume the bank's debts to the Federal Reserve.

Auto Industry Slump

One of the U.S. industries hit hardest by inflation and recession in 1974 was the automobile manufacturing industry. A drop in sales resulted in reductions of output, the layoff of thousands of workers and sharp declines in profits. Prices of cars, however, continued to climb.

In 1974 U.S. auto sales totaled 8.9 million cars, or 22% below 1973's record level. Sales in 1974 were lower than for any year since 1970 (when a General Motors strike crippled production) and for any non-strike year since 1963.

Production curtailed. Chrysler Corp. disclosed Oct. 17 that it planned a major cost cutting program, including closing one of six of its car assembly plants for three weeks between November and Christmas. Nearly 4,000 employes would be laid off. It was the first significant layoff since spring, when the continuing effects of the oil embargo forced widespread cutbacks in the auto industry.

More than 51,000 industry employes remained on indefinite layoff, according to the New York Times Oct. 18. Ford Motor Co. and General Motors Corp. also disclosed Oct. 17 that their white collar work force had been reduced in the last year. GM had cut its numbers by 10,000 to 130,000. Ford had reduced its work force by 2,000 to total 63,000. Chrysler had laid off 2,400 white collar workers in the previous 12 months. GM Oct. 24 announced scheduled layoffs of at least 6,000 more workers to bring the number of GM employees on indefinite layoff to more than 36,000.

Sales decline brings new cutbacks. The auto industry reported Nov. 5 that in October 1974, new-car sales had fallen nearly 27% from 1973's level. It was the industry's worst sales performance for a new model year in 10 years.

With sales continuing to fall and production off 23.4% from the previous year, massive new layoffs were scheduled.

Ford Motor Co. announced Nov. 1 that 12,000 workers would be idled for one week at assembly plants for small cars and 1,400 other employes were given notice of an indefinite layoff. After two more layoff plans were issued Nov. 7 and 8, the total number of Ford workers on indefinite furlough had risen to 8,400, with another 3,000 parts plant workers laid off an extra week.

General Motors Corp., the largest carmaker and hardest hit by declining sales, had placed 30,000 workers on indefinite layoff by Nov. 8 and then added 5,300 workers to the list during the following week.

Chrysler Corp. had laid off 17,000 workers indefinitely by Nov. 8 and two assembly plants employing 11,800 workers were scheduled for a temporary shutdown.

American Motors Corp., which emphasized small car production, was the only U.S. car maker to report a rise in sales and announce plans to increase production. In a financial report of its fourth fiscal quarter Nov. 13, AMC announced that sales were up 15% for the year but because of a strike in the final period, the firm lost $7 million. For the 1973 fiscal year, net income was $27.5 million—a 38% drop in profits from fiscal 1972.

General Motors had announced Oct. 25 that its net earnings fell from a record $266.6 million in the third quarter of 1973 to $16.7 million in the same period of 1974. It was GM's second lowest income level since World War II.

Ford Motor Co. announced Oct. 30 that its quarterly earnings dropped 50% from the third quarter of 1973 to $47.4 million. Sales were up 21% compared with 1973 to $6.02 billion.

Chrysler announced Nov. 19 that it would close five of its six assembly plants in the U.S. from Thanksgiving until early in January 1975 in an effort to reduce its new car inventories.

The cutbacks would temporarily idle 35,000 employes; another 8,400 workers were scheduled for permanent layoffs, in addition to the 22,000 already on indefinite furlough. Production in the fourth quarter would be slashed 41% from the original schedule and 53% from the comparable period of 1973.

General Motors Corp. also announced continuing cutbacks. Officials said Nov. 14 that car production at its Lordstown,

Ohio small car assembly plant would be halted for two weeks, idling 6,000 workers. One-week closings, affecting another 7,200 employes, were planned for three other plants.

American Motors Corp. announced Nov. 20 that it would shut down two assembly plants for a three-day period.

U.S. car sales in November 1974 were 34% below November 1973 levels, and the big-three car makers produced 31% fewer autos than they had done in November 1973. As inventories mounted, new production cuts and layoffs were scheduled.

General Motors announced Nov. 21 that it had ordered one- and two-week shutdowns of nine of its 22 assembly plants for December and that 30,000 workers would be laid off.

Plans for additional GM closings were disclosed Nov. 29 after it was decided that production in January would be reduced to 337,500 cars. The move, including the elimination of several work shifts and temporary closure of some plants, would temporarily idle 41,000 assembly plant workers and cause 64,000 GM employes to be laid off indefinitely.

Chrysler Corp. confirmed Nov. 22 that 20,000 white collar workers would be laid off temporarily during December, bringing the total number of Chrysler employes without work to more than 80,000. At the same time, it was announced that top Chrysler officials would "forgo a portion of their salaries" during December.

Ford Motor Co. announced Nov. 22 that production would be cut back at 11 of the company's 20 assembly plants in the U.S. and Canada, temporarily idling more than 32,000 workers. (More than 3,000 Canadian workers were affected by the move.) Another 2,500 employes were laid off indefinitely. Ford officials then disclosed Nov. 27 that an additional 25,000 workers were being laid off, either on a temporary basis or permanently. The action raised the number of Ford factory employes without jobs for an indefinite period to 15,500 and the number of laid off salaried workers to about 3,000. A total of 21,400 employes were on temporary layoff.

American Motors Corp. officials said Nov. 22 that 8,000 workers in two small car assembly plants in the U.S. and Canada would be laid off for a week during December.

By Dec. 18, 142,000 workers were on permanent layoff and another 76,000 were temporarily without work throughout the industry.

Ford, auto industry leaders confer. Auto industry officials met with President Ford at the White House Dec. 11 to ask that he extend special aid to the distressed industry. Ford Motor Co. President Lee Iacocca proposed that the Administration freeze federal emission and safety requirements for five years and cut taxes in order to stimulate car sales.

Industry leaders also sought a "one shot" 20% investment tax credit, removal of the federal excise tax on heavy trucks and a general easing of the nation's money supply to make financing of car purchases easier. United Auto Workers President Leonard Woodcock, who also attended the meeting, backed the industry's position and said he would support a "pause" in federal auto standards.

According to White House Press Secretary Ron Nessen, Lynn Townsend, chairman of Chrysler Corp., and Thomas A. Murphy, chairman of General Motors Corp., called on the President to restore public confidence in the economy. Some "highly visible innovations" of this kind were needed to "jolt the public into buying cars," Townsend said.

Nessen added, however, that the auto makers did not offer to stimulate car sales by cutting prices.

Participants at the meeting said afterward that President Ford expressed vehement opposition to a gasoline tax increase because it would be "inequitable."

Henry Ford 2nd, chairman of Ford Motor Co., Dec. 9 called for an immediate 10% income tax cut and asked the government to consider reviving the Reconstruction Finance Corp. of the 1930s to pull the nation out of the current "severe recession." A "lender of last resort" was needed, Ford said, to "make large amounts of capital available to industrial firms, utilities and banks which are unable to obtain badly needed financing today, even though their business is in sound condition, because of the collapse of the equity markets and shortage of loan funds."

The same day, the company announced its third cut in 1975 spending plans. In the latest projection, capital expenditures were set at $800 million, more than $100 million below the original estimate.

Ford dealers ask price cut—An independent organization of Ford dealers Dec. 10 called on the car manufacturer to cut wholesale car prices $200–$400 in an effort to bolster sales.

Contending that they had been forced to absorb much of the industry loss from the steep drop in car sales, spokesmen for the Ford Dealers Alliance blamed the sales slump on the manufacturer's decision to pass on inflationary cost increases rather than reduce its profit margin.

Edwin J. Mullane, president of the association which claimed to represent 1,500 of the nation's 5,700 Ford dealers, said Ford's profit per car was $600–$700.

"Give the law of supply and demand a chance to work," Mullane said. Otherwise, he added, the industry faced the prospect of "massive" new inventory buildups of new cars.

Layoffs & Jobless Benefits

Jobless claims & layoffs mount. The Labor Department said Dec. 18, 1974 that initial claims for unemployment benefits totaled 693,600 in the week ending Dec. 7, up from 169,500 in the week ending Nov. 30, when about 3 million persons were already receiving jobless benefits.

Companies scheduling heavy layoffs included: General Electric Co., which announced Nov. 6 that 11,200 workers would be placed on temporary furlough; Polaroid Corp. said Nov. 6 that 1,000 employes would be laid off by mid-November, adding that 500 part time jobs already had been eliminated; Hershey Food Corp. announced Nov. 7 that 1,000 workers would be laid off temporarily.

In announcements Nov. 21: Goodyear Tire & Rubber said 2,000 of its 12,000 workers would be laid off; and Libby-Owens-Ford Co. told 1,220 employes that they were placed on indefinite layoff.

The continuing coal strike was disrupting shipments to the steel industry and causing the nation's largest steel makers, U.S. Steel Corp. and Bethlehem Steel Corp., to schedule stepped up production cutbacks. By Nov. 22, Bethlehem had laid off 2,800 workers and U.S. Steel had laid off 18,000. The Norfolk & Western Railway, the nation's largest coal-carrying railroad, had announced Nov. 19 that 1,800 workers had been laid off because of the strike.

Celanese Corp. disclosed Nov. 28 that 13,300 workers, nearly 13% of its work force, had been laid off indefinitely because of the "unprecedented sharpness in the reduction of demand" for textile goods.

GE announced plans Nov. 25 to lay off 6,800 employes for a week during December. Magnavox Co. officials said Nov. 22 that 1,140 workers, or about 20% of its work force, were being laid off because of production cutbacks.

Texas Instruments Inc. Nov. 22 announced a drastic curtailment of its worldwide operations. Because of partial or complete plant shutdowns during the remainder of the year, about 50% of the firm's 73,800-person work force would be laid off until Dec. 22 and about 20% of the firm's employes would be without jobs from late December until Jan. 5, 1975.

Quasar Electronics Corp., a unit of Matsushita Electric Industrial Co. of Japan, announced Nov. 28 that three plants would be shut down during the next two months, idling more than 1,500 employes.

Owens-Corning Fiberglass Corp. said Dec. 9 that 2,600 workers, about 20% of its domestic work force, had been laid off indefinitely.

Indefinite layoffs were also scheduled for 2,900 General Electric Corp. employes in January, it was reported Dec. 9. Since mid-summer, when 23,000 persons had worked for GE, its work force had shrunk to about 18,000.

Xerox Corp. officials said Dec. 10 that 6,000 workers would be laid off for two weeks while a major manufacturing facility was shut down and secondary plants remained closed. A permanent work force reduction involving 500 persons was planned for January 1975.

Motorola Inc. announced Dec. 10 that 1,550 employes would be laid off, bringing the total layoffs to more than 5,000 of Motorola's 20,000 personnel.

A two week shutdown was announced by the Hammermill Paper Co. Dec. 16. The production cutback involved 1,120 workers.

It was reported Dec. 16 that a unit of General Dynamics Corp. would lay. off 2,500 production and clerical workers at four plants until Jan. 6, 1975.

It was announced by the Weyerhaueser Co. Dec. 17 that some 4,200 of its 13,000 employes in forest products plants in Washington, and 6,000 of its 7,300 workers in Oregon would be idled temporarily when facilities were shut down for up to 11 days. Weyerhaeuser then extended its production cuts Dec. 23, laying off 3,400 employes for up to two weeks.

Officials of the Alabama Power Co. announced Dec. 19 that 3,000 employes would be laid off for two weeks, beginning Dec. 30.

An estimated 6,700 production workers at American Standard Inc.'s plumbing and heating operations would be laid off or placed on a reduced work schedule during the holidays, officials said Dec. 19.

B. F. Goodrich Co. announced Dec. 19 that 1,800 workers would be laid off for up to 28 days during January 1975.

The Singer Co. announced Dec. 23 that 20,000 workers would be laid off temporarily by the one-to-three-week closings of plants in the U.S. and abroad.

Bethlehem Steel Corp. employes who were without work totaled 5,525 Dec. 23 when it was announced that another 1,600 workers had been furloughed for one week.

The Black & Decker Manufacturing Co. announced Dec. 27 that its operations in the U.S. would be shut down for one week beginning Jan. 13, idling 7,500 employes.

The Celanese Corp. also announced Dec. 27 that it would close two of its fiber plants for six weeks Jan. 4, laying off more than 1,400 workers.

Aluminum Co. of America announced Dec. 30 that it would reduce its primary aluminum production 2.9%. Alcoa had earlier closed three primary production lines, totaling 6.2% of its capacity.

The airline industry, which had been beset by rising fuel costs and declining passenger loads throughout the year, announced plans Dec. 30 to reduce flight schedules and cut back personnel. American Airlines, Allegheny Airlines and Southern Airways were the first carriers to institute the cutbacks.

Price Movements

Inflation rate 10.3% in 1974. Revised statistics made public by the Labor Department Feb. 20, 1975 indicated that the rate of inflation in the U.S. during 1974 was 10.3%, the highest figure since the 11.9% rate of 1947. During the final quarter of the year, prices were increasing at an annual rate of 14.4%.

Taxes led 1974 cost rises. A survey by the Congressional Joint Economic Committee, made public Feb. 9, 1975, found that increases in taxes outpaced all other price rises in the average consumer budget of 1974. Moreover, this rise had greater impact on low- and middle-income taxpayers than on the wealthy, the survey indicated.

The survey, entitled "Inflation and the Consumer in 1974," found that for a family with an "intermediate income" of $14,466, personal federal, state and local income taxes rose 26.5%, and Social Security taxes went up 21.6%. This compared to an overall 1974 inflation rate of 10.2%.

Other highlights of the survey:

Prices for food consumed by low-income families rose faster than food costs for other income groups. Tax collections, swollen by inflation, reduced consumer demand. (In other recessions, the survey noted, tax burdens had declined, providing consumers with more real disposable income.) Real weekly earnings dropped 4.6% in 1974 and real disposable income declined 3%.

As an example of how inflation "perversely" affected the consumer, the survey pointed out that a family of four with an income of $9,320 had to pay taxes in 1974 that were 31% higher than the year before. Yet a family of four with a 1974 income of $20,883 experienced a 26.5% increase in taxes.

Prices of Raw and Crude Industrial Commodities

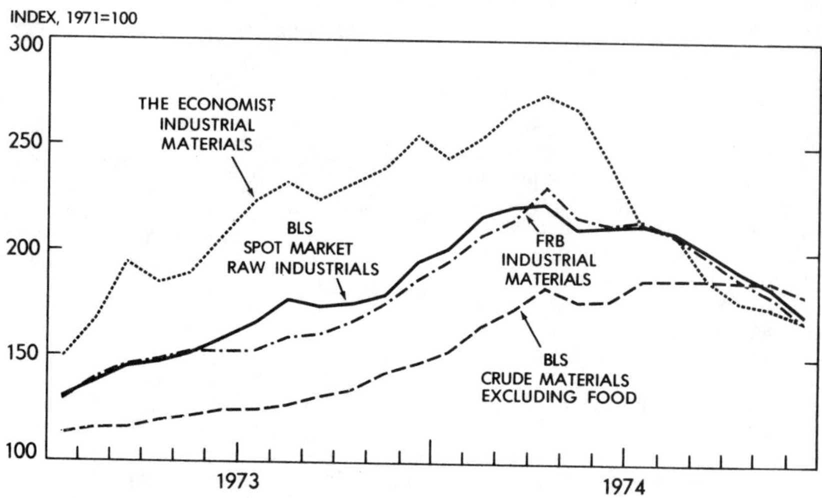

SOURCES: DEPARTMENT OF LABOR, BOARD OF GOVERNORS OF THE FEDERAL RESERVE SYSTEM, AND THE ECONOMIST.

Changes in Wholesale Industrial Prices

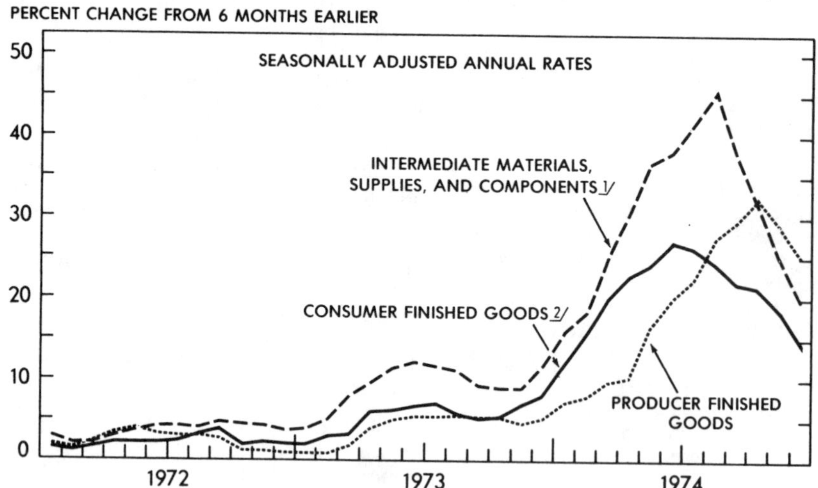

1/EXCLUDES INTERMEDIATE MATERIALS FOR FOOD MANUFACTURING AND MANUFACTURED ANIMAL FEEDS.
2/EXCLUDES FOOD.

SOURCE: DEPARTMENT OF LABOR.

The survey was especially gloomy about the future effects of inflation on the less affluent: "Lower income families are more likely to face budget cost increases higher than those faced by families at higher income levels in 1975 since food, which constitutes a large share of their budgets, is expected to rise faster than other items."

It concluded: "The spiraling inflation of the past three years has had an adverse effect on all consumers, but the poor have clearly borne a greater burden. Not only are they less able to cope with inflation because of their limited discretionary incomes, but low income families and individuals have also suffered price increases significantly greater than those by upper income consumers."

Family costs up 13.5% in '73–'74. The average urban family of four spent $14,-333 during a 12-month period ended in the fall of 1974 to maintain a "moderate" standard of living, the Labor Department said April 8, 1975. Compared with the previous 12-month period, family support costs rose a record 13.5%.

The same hypothetical family on a low budget spent $9,198, up 12.4% from the 1973 period; for families on a more luxurious budget, annual costs rose 14.2% to $20,777.

The figures were based on the budgetary needs of a 38-year-old husband who was an experienced, full-time worker, his wife who was not employed outside the home, a 13-year-old son and an eight-year-old daughter. Family budgets were lowest for those living in the South. Costs were 8%–18% higher in metropolitan areas than in non-metropolitan areas.

Rising food prices had the strongest impact on families with low budgets where food accounted for a large proportion of total costs. Food prices rose 13.2% in the low budget compared with 10.8% in the high budget.

Higher housing costs were felt most severely in the moderate budget, where costs were up 12%, compared with 8.1% in the low budget. Increased transportation costs hit high-income families hardest, rising 15.7% over 12 months. Taxes accounted for the largest increases in all three budgets. Personal income taxes rose 25.7% for those with a low budget, 25.1% in the moderate budget and 26.6% in the high budget.

Indexes soared in '74. The Consumer Price Index (sometimes called the "cost-of-living" index) rose by 12.2% during 1974 and, in December 1974, reached a record level of 155.4% of the 1967 average. The year's increase was exceeded only by the 18.2% rise recorded in 1946 when World War II price controls ended.

Food prices, a major component of the index, rose .7% during December. For the year, food prices were up 12.2%. The rise in nonfood costs abated during December, increasing .4%, the smallest gain since September 1973. For the entire year, however, nonfood costs rose 13.6%. The price of gasoline and other fuels declined for the fourth consecutive month, falling .4%, but for all of 1974, fuel costs rose 20.2%. Fuel oil and coal costs showed a similar pattern, declining .3% in December, but rising 32.4% throughout the year.

Service costs were up .9% during December and climbed 11.3% during all of 1974. A broad range of items in the index showed large yearly increases: shelter costs were up 11.3%; clothing costs were 8.7% higher; transportation was up 13.3%; medical care, up 12.4%. In an exception to this trend, the cost of beef declined 3.1% during 1974.

The Wholesale Price Index (WPI) in December 1974 declined a seasonally adjusted .5%, its first monthly drop since October 1973. For 1974 as a whole, however, wholesale prices rose 20.9%, the steepest yearly rise since 1946's 31.1% increase.

Administration officials attributed the December decline to the mounting effects of the current recession. The downturn should mean "some slowdown in the rate at which consumer prices will increase in the months ahead," said Gary Seevers, a member of the President's Council of Economic Advisers.

Improvement in three areas of the December index gave rise to this optimism: for the month, farm prices declined 4.1% and the cost of processed foods and feed was off 2.5%; the prices of industrial commodities showed no gains (prices had been rising steadily since late 1972); and the wholesale cost of consumer finished goods, items which were represented in the Consumer Price Index (CPI), declined .4%, the first drop since July 1973.

Among industrial commodities, the price of metal and metal products declined 1.1% during December, the largest decrease since May 1968, and textile and wholesale clothing costs were off 1%. Items which rose in price during the month included autos, up 1.3%, fuels, up .7%, and machinery and equipment, up .9%. Over a 12-month period, industrial commodity prices surged 25.6%.

The December WPI for all items was 171.5% of the 1967 base period, meaning that items which had cost $100 at wholesale in 1967 currently cost $171.50.

Buying power dropped—The average manufacturing worker's purchasing power declined 5.4% during 1974—the steepest one-year drop since records were first compiled in 1964. "Real" spendable earnings for the typical worker with three dependents rose .4% in December following five consecutive monthly declines.

Auto makers raise prices. General Motors Corp. said Aug. 9, 1974 that its 1975 model cars and trucks would cost an estimated $500, or nearly 10%, more than the current level. (The price of cars and trucks for the 1974 model year were $500 to $600 higher than those for the 1973 model year.)

The increase, the largest single price hike ever planned by the auto industry, included a $480 rise in the base sticker price, higher optional equipment prices and an additional $15–$20 charge for shipping.

In a letter to its dealers, GM claimed it had "no alternative" but to implement the "substantial increase" because of rising material and labor costs.

In justifying its decision, GM said an average $130 increase was needed to cover the cost of catalytic converters required by the government to remove pollutants from cars' exhaust; another 7% was required to partly pay for "known cost increase" on new models. Materials would cost the automaker an additional 13%, GM said, citing a 29% rise in the cost of steel, and 14%–25% increases in the prices of other metals. Wage and employe benefit costs were expected to rise 10%, GM stated. Another factor contributing to the need for a large increase this time, officials added, was that their prices had been subject to "artificial restraint" by the now defunct Cost of Living Council since the August 1971 freeze was imposed on all prices.

President Ford Aug. 12 issued a statement assailing the GM price increase. In response to Ford's statement, GM announced Aug. 21 that it was cutting the planned increase by an average of $54 per car.

Instead, an increase totaling an average $416, or 8.2%, would take effect. Despite the partial rollback, it remained the largest single price boost in recent industry history.

Ford was "encouraged" by the partial rollback, Press Secretary J. F. terHorst said Aug. 21, but he added, "obviously the President would like to see an even larger reduction, if that were possible."

The price reduction affected cars only, according to GM spokesmen. New truck prices actually were raised again, with a $624, or 10.9%, increase earmarked for the 1975 models. It was reported Aug. 27 that the bulk of the car price increases would be attached to the small car market. Some of the overall price hikes totaled $1,316 (for Cadillac limousines) and 19% (for a small Pontiac model). (A few small cuts averaging about 1% were also planned for a few models.)

An average price increase of more than 8.5% on 1975 model cars was announced Sept. 11 by Chrysler Corp. The $415 price hike represented a $350 increase in the base sticker price, a $50 increase for higher optional costs and optional equipment now included as standard items; and a $15 rise in shipping charges. Chrysler also eliminated several cheaper big car models and affixed large price increases to its more popular small car models, while raising the price of big car models by smaller amounts. (A Dodge subcompact would cost $694 or 21% more than the 1974 version; the price of the full-sized Chrysler Newport was raised $177 or 3.8%.)

American Motors Corp. announced Sept. 11 that it planned to raise 1975 model prices 7.7%, or an average $300.

It was the smallest percentage or dollar increase planned by the auto industry. In another departure from the industry's pricing strategy, American also announced it would produce only small cars in 1975. The sticker price of American's subcompact model, Gremlin, would be raised $300, or 12%, to $2,781.

Ford Motor Co. said Sept. 12 that it would raise prices of new cars and trucks an average of $407, or 8%. Spokesmen said the increase did not reflect the effect on consumers of Ford's decision to drop its 19 lowest price subcompact and full-sized models that were offered in 1974, or its decision to make option packages standard on its lowest price mid-sized models.

The lowest priced 1975 Torino, a mid-sized car, carried a sticker cost of $3,954—$718 or 22% more than the cheapest 1974 Torino. Ford's lowest priced car, the subcompact Pinto, would cost $2,919 in 1975—an increase of $392 or 16% over the 1974 model.

AMC and Ford soon raised their prices again.

American Motors said Oct. 7 that it was increasing the price of its 1975 model cars an average $414—about 10% above average 1974 prices. The increase included the September price boost.

AMC's percentage increase was larger than those announced by the major automotive makers, but its dollar range was comparable to their price increases. Although the price of AMC's cheapest car was raised nearly 13%, it remained the least expensive small car made by U.S. manufacturers, selling for an estimated $2,800.

Ford then quietly raised prices of its 1975 model cars and trucks another 2%, or about $75 a unit, the Wall Street Journal reported Nov. 20.

The annoucement of the price increase, confirmed by Ford officials Nov. 20, was made in a private letter to car dealers. They were told that Ford was raising prices by increasing shipping costs, charging dealers extra for antifreeze that formerly was free, and adding the price of certain optional equipment into the base sticker price, unless the purchaser specifically ordered the model without the optional equipment. This pricing practice, known as "delete option," allowed Ford to continue to advertise its vehicles at the previous lower price.

In a public announcement Nov. 21, Ford reduced the base price of its lowest priced small car by an average $150 or 5.1%. It was the first price cut made by any U.S. carmaker since the fall of 1973.

Ford wins cut in steel price boost. In late 1974 President Ford prevailed on steelmakers to curtail announced increases in steel prices.

The President Dec. 17 had demanded that U.S. Steel justify in writing its planned price increases for two-thirds of its product line. The increases announced Dec. 16 were selective, focusing on items in heavy demand, and ranged from an average 8% on tubular products to 11.6% on standard structural steel. They became effective Dec. 18.

The White House, which had no advance warning of the increases, reacted quickly to U.S. Steel's announcement. White House Press Secretary Ron Nessen said Ford was "concerned and disappointed" about the action and had directed the Council on Wage and Price Stability to launch an immediate investigation of the price increases.

Although the council lacked the authority to order a rollback, Ford increased the pressure on U.S. Steel Dec. 18, asking the firm to rescind part of the increases.

In a reply to the White House issued the same day, U.S. Steel stated that the "increases are fully justified. Our costs continue to rise and our prices for a considerable time have been generally below those already being charged in the marketplace."

Sen. William Proxmire (D, Wis.), chairman of the Joint Economic Committee of Congress, urged the President Dec. 18 to use the "full power of his office to roll back the totally unjustified and unconscionable increases in steel." Proxmire also charged that the firm's decision was in violation of promises made to the joint committee that steel prices would not be raised unless justified by cost increases.

U.S. Steel yielded within a week and announced Dec. 23 that it had reduced its average price increase from 4.7% to 4%.

The firm, the nation's largest steel maker, also said the average level of its steel prices would not be raised for six months, barring "unforeseen major economic events."

In announcing the partial rollback, which totaled about 20% of the planned increases, U.S. Steel said the action was taken "to aid the nation in its fight against double digit inflation."

U.S. Steel's decision to scale down its planned increases followed a meeting Dec. 20 between Albert Rees, chairman of the Council of Wage and Price Stability, and Edgar B. Speer, U.S. Steel chairman. Rees, who had been directed by Ford to seek written justification for the planned increases, was provided with U.S. Steel's confidential cost data. Following the meeting, Rees said a "portion" of the increase was "clearly cost-justified," but added that more time would be needed to analyze all the data.

In data released Dec. 20, U.S. Steel contended that the average price increase planned for two-thirds of its product line was 4.7%. Since Sept. 1, the steel producer said costs had risen more than $20 a ton, and with the latest increases, only $15 a ton in costs would be recouped. Sharply higher labor costs accounted for $5 of that cost breakdown, Speer said, with the remaining $15 accounted for in higher materials costs, particularly iron ore imported from Venezuela.

The Administration extended its efforts to limit steel industry price increases when a small steel producer, CF&I Corp. of Pueblo, Colo., agreed Dec. 20 to provide the wage and price council with written justification for its price increases, announced Dec. 17.

Just prior to U.S. Steel's announcement of a partial price rollback, its chief rival, Bethlehem Steel Corp., announced that it would meet U.S. Steel's original, higher price quotes by implementing an average "overall" increase of 2.5% for rolled steel products. Rees immediately demanded a "full explanation and justification" for the price hike, and asked Bethlehem and CF&I to reconsider their recently announced price increases in light of the U.S. Steel rollback.

Bethlehem Dec. 28 also announced a 20% rollback in its planned price increases and pledged not to raise prices before June 1, 1975, as requested.

The decision to implement a partial rollback was made after a meeting Dec. 27 with wage and price council officials.

Bethlehem had claimed its average "overall" price increase would total 2.5%. According to the New York Times Dec. 28, independent calculations set the average increase at about 5%. In announcing the partial rollback, Bethlehem said it would forego a scheduled increase on tin plate and steel rails, but permit a 4% increase on plate steel and a 6% increase on structural steel to take effect.

Amtrak fares to rise 10%. Amtrak, the nation's passenger railroad corporation, announced Oct. 26 that it was increasing fares on most of its routes by 10%, effective Nov. 15. The need for the increase was blamed on rising fuel, labor and materials costs. Inflation had also been cited as the need for an earlier nationwide fare increase of 5% that had taken effect in April.

CAB OKs 4% air-fare boost. The Civil Aeronautics Board (CAB) Oct. 31, 1974 approved a new 4% increase in the price of domestic air fares and made permanent a 6% fare increase granted earlier on an interim basis.

The CAB also approved an amended agreement submitted by the International Air Transport Association (IATA) calling for a 6%–11% fare increase on transatlantic flights.

The fare increase was approved on a 3–2 vote. The dissenters, Lee R. West and G. Joseph Minetti, criticized the increase as inflationary and "clearly contrary to the national interest." The airlines had contended that the sharp rise in fuel costs required a fare increase, but West and Minetti replied that domestic fuel prices had leveled off recently and that airlines had already been compensated for previous fuel cost hikes. Domestic air fares had increased approximately 25% in the past 12 months.

A group of 25 congressmen charged Nov. 13 that the fare boost was improper and asked the CAB to roll back the increase. The spokesman for the group, Rep. John E. Moss (D, Calif.), contended that the CAB had wanted to reject the airlines' request for another fare increase, but instead approved it after communicating informally with the carriers and winning their agreement to set an expiration date of June 30, 1975 on the increase.

The CAB rebuffed the Congressional petition Nov. 14 and defended the expiration date as an effort to protect airline passengers from "excessive charges" in the event that the industry's profits climbed by mid-1975.

In a report issued Nov. 6, the Brookings Institution charged that airline passengers had paid up to $538 million in "excess fares" annually because of the CAB's inefficient and rigid regulation of the airline industry. "The principal sources of economic inefficiency in air service may be ascribed to regulator-imposed restraints on competition," the report stated.

The study also urged deregulation of the airline industry "to the degree politically feasible." Airlines operating within Texas and California were subject only to the authority of state utility commissions and offered fares at less than half the cost per mile of scheduled (federally regulated) airlines, the study noted.

Wages Up

'74 wage gains topped 1973. Major collective bargaining agreements negotiated during the first nine months of 1974 for 4.1 million workers exceeded wage gains won in 1973, the Department of Labor reported Oct. 25, 1974.

During the nine-month negotiating period, wage increases won in the settlements averaged 9.6% for the first year of the contract, compared with 5.8% in 1973, and 7.2% over the life of the contract, compared with 5.1% in 1973. The data applied to 918 settlements in the private nonfarm economy, affecting 1,000 workers or more, and excluded possible cost of living adjustments.

In contracts covering 5,000 workers or more, the wage and benefit gains were greater, averaging 10.1% for the first year, compared with 7.1% in 1973, and 7.5% over the life of the contract, compared with 6.1% in 1973.

Cost of living provisions were adopted in 110 settlements, affecting more than 600,000 workers, during the first nine months of 1974. It was estimated that escalator clauses currently covered 5 million workers in major bargaining units (49% of the total).

Contracts containing cost of living clauses provided annual wage increases (exclusive of potential cost of living benefits) of 5.9% over the life of the contract, compared with wage gains of 4.9% won in 1973. Contracts without cost of living adjustments had annual wage increases averaging 8.9%, compared with 5.3% won during the previous year.

First year negotiated increases and cost of living adjustments already put into effect averaged 11% in settlements containing escalator provisions that were reached during the first nine months of 1974.

According to a study by the Council on Wage & Price Stability (reported in the Wall Street Journal Aug. 20, 1975), cost-of-living clauses accounted for only a fraction of wage-cost increases in 1974.

The report said, however, that added reliance on the escalator clauses, which tied wage increases to consumer price increases, could make inflation more difficult to control in the future.

By the end of 1974, contracts for an estimated 7.7 million workers, about 10% of the nation's nonagricultural workforce, contained cost-of-living clauses, the study noted. The clauses accounted for 20% of the average wage increases won for all workers covered by major collective-bargaining agreements. From 1968 through 1974, the study said, escalator provisions permitted workers to regain about 50% of their buying power that was lost to inflation.

According to another study, prepared by Arthur Young & Co. (released Sept. 3, 1975), the average salary of middle- and top-management executives increased 12% in 1974, the highest rate ever recorded. The study was based on a survey of salary and bonus compensation paid by 1,100 companies. (In 1971–1972, compensation had increased 8.7%.)

Copper strikes bring raises. New three-year contracts with the major copper producers were concluded by Aug. 15, 1974 after an intensive two-month period of bargaining marked by strikes. The wage agreement was said by union spokesmen to compare with that in the steel industry reached earlier in the year by the AFL-CIO United Steelworkers of America. The USW was the major component of the 26-union Nonferrous Industry Conference, which conducted the copper negotiations.

Anaconda Co. was the first of the "Big Five" copper producers to settle; an agreement covering its 7,000 workers was reached June 25 before the contract deadline June 30. The new pact called for across-the-board wage increases of 28¢ an hour in the first year, 16¢ in the second year and 17¢ in the third year. It also incorporated into the base wage another 62¢ an hour the workers already were receiving as cost-of-living increments under previous pacts. The basic monthly pension was raised from $7.50 to $11 for each year of service.

The basic wage increase was boosted to about 86¢ an hour by adjustment of job classifications and corresponding wage differentials.

After the Anaconda settlement, the strike deadline for the other producers was extended to July 14. However, walkouts at some locations of Kennecott Copper Corp. and American Smelting & Refining Co. (Asarco) began July 2. A full strike against four of the "Big Five" firms—Phelps Dodge Corp. and Newmont Mining Corp.'s Magma Copper Co. as well as Kennecott and Asarco—were launched July 15. Kennecott reached a settlement covering its 10,000 workers later in the day. A settlement with Magma (4,600 workers) was reached Aug. 14, with Asarco (5,000 workers) Aug. 15, with Phelps Dodge (6,000 workers) later Aug. 15.

All settlements were said to be in the Anaconda pattern. The average wage scale in the industry before the settlements was $4.30 to $4.61 an hour, excluding the cost-of-living increments built into the new pacts. The new range after three years would be $5.78 to $6.09.

East Coast dock pact. Dock workers in Baltimore voted ratification Sept. 5, 1974 of a new three-year labor contract covering some 35,000 longshoremen from Portland, Me. to Hampton Roads, Va. The master contract, between the AFL-CIO International Longshoremen's Association and the Council of North Atlantic Shipping Associations, had been worked out in negotiations June 21. It called for an increase of $2.72 an hour, $1.90 to be applied to wages and 82¢ to pension and welfare funds. The base hourly wage rate would rise from the current $6.10 to $8 in the third year of the new pact.

Rank-and-file union approval was announced Aug. 21 for the ports of New York-New Jersey, Boston, Providence, Philadelphia and Hampton Roads. But the pact was rejected by the Baltimore dock workers, who were seeking a guarantee of more hours pay for workers called to a job and more hours of guaranteed pay annually. Under the new pact, the guaranteed annual pay, negotiated in 1964, ranged from a total of 2,080 hours in New York-New Jersey docks to 1,250 hours in South Atlantic ports. The Baltimore dock workers, whose guaranteed pay would remain 1,900 hours, approved the new pact Sept. 5.

During the negotiations, which had begun in March, management agreed May 13 to restore to the dockworkers a 15¢-an-hour pay increase that had been cut by the federal Pay Board from a 70¢ increase arranged in 1972. About 12,000 West Coast dock workers, members of the International Longshoremen's and Warehousemen's Union, won a 30¢ hourly wage boost May 7 on similar grounds after staging a one-day work stoppage May 1, closing ports from Seattle to San Diego. The 30¢ had been cut by the Pay Board from a pay increase negotiated in 1972.

Great Lakes dock pact—Negotiators for the AFL-CIO International Longshoremen's Association and Great Lakes stevedoring companies reached agreement Dec. 20 on their first master contract for some 12,000 longshoremen and 65 employers. It called for wage and fringe benefits to be boosted a total of $2.72 to the $10.57 level ($7.80 in wages) by 1977.

Boeing contract. The Boeing Co. and the AFL-CIO International Association of Machinists (IAM) agreed on a new three-year contract Sept. 30 covering 27,000 employes in Seattle, Wichita, Kan. and Cape Canaveral, Fla. The pact, ratified by the union membership Oct. 2, called for wage increases averaging 11½% the first contract year and 3% in each of the next two years. Cost-of-living adjustments in pay based on the consumer price index (1¢ an hour for each .3% rise in the index) would be made on a quarterly basis. Under the old contract, which expired Oct. 1, they were made annually. The first-year wage rise included incorporation into the base wage of a 33¢ an hour cost-of-living increase. The base hourly wage scale under the new pact would rise to $4.50–$7 in the first year.

American Motors raise. Agreement on raises and a new two-year contract was reached Oct. 1, 1974 by negotiators for American Motors Corp. (AMC) and the United Auto Workers (UAW). The strike-ending agreement was ratified by the union membership Oct. 6 and the strikers, who had walked out Sept. 16 when the old contract expired, returned to work Oct. 7. Negotiations for the new pact had begun July 25.

The new pact, covering about 15,000 workers, would raise the AMC wage and benefit package to that set in the Big Three negotiations in 1973. Under the pact, wages for an assembler would rise from about $5 an hour to $5.91, all but 19¢ of it cost-of-living boosts built into the base pay rate. Supplemental unemployment benefits, a 30-years-and-out retirement plan, pension and insurance plans were also to be made equivalent to Big Three standards.

Raise ends bus strike. Greyhound Lines Inc. bus service was shut down for a week by a strike of drivers and terminal workers Nov. 18–24. Some 16,000 employes were idled by the strike, the first on a nationwide basis against Greyhound. The nation's largest intercity bus system normally carried 190,000 daily passengers.

The strikers, members of the AFL-CIO Amalgamated Transit Union, began returning to work shortly after an accord was reached Nov. 24 on a new three-year contract to provide an additional 16% in wages and benefits. Under the old pact, drivers were paid $5.75 an hour or 21.8¢ a mile, whichever was higher.

Coal settlement. United Mine Workers President Arnold R. Miller signed a new national coal contract Dec. 5 and officially ended the miners' 24-day strike.

Miller announced that 56% of the 79,495 miners voting on the new pact had approved it. It was the first contract in the union's history to be subject to rank and file ratification. About two-thirds of the union's 120,000 members had voted.

The contract with the Bituminous Coal Operators Association would provide for a 54% increase over the three years in the $8.11 average hourly compensation. The increase included wages and fringe benefits and assumed an 8% annual rate of inflation, or the maximum increments written into the contract in the cost-of-living escalator clause.

An earlier agreement had been reached by the negotiators Nov. 13, one day after the start of the strike, but it was revised Nov. 24, with the aid of Treasury Secretary William E. Simon, after the union's 38-member bargaining council had demanded improvements in the Nov. 13 pact.

Simon intervened in the negotiations Nov. 24. "A prolonged coal strike would have very serious economic implications," he said, "so as the chief economic spokesman, I consider this my very deep responsibility to attempt to work toward a resolution of this issue." He met at the Treasury Department with industry executives and later, at management's request, went to the hotel where negotiations were being conducted. W. J. Usery Jr., director of the Federal Mediation and Conciliation Service, also joined the negotiations Nov. 24.

Agreement on a revised contract was reached later Nov. 24. The major revision was in wages and a vacation provision. The original terms for wage increases of 9% the first year, 3% the second and 3% the third year of the contract were changed to 10%, 4% and 3%. Quarterly cost-of-living increments to be initiated in the second year were to begin February 1975. Instead of splitting two basic weeks of vacation as proposed in the original agreement—one in the summer and one at Christmas, when absenteeism traditionally was high—the contract would permit the miners to take the two weeks in the summer, as in the past.

The revised contract was put before the UMW bargaining council Nov. 26. It rejected it by a vote of about 2–1, reportedly on the wage issue. Miller said he believed the members of the union "should have the right to express their will." He reconvened the council, which reversed itself and approved the contract.

Simon, asked Nov. 25 if the new contract was not "pretty inflationary," said "we must recognize that inflation is one of the major problems that we have in this country today and that the real wages in the past year have declined for all workers in the United States. And there has to be some recognition of that fact taken in every settlement."

New York milk strike. An 11-day strike by milk drivers and plant employes in the New York City area ended Dec. 14 with ratification of a new contract calling for the weekly base wage of plant workers to rise from $216 to $270 in two years. The drivers retained their commission of 1.5% of the dollar volume of sales and would receive an $8 raise in weekly base pay in the second contract year. The strike, by members of the International Brotherhood of Teamsters, affected 115 milk processors and distributors and some 10 million consumers.

Washington paper votes 4-day week. Editorial and business employes of the Washington Star-News, the city's only afternoon daily newspaper, voted overwhelmingly Dec. 9 to accept a 20% pay cut by working a 4-day week for 4 days' pay. The move had been initiated by the paper's unit of the Washington-Baltimore Newspaper Guild in response to a cost-saving plan developed by the paper's management calling for the dismissal of 100 employes, 20% of the Guild's Star-News membership.

The newspaper had reported losses totaling nearly $15.5 million over the last four years, including nearly $5 million in 1973. The 4-day week was the first imposed by a major U.S. newspaper since the Depression.

Despite the cutback, other provisions of the current contract between the paper and the union would take effect, including cost of living wage increases and raises due in April 1975.

Production, Income & Other Developments

Total GNP up but 'real' GNP down in 1974. Revised statistics made public by the Labor Department Feb. 20, 1975 revealed that the U.S. Gross National Product (GNP) totaled $1.397 billion in 1974. Although this "total" output of goods and services exceeded the 1973 total by 7.9%, all of the increase was due to inflation, and 1974's "real" GNP (adjusted for soaring prices) was reported to have been 2.2% below 1973's.

In releasing earlier statistics on the economic developments of 1974, Commerce Department officials had indicated Jan. 16 that they considered the current recession and inflation the worst the U.S. had experienced for many years.

"The current situation is extremely bad. Everything is bad," a Commerce Department spokesman said, and he added, the "breadth of the decline and other evidence suggests that real output may decline again in the current quarter" as business inventories continued to mount and new orders were slashed.

Some officials contended that the current recession was the worst since the 1930s, noting that since the downturn began at the end of 1973, demand and production had fallen 5%, compared with a 3.9% decline during the 1957–1958 slump.

The depressed states of two major industries accounted for most of the quarterly decline in economic activity, officials said. Half of the three-month downturn in total production came in the auto industry and one-fourth was in the housing industry.

The Federal Reserve Board had reported Jan. 15 that production in the nation's factories, mines and utilities had declined by

6.5% during 1974. This was the sharpest 12-month decline in industrial output since the 7.2% decline of October 1969 to October 1970. Production had dropped 2.8% during 1974's final month.

The December decline was the largest one-month drop since August 1959 when there was a nationwide steel strike. Production during the 4th quarter of 1974 was off 12.1% at an annual rate, the sharpest fall since World War II.

According to officials, there were sharp declines in production in a "wide range of industrial materials" during the month. Automobile production dropped 25%. Coal output, which had declined 32% during November because of a nationwide strike, increased only 9% over the earlier depressed level.

Productivity shows first yearly decline. Productivity of the nation's work force declined 2.7% throughout 1974, the Labor Department said Jan. 27, 1975. It was the first yearly decline in the measure of output per manhour since records were first compiled in 1947. Officials attributed the decline to the worsening recession and a drop in output, rather than to changing work habits.

For the 4th quarter of 1974, productivity plunged at an annual rate of 5.1%, the second largest decline on record. In the manufacturing sector, however, productivity increased at an annual rate of .6% during the 4th quarter and gained .8% for the year. The improvement was largely a reflection of increased layoffs during the final period of 1974, when a sharp drop in hours work offset a decline in output.

In the nonfarm sector, productivity was off 2.8%for the year and 3.7% at an annual rate during the 4th quarter. (It was the seventh quarterly drop in a row and the longest period of decline on record, according to officials.)

The private economy's unit labor costs increased at an annual rate of 14.7% during the 4th quarter. In the nonfarm sector, the quarterly gain was 13.3% and in manufacturing, costs were up 12.9%.

"Real" compensation per manhour, adjusted to reflect the effects of inflation, declined 2.8% at an annual rate during the 4th quarter and dropped 2.1% throughout the year. In manufacturing, real compensation rose 1.4% during the quarter but declined 1.3% throughout the year. The nonfarm sector registered a 2.6%

Gross National Product & Major Components

		Personal Consumption Expenditures						
Year	Total GNP	Durable Goods	Nondurable Goods	Services	Total	Government Purchases	Domestic Investment	Net Exports
				(Billions of current dollars)				
1960	503.7	45.3	151.3	128.7	325.2	99.6	74.8	4.0
1965	684.9	66.3	191.1	175.5	432.8	137.0	108.1	6.9
1970	977.1	91.3	263.8	262.6	617.6	219.5	136.3	3.6
1971	1,055.5	103.6	278.7	284.9	667.2	234.3	153.2	0.8
1972	1,158.0	118.4	299.7	310.9	729.0	255.7	179.3	−6.0
1973	1,294.9	130.3	338.0	336.9	805.2	276.4	209.4	3.9
1974	1,397.3	127.5	380.2	369.0	876.7	309.2	209.4	2.0
Year				(Billions of constant 1958 dollars)				
1960	487.7	44.9	149.6	121.6	316.1	94.9	72.4	4.3
1965	617.8	66.6	178.6	152.5	397.7	114.7	99.2	6.2
1970	722.5	83.8	206.5	187.2	477.5	139.3	103.4	2.3
1971	745.4	92.2	211.6	192.4	496.3	138.4	110.3	0.4
1972	792.5	104.9	220.2	202.2	527.3	143.1	125.0	−3.0
1973	839.2	113.6	228.6	209.9	552.1	144.4	138.1	4.6
1974	821.1	103.1	223.7	212.6	539.5	146.0	126.7	9.0

Source: U.S. Department of Commerce.

Note: Parts may not add to totals due to rounding.

Table from National Consumer Finance Association, 1975 Finance Facts Yearbook

Indexes of Productivity & Related Data

[1967=100]

Item	1950	1955	1960	1965	1966	1967	1968	1969	1970	1971	1972	1973	1974
Total private:													
Output per hour of all persons	59.7	69.9	77.9	94.1	98.0	100.0	103.0	103.5	104.3	108.4	112.3	115.1	112.0
Compensation per hour	42.9	56.2	72.1	88.7	94.8	100.0	107.8	115.7	123.9	132.1	140.2	150.9	164.0
Real compensation per hour	59.5	70.1	81.4	93.8	97.5	100.0	103.4	105.4	106.5	108.9	111.9	113.4	111.1
Unit labor costs	71.8	80.4	92.6	94.2	96.7	100.0	104.7	111.8	118.8	121.8	124.8	131.1	146.5
Unit nonlabor payments	69.3	78.6	84.5	95.7	97.9	100.0	102.0	102.8	105.3	112.5	116.4	124.2	134.0
Implicit price deflator	70.8	79.7	89.5	94.8	97.2	100.0	103.6	108.3	113.6	118.2	121.6	128.4	141.6
Private nonfarm:													
Output per hour of all persons	65.1	73.8	80.0	94.9	98.5	100.0	103.0	103.0	103.3	107.2	111.2	113.6	110.4
Compensation per hour	45.4	58.9	74.2	89.5	94.8	100.0	107.4	114.9	122.5	130.6	138.7	148.8	161.9
Real compensation per hour	63.0	73.4	83.7	94.7	97.5	100.0	103.1	104.6	105.3	107.7	110.7	111.8	109.6
Unit labor costs	69.7	79.8	92.8	94.2	96.2	100.0	104.3	111.6	118.6	121.9	124.8	130.9	146.6
Unit nonlabor payments	68.7	78.9	84.1	95.6	97.7	100.0	102.3	102.6	105.3	112.7	115.3	117.9	129.2
Implicit price deflator	69.3	79.5	89.5	94.7	96.8	100.0	103.5	108.1	113.5	118.4	121.2	126.0	140.0
Nonfinancial corporations:													
Output per all-employee hour	(1)	(1)	79.2	96.5	99.0	100.0	104.2	106.0	106.9	112.0	116.9	120.5	117.7
Compensation per hour	(1)	(1)	75.1	90.2	95.0	100.0	107.2	114.6	122.8	131.4	139.7	149.9	163.0
Real compensation per hour	(1)	(1)	84.8	95.4	97.6	100.0	102.8	104.4	105.5	108.4	111.5	112.7	110.4
Unit labor costs	(1)	(1)	94.8	93.4	95.9	100.0	102.8	108.1	114.9	117.4	119.6	124.4	138.4
Unit nonlabor payments	(1)	(1)	88.6	99.3	99.5	100.0	102.1	100.2	101.3	107.8	110.0	112.2	119.2
Implicit price deflator	(1)	(1)	92.6	95.6	97.2	100.0	102.5	105.3	110.0	113.9	116.1	120.0	131.5
Manufacturing:													
Output per hour of all persons	64.3	73.6	79.8	98.3	99.8	100.0	104.6	107.4	107.8	115.2	121.7	128.3	129.2
Compensation per hour	44.5	59.9	76.5	91.1	95.2	100.0	107.1	114.1	122.0	130.4	137.6	147.2	161.1
Real compensation per hour	61.8	74.7	86.3	96.4	97.8	100.0	102.8	103.9	104.9	107.5	109.8	110.6	109.0
Unit labor costs	69.2	81.3	95.8	92.7	95.4	100.0	102.3	106.2	113.2	113.2	113.1	114.8	124.6
Unit nonlabor payments	81.1	86.9	90.1	102.4	101.6	100.0	102.2	94.4	91.3	97.3	99.2	98.4	(1)
Implicit price deflator	72.9	83.1	94.1	95.6	97.3	100.0	102.3	102.6	106.5	108.3	108.8	109.7	(1)

[1] Not available.

Table from Bureau of Labor Statistics, Monthly Labor Review, February 1976

quarterly decline and a 2.1% drop during the year.

Personal incomes up. Personal incomes in the U.S. rose by 9% ($95.4 billion) during 1974 to a $1.15 trillion total for the year.

Incomes increased $5.2 billion in December to a seasonally adjusted annual rate of $1.19 trillion, according to the Commerce Department Jan. 15, 1975. However, officials cautioned that the small gain was a result of a large rise in government benefit payments that offset a second consecutive decline in payroll outlays.

Wages and salaries declined .3% during the month to an adjusted annual rate of $765.4 billion, following a .7% decline in November. Manufacturing payrolls were off 2.3% in December and 2.4% in November. Government transfer payments—chiefly Social Security, veterans aid and welfare—expanded by $6.1 billion (4.1%) throughout the month.

'Real' family income fell in 1974. The average family's income increased 6.5% during 1974, but because of double-digit inflation, failed to keep pace with inflation, the Commerce Department reported July 23, 1975. While medium income for 1974 was $12,840, compared with $12,051 in 1973, real income adjusted for price changes declined 4% from the 1973 level.

The number of persons with incomes below the poverty line increased by 1.3 million (5.6%) in 1974 to 24.3 million, despite an increase in the official poverty line for a nonfarm family of four to $5,038 from $4,540 in 1973. Those who were officially designated "poor" represented 11.6% of the population.

Whites accounted for 1.1 million out of the 1.3 million rise in the poverty population; 15.7% of all persons 65 and older were classified as poor in 1974, 8.9% of whites, 31.4% of blacks, 15.5% of all children under 18, and 40.7% of all black children under 18.

The top 20% of the population had incomes of more than $20,445. Those with incomes over $31,948 were in the top 5% and persons with incomes exceeding $50,000 were in the top 1.1%.

1974's profits slump. Revised figures issued by the Commerce Department April 17, 1975 indicated that after-tax corporate profits declined 15.7% in the 4th quarter of 1974 to a seasonally adjusted annual rate of $79.5 billion. The quarterly drop in earnings was the steepest since the 16.5% decline of 1958's first quarter.

According to officials, the falloff in after-tax profits reflected a sharp reduction in inventory profits. During the year, many companies tried to adjust their inventory profits, swollen by inflationary price changes, by adopting a new accounting method that tended to depress earnings.

Supermarket profits at 3-year high. Supermarket profits during 1974 were at their highest level since 1971, according to an industry survey May 5, 1975. Net earnings as a return on total assets were 4.1% in 1974, compared with 2.5% in 1973, 4% in 1972 and 5.3% in 1971. The report marked the first time the industry had provided a breakdown of profits as a return on investments and assets, as well as in terms of a percentage of sales.

Consumer confidence at record low. Consumer confidence was at its lowest level since attitudes were first measured following World War II, according to the University of Michigan's Survey Research Center Dec. 12, 1974.

Consumer confidence had been falling since 1972, analysts said, declining sharply in February at the height of the Arab oil embargo, and during October. Pessimism appeared to be growing as industry layoffs increased and sales worsened.

Record drop in consumer credit. The Federal Reserve Board said Jan. 6, 1975 that consumer borrowing during November 1974 showed its first downturn in four years, declining a seasonally adjusted $402 million. It was the largest monthly drop on record, exceeding the previous record decline of $376 million set in June 1942. The fall was much steeper in 1942, however, when the monthly decline repre-

Consumer Credit Outstanding, Year End

(In billions of dollars)

	1965	1970	1971	1972	1973	1974
Total	89.9	127.2	138.4	157.6	180.5	190.1
Installment	70.9	102.1	111.3	127.3	147.4	156.1
Noninstallment	19.0	25.1	27.1	30.3	33.0	34.0
Single-payment loans	7.7	9.7	10.6	12.3	13.2	13.0
Commercial banks	6.7	8.5	9.3	10.9	11.7	11.5
Other financial institutions	1.0	1.2	1.3	1.4	1.5	1.5
Charge Accounts	6.4	8.0	8.3	9.0	9.8	10.1
Retail outlets	5.7	6.2	6.4	7.1	7.8	8.0
Credit cards*	0.7	1.8	1.9	1.9	2.0	2.1
Service credit	4.9	7.4	8.2	9.0	10.0	10.9

Consumer Installment Credit, By Type

	1965	1970	1971	1972	1973	1974
Outstanding at year end	70.9	102.1	111.3	127.3	147.4	156.1
Retail automobile paper	28.4	35.2	38.7	44.1	51.1	51.7
Other consumer goods paper	18.5	31.5	34.3	40.1	47.5	52.0
Personal loans	20.2	30.3	32.9	36.9	41.4	44.3
Home improvement loans	3.7	5.1	5.4	6.2	7.4	8.2
Extensions during year	78.6	112.2	124.3	142.9	164.9	166.5
Retail automobile paper	27.2	29.8	34.9	40.2	46.5	42.8
Other consumer goods paper	22.8	43.9	47.8	55.6	66.7	71.1
Personal loans	26.3	35.5	38.3	43.2	47.0	48.0
Home improvement loans	2.3	3.0	3.2	4.0	4.7	4.7
Repayments during year	70.5	107.2	115.1	126.9	144.8	157.8
Retail automobile paper	23.7	30.1	31.4	34.7	39.5	42.2
Other consumer goods paper	20.7	40.7	44.9	49.9	59.3	66.6
Personal loans	24.0	33.9	35.8	39.1	42.5	45.2
Home improvement loans	2.1	2.5	2.9	3.2	3.6	3.8
Net increase or decrease in credit outstanding	8.1	5.0	9.2	16.0	20.1	8.7
Retail automobile paper	3.5	−0.3	3.5	5.5	7.0	0.6
Other consumer goods paper	2.1	3.2	2.9	5.7	7.5	4.5
Personal loans	2.3	1.6	2.5	4.1	4.5	2.8
Home improvement loans	0.2	0.5	0.3	0.8	1.1	0.9

Source: Federal Reserve Board.

Note: Parts may not add to totals due to rounding.

* *Service station and miscellaneous; bank credit card accounts are included under installment credit outstanding.*

Table from National Consumer Finance Association, 1975 Finance Facts Yearbook

sented a 5% contraction in consumer borrowing. The current decrease represented a .2% drop in credit outstanding, which totaled $188.08 billion in November.

The month's decrease was chiefly a reflection of a $361 million decline in auto debt, the sharpest drop on record, and a $174 million reduction in personal loans outstanding, the first such decrease since February 1945. According to a government analyst, the November figures suggested "a very substantial degree of consumer caution" and renewed efforts to pay off existing obligations.

Consumer debt then contracted an additional $877 million (seasonally adjusted) in December. It was the first time since 1958 that borrowing had fallen in two consecutive months.

Dow Jones closes at 616.24. The Dow Jones industrial average closed at 616.24 points on the New York Stock Exchange Dec. 31, up 12.99 for the day and ending 1974 with a mild recovery. Since the close on Dec. 31, 1973, the Dow had plunged 26.6%, losing 234.62 points, and hitting a new 12-year low of 577.6 Dec. 6. (The Dow had closed at 569.02 on Oct. 26, 1962 during the Cuban missile crisis.) Announcement of a 6.5% unemployment rate during November and reports of mounting layoffs triggered the decline Dec. 6, when the Dow was off by 9.46 points.

Utilities' construction cutbacks mount. A private study, conducted by National Economic Research Associates Inc. and published Oct. 11, 1974, showed that the nation's utilities had reduced their construction budgets by 18% through 1978 because of rising costs and a slowdown in the growth of energy consumption.

The spending cutbacks, some of which reflected cancellations but most of them visible as postponements, totaled $16.1 billion as of Oct. 1 and represented 132,490,000 kilowatts of capacity. Utilities' projected construction budgets through 1978 totaled $88.1 billion.

Planned cutbacks in nuclear energy were extensive and could seriously jeopardize the government's Project Independence, which aimed at achieving national self-sufficiency in energy supplies by 1980. According to the report, "a little more than half of the 175,918,000 kilowatt total of all nuclear capacity being planned" had been postponed or canceled—an amount that was "equal in magnitude to a half dozen Tennessee Valley Authorities and is enough capacity to serve a dozen New York Cities."

The Atomic Energy Commission earlier had anticipated that nuclear generating plants could provide 15% of the nation's energy supplies by 1980, compared with the current rate of 7.4%.

According to the report, only four of the nation's 15 largest utilities had not yet announced cutbacks; 39 utilities across the country had announced cuts in their construction budgets.

One of the hardest hit utilities, Detroit Edison Co., announced Nov. 7 that it was essentially halting all major construction projects and cutting its 1975 construction budget for the fourth time in 1974. The new 1975 spending allocation was $230 million, down from the original projection of $558 million. A total of 3,500 jobs would be lost because of the cutbacks.

According to the utilities industry, the cutbacks resulted from new, scaled-down estimates of energy consumption, the nation's generally gloomy economic trends, the high cost of borrowed money, and a widespread slump in the securities market, in which equity securities of many utilities were selling at less than book value.

Because of these financial considerations, utilities had coupled spending cutbacks with sharply higher rate increases. According to the National Utility Service Inc. Oct. 14, electricity rates at the nation's 50 largest utilities had climbed an average 55.4% during the first half of 1974. For all of 1973, the average rate increase was 12.3%.

In the first six months of 1974, 46 utilities obtained rate increases valued at $1.38 billion, and 41 were awaiting approval of $1.02 billion in increases. During all of 1973, 128 rate increases were approved totaling $1.08 billion.

Fortune ranks 500 largest industrials. "Oil, inflation and recession had—not surprisingly—a lot to do with the record turned in by the 500 largest industrials in 1974," Fortune magazine reported in its May 1975 issue.

The performance of the petroleum-refining industry dominated the list, just as higher oil prices had a dominant impact on the national economy during 1974. Exxon Corp., the group's standard-bearer, was ranked No. 1 in sales, surpassing General Motors Corp., the nation's sales leader for 40 years. Exxon was also the 1974 leader in assets, net income and stockholders' equity.

As a group, the petroleum refining industry reported an 80.4% median increase in sales during 1974—the largest gain registered by any industry since records were first compiled in 1955. Five of the seven largest companies on the list were oil companies. Among the top 50 industrials, 16 were oil companies; three of them, Sun Oil Co., Amerada Hess Corp., and Ashland Oil Corp., were new to the top-50 group, but each of the 16 oil companies moved up in rank.

Higher oil prices had a double effect on the sales ranking, Fortune noted, swelling the oil firms' sales while depressing sales in other key industries, chiefly the automotive group.

Combined sales of the 500 largest industrials increased by 25% over the previous year. According to Fortune, this gain was "illusory," since a government index showed that manufactured goods rose 19.3% in price during the year. When adjusted to reflect inflation's effect, the group's "real" sales gain for 1974 was only 5.7%, slightly below the 20-year average. Non-oil companies reported a 4.7% decline in real sales.

Of the 500 largest industrials, 471 posted sales gains, with the greatest median increases, aside from advances made by the oil group, reported in mining (up 60.9%), chemicals (up 31%), and metal manufacturing (up 27.9%). Kaiser Industries registered the largest single yearly sales gains. Consolidation with Kaiser Steel caused the firm's sales to rise 335.8%. Of the remaining top-10 sales leaders, eight were in coal or oil.

Fortune reported that 203 industrials had sales in excess of $1 billion during 1974—36 more than in 1973. Sales of 24 companies were greater than $5 billion and 11 firms had sales of more than $10 billion.

Despite the huge profits reported by oil companies in 1974, the petroleum refining industry ranked only fourth in terms of an annual earnings increase. The group's profits for 1974 were only 39.6% higher than in 1973, compared with a record 100.8% median increase in the mining industry's earnings. Metal manufacturers ranked second with a 78.6% median increase in profits and the chemicals group posted a 40.5% median gain.

Profits for the 500 increased 12.8%, but non-oil companies showed only 4.1% gain. Six industries reported a median decline in profits; 21 companies lost money, with Chrysler the biggest loser.

As a group, the 500 posted a 4.3% median return on sales, down from 4.5% in 1973. The mining industry led the list with a 13% median margin, followed by pharmaceuticals with 8.8%. The highest single margin was reported by Texasgulf, which benefitted from a worldwide shortage of phosphate fertilizers.

The median return on stockholders' equity for the entire group was a record 13.6%. The mining industry again was the leader with a 23.2% return.

The 500's median total return during 1974 was a minus 22.35%. For 1973, the median total return had been a minus 25.49%. Soaring interest rates, which made common stocks less attractive as investments, were blamed for much of the decline. The company with the highest single return, 177.42%, was Lykes-Youngstown Corp., a steel maker.

The poor returns posted in 1973 and 1974 had a negative impact on the results of the 1964–1974 period. Over the decade, the 500's total return was 1.83%.

The nation's 500 largest industrial corporations employed 276,137 fewer workers in 1974, a decline of 1.8% over the previous year. More than a third of that reduction was concentrated in the auto industry.

Although the 500 largest industrials represented 66% of the sales of all U.S. industrials during 1974, compared with 65% in 1973, their share of industrial profits declined from 79% in 1973 to 72% in 1974. "The devastation inflicted on the auto industry was a major reason for that setback," Fortune reported.

Ford's Program Evolves

Plans for Economic Recovery & Independence in Energy

President Gerald R. Ford's program for starting the U.S. back on the way to economic recovery began to take visible shape early in 1975. In a televised address to the nation Jan. 13 and in his State-of-the-Union message to Congress Jan. 15, Ford presented a plan to fight inflation and recession and to make the U.S. independent in energy.

Ford outline to nation. President Ford outlined to the nation Jan. 13 his program to revive the economy and lessen the nation's dependence on foreign oil supplies. The President disclosed his plans, involving a drastic shift in his economic policy, in a nationally televised address from the White House library.

He proposed a federal income tax cut of $16 billion, $12 billion of it to individual taxpayers as a cash rebate amounting to 12% of their 1974 tax, up to $1,000 in rebate. If Congress acted by April 1, Ford said, half the rebate could be paid in May and the rest by September.

The $4 billion remainder of the tax cut was to go to business taxpayers, including farmers, by increasing the investment tax credit from 7% to 12% for one year to promote plant expansion and job creation. He promised "special provisions" to assist public utilities in increasing their energy capacity.

The President also called for higher taxes on oil as well as on natural gas and for a return of this revenue, estimated at $30 billion, to the economy in the form of additional payments and credits to business, to state and local governments and to individuals, including those who paid no income taxes because of low earnings.

"We must wage a simultaneous three-front campaign against recession, inflation and energy dependence. We have no choice," Ford said. "We must turn America in a new direction."

"We need, within 90 days the strongest and most far-reaching energy conservation program we have ever had," Ford emphasized. He conceded that gasoline and oil would cost "even more than they do now." To get started on "an urgent national energy plan," Ford said he would use his emergency powers to raise import fees on each barrel of foreign crude oil by $1–$3 over the next three months. "A more comprehensive program of energy conservation taxes on oil and natural gas, to reduce consumption substantially, must be enacted by the Congress," he said.

Other facets of the program: to utilize oil allocation authority to avoid undue hardships in specific areas or industries, to take steps to prevent windfall profits by producers and to speed development of non-petroleum domestic energy resources. The President said he also intended to ask Congress for a five-year delay on higher automobile pollution standards so that a 40% improvement in miles per gallon could be attained. "There must also be voluntary efforts to cut gasoline and other energy use," Ford said.

The program "requires personal sacrifice," he said, but it would enable the country to reach its goal of reducing foreign oil imports by one million barrels a day by 1976 and by two million barrels by 1978.

Ford cited his distaste for federal deficits but said unless the economy revived, future deficits would be even larger than under his plan. He pointed toward eventual reform of existing federal programs, built into the system, that would produce, if unchecked, Ford said, federal deficits of $30 to $50 billion in 1975 and 1976. Reform of these would take time, he said, and in the interim he did not intend to propose any new federal spending programs except for energy. Urging public support, he called for "a one-year moratorium on new federal spending programs."

The President said he would "insist" on a 5% limit on federal pay increases in 1975; Congress would be asked to put a 5% ceiling on automatic cost-of-living increases in government, military retirement pay and Social Security.

"We are in trouble," Ford declared. "But we are not on the brink of another Great Depression." He urged business, labor and governments to exercise "self-restraint." He promised to see that individuals or special interests did not prosper "from our common distress."

Ford's State of the Union message. President Ford delivered a somber State of the Union message to Congress Jan. 15. He proposed immediate revision of economic policy to combat recession and a massive effort to achieve energy independence for the nation.

In his message Jan. 15, addressed to a joint session of Congress and televised nationally, Ford asked Congress not to legislate restrictions on his conduct of foreign policy, which he said was the responsibility of the president. He deplored the growth of the federal budget to "shocking" proportions and cautioned Congress he would veto any new spending programs it may adopt in 1975. He would propose no new spending programs, he said, except in energy and would present legislation "to restrain the growth of a number of existing programs."

Part of the trouble, Ford said, was that the nation had been "self-indulgent," voting "ever-increasing levels of government benefits." "And now the bill has come due," he said. "We have been adding so many new programs that the size and the growth of the federal budget has taken on a life of its own."

The President said he would send separate messages to Congress later on domestic legislation, such as revenue sharing and voting rights.

"I must say to you that the state of the union is not good," he told Congress. The economy was beset with unemployment, recession and inflation. Federal deficits of $30 billion in fiscal 1975 and $45 billion in fiscal 1976 were anticipated. The national debt was expected to rise to over $500 billion. Plant capacity and productivity were not increasing fast enough. "We depend on others for essential energy," Ford said, and "some people question their government's ability to make hard decisions and stick with them."

The nation still was better able to meet the needs of its people, Ford said, paraphrasing President Truman in 1949. Since then, 26 million more Americans had jobs, and the average family income had doubled. But, he said, "I've got bad news, and I don't expect much, if any, applause. The American people want action and it will take both the Congress and the President to give them what they want."

Before concluding his speech, Ford stressed the international role of the U.S. and urged Congress not to limit presidential conduct of foreign affairs. On his part, he pledged "the closest consultation" with Congress. The nation's plight today, he said, could be "one of the great creative moments of our nation's history. The whole world is watching to see how we respond. A resurgent American economy would do more to restore the confidence of the world in its own future than anything else we can do. The program that this Congress passes can demonstrate to the world that we have started to put our own house in order."

"Quite frankly," Ford said, referring to

the world leadership role of the nation, "at stake is the future of the industrialized democracies."

Economic revival plans—The President proposed a one-year tax reduction of $16 billion. This would be coupled with higher taxation of oil and natural gas. The latter proposal, whose purpose was to encourage conservation, was expected to produce revenues of some $30 billion which would be "refunded to the American people in a manner which corrects distortions in our tax system wrought by inflation." State and local governments would receive $2 billion of this in additional revenue-sharing to offset increased energy costs.

In addition, both corporate and individual income taxes would be reduced in the future. The corporate tax rate of 48% would be reduced to 42%. Individual income taxes would be reduced by $16.5 billion. (Administration officials, in disclosing Ford's plans Jan. 14, said the $16.5 billion reduction was intended to be applied to the tax rates for 1975 and later years.) This would be done by raising the low-income allowance and reducing tax rates, primarily to benefit lower-and-middle-income taxpayers, the President said. He gave these examples: a typical family of four with gross income of $5,600 paying $185 in federal income taxes would, under his plan, pay nothing; a family of four with gross income of $12,000, paying $1,260, would pay $300 less; families grossing $20,000 would pay $210 less. Those with the very lowest incomes, he said, would receive compensatory payments of $80.

Energy conservation program—Ford expressed confidence that his program would begin to restore the nation's status of "surplus capacity in total energy" that it had in the 1960s. But he cautioned that it would impose burdens and require sacrifices. He assured that "the burdens will not fall more harshly on those less able to bear them."

The goals were to reduce oil imports to "end vulnerability to economic disruption by foreign suppliers by 1985" and to develop energy technology and resources.

Immediate action was needed to cut imports, Ford said, and he urged quick action on legislation to allow commercial production at the Elk Hills, Calif. Naval Petroleum Reserve.

He would submit legislation to enable more power plants to convert to coal.

Using presidential power, he would raise the fee on all imported crude oil and petroleum products. Crude oil fee levels would be increased $1 per barrel on Feb. 1, by $2 per barrel on March 1 and by $3 per barrel on April 1.

These were "interim" actions, he said, pending a broader program he requested that Congress enact within 90 days. This would include:

- Excise taxes and import fees totaling $2 per barrel on product imports and on all crude oil.
- Deregulation of new natural gas and a natural gas excise tax.
- A windfall profits tax. Ford asked for the windfall profits tax by April 1 since he planned to act to decontrol the price of domestic crude oil on that date.

The President said he was prepared to use presidential power to limit imports as necessary to guarantee success of his energy conservation program.

Before deciding on the program, he said, he considered rationing and higher gasoline taxes as alternatives but rejected them as ineffective and inequitable.

Ford spoke of "a massive program" that must be launched to attain energy independence within a decade. The largest part of increased oil production, he said, must come from "new frontier areas" on the outer continental shelf and from the Naval Petroleum Reserve in Alaska. He planned "to move ahead" with development of the outer-shelf areas "where the environmental risks are acceptable."

On coal, Ford recommended "a reasonable compromise on environmental concerns." He said he would submit legislation to allow "greater coal use without sacrificing clean air goals." Referring to his veto of strip-mining legislation, Ford said he would sign a version "with appropriate changes."

As for nuclear power, he would submit legislation to expedite leasing and rapid selection of sites.

For utilities, whose financial problems were worsening, Ford said, he proposed that the one-year investment tax credit of 12% be extended for an additional two years "to specifically speed the construction of power plants that do not use natural gas or oil." He also would submit proposals for selective reform of state utility commission regulations.

To provide stability for production, Ford said he planned to request legislation to authorize and require tariffs, import quotas or price floors to protect domestic energy prices.

To cut long-term consumption, Ford proposed:

- Mandatory thermal efficiency standards for new buildings.
- A tax credit of up to $150 for homeowners installing insulation.
- Aid to low-income families to buy insulation.
- Revision and deferment of automotive pollution standards for five years "which will enable us to improve new automobile gas mileage by 40% by 1980."

As a foil against foreign disruption, Ford requested stand-by emergency legislation and a strategic storage program of one billion barrels of oil for domestic needs and 300 million barrels for defense.

The President listed these goals to be attained by 1985: one million barrels of synthetic fuels and shale oil production per day; 200 major nuclear power plants; 250 major new coal mines; 150 major coal-fired power plants; 30 major new refineries; 20 major new synthetic fuel plants; thousands of new oil wells; insulation of 18 million homes; and sale of millions of new automobiles, trucks and buses using "much less fuel."

Excerpts from Ford's 1975 State-of-the-Union message:

. . . The state of the union is not good.

Millions of Americans are out of work. Recession and inflation are eroding the money of millions more. Prices are too high and sales are too slow. This year's federal deficit will be about $30 billion; next year's probably $45 billion. The national debt will rise to over $500 billion. Our plant capacity and productivity are not increasing fast enough. We depend on others for essential energy. . . .

The moment has come to move in a new direction. We can do this by fashioning a new partnership between the Congress on the one hand, the White House on the other, and the people we both represent. Let us mobilize the most powerful and most creative industrial nation that ever existed on this earth to put all our people to work. The emphasis on our economic efforts must now shift from inflation to jobs.

To bolster business and industry and to create new jobs, I propose a one-year tax reduction of $16 billion. Three-quarters would go to individuals and one-quarter to promote business investment. This cash rebate to individuals amounts to 12% of 1974 tax payments—a total cut of $12 billion, with a maximum of $1,000 per return.

I call on the Congress to act by April 1. If you do, and I hope you will, the Treasury can send the first check for half the rebate in May and the second in September.

The other one-fourth of the cut, about $4 billion, will go to business, including farms, to promote expansion and to create more jobs. The one-year reduction for businesses would be in the form of a liberalized investment tax credit increasing the rate to 12% for all business.

This tax cut does not include the more fundamental reforms needed in our tax system. But it points us in the right direction—allowing taxpayers rather than the government to spend their pay.

Cutting taxes now is essential if we are to turn the economy around. A tax cut offers the best hope of creating more jobs. Unfortunately, it will increase the size of the budget deficit. Therefore, it is more important than ever that we take steps to control the growth of federal expenditures.

Part of our trouble is that we have been self-indulgent. For decades, we have been voting ever-increasing levels of government benefits—and now the bill has come due. We have been adding so many new programs that the size and the growth of the federal budget has taken on a life of its own. One characteristic of these programs is that their cost increases automatically every year because the number of people eligible for most of the benefits increases every year. When these programs were enacted, there was no dollar amount set. No one knows what they will cost. All we know is that whatever they cost last year, they will cost more next year.

It is a question of simple arithmetic. Unless we check the excessive growth of federal expenditures or impose on ourselves matching increases in taxes, we will continue to run huge inflationary deficits in the federal budget.

If we project the current built-in momentum of federal spending through the next 15 years, state, federal and local government expenditures could easily comprise half of our gross national product. This compares with less than a third in 1975.

I've just concluded the process of preparing the budget submissions for fiscal year 1976. In that budget, I will propose legislation to restrain the growth of a number of existing programs. I have also concluded that no new spending programs can be initiated this year, except for energy. Further, I will not hesitate to veto any new spending programs adopted by the Congress.

As an additional step toward putting the federal government's house in order, I recommend a 5% limit on federal pay increases in 1975. In all government programs, tied to the Consumer Price Index—including Social Security, Civil Service and military retirement pay, and food stamps—I also propose a one-year maximum increase of 5%.

None of these recommended ceiling limitations, over which Congress has final authority, are easy to propose, because in most cases they involve anticipated payments to many, many deserving people. Nonetheless, it must be done. I must emphasize that I am not asking to eliminate, to reduce, or to freeze these payments. I am merely recommending that we slow down the rate at which these payments increase and these programs grow. Only a reduction in the growth of spending can keep federal borrowing down and reduce the damage to the private sector from high interest rates. Only a reduction in spending can make it possible for the Federal Reserve System to avoid an inflationary growth in the money supply and thus restore balance to our economy. A major reduction in the growth of federal spending can help dispel the uncertainty that so many feel about our economy, and put us on the way to curing our economic ills.

If we don't act to slow down the rate of increase in federal spending, the United States Treasury will be legally obligated to spend more than $360 billion in fiscal year 1976—even if no new programs are enacted....

The economic disruptions we and others are experiencing stems in part from the fact that the world price of petroleum has quadrupled in the last year. But, in all honesty, we cannot put all of the blame on the oil exporting nations. We, the United States, are not blameless. Our growing dependence upon foreign sources has been adding to our vulnerability for years and years. And we did nothing to prepare ourselves for such an event as the embargo of 1973.

During the 1960s, this country had a surplus capacity of crude oil, which we were able to make available to our trading partners whenever there was a disruption of supply. This surplus capacity enabled us to influence both supplies and prices of crude oil throughout the world. Our excess capacity neutralized any effort at establishing an effective cartel, and thus the rest of the world was assured of adequate supplies of oil at reasonable prices.

By 1970 our capacity, our surplus capacity had vanished, and as a consequence the latent power of the oil cartel could emerge in full force. Europe and Japan, both heavily dependent on imported oil, now struggle to keep their economies in balance. Even the United States, our country, which is far more self-sufficient than most other industrial countries, has been put under serious pressure.

I am proposing a program which will begin to restore our country's surplus capacity in total energy. In this way, we will be able to assure ourselves reliable and adequate energy and help foster a new world energy stability for other major consuming nations.

But this nation and, in fact, the world must face the prospect of energy difficulties between now and 1985. This program will impose burdens on all of us with the aim of reducing our consumption of energy and increasing our production. Great attention has been paid to the considerations of fairness, and I can assure you that the burdens will not fall more harshly on those less able to bear them....

I have set the following national energy goals to assure that our future is as secure and as productive as our past:

First, we must reduce oil imports by one million barrels per day by the end of this year and by two million barrels per day by the end of 1977.

Second, we must end vulnerability to economic disruption by foreign suppliers by 1985.

Third, we must develop our energy technology and resources so that the United States has the ability to supply a significant share of the energy needs of the free world by the end of this century....

I want you to know that before deciding on my energy conservation program, I considered rationing and higher gasoline taxes as alternatives. In my judgment, neither would achieve the desired results and both would produce unacceptable inequities.

Now, let me turn, if I might, to the international dimensions of the present crisis. At no time in our peacetime history has the state of the nation depended more heavily on the state of the world. And seldom if ever has the state of the world depended more heavily on the state of our nation.

The economic distress is global. We will not solve it at home unless we help to remedy the profound economic dislocation abroad. World trade and monetary structure provides markets, energy, food and vital raw materials—for all nations. This international system is now in jeopardy....

We are a great nation—spiritually, politically, militarily, diplomatically and economically. America's commitment to international security has sustained the safety of allies and friends in many areas—in the Middle East, in Europe, in Asia. Our turning away would unleash new instabilities, new dangers around the globe, which in turn, would threaten our own security....

A resurgent American economy would do more to restore the confidence of the world in its own future than anything else we can do. The program that this Congress passes can demonstrate to the world that we have started to put our own house in order. If we can show that this nation is able and willing to help other nations meet the common challenge, it can demonstrate that the United States will fulfill its responsibility as a leader among nations.

Quite frankly, at stake is the future of the industrialized democracies, which have perceived their destiny in common and sustained it in common for 30 years.

The developing nations are also at a turning point. The poorest nations see their hopes of feeding their hungry and developing their societies shattered by the economic crisis. The long-term economic future for the producers of raw materials also depends on cooperative solutions.

Our relations with the Communist countries are a basic factor of the world environment. We must seek to build a long-term basis for coexistence. We will stand by our principles; we will stand by our interests; we will act firmly when challenged. The kind of world we want depends on a broad policy of creating mutual incentives for restraint and for cooperation.

As we move forward to meet our global challenges and opportunities, we must have the tools to do the job. Our military forces are strong and ready. This military strength deters aggression against our allies, stabilizes our relations with former adversaries and protects our homeland. Fully adequate conventional and strategic forces cost many, many billions, but these dollars are sound insurance for our safety and for a more peaceful world.

Military strength alone is not sufficient. Effective diplomacy is also essential in preventing conflict and building world understanding....

Let me sum it up:

America needs a new direction which I have sought to chart here today—a change of course which will:

Put the unemployed back to work.

Increase real income and production.

Restrain the growth of federal government spending.

Achieve energy independence.

And advance the cause of world understanding....

House Democrats present plans. The Democratic leadership in the House Jan. 13 presented "emergency" economic and energy proposals designed to halt recession, check inflation and conserve energy. The plan, devised by a 10-member task force of the Democratic Steering and Policy Committee, was introduced by House Speaker Carl Albert (D, Okla.) at a news conference only hours before

President Ford presented the Administration proposals.

The Democrats' plan included a $10 billion–$20 billion tax cut for low and middle income persons, elimination of corporate tax loopholes, expanded credit and reduced interest rates, increased public service jobs and more public works projects, and aid to the housing industry.

The Democrats urged a "tough but selective program to halt the current wage-price spiral," one that occupied a middle ground between the policy extremes of the Nixon and Ford Administrations. Nixon's Phase 1 and 2 "controlled wages with a vengeance while permitting prices to rise, resulting in a cruel diminution of the wage-earners' purchasing power," according to the study group. "There must be no return to such a policy," the Democrats declared, but they also rejected the present Ford Administration approach to inflation control, labeling the current Council on Wage and Price Stability a "toothless tiger."

The Democrats urged establishment of an "independent agency with subpoena power, the resources to hold extensive hearings, the authority to delay price increases up to 90 days, and, in extreme cases, the authority to impose controls more permanently on a selective basis, . . . aimed at those industries where near-monopoly and 'administered' prices render the forces of true competition inoperable."

Among the energy saving measures offered for consideration by the House Democrats were mandatory allocation of petroleum and other forms of energy, increased gasoline taxes, rationing of gasoline and home heating oil, higher excise taxes on power boats and high powered cars, a ban on weekend sales of gasoline, subsidized loans for home insulation and a redesign of utility rates to discourage excess use. "Voluntary [fuel] restrictions simply have not worked," party spokesmen said.

Rep. James Wright (D, Tex.), chairman of the Democratic study group, said the leadership's decision to launch its own program without waiting for President Ford to submit his legislative proposals "does not mean we are seeking confrontation with the executive . . . but solutions." Albert also pledged cooperation with the White House in solving the nation's economic and energy problems, but criticism of Ford's handling of the situation was implicit in the study group's report. The state of the economy had been allowed to "drift, devoid of purposeful direction" "for too long," the Democrats declared. In that void, their report added, Congress must "assume a responsibility for decisive and resourceful leadership."

Ford begins bid for support. President Ford met separately Jan. 16 with Congressional leaders and with governors, mayors and other local leaders to seek support for his economic program.

White House Press Secretary Ron Nessen reported that Ford had found "common ground" with the Congressional leaders and that both Democrats and Republicans recognized the urgent need to reach agreement on a program. Ford appealed for support of his total plan and urged quick enactment of it or legislation that resembled it, Nessen said.

However, criticism of specific sections of the program was widespread. It came from spokesmen from oil-producing states, and oil-consuming states, particularly in the Northeast. Conservatives objected to the huge proposed budget deficits. Liberals insisted on restricting tax rebates to low-income families. New England legislators decried the prospect of even higher prices for petroleum products. Petroleum industry spokesmen warned that the windfall profits tax would dry up the search for new domestic oil supplies. National Association of Manufacturers President E. Douglas Kenna said Jan. 14 his members had "serious reservations" about the program because of its resultant federal deficits. AFL-CIO President George Meany said Jan. 14 the proposed 12% tax rebate for individuals was "peanuts for the poor," and added Jan. 15 that the entire Ford program was "insupportable."

In Congress, Rep. Al Ullman (D, Ore.), incoming chairman of the House Ways and Means Committee, where tax legislation must originate, said Jan. 15 a $17 billion tax cut plan would be prepared for floor consideration by March, "but it's going to be a greatly different plan from the one the President advocated, funneled far more to low-income and middle-income citizens." Ford's program as a whole, he said, "fell far short of the program that would turn America around. It's too much of a scattergun approach rather than a comprehensive approach that gets to the heart of the problem. Much of it can be enacted, but it is not an energy program and it is not an economic program."

Dismay about the projected budget deficits even came from within the Administration. Treasury Secretary William E. Simon told reporters Jan. 16 "the size of the deficit horrifies me." However, the Administration, he stressed, was "fully united behind our President" and "we are united behind his proposals." Like the President, he was alarmed at the automatic nature of growth of the federal budget. "We have to get this crazy government spending under control," he said.

Albert, Humphrey give Democratic reply. Two prominent Democrats in Congress replied to President Ford's plan for reviving the economy and reducing dependence on foreign oil; both criticized his tax rebate and energy saving proposals.

House Speaker Carl Albert (D, Okla.) Jan. 20 asked, "What conceivable good will it do for a family to receive a $75–$100 tax rebate if the same family is then required to pay $250–$300 more during the year to get to and from work and to heat their home?" According to Albert's calculations, the richest 17% of the population would receive 43% of the refund from 1974 taxes.

Instead, Albert asked for support for the Democrats' tax cut program favoring low and middle income persons. He also warned that the party would seek a progressive tax on interest income if the Administration did not take steps to force a reduction in interest rates and apportion credit toward "productive" uses."

Albert said the Democrats had "serious reservations" about Ford's energy proposals, particularly his plan to tax oil imports, a measure which Albert said would have an "astounding inflationary impact" on the economy. The Democrats favored a "more moderate approach" which combined gasoline rationing, an excise tax on automobiles, gasless days and other measures, he said.

Albert's speech was broadcast live on national radio, but the three major television networks refused to give him equal time to respond to Ford's nationally televised address Jan. 13. NBC televised Albert's speech on a delayed basis Jan. 20. ABC broadcast the speech Jan. 21.

CBS asked Sen. Hubert H. Humphrey (D, Minn.) to deliver a reply Jan. 22 to the President's program. Humphrey rejected Ford's energy proposals as "the least desirable set of alternatives," charging that they would cost consumers $45 billion a year.

Ford's tax rebate plan would not provide the quick remedy that was needed to stimulate the economy, Humphrey charged. Instead, he urged Congress to cut 1975 withholding rates, retroactive to Jan. 1, in order to cut individual income taxes by $18.5 billion and reduce corporate taxes $2.5 billion.

Ford steps up defense of program. President Ford embarked on the first of a series of speaking engagements to sell his plan of action to the public and defend it against Democratic opponents in Congress.

In a Washington address Jan. 22, Ford told the Conference Board, a nonprofit institute for business and economic research, that the Democrats' emphasis on tax relief favoring low income persons would penalize "hard working middle income Americans" and "strip incentives" from "upward bound millions who are struggling to improve their lives and their childrens' lives."

Ford repeated his pledge to veto new domestic spending programs passed by Congress. He criticized Democrats for supporting "massive federal spending" on social problems while contending that "all we need to do to get federal spending back in line is to hack away at our defense establishment."

"The fashion is to deride excessive defense spending," Ford said. "The fact of the matter is that defense outlays have been a dwindling part of our Gross National Product [GNP], falling from 8.9% in 1968 to less than 6%" projected for fiscal 1976, beginning July 1.

In contrast, Ford said, government transfer payments—money collected in taxes and redistributed to other citizens in the form of veterans and Social Security benefits, welfare payments and other checks—had been growing at an annual rate of 9% for the last 20 years. According to Ford, transfer payments, totaling $138 billion, were expected to comprise 44% of the fiscal 1976 budget. "At this rate, he said, total federal, state and local government spending, which currently equaled about one-third of the GNP, "could eat up more than half of the GNP" in another 20 years.

(In his press conference Jan. 21, Ford had urged Congress to set a 5% ceiling on cost of living increases slated for Social Security recipients. He defended an Administration action in raising the cost of food stamps. Recipients who then paid about 23% of their net incomes for food relief would have to pay 30% starting March 1.)

Ford also renewed his attack on gasoline rationing proposals, expanding his veto threat to include any "mandatory rationing program" involving petroleum products.

Greenspan gives gloomy assessment. Alan Greenspan, chairman of the President's Council of Economic Advisers, had told the Joint Economic Committee of Congress Jan. 6 that the economic outlook for 1975 was "neither pleasant nor reassuring." He warned that a "sharp contraction in production and employment . . . still has several months to run," causing the economy to continue to "decline into the summer."

Greenspan said a "bottoming out" of the economy was expected at midyear, but he added that the "timing and strength" of the subsequent turnaround were "still very uncertain." An upturn during the second half of the year was conditional on recoveries in the auto and housing industries and the end of inventory liquidation, Greenspan said.

According to Greenspan, the current recession was having a braking effect on the nation's prices—inflation was expected to slow to 6%-7% at an annual rate by mid-1975. He added, however, that he expected little improvement in the unemployment rate, and warned that joblessness could peak at "close to 8%" during 1975. A recovery during the second half of the year was "unlikely to provide much of a reduction in unemployment this year," he said.

Greenspan admitted that the recession "has come upon us much more suddenly than we generally anticipated." He declined to answer questions about President Ford's latest plans to counter the worsening economic situation, but Greenspan agreed with committee members that strong actions were required to "dissipate the extraordinary sense of uncertainty and gloom that businessmen and housewives have about the economy."

AFL-CIO urges alternate program. The AFL-CIO leadership proposed Jan. 23 an antirecession and energy conservation program featuring a tax cut of "at least" $20 billion and a ban on Arab oil imports. The leadership, at a general board meeting, its first since 1968, rejected President Ford's proposals. Also rejected were those of the Congressional Democrats, considered too vague. AFL-CIO President George Meany dismissed them as "press statements."

Meany criticized the government's reaction to the Arab oil embargo. "Every American schoolchild could have told the government how to handle the blackmail demands of the Arab oil sheiks," he said. "The response should have been very simply: 'Not one cent for tribute.' Instead, [Secretary of State] Henry Kissinger had a new quotation for the history books: 'Pay.' " Meany said there should be "no tribute, no foreign aid, no trade, no jet fighters—nothing, until the blackmail stops."

The AFL-CIO proposal was for "a ban on such imports originating in those countries that embargoed oil" to the U.S. and the Netherlands in 1973-74. Oil importing itself was to be "taken out of private hands" and handled by the government, which was to have authority to set import quantities, negotiate price and allocate. The federation leaders also endorsed rationing, federal regulation of investment in the U.S. by Arab oil interests, establishment of a petroleum stockpile, continued regulation of natural gas, speed-limit enforcement and excess profits taxes.

Its tax cut proposal was for a $15 billion cut in individual income taxes through lower withholding rates and a $5 billion cut for business by raising investment tax credits from 7% to 12% in general and from 4% to 12% for utilities.

The AFL-CIO also urged immediate Presidential action to lower interest rates and allocate credit to housing and other "high priority" areas; a $2 billion public works program; release of most of $19 billion in currently impounded public works funds; trade quotas to protect jobs; and improvements in the unemployment compensation system.

Teamsters urge economic plan—A call for urgent federal action to stimulate the economy came out of an emergency economic conference held in Washington Feb. 13 by the International Brotherhood of Teamsters. The conference, which was attended by about 500 Teamsters delegates, adopted a program that included calls for:

■Immediate price controls and a restraint on wages after "catch-ups" to balance purchasing power with prices.

■A public-service jobs program—half-a-million to be created by July, and an additional half-million for each half percentage point rise in the jobless rate above 7%.

■Strengthened aid to the unemployed, such as 52 weeks of benefits; hospitalization insurance; and federally-backed loans for the elderly, the poor and students.

■Accelerated public works projects, credit allocation to industries hard hit by unemployment.

■Emergency tax rebates of 12%, with a rebate ceiling of $350, and no rebates for those with incomes exceeding $30,000 a year; permanent income tax reduction for individuals; a $5 billion cut in corporation taxes; an end to the oil depletion allowance and foreign credits for oil firms.

■Gas rationing without price increases rather than President Ford's plan to cut down on gas use by increasing oil tariffs; a mandatory 40% improvement in car-engine gas mileage.

Teamsters President Frank Fitzsimmons called President Ford's economic ideas "outdated" and said oil companies should be nationalized if they failed to act in the national interest.

The Budget

Continued recession seen. Submitting his fiscal 1976 budget to Congress Feb. 3, 1975, President Ford foresaw no recovery from the recession until the end of the current year. His $349.4 billion budget envisaged a deficit of $51.9 billion for fiscal 1976. The deficit for fiscal 1975 (July 1, 1974–June 30, 1975) was estimated at a peacetime record of $34.7 billion.

The expenditures budgeted represented a 11.5% increase over the previous year, although Ford proposed $17 billion in spending cutbacks and presented no new programs except in energy. The budget was predicated on the President's previously disclosed antirecession and energy program.

The budget forecast for 1975 was for deep recession—production further ebbing (down 3.3% after adjustment for inflation), double-digit inflation (11.3%), and the highest unemployment rate (8.1%) since 1941. Corporate profits were expected to fall more than 18% to $115 billion, on a pretax basis.

In comments made on signing the Budget Message, the President said he expected the economy to turn "in a new and more favorable direction" well before the end of 1975. But recovery would be slow, he warned.

For 1976, the "real" growth in gross national product (GNP), or total output of goods and services, was forecast at 4.8% after discounting inflation, a relatively low level of increase for a period of recovery from recession. Inflation was expected to average 7.8%, unemployment 7.9%. Corporate profits were expected to jump by 26% over 1975.

The Administration also offered, for the first time in a budget presentation, several long-range economic "projections" that it distinguished from forecasts. These indicated gradual improvement: a "real" GNP growth ranging from 5.6% in 1977 to 6.5% in 1980, unemployment reduction from 7.5% in 1977 to 5.5% in 1980, an inflation rate drop from 6.6% in 1977 to 4% in 1980.

The projected deficit was attributed to the recession. Roy L. Ash, director of the Office of Management and Budget, at a budget briefing Feb. 3, estimated that the fiscal 1976 budget would have showed a small surplus instead of a record deficit if the economy were running at the employment and production levels of 1974.

The budget remained stable as a percentage of the total economy, or GNP—21.9% for both fiscal 1975 and fiscal 1976. The $35.9 billion increase in spending planned in fiscal 1976 was matched almost entirely by inflation and expected inflation. A quarter of the increase, $8.7 billion, was for defense. It was "no longer realistically possible," Ford said in the Budget Message, "to offset increasing costs of defense programs by further reducing military programs and strength."

Ford said defense outlays represented "a decreasing share of our gross national product, falling from 8.9% in 1969 to 5.9% in 1976." Federal nondefense spending, he said, had increased during that period from 11.6% of GNP in 1969 to an estimated 16% in fiscal 1976.

Increases for other major budget items included Social Security ($6.5 billion), Medicare and Medicaid ($1.6 billion), unemployment insurance ($3.5 billion) and interest on the debt ($3.1 billion). The $1.7 billion budgeted for fiscal 1976 spending for energy research and development represented an increase of 36% over the previous year's outlays.

Ford urged Congress to accept his recommendation for a 5% "cap" on increases in federal pay and some social welfare programs and he appealed to the private sector, labor and management, "to follow this example and minimize price and wage increases."

In compliance with legislation adopted in 1974, the budget provided for a change in the dates of the federal fiscal year beginning with fiscal 1977, which would begin Oct. 1, 1976. Since fiscal 1976 would end June 30, 1976, the Administration also presented a "transition budget" for the extra three months. It envisioned outlays of $94.26 billion and receipts of $84.41 billion with a deficit of $9.85 billion. This would bring the total federal debt to an estimated $616.77 billion. The change in fiscal year was intended to allow Congress more time to review the executive branch's budget proposals.

The budget incorporated $17 billion in spending reductions, $12.3 billion of which required Congressional action. A large part of the saving, $6 billion, would come from a proposed "cap" of 5% on increases in federal civilian and military pay and on automatic increases in benefit programs tied to consumer prices, which included Social Security, railroad retirement, federal employe retirement and disability, military retired pay, supplemental security income and food stamp and child nutrition programs.

Among details of the budget:

Taxes—The President's previously announced plans for a $16 billion antirecession tax cut became, in final form, a $16.3 billion reduction in the budget—a $6.1 billion reduction in fiscal 1975 and a $10.2 billion reduction in fiscal 1976. The proposed income-tax rebates for individuals—12% of the taxpayer's 1974 payment, up to a $1,000 limit, rebated in two installments—would cause a revenue loss of $4.9 billion in fiscal 1975 and of $7.3 billion the next year. The one-year increase in the investment tax credit for business—to 12%—would lower revenues by $1.2 billion in fiscal 1975 and $2.9 billion the next year.

Other tax relief proposed included an increase in the $1,300 minimum standard deduction, retroactive to Jan. 1, 1975, to $2,000 for individuals and $2,600 for families. This would cut tax receipts by $600 million in fiscal 1975 and by $8.1 billion in fiscal 1976.

A reduction in individual tax rates for individuals was to be made retroactive to Jan. 1, 1975, but the change in withholding

---

The Budget Dollar

Where it comes from:

Individual income taxes	30¢
Social insurance receipts	26¢
Corporation income taxes	14¢
Excise taxes	9¢
Borrowing	15¢
Other	6¢

Where it goes:

Benefit payments to individuals	39¢
National defense	27¢
Grants to states and localities	16¢
Other federal operations	11¢
Net interest	7¢

from paychecks was to be delayed until June, making the projected revenue loss from it only $800 million in fiscal 1975. The loss in fiscal 1976 was estimated at $16.3 billion.

The proposed reduction in the corporate income tax rate to 42%, retroactive to Jan. 1, 1975, was expected to reduce tax revenues $1.8 billion in fiscal 1975 and $6.6 billion in fiscal 1976.

The projected tax credit for home improvements to save energy, such as insulation, of 15% of the cost up to a $150 credit over three years, would cut $500 million from fiscal 1976 tax receipts.

The budget also incorporated the Administration's plans to increase energy taxes by $30 billion annually and return these monies to the economy. In addition to the temporary increase in the federal fee on imported oil, already ordered, the plans included an excise tax of $2 a barrel on domestic and imported oil; an excise tax of 37 cents a thousand cubic feet on natural gas; ending federal price controls on domestic oil April 1; a windfall-profits tax on oil firms, and ending price regulation of newly discovered natural gas.

Energy—The President requested legislation to permit commercial production of oil from military petroleum reserves. The revenue from sale of the oil would finance exploration of further federal reserves in Alaska and the cost of setting up a national strategic oil stockpile.

A stepped-up program for development of oil and gas from federal offshore areas was planned. The leasing revenues, which totaled $6.7 billion in fiscal 1974, were estimated at $5 billion in the current fiscal year and $8 billion the next. The areas designated for development were off the East and California coasts and in the Gulf of Alaska.

A supplemental appropriation of $3 million was requested for fiscal 1975 to help the states prepare for offshore oil and gas development.

Federal spending for civilian energy research and development was projected at $2.1 billion in fiscal 1976, a 33% increase.

Budget Receipts and Outlays

In millions of dollars

Receipts by Source	**1974 actual**	**1975 estimate**	**1976 estimate**
Individual income taxes	118,952	117,700	106,300
Corporation income taxes	38,620	38,500	47,700
Social insurance taxes and contributions	76,780	86,225	91,550
Excise taxes	16,844	19,947	32,145
Estate and gift taxes	5,035	4,800	4,600
Customs duties	3,334	3,910	4,300
Miscellaneous receipts	5,369	7,668	10,925
Total receipts	**264,932**	**278,750**	**297,520**
Outlays by Function	**1974 actual**	**1975 estimate**	**1976 estimate**
Military	78,569	85,276	94,027
International affairs	3,593	4,853	6,294
General science, space, and technology	4,154	4,183	4,581
Natural resources, environment, and energy	6,390	9,412	10,028
Agriculture	2,230	1,773	1,816
Commerce and transportation	13,100	11,796	13,723
Community and regional development	4,910	4,887	5,920
Education, manpower, and social services	11,600	14,714	14,623
Health	22,074	26,486	28,050
Income security	84,431	106,702	118,724
Veterans benefits and services	13,386	15,466	15,592
Law enforcement and justice	2,462	3,026	3,288
General government	3,327	2,646	3,180
Revenue sharing and general purpose fiscal assistance	6,746	7,033	7,249
Interest	28,072	31,331	34,419
Allowances*	...	700	8,050
Offsetting receipts	−16,650	−16,839	−20,193
Total outlays	**268,392**	**313,446**	**349,372**
Budget surplus or deficit (−)	**−3,460**	**−34,696**	**−51,852**

*Includes allowances for energy tax equalization payments, cilivian agency pay raises, and contingencies

Source: Office of Management and Budget

Of the $1.6 billion requested for nuclear energy development, $261 million was for a liquid-metal fast breeder reactor.

Other energy research received considerable boosts in the new budget over previous levels of funding. Solar-energy projects were allotted $57 million, up 551%; geothermal projects $28.3 million, up 105%; coal projects, principally in liquefaction, $279 million, up 60%; oil shale projects $311 million, up 135%. Research in energy conservation was budgeted at $32.1 million, up 93%.

Unemployment aid—The number of persons drawing unemployment benefits, 6.6 million in fiscal 1974, was expected to soar to between 14.1 million and 14.2 million persons in the next two years. The cost of direct assistance, much of it absorbed by state trust funds, would soar as well for the period from $6.1 billion to between $15.3 billion and $18.8 billion by fiscal 1976. The federal share of this was budgeted at $4 billion for fiscal 1976, a rise from $1.9 billion in fiscal 1975. A supplemental appropriation was planned for the funding.

The public-service jobs program was funded at $1.3 billion, which would produce 141,000 jobs, fewer than the 161,000 planned for fiscal 1975. The program itself was said to be operating at the 100,000-job level, and was expected to jump to the 320,000 level by April and to exceed the budgeted resources by late 1975.

The federal job-training effort, at a $2.8 billion level in the current fiscal year, would decline slightly to $2.7 billion for fiscal 1976.

Income maintenance—Budget outlays for income maintenance, mainly Social Security payments, were scheduled to amount to $92.3 billion in fiscal 1976, a rise of $4 billion. The cost of Social Security was expected to rise 8.7% or $2.6 billion if Congress refused the President's request for a 5% limit in fiscal 1976 on benefit increases.

The President planned a reduction of public welfare payments by the federal government. Congress was asked to cut to 50% the 75% federal share of the cost of state-provided service programs for welfare recipients. The federal budget's outlays for public welfare payments would drop $300 million to $6.3 billion in fiscal 1976.

Federal welfare aid for the aged, blind and disabled was put at $4.6 billion for fiscal 1976, up $500 million despite the proposed 5% cap.

Defense—The fiscal 1976 defense budget of $92.8 billion represented an $8 billion increase over the prior year attributed almost entirely to anticipated inflation. In terms of total obligational authority—the commitment by Congress of new appropriations that would not all be spent in fiscal 1976 plus defense funds appropriated in prior years but still unexpended—the defense budget would rise $15.7 billion to $104.7 billion. Of this increase, $8.2 billion comprised "real" growth above the inflation factor.

A Pentagon projection of defense spending envisioned $104 billion in expenditures for fiscal 1977 and $140 billion by fiscal 1980.

The budget did not provide for any major new weapons program or expansion of forces. The Army planned to add two divisions, for a total of 16, by the end of fiscal 1976, mainly through a shift of units from support into combat positions.

The budget for foreign military aid included a previously requested $522 million supplemental appropriation for Indochina plus a fiscal 1976 request for $1.3 billion more for South Vietnam. The President also sought $300 million to procure weapons for sale or grant to allies in emergencies.

The procurement figure in the defense budget was $24.7 billion, a $7.3 billion increase over fiscal 1975, $2.7 billion of it in excess of the inflation factor.

Defense research and development was allotted $9.4 billion, a $1.7 billion rise or $1.1 billion in "real" growth minus the inflation catch-up.

The budget would expand expenditures for general-purpose, or conventional, forces by $7.7 billion to $35.9 billion in fiscal 1976. A $300 million increase, to $7.7 billion, was requested for strategic, or nuclear deterrent, forces.

The budget would support uniformed armed forces of 2,100,000 by June 30, 1976, a decline of 22,000 in the Air Force and 7,000 in the Navy.

The service budgets: Army, $25.1 billion; Air Force, $30.6 billion; Navy, $34.1 billion.

Because of the change in the fiscal year, beginning in 1977, to an Oct. 1 starting date, the Pentagon submitted a three-month transition budget for July 1–Sept. 30, 1976. This called for outlays of $25.4 billion and total obligational authority of $24.6 billion.

Among items in the defense budget (in terms of total obligational authority):

Trident missile submarine: More than $2.1 billion was requested for the Trident submarine program in fiscal 1976, almost $1.2 billion for construction and $968.2 million for the sub's long-range missiles. The transition budget included another $620.7 million for the Trident. The budget covered construction of one submarine. A "lower cost alternative to the Trident" was broached again in the budget despite rejection in 1974 by Congress.

B1 bomber: $749.2 million, an increase of $304.2 million, was requested for continued development work. Another $199.3 million was in the transition budget. A production decision was scheduled for November, 1976. Current estimate of the plane's cost: $76.4 million each.

Minuteman missiles and site defense: $779.9 million, up $51.2 million over the previous year, was budgeted for the Minutemen III. Another $104.5 million was allocated to it in the transition budget. In addition, $41.2 million was requested for research on a new generation of intercontinental ballistic missiles that could be land-based or launched from ground vehicles or planes. $15.3 million was allocated to the project in the transition budget.

Anti-ballistic-missile (ABM) defense: The ABM program was to receive $140 million, up $25.1 million over fiscal 1975, in fiscal 1976 and $38 million in the three-month transition period.

Cruise missiles: $102 million, an increase of $64 million, was proposed for development of a submarine-launched low-trajectory Cruise missile. An air-launched Cruise missile was budgeted at $51 million, down $3.6 million, for fiscal 1976 and $13 million in the transition period.

SAM-D missile: Continued development of the SAM-D, battlefield antiaircraft missile system, was budgeted at $130 million, up $25 million.

M60 tanks: $498 million, up $242 million over 1975, was proposed for purchase of 816 M60 tanks in fiscal 1976. Purchase of another 248 tanks for $171 million was covered by the transition budget.

Airborne command post: $42 million, a cut of $40 million, was budgeted for continued development of the flying command post, a communications-laden Boeing 747. $194 million was in the transition budget for procurement of three planes.

AWACS warning plane: $690 million, up $72 million, was requested for the AWACS warning and command system to control fighter planes in tactical situations. $85 million more was allocated for the project in transition budget.

Aircraft: $1.7 billion, up $587 million, was budgeted to buy 108 F15 fighters; and another $356 million in the transition budget for 27 more F15s. $460 million, an increase of $199 million, was requested to buy 61 A10 attack planes for troop-support in battle; the transition budget asked another $107 million for 33 A10s. $622 million, down $111 million, was requested to purchase 36 F14 fighters for the Navy; nine more planes were to be purchased in the three-month transition budget for $138 million. $273 million, up $241 million, was budgeted for development of the F16 combat fighter for Air Force; $83 million more was asked for the project in the transition budget. The Navy budgeted $110 million, up $90 million, for work on the carrier-based version of the F16. The carrier-based S3A antisub plane was budgeted for $517 million, down $44 million, for purchase of 41 planes.

Ships: Almost $1.1 billion, up $909 million, was budgeted for first construction of 10 PF patrol frigates. $819 million, up $274 million, was requested for SSN688 nuclear-powered attack submarines; $192 million more was asked in the transition budget. $397 million, up $142 million, was requested for the DLGN38 nuclear frigate program, and $436 million, up $325 million, for two destroyer tenders. $220 million, up $112 million, was budgeted for a first purchase of two patrol hydrofoils in fiscal 1976. $232 million, up $231 million, was budgeted for a fleet oiler project.

Space—**The National Aeronautics & Space Administration's budget was increased by $291 million over 1975, to $3.5 billion for fiscal 1976. The space budget was designed to maintain the timetable for**

a first manned space shuttle flight in mid 1979. Some existing tracking stations would be closed down and employes laid off and for the first time in a decade the new budget contained no funds for new space projects.

Some 28 launches were planned, among them a joint U.S.-Soviet link-up in earth orbit in July.

Health—The Administration requested $27.3 billion for fiscal 1976 spending on health programs. The total was $1.5 billion above previous-year funding although the department's (Health, Education & Welfare) fiscal plans were being shaped by an intensive cost-control effort.

A 20% spending cut was imposed on direct service programs such as neighborhood health centers, maternal and child health and community mental health centers. The department expected state and local governments to provide the deleted funds. The spending reductions would hit migrant health care, family planning, drug abuse, alcohol control, immunization and venereal disease programs.

For Medicare, Congress was asked to endorse a cost-control plan to limit the rate of increase in average daily costs reimbursable to hospitals from the government. The Administration also was seeking legislation for authority to raise the monthly premium for Medicare paid by the aged as well as legislation to increase the non-premium, or out-of-pocket, payments by the aged for Medicare benefits, up to an annual ceiling of $1,500.

The Administration further requested legislation to reduce to 40% the current 50% federal share of Medicaid programs funded in cooperation with the states.

Federal spending on health research would be augmented, with about half the total going to the drive against cancer.

Education—HEW planned to hold education outlays in fiscal 1976 at the fiscal 1975 level of $6.2 billion. To do this despite the impact of inflation, cutbacks were required. The targets, successfully defended against cuts in the past by their Congressional supporters, were college scholarship programs and the impacted-aid program for school districts with large numbers of children of federal employes. The Administration sought a $260 million a year reduction in the impacted-aid program. It wanted to drop the national defense education loan program, currently funded with $320 million, and a $240 million annual scholarship-grant program. However, the much larger basic opportunity grant program for low-income college students was to be expanded from its $660 million level to $1.1 billion.

HEW planned to tighten administrative control of defaults in the guaranteed student loan program, set in fiscal 1976 at $1.65 billion for federally insured loans. The default rate was running 11.3%,

DOMESTIC TRANSFER PAYMENTS
(in billions of dollars)

Fiscal year	Total	Retirement and disability [1]	Hospital and supplementary medical insurance	Food stamps	Veterans benefits and insurance	Unemployment benefits	Other
1965	28.3	20.2	--------	*	4.7	2.5	0.9
1966	31.8	23.8	--------	0.1	4.7	2.1	1.1
1967	37.3	25.3	3.2	.1	5.3	2.1	1.3
1968	42.7	28.0	5.1	.2	5.6	2.2	1.7
1969	48.5	32.2	6.3	.2	6.1	2.2	1.6
1970	54.8	35.6	6.7	.6	6.9	3.0	2.0
1971	67.4	42.4	7.4	1.5	8.0	5.6	2.3
1972	75.7	47.9	8.3	1.8	8.8	6.5	2.5
1973	86.7	58.5	9.0	2.1	9.7	4.8	2.5
1974	101.3	69.1	10.9	2.7	10.4	5.4	2.7
1975 estimate	128.2	82.6	13.2	3.3	11.9	13.7	3.5
1976 estimate	143.0	91.3	14.1	3.1	11.6	17.2	[2] 5.7

* Less than $50 million.
[1] Includes black lung benefits, supplemental security income benefits, and military retired pay.
[2] Includes allowances for energy tax equalization payments in 1976 and contingencies in 1975 and 1976.

costing $89 million in fiscal 1974, and was expected to become 14.1% in fiscal 1976, at a cost of $262 million.

Transportation—The Transportation Department's budget request for fiscal 1976 showed a 9.3% increase to $9.99 billion. Mass transit outlays would rise 34%, road construction outlays about 7%, airport-grant outlays 24%, ship-construction subsidies 23% and merchant-vessel operating subsidies 30%.

Requested obligations for new programs of the Urban Mass Transportation Administration were 19.3% above this year to $1.72 billion for fiscal 1976. The capital-grant budget authority was increased to $1.1 billion, from $1.05 billion in the current fiscal year. $300 million of $1.35 billion appropriated by Congress in fiscal 1975 was to be rechanneled to a new program permitting cities to use the funds either for capital projects or for operating expenses. The same option was applied to $500 million in the fiscal 1976 budget. Another $200 million was designated for transit in cities opting to switch the funds from highways to mass transit.

For highways, spending on the Interstate Highway System would be increased in an effort to complete link-ups. Other federally aided road projects were to be removed from the trust-fund outlays beginning in fiscal 1978. The administration sought to combine over 30 highway-grant programs into four areas—interstate, urban, rural, safety—with states getting more say in spending decisions.

For railroads, the budget contained requests for legislation to guarantee $2 billion in loans for track and equipment and to ease Interstate Commerce Commission control over freight-rate increases and route abandonment. Amtrak was to receive $350 million in grants to cover losses. The operating grant for fiscal 1975 was estimated at $298 million, $77.9 million of which was to be sought in an imminent supplemental appropriation. Instead of loan guarantees for capital projects, as sought in the past, a $110 million grant was requested for Amtrak in fiscal 1976 for locomotives, passenger cars and track upgrading.

For aviation, $350 million was budgeted for new airport grants, an increase of $25 million over fiscal 1975. The Administration planned to fund the projects entirely instead of requiring 25%-50% from airport authorities.

Some transportation tax changes were proposed: to reduce the airline passenger ticket tax to 7% from 8%; raise the boarding fee for international flights to $5 from $3; to charge private flights a "departure fee" of $5 to $10; lower the aviation fuel tax, in October 1977, to 2¢ a gallon from 7¢ with the states getting the option of imposing the 5¢ difference themselves.

Environment—The Environmental Protection Agency budget for fiscal 1976 was $743 million, a $47 million rise from the previous year. Research and development activity was reduced by $22 million to about $112 million.

The effort would focus on the effects of energy extraction and conversion, pollution control techniques and the consequences of alternative methods for pollution control in energy systems.

The only substantial new direction in funding was $25 million requested for a program to establish national standards for drinking water.

The budget provided for allotment to the states of some $4 billion impounded in 1974 for construction of municipal waste-treatment plants. Another $5 billion remained withheld out of $18 billion Congress had authorized for a water-pollution cleanup program originally designed to end in 1975.

Urban development—The fiscal 1976 program for the Housing and Urban Development Department was augmented by 29% to $7.1 billion from $5.5 billion for fiscal 1975. The community development program authorized by Congress in 1974 accounted for much of the increase. It was projected to expand from $225 million in fiscal 1975 to $1.3 billion for the first full year of spending.

Housing subsidies for the poor were to rise from $2.1 billion to $2.6 billion in fiscal 1976, with the government paying the difference between the fair market rental for apartments and the 15%-25% of income required from eligible families.

Subsidies for new and existing apartments were expected to be in the 200,000-unit range for fiscal 1975 and 400,000-unit range for fiscal 1976.

HUD would continue to carry the heavy burden of a discontinued program of insured home loans to low-income buyers in the inner cities. Net outlays for mortgage defaults under the program were budgeted at $792 million in fiscal 1975, $730 million in fiscal 1976.

"Tandem plan" programs begun in 1974 to spur the housing market were responsible for a deficit in HUD's special assistance programs, which required $390.4 million for fiscal 1975 and $513.2 million for fiscal 1976. Under the "tandem plan," HUD subsidized below-market mortgage rates by offering to buy low-interest loans from lenders. The loans subsequently were sold by HUD to private investors.

The budget for fiscal 1976 was predicated on the assumption "that as conditions in the mortgage market return to normal, there will no longer be a need for these temporary programs."

Agriculture—The budget programmed a dramatic decline in spending for direct payments to farmers and for food programs. The latter, including food stamps and child nutrition programs, were allocated $5.4 billion in fiscal 1976, a $411 million drop from the previous year. A proposed increase in the cost of food stamps, opposed in Congress, was to save the government $215 million in fiscal 1975 and, combined with tightened eligibility rules, $650 million in fiscal 1976. Expenditures for the program were budgeted at $3.7 billion for fiscal 1975 and $3.6 billion in fiscal 1976.

Direct federal payments to farmers were budgeted at $401 million, a $605 million decline from fiscal 1975. No payments under the "target price" program for major crops were scheduled for fiscal 1976 because of the anticipation that prices would remain above the price-support trigger.

Foreign aid—The President requested $4.1 billion for the foreign economic assistance program in fiscal 1976. For fiscal 1975, the total was $3.9 billion.

A substantial portion was requested for Indochina reconstruction—$508 million in fiscal 1975 and $762 million the next fiscal year.

Reconstruction aid for the Middle East also was planned: $331 million in fiscal 1975 and $410 million the following year.

The budget for the Agency for International Development was set at $1.1 billion for fiscal 1976, about $95 million more than in the prior year.

The foreign food aid expenditures under Public Law 480 were planned at $1.1 billion for fiscal 1976, a decrease of $273 million. The Administration planned a substantial increase in total obligational authority for the program of $1.34 billion in fiscal 1976, a rise from fiscal 1975's authorization of $778 million.

Tax preferences listed—A listing of "tax expenditures" was provided by the budget for the first time, as required under 1974 legislation. The items were tax preferences granted to individuals and corporations that could be viewed as federal spending in that they were revenues lost to the government.

The items listed by the Administration amounted to $81.4 billion in fiscal 1975—$62.1 billion for individuals, $19.3 billion for corporations—and $91.7 billion in fiscal 1976—$70.9 billion for individuals and $20.8 billion for corporations.

Among the items (fiscal 1975): Corporations—Investment tax credit, $4.2 billion. Lower tax rate (22%) on first $25,000 of corporate earnings, $3.6 billion. Tax exempt status of state and municipal bonds, $3.2 billion. Mineral depletion allowances, such as for oil and gas, $2.2 billion. Tax deferrals for export sales, $1.1 billion. Bad-debt reserve write-offs allowed for financial institutions, $1 billion.

Individuals—Deductions for state and local taxes other than on property and gasoline, $8.8 billion. Mortgate interest payment deductions, $5.6 billion. State gasoline-tax deductions, $850 million. Excluding pension contributions from taxable income, $5.2 billion. Property tax write-offs, $4.7 billion. Deductions for charitable contributions, $4.5 billion. Special rate for capital gains, $3.3 billion. Consumer credit interest deductions, $2.9 billion.

Democrats call budget 'misguided.' President Ford's $349.4 billion budget for fiscal 1976 drew expressions of shock from leading Democrats in Congress Feb. 3. Their criticism focused largely on the big projected deficit and on the budget's assumption of high and protracted unemployment.

Sen. Hubert H. Humphrey (D, Minn.), chairman of the Joint Economic Committee, called the budget "completely unacceptable." He told the Senate it was "unbelievable" that the President could propose record deficits and "not put America back to work." House Majority Leader Thomas P. O'Neill Jr. (D, Mass.) said the budget was based on "misguided priorities" and that Congress would "re-order" them "in light of our urgent human needs and our need to get the economy working again."

Chairman George H. Mahon (D, Tex.) of the House Appropriations Committee called the projected deficit "shocking." He predicted reductions, "sharp reductions," in the President's defense requests.

Cities' report calls budget 'inept'—The budget was described as "inept and insensitive" in a joint analysis issued Feb. 8 by the National League of Cities and the United States Conference of Mayors. The report said the budget projected reduced federal spending in many areas on the unrealistic assumption that the slack would be taken up by hard-pressed local governments.

It said the budget "sets forth economic recovery policies that both help and rely heavily upon the private sector. . . . Thus the President proposes to shift some billions of dollars in purchasing power to private business and to individuals." Such a policy, the report said, "means that the urgent needs of the cities will go largely unmet." The President's budget itself, it said, "creates emergency fiscal conditions in cities."

The report noted critically that the budget projected high employment which struck especially hard at "vulnerable" members of the work force, such as blacks and youth, but it failed to focus any emergency programs on these groups. It also objected to the fact that defense funds had been raised 10% to offset inflation while other expenditures, such as those for housing and transportation, did not get the inflation increment.

Fiscal '75 deficit at 30-year high. The federal deficit for fiscal 1975, ended June 30, totaled $44.21 billion, the biggest since 1945 when the budget deficit was $47.47 billion, according to Budget Director James Lynn July 28.

The final figures on deficit spending by the government exceeded the Administration's most recent forecast by about $2 billion and were nearly $10 billion above the February estimate.

Receipts during fiscal 1975 totaled $280.92 billion, up from $264.93 billion in the previous year. Outlays were $325.13 billion, compared with $268.39 billion in fiscal 1974.

1975 Economic Reports

President's report. "The economy is in a severe recession," President Ford told Congress in the opening sentence of his annual Economic Report Feb. 4. Unemployment, inflation and interest rates were all too high, he said, and the nation faced an energy problem demanding conservation and development of new energy sources.

Ford advocated passage of his tax and energy proposals to help stabilize the economy. While "they will not produce swift and immediate results," he said, they would be effective, and he urged Congress "to adopt them and to help me follow through with further measures that changing circumstances may make desirable."

The President stressed the need to curb the growth of federal spending and to reduce the federal deficit as the economy moved toward recovery and full employment.

Ford emphasized the need for Americans to adjust to higher pricing for energy products and to reduce U.S. dependence on unreliable sources of oil. He reiterated his stand that long-term energy rationing would be "both intolerable and ineffective," and he noted his proposal for a program of permanent tax cuts to compensate consumers for the coming higher costs of energy.

The President conceded that his proposed $16 billion anti-recession tax cut "might delay achieving price stability" but he called the tax cut "essential."

As for fiscal and monetary policies, they "must support the economy during 1975," Ford insisted. He added that, "In supporting the economy, however, we must not allow victory in the battle against inflation to slip beyond our grasp. It is vital that we look beyond the unemployment problem to the need to achieve a reduction in inflation not only in 1975 but also in 1976 and beyond."

Text of Ford's 1975 Economic Report:

The economy is in a severe recession. Unemployment is too high and will rise higher. The rate of inflation is also too high although some progress has been made in lowering it. Interest rates have fallen from the exceptional peaks reached in the summer of 1974, but they reflect the rate of inflation and remain much too high.

Moreover, even as we seek solutions to these problems, we must also seek solutions to our energy problem. We must embark upon effective programs to conserve energy and develop new sources if we are to reduce the proportion of our oil imported from unreliable sources. Failure or delay in this endeavor will mean a continued increase in this nation's dependence on foreign sources of oil.

We therefore confront three problems: the immediate problem of recession and unemployment, the continuing problem of inflation, and the newer problem of reducing America's vulnerability to oil embargoes.

These problems are as urgent as they are important. The solutions we have proposed are the result of careful study, but they will not produce swift and immediate results. I believe that these programs and proposals will be effective. I urge the Congress to adopt them and to help me follow through with further measures that changing circumstances may make desirable.

In our efforts we must recognize that the remedies we devise must be both effective and consistent with the long-term objectives that are important for the future well-being of our economy. For the sake of taking one step forward we must not adopt policies which will eventually carry us two steps backward.

As I proposed to you in my State of the Union Message, the economy needs an immediate one-year tax cut of $16-billion. This is an essential first move in any program to restore purchasing power, rebuild the confidence of consumers, and increase investment incentives for business.

Several different proposals to reduce individual taxes were considered carefully in our search for the best way to help the economy. We chose the method that would best provide immediate stimulus to the economy without permanently exacerbating our budget problem.

Accordingly, I recommended a 12% rebate of 1974 taxes, up to a maximum of $1,000. The rebate will be paid in two large lump-sum payments totaling $12 billion, the first beginning in May and the second by September.

I have also proposed a $4 billion investment tax credit which would encourage businessmen to make new commitments and expenditures now on projects that can be put in place this year or by the end of next year.

The prompt enactment of the $16 billion tax reduction is a matter of utmost urgency if we are to bolster the natural forces of economic recovery. But in recognizing the need for a temporary tax cut, I am not unmindful of the fact that it will increase the size of the budget deficit. This is all the more reason to intensify our efforts to restrain the growth in federal spending.

I have asked Congress to institute actions which will pare $17 billion from the fiscal 1976 budget. Even so, we foresee a deficit of more than $50 billion for the fiscal year beginning July 1. Moreover, even without new expenditure initiatives, the budget deficit is likely to remain excessively large in fiscal 1977. As a consequence, I will propose no new expenditure programs except those required by the energy program.

I am also asking the Congress to join me in finding additional ways to slow the rate of increase in federal spending. Budget outlays for new programs or for expansion of existing ones would have their economic effect long after the economic recovery gets under way. It is essential that the deficit be reduced markedly as the economy begins to return toward full employment. Control of expenditures is the only way we can halt an extraordinary increase in the portion of our incomes which government will take in the future.

A simple calculation shows the size of the problem which we face. Transfer payments to individuals by the federal government have increased, after adjustment for inflation, by almost 9 per cent annually during the past two decades. A continuation of this trend for the next two decades, along with only modest increases in other federal expenditures and in those of state and local governments, would lift the expenditures by government at all levels from about one-third of the gross national product to more than one-half.

Spending on this scale would require a substantial increase in the tax burden on the average American family. This could easily stifle the incentive and enterprise which is essential to continue improvements in productivity and in our standard of living.

The achievement of our independence in energy will be neither quick nor easy. No matter what programs are adopted, perseverence by the American people and a willingness to accept inconvenience will be required in order to reach this important goal. The American economy was built on the basis of low-cost energy. The design of our industrial plants and production processes reflect this central element in the American experience. Cheap energy freed the architects of our office buildings from the need to plan for energy efficiency. It made private homes cheaper because expensive insulation was not required when energy was more abundant. Cheap energy also made suburban life accessible to more citizens , and it has given the mobility of the automobile to rural and city dwellers alike.

The low cost of energy during most of the twentieth century was made possible by abundant resources of domestic oil, natural gas and coal. This era has now come to an end. We have held the price of natural gas below the levels required to encourage investment in exploration and development of new supplies, and below the price which would have encouraged more careful use.

By taking advantage of relatively inexpensive foreign supplies of oil, we improved the quality of life for Americans and saved our own oil for future use. By neglecting to prepare for the possibility of import disruptions, however, we left ourselves overly dependent upon unreliable foreign supplies.

Present circumstances and the future security of the American economy leave no choice but to adjust to a higher relative price of energy products. We have, in fact, already begun to do so, although I emphasize that there is a long way to go. Consumers have already become more conscious of energy efficiency in their purchases.

The higher cost of energy has already induced industry to save energy by introducing new production techniques and by investing in energy-conserving capital equipment. These efforts must be stimulated and maintained until our consumption patterns and our industrial structure adjust to the new relationship between the costs of energy, labor, and capital.

This process of adjustment has been slowed because U.S. energy costs have not been allowed to increase at an appropriate rate. Prices of about two-thirds of our domestic crude oil are still being held at less than half the cost of imported oil, and natural gas prices are being held at even lower levels. Such artificially low prices encourage the wasteful use of energy and inhibit future production.

If there is no change in our pricing policy for domestic energy and in our consumption habits, by 1985 one-half of our oil will have to be imported, much of it from unreliable sources. Since our economy depends so heavily on energy, it is imperative that we make ourselves less vulnerable to supply cutoffs and the monopolistic pricing of some foreign oil producers.

The need for reliable energy supplies for our economy is the foundation of my proposed energy program. The principal purpose is to permit and encourage our economy to adjust its consumption of energy to the new realities of the market-place during the last part of the twentieth century.

The reduction in our dependence on unreliable sources of oil will require Government action, but even in this vital area the role of Government in economic life should be limited to those functions that it can perform better than the private sector.

There are two courses open to us in resolving our energy problem: the first is administered rationing and allocation; the second is use of the price mechanism. An energy rationing program might be acceptable for a brief period, but an effective program will require us to hold down consumption for an extended period.

A rationing program for a period of five years or more would be both intolerable and ineffective. The costs in slower decision-making alone would be enormous. Rationing would mean that every new company would have to petition the government for a license to purchase or sell fuel. It would mean that any new plant expansion or any new industrial process would require approval. It would mean similar restrictions on homebuilders, who already find it impossible in much of the nation to obtain natural gas hookups. After five or 10 years such a rigid program would surely sap the vitality of the American economy by substituting bureaucratic decisions for those of the marketplace. It would be impossible to devise a fair long-term rationing system.

The only practical and effective way to achieve energy independence, therefore, is by allowing prices of oil and gas to move higher—high enough to discourage consumption and encourage the exploration and development of new energy sources.

I have, therefore, recommended an excise tax on domestic crude oil and natural gas and an import fee on imported oil, as well as decontrol of the price of crude oil. These actions will raise the price of all energy-intensive products and reduce oil consumption and imports. I have requested the Congress to enact a tax on producers of domestic crude oil to prevent windfall profits as a result of price decontrol.

Other aspects of my program will provide assurances that imports will not be allowed to disrupt the domestic energy market. Amendments to the Clean Air Act to allow more use of coal without major environmental damage, and incentives to speed the development of nuclear energy and synthetic fuels will simultaneously increase domestic energy production.

Taken as a whole, the energy package will reduce the damage from any future import disruption to manageable proportions. The energy program, however, will entail costs. The import fee and tax combination will raise approximately $30 billion from energy consumers.

However, I have also proposed a fair and equitable program of permanent tax reductions to compensate consumers for these higher costs. These will include income tax reductions of $16 billion for individuals, along with direct rebates of $2 billion to low-income citizens who pay little or no taxes, corporate tax reductions of $6 billion, a $2 billion increase in revenue-sharing payments to state and local governments, and a $3 billion increase in Federal expenditures.

Although appropriate fiscal and energy policies are central to restoring the balance of our economy, they will be supplemented by initiatives in a number of other areas.

I was pleased to sign into law in December unemployment compensation legislation which provides extended benefits and expanded coverage for the unemployed. The budget also provides for a significant expansion in public service employment. I also urge the Congress to remove the remaining restrictions on agricultural production and enact legislation to strengthen financial institutions and assist the financial position of corporations.

I have also asked for actions to strengthen the Administration's antitrust investigative power and to permit more competition in the transportation industry.

We sometimes discover when we seek to accomplish several objectives simultaneously that the goals are not always completely compatible. Action to achieve one goal sometimes works to the detriment of another. I recognize that the $16 billion antirecession tax cut, which adds to an already large Federal deficit, might delay achieving price stability. But a prompt tax cut is essential. My program will raise the price of energy to consumers; but when completed this necessary adjustment should not hamper our progress toward the goal of a much slower rate of increase in the general price level in the years ahead.

As we face our short-term problems, we cannot afford to ignore the future implications of our policy initiatives. Fiscal and monetary policies must support the economy during 1975. In supporting the economy, however, we must not allow victory in the battle against inflation to slip beyond our grasp. It is vital that we look beyond the unemployment problem to the need to achieve a reduction in inflation not only in 1975 but also in 1976 and beyond.

The future economic well-being of our nation requires restoring a greater measure of price stability. This will call for more responsible policies by your government. The stakes are high. Inflation reduces the purchasing power of our incomes, squeezes profits, and distorts our capital markets. The ability of our free economy to provide an ever higher standard of living would be weakened. We must not be lulled into a belief that inflation need no longer be a major concern of economic policy now that the rate at which prices are increasing appears to be slowing.

The proposals I have made to deal with the problems of recession, inflation, and energy recognize that the American economy is more and more a part of the world economy. What we do affects the economies of other nations, and what happens abroad affects our economy. Close communication, coordination of policies, and consultations with the leaders of other nations will be essential as we deal with our economic and financial difficulties, many of which are common to all the industrial countries of the Western world.

We are already cooperating to insure that the international monetary system withstands the pressure placed on it by higher oil prices. The passage of the Trade Reform Act of 1974 will make it possible to begin critical negotiations this year on further liberalizing the international trading system, and we will continue to work with other counties toward solutions to the special problems of food and energy.

The economic problems that have emerged during the 1970's are difficult. Some of them reflect years of misdirection. Our efforts to solve the nation's economic difficulties must be directed toward solutions that will not give rise to even bigger problems later. The year 1975 must be the one in which we face our economic problems and start the course toward real solutions.

Economic advisers' report. The report Feb. 4 of the President's Council of Economic Advisers forecast with reservations that the economy would "move onto the road of recovery in the second half" of the year. But the report, which accompanied the President's Economic Report to Congress, cautioned about the uncertainties of the forecast. Because of the sudden steepness of the economic decline, the imponderables of consumer and business confidence and money-management policies of the independent Federal Reserve Board, its predictions were "subject to an unusually wide margin of error," the council noted.

First, the economy would continue to decline "several more months," it said, and the decline in the closing months of 1974 "gathered so much momentum that developments beyond the current quarter are difficult to gauge." "It is quite likely, however, that the contraction of business activity and rising unemployment will continue for several more months."

"The most pressing concern of policy," the report continued, "is to halt the decline of production and employment." But, it said, "the momentum of the decline is so great that a quick turnaround and a strong recovery in economic activity aren't yet assured." Furthermore, it said, even if the second-half upturn transpired, the first-half decline would be so "severe" that the full year would show a decline. It estimated that "real" gross national product, or output of goods and services after adjustment for inflation, would decline about 3% from the 1974 level. (The GNP had declined 2.2% in 1974.) Total GNP in current dollars was expected to grow about 7.25% to $1.5 trillion, with the increase attributed entirely to inflation.

The council expected some progress in reducing the inflation rate. It predicted that consumer prices would average about 11% higher than in 1974, but the rate of increase would slow to about 7% in the fourth quarter.

The advisers conceded that the Administration's energy program would increase the consumer price level, perhaps by two percentage points or more. This would be "a special problem" for the Federal Reserve Board, the council noted. The spread of higher energy costs throughout the economy, it said, would require a flow of more money from the Federal Reserve System "to avoid a contractive effect." The council urged a "flexible" monetary policy for easier credit and lower interest rates in 1975 than in 1974. The council advocated "reasonable growth in money and credit," without specifying any rates.

"Consumers hold the key to the strength of the economic recovery," the council concluded. It estimated consumer spending would rise about 10% in dollar terms, but might be less than in 1974 in "real" terms after adjusting for inflation. Consumer savings were expected to be at a higher rate in 1975 than in 1974, especially in view of the proposed tax rebates.

As for business, the council said, "the behavior of inventory investment is likely to be the dominant influence on the course of production over the coming year." The volume of inventories at the beginning of 1975 in relation to GNP, it noted, "was the highest since the end of World War II." A sell-off of excess inventories was predicted for "most and perhaps all of the coming year," with total business inventories dropping $5 billion in 1975 after a $13.4 billion increase in 1974.

Business outlays for plant and equipment were expected to fall, in real terms, in the first half, but edge upward late in the year. A 4% increase (current dollars) in 1975 for fixed investment outlays by business would result, the council said, in a decrease of 9% in real dollars after adjusting for inflation.

Housing activity was expected to pick up, beginning in spring, and to reach an annual rate of 1.6–1.7 million by the final quarter making the 1975 total about 1.3 million starts, about the same as in 1974. The rate in December 1974 was less than 900,000 starts.

Among its recommendations, the council called for less federal regulation in the transportation, natural gas and financial industries. Current controls—in transportation especially—were "imposing significant costs on the economy," it said. Precise estimates of the costs were not available, it said, "but existing evidence suggests that this may range up to 1% of the Gross National Product, or approximately $66 per person per year."

Greenspan warns vs. larger deficit. Alan Greenspan, chairman of the Council of Economic Advisers, cautioned at a press briefing Feb. 4 against Congressional action that would enlarge the projected federal budget deficit of $52 billion. A deficit in the $70 billion range, he said, "will put a very severe strain on the credit markets." And "if we stimulate beyond what the President is suggesting, we would be trading off some small reduction in unemployment for inflation later and an average level of unemployment higher than we want."

Greenspan said the council's report forecast a sharp decline in the current quarter, "some stabilization" in the second quarter and a recovery of "reasonably good proportions" in the second half of the year. He estimated that the unemployment rate would peak at 8.5% and not fall below 8% until the first quarter of next year. Greenspan commented on the uncertainty of the predictions. "It may turn out that our numbers are too pessimistic," he said, and the economy "could come back a lot faster."

Policy Issues

Ford seeks support on tours. President Ford sought support for his anti-recession and energy program in a series of regional visits, speeches, press conferences and meetings with groups of governors Feb. 3-13, 1975.

But Ford indicated that his programs were subject to improvement.

At a press conference held in Atlanta Feb. 4, the President stressed continued opposition to going beyond his spending proposals in efforts to spur the economy. This would include any new spending to reduce unemployment. He specifically rejected a Jan. 31 appeal from the U.S. Conference of Mayors for $15 billion in aid to cities despite a warning from Milwaukee Mayor Henry W. Maier that there would be "blood in the streets" unless the federal government did something to relieve urban pressures.

In Houston Feb. 10, Ford promised independent oil producers more tax relief to permit new exploration. In Topeka Feb. 11, he promised farmers "a rebate program to compensate for increased energy costs caused by our conservation program." In Topeka, at a news conference, Ford gave details of the tax relief for oil producers. There was "some justification," he thought, to amend his "windfall profits" tax proposal to grant exemption for profit plowed back into exploration and development of additional sources of oil. This would reduce the proposed $12 billion of additional tax by some $3-$4 billion, he said, which was not "a serious change" but one that would have to be offset elsewhere in his energy program.

Ford said a revision of the oil proposal had been advocated "by individuals both in and out of government" whom he saw in Houston and Topeka. The President was flanked at a Houston dinner Feb. 10 by Govs. Dolph Briscoe (D, Tex.) and David Boren (D, Okla.). Boren said next day he and Briscoe had pleaded at length for easing the Administration's proposed tax increases for the oil industry.

In an address before the New York Society of Security Analysts in New York Feb. 13, Ford sought to soften the somber forecast of his budget.

"Forecasts are only forecasts," he reminded them, and the nation's economic future did not "depend on paper projections." "If we approach it with practical, tough-minded optimism," he said, "we can cope."

Ford said he hoped unemployment would be "moving down" by the end of the year but he cautioned that "we must not fight recessionary problems with inflationary cures." While unemployment was "the biggest concern" of the 8.2% of workers out of work, he said, inflation was "the universal enemy of 100% of our people."

Highway funds released—Ford announced—before a joint session of the Kansas Legislature Feb. 11—release of up to $2 billion in impounded highway construction funds through June 30 to spur the economy. The action derived from a request from governors, Ford said.

In releasing the funds, Ford said he was urging they be applied first to producing jobs, then to highway safety and completion of key links in the interstate system. Another priority could be given to urban mass transit projects that state and local officials agreed "should be substituted for less critical highway projects," he said.

At the Feb. 11 news conference, Ford defended the move, in light of the need to conserve fuel. "Better highways conserve fuel" he said, and so did mass transit, which was an option open to state and local officials in using the money.

(U.S. Judge John Lewis Smith Jr. of the District of Columbia ruled Feb. 12 that impoundment by the Executive branch of highway funds apportioned to the states by Congress was illegal. The federal-aid highway act, he said, did not allow such withholding "for reasons unrelated to the merits of a project itself." The suit was brought by 12 states which claimed a total of $2.1 billion as their share of $11.1 billion in road funds impounded under three Administrations as anti-inflationary action. Smith ordered the Federal Highway Administration to determine the allotments and release the funds. The Washington Post Feb. 13 reported federal officials as saying the $2 billion released by Ford would be ultimately deducted from the amount due the states on Smith's ruling. The states: Pennsylvania, Alaska, Arizona, Idaho, Louisiana, Michigan, Nevada, Oklahoma, Texas, Utah, Washington and Wisconsin.

(In a similar case, U.S. Judge George Templar ordered release of $121 million in road funds claimed by Kansas. The ruling was issued in Topeka Feb. 6.)

WIN slogan abandoned. The Citizens Action Committee Inc., which was organized by President Ford in October 1974 as a volunteer program designed to spur consumer involvement in the Administration's efforts to fight inflation, March 8 quietly discarded its Whip Inflation Now (WIN) slogan and announced that its efforts would be redirected toward encouraging energy conservation.

The committee said its aim was to establish local organizations in 40 key cities to promote energy-saving activities. About $14,000 in contributions already had been received and efforts were underway to win federal funding for the volunteer program.

Ford not to veto food stamp freeze. President Ford announced Feb. 13 that he would allow a bill barring an increase in the cost of food stamps through 1975 to become law without his signature. Ford said he would not fight "the clear will of Congress" on the bill, which passed by 374–38 House vote Feb. 4 and 76–8 Senate vote Feb. 5.

The bill blocked Ford's plan to raise the cost of the stamps March 1.

The President expressed disappointment that Congress not only rejected his plan but failed "to advance a constructive proposal of its own." If Congress continued such practice "an unthinkable [budget] deficit will result and there will be no mistaking where the responsibility lies," Ford said.

The President's decision was announced as a federal court considered two suits filed against the increase. Judge William B. Jones had said Feb. 11 he would issue a temporary injunction against the increase unless informed by Feb. 13 the bill would not be vetoed. The suits, brought by Consumers Union and the Food Research & Action Center of New York, were dismissed after Ford's announcement.

Ford signs reduced foreign aid bill. President Ford March 26 signed into law legislation appropriating $3.7 billion in foreign aid for fiscal 1975. (Programs, which otherwise would have been shut down for lack of funding, had been kept running by a series of emergency appropriations resolutions while Congress completed action.)

Ford said he was signing the bill, which was $2.3 billion less than requested, despite "considerable misgivings" about reductions in overseas assistance programs. He expressed regret over the cutting of the Administration's request for postwar Indochina reconstruction funds from $939 million to $440 million. Similarly, he warned that Congress' refusal to appropriate even half of $1.207 billion requested for the Military Assistance Program would jeopardize its continuing existence. "Programs of a humanitarian or developmental nature cannot be productive if our friends and allies are unable to defend themselves," he said.

Approved March 24 in the Senate by voice vote without debate, the bill faced opposition in the House, where it passed March 24 by a narrow margin of 193–185. Opponents of the bill argued that the money could be better used in the U.S. to help fight the current recession and to help lower the projected federal spending deficit.

The bill contained funds for developmental assistance, postwar reconstruction of Indochina, military aid grants and credit sales, international banks, refugee and disaster aid and United Nations development programs. It gave more than $1 billion in economic and military assistance to the Middle East. Of that amount, $324.5 million was earmarked for Israel, $250 million for Egypt and $77.5 million for Jordan.

Besides drastically cutting Administration requests for postwar Indochina reconstruction aid and for military assistance, Congress appropriated $300 million for food and nutrition, $246 million less than asked; $17.5 million for international narcotics control, $25 million less than the initial request; $74 million for the Asian Development Bank, $96 million less than asked and $225 million for the Inter-American Development Bank, $275 million less than the Administration had first sought.

Debt limit raised. The Senate Feb. 18 passed and sent to the White House a bill increasing the ceiling on the federal debt to $531 billion through June 30. President Ford signed the legislation Feb. 20. The Senate action came just as the Treasury exceeded the current $495 billion debt limit with delivery of $3.55 billion of debt securities to purchasers of the Treasury's notes and bonds.

Sale of the debt issues had been made in January, but delivery was postponed until there was final Congressional action on the debt ceiling, thereby allowing the government to continue its borrowing operations and to meet payrolls.

The House vote for temporarily lifting the debt ceiling by $36 billion had been 248–170 Feb. 5.

Making an even higher increase, the Senate June 26, by a 72–21 vote, approved and sent to the White House legislation raising the national debt ceiling $46 billion to $577 billion through Nov. 15. The bill had first been passed in the House June 25 on a vote of 223–196. Had Congress failed to act, the ceiling would have reverted to $400 billion July 1, although outstanding government debt was well above that amount.

Tax cut gets Ford's reluctant OK. President Ford March 29 reluctantly signed a $22.8 billion tax cut bill passed by the House and Senate, but warned the Democratic majority in Congress that tax cuts must be tied to spending cuts. Ford said he would not accept any more Congressional spending initiatives that would raise the federal budget deficit above an estimated $60 billion level, thereby jeopardizing the nation's recovery from recession by spurring inflation.

The bill-signing ceremony was nationally broadcast. Ford told his radio and television audience that the tax relief provisions, which provided for the largest tax cut in the nation's history, represented a "reasonable compromise" between the $16 billion tax cut proposal he had submitted to Congress and the $30.6 billion tax cut and spending legislation originally passed by the Senate.

Ford and Congress had both considered a tax cut a desirable way to stimulate the economy.

But Ford also noted his objections to features that had prompted Republican legislators to urge a presidential veto. Chief among the bill's defects, Ford said, were "extraneous changes [made] in our tax laws . . . which were adopted in a hectic last-minute session" before Congress broke for its Easter recess. Ford also said he opposed the bill's distribution of tax cuts. The legislation "fails to give adequate relief to the millions of middle-income taxpayers who already contribute the biggest share of federal taxes," he said.

Citing these objections, Ford said he was signing the bill "despite [its] serious drawbacks" because "any damage they do is outweighed by the urgent necessity of an anti-recession tax reduction right now."

(Ford also referred to the "take-it-or-leave-it" position he said he was forced to assume on the bill, noting that if a veto were sustained, there was no assurance that Congress "would send me a better bill—it might even be worse.")

In signing the compromise bill, Ford avoided an open clash with Congress on the politically volatile tax cut issue, but he took a hardline stand on a related issue—the burgeoning federal deficit.

Ford reminded the Democratic majority that his $16 million tax cut proposal had been coupled with a plan for cutting spending on existing federal programs by $17 billion and setting a one-year moratorium on all new government spending programs except in the energy field.

If renewed efforts were not made toward reducing the federal budget, Ford warned, "another round of inflation due to giant and growing deficits would cancel out all expected gains on economic recovery."

"If Congress had accepted all my economic recovery proposals, both for tax cuts and spending cuts," Ford said, "the estimated federal deficit for fiscal year 1976 [beginning July 1] would have been about $52 billion." The tax cut bill and "other changes," however, had raised the estimate to $60 billion.

According to Ford, if Congress failed to implement the spending cutbacks requested by the Administration, the deficit could reach $72 billion. New spending proposals under consideration in Congress would add another $30 billion, bringing the deficit to the "enormous total of $100 billion," Ford warned.

"Deficits of this magnitude are far too dangerous to permit. They threaten another vicious spiral of run-away double digit inflation which could well choke off any economic recovery," the President said.

Pointing to a chart to illustrate his message, Ford declared "I am drawing the line right here [at $60 billion], serving notice that this is as high as our fiscal 1976 deficit should go."

"This is as far as we dare go," Ford said. "I will resist every attempt by Congress to add another dollar to this deficit by new spending programs. I will make no exceptions, except where our long-range national security interests are involved as in the attainment of energy independence."

Congressional action—House and Senate conferees had completed work March 23 on a compromise version of widely divergent tax cut measures passed by each chamber. Over the protests of outnumbered Republicans, the conference report was rushed to the floor for a final vote March 26 so that Congress could begin its Easter recess.

The House vote in favor of the bill's final version was 287–125 (232 D & 55 R vs 43 D & 82 R). In subsequent Senate action, the vote in favor of adopting the conference report was 45–16 (34 D & 11 R vs 2 D & 14 R).

Several controversial amendments in the House and Senate bills were retained in modified form in the final bill, including repeal of the 22% depletion allowance for major oil and gas producers, restrictions on use of foreign tax credits, $50 bonus payments to Social Security recipients, railroad retirees and those on welfare and disability support, and a 5% tax credit for buyers of new homes.

The tax cut bill would reduce federal revenues by about $20.9 billion with tax cuts for individuals totaling $18.1 billion, business tax cuts of $4.8 billion and an offsetting $2 billion increase in the oil industry's taxes. The bill also increased federal spending by $1.9 billion for the calendar 1975. The $22.8 billion figure represented the bill's net cost. (Actual tax cuts totaled $22.9 billion.)

Individual taxes—$8.1 billion would be refunded to individuals. Taxpayers would receive a 10% rebate on 1974 individual taxes up to a maximum $200. The minimum rebate was $100—or an individual's total tax payment if it were less than $100. The $200 maximum would be phased downward for taxpayers with income of $20,000 or more. Individuals earning $30,000 or more would receive a maximum $100 rebate.

The percentage standard deduction on 1975 taxes was increased to 16% of adjusted gross income with a maximum of $2,300 for single persons and $2,600 for joint returns. The previous maximum had been 15% up to $2,000. The low-income allowance—a minimum standard deduction designed to free poverty-level families from paying federal taxes—was increased to $1,600 for single persons and to $1,900 for joint returns. The previous maximum had been $1,300 for single and joint returns. Total cost in lost revenue for the changes in standard deductions—$2.6 billion.

Individuals were allowed a $30 credit against taxes owed in 1975 income for each taxpayer and dependent. Cost—$5.2 billion.

A negative income tax provided a refundable 10% tax credit up to $400 on earned income of $4,000 or less for a family with at least one dependent child. The credit would be phased down in higher incomes and eliminated at the $8,000 level. Cost—$1.5 billion.

Individuals who purchased a newly built home that was finished or under construction by March 26, 1975 were entitled to a 5% tax credit up to $2,000. The credit was available for principal residences bought between March 13, 1975 and Dec. 21, 1976. Cost—$600 million.

A tax credit for homeowners installing fuel-saving insulation or solar heating devices was omitted from the final bill.

Business taxes—The business investment tax credit was increased to 10% in 1975 and 1976 from the existing levels of 4% for public utilities and 7% for other businesses. Total cost in lost revenue from changes in the investment tax credit—$3.3 billion.

Corporations were allowed to take an 11% credit on investments during 1975 and 1976 provided that benefits from the additional 1% credit were contributed to an employes' stock ownership plan.

The existing $50,000 limit on the amount of used property qualifying for the investment tax credit was increased to $100,000 for 1975 and 1976.

The limit on the amount of investment credit taken by a utility during one year was increased from the existing ceiling of 50% tax liability above $25,000 to 100% of tax liability in 1975 and 1976. After that two-year period, the limit would phase back to 50% over a five year period.

Businesses were allowed to claim the investment credit for progress payments made during one year toward construction of investments taking several years to complete.

Public utilities that had elected immediately to pass along to consumers through lower rates the benefits of the existing 4% credit were allowed to choose to keep for their own purposes the benefit of the additional credit provided by the increase to 10%. If a state regulatory agency required that the benefits be passed on to consumers immediately, the increased credit would be denied.

The amount of corporate income exempt from the 26% corporate tax surcharge was increased from the existing $25,000 level to $50,000 for 1975. Cost—$1.2 billion.

The normal 22% corporate income tax rate was reduced to 20% on the first $25,000 in income during 1975. Cost—$300 million.

Individuals and business—Self-employed persons were allowed to deduct from their 1975 taxable incomes contributions to qualified pension plans made after the end of the year but before their 1975 tax returns were filed.

A tax credit was allowed for 20% of the wages paid between the date of enactment and July 1, 1976 to hire a recipient of federal aid to families with dependent children (AFDC). Individual taxpayers hiring AFDC recipients for personal services rather than for a business were allowed a tax credit limited to $1,000 for each employe hired.

Oil and gas depletion—The 22% depletion allowance on oil and gas production was repealed retroactive to Jan. 1, 1975. However, the allowance was retained until July 1, 1976 for natural gas sold under federal price regulations (or until the controlled price was raised to take account of repeal of depletion). The allowance also was retained for natural gas sold under fixed price contracts until the price was raised.

Small producers were provided a permanent exemption that allowed independent oil companies to continue taking the depletion allowance on a basic daily output of oil and natural gas, averaging 2,000 barrels of oil or 12 million cubic feet of natural gas or an equivalent quantity of both oil and gas.

The daily production eligible for depletion would be reduced by 200 barrels a day for each year between 1976 and 1980, leaving the small-producer exemption at a permanent level of 1,000 barrels of oil per day or 6 million cubic feet of natural gas.

The depletion rate available for the small producers would be reduced to 20% in 1981, 18% in 1982, 16% in 1983, and to a permanent 15% rate in 1984.

The 22% depletion rate would be kept until 1984 for production of up to 1,000 barrels a day through costly secondary or tertiary recovery methods used to extract remaining oil and gas from wells that were mostly pumped out.

The deduction taken under the small-producer exemption would be limited to 65% of the taxpayer's income from all sources. The small-producer exemption would be denied to any taxpayer who sold oil or gas through retail outlets or operated a refinery processing more than 50,000 barrels of oil a day.

Foreign Income—The amount of foreign tax payments on oil-related income that an oil company could take as a credit against U.S. taxes was limited to 52.8% of its 1975 income from foreign oil operations. The limit would be reduced to 50.4% in 1976 and 50% thereafter. Use of excess credits within those limits was allowed only to offset U.S. taxes on foreign oil-related income, not on income from other foreign sources.

After 1975, oil companies were denied the use of the per-country limitation option that allowed a company to compute its maximum foreign tax credits on a country-by-country basis.

It was required that oil companies recapture foreign oil-related losses that were deducted from income subject to U.S. taxes by taxing an equivalent amount of subsequent foreign oil-related profits as if earned in the U.S. (and therefore not eligible for deferral until transferred to the U.S.). The credit for foreign taxes on the subsequent profits also would be reduced in proportion to the amount treated as U.S. profits.

The foreign tax credit was denied for any taxes paid to a foreign country in buying or selling oil or gas from property that the nation had expropriated. Domestic international sales corporations (DISCs) were denied the deferral of taxes on half of the profits from exports of natural resources and energy products. Effective in 1976, certain existing exemptions were repealed from a 1962 law requiring current U.S. taxation of profits earned by subsidiaries set up by a U.S. corporation in tax haven countries that imposed little or no taxes. Allowance was made for deferral of U.S. taxes on all earnings by a foreign subsidiary if less than 10% of its income was defined as tax haven income.

Non-tax provisions requiring new federal spending—A $50 bonus payment out of general Treasury revenues was granted to each recipient of Social Security retirement, railroad retirement or supplemental security income benefits.

An additional 13 weeks of emergency unemployment benefits was provided jobless workers in nine states that had exhausted their available 52 weeks of regular and extended benefits. (An estimated 375,500 workers in California, New York, New Jersey, Rhode Island, Washington, Oregon, Massachusetts, Pennsylvania, and Michigan were expected to benefit from the added jobless aid.)

Ford bids nation remain optimistic. President Ford said April 7 he rejected the view that the nation faced "nothing but a grim future of depression at home and disintegration abroad." His vision, he said, was "one of growth and development worldwide through increasing interdependence of nations of the world."

"During my administration," he continued, "Americans will neither resign from the world nor abandon hope of peaceful and constructive relationships with all peoples."

Ford made the remarks in a speech in Las Vegas before the convention of the National Association of Broadcasters. He was critical in his speech of "unfair" tax reductions in the recently enacted tax bill and urged Congress to limit federal spending so as not to exceed the proposed fiscal 1976 budget deficit of $60 billion.

On the tax bill, Ford protested that the tax reductions were "unfairly concentrated in the very lowest income brackets." "Low-income people should indeed be helped," he said, "but not to the exclusion of the rest of the population." The bill also "took some six million Americans off the tax rolls," he said. "We cannot afford to have this nation divided between taxpayers and nontaxpayers. This is most unfair."

On federal spending, he said if Congress exceeded the proposed $60 billion deficit it could make "a solid, sustainable and noninflationary recovery in our nation impossible." If the current trend in Congress continued, he cautioned, "a possible deficit of $100 billion is projected" and "that would be a disaster." "Running a deficit of $100 billion is gambling with the nation's economic strength," he said.

Ford signs rescissions legislation. President Ford April 8 signed into law legislation rescinding $259 million in fiscal 1975 budget appropriations. The amount rescinded was far smaller than the $2.1 billion originally requested by the Administration. Contained in two separate bills, the rescissions were approved by the House March 25 and the Senate March 26.

Most of the rescissions sanctioned by Congress came from Defense Department funds. Included were rescissions of $123 million for the procurement of 12 F-111 fighter bombers and $60 million for department operation and maintenance efforts.

Among other rescissions granted: $17.8 million in Agriculture Department funds, $9.4 million in Justice Department funding, $19.3 million for the Commerce Department and $5 million from the Executive Office of the President.

Both houses firmly opposed proposed rescissions of $1.2 billion for several health, education and welfare programs and $264 million for housing assistance.

Congress sets $367 billion target. Congress May 14 completed action on a concurrent resolution setting a $367 billion spending target for fiscal 1976. The measure was passed by voice vote in the Senate and by a 230–193 margin in the House.

The first attempt by Congress to establish overall spending goals to guide individual committees as they considered federal outlays for the coming fiscal year, the resolution called for a total expenditure of $367 billion, with projected revenues of $298.1 billion and a resulting deficit of $68.8 billion.

The deficit was above the $60 billion figure President Ford had said was the maximum he would accept, but Congressional proponents of the resolution claimed that differences between their amount and Ford's were due almost entirely to disagreement over expenses and receipts beyond the government's control, as well as the state of the economy.

Jobs bill vetoed. A $5.3 billion job-producing bill was vetoed by President Ford May 29 as "not an effective response to the unemployment problem."

Noting that the bill authorized spending $3.3 billion above his budget request, almost half of that in fiscal 1976, Ford said the bill "would exacerbate both budgetary and economic pressures and its chief impact would be felt long after our current unemployment problems are expected to subside."

"Economic recovery is expected to be well under way by the end of 1975," Ford said in his veto message, "and the accelerative influences of this bill would come much too late to give impetus to this recovery."

The President urged Congress to act quickly on a bill to provide funds for "immediate and temporary employment through the public sector and summer youth jobs." The vetoed bill contained such provisions, but it also had "a host of provisions of questionable value," according to Ford.

Veto sustained by House—The veto was sustained by the House June 4. A vote to override was 277–145, five short of the two-thirds majority of those present and voting required to carry. The totals included 22 Democrats voting to uphold the veto and 19 Republicans voting to override. The latter contrasted with 48 Republicans voting for passage originally.

Party lobbying before the vote was intense. President Ford telephoned several members—some Southern Democrats as well as Republicans, whose votes were uncertain—from aboard his plane. House Speaker Carl Albert (D, Okla.) made a rare appearance in a floor debate to plead with the House to override "to show we are a legislative body."

House Democratic Leader Thomas P. O'Neill Jr. (Mass.) told the House Democrats at a caucus June 4 "we will not be faced again this session with so clear a confrontation between the philosophy and ideals of the Republican and Democratic parties."

On the floor later, O'Neill rebutted Ford's budgetary argument for veto, that the bill was $3.3 billion more than his budget, by claiming Ford's economic policies had "cost the government $56 billion" in eight months of office. This was based on the increase in the unemployment rate since Ford took office; the rate rose from 5.4% to 8.9%. House Appropriations Committee chairman George H. Mahon (D, Tex.), floor manager of the override vote, had said that each 1% increase in unemployment increased the federal deficit $16 billion—$14 billion in lost income tax revenue and $2 billion paid out in unemployment benefits.

On the other side, House Republican Leader John J. Rhodes (Ariz.), attributing the current economic condition to the Democrats, who controlled the last two Congresses, referred to the "93rd and 94th Congressional recession."

O'Neill rose to say the current recession "happened because of a corrupt Nixon Administration that the American people lost confidence in."

Summer job funds approved. The Senate June 12, by voice vote, passed and sent to the White House legislation appropriating $473 million for summer jobs for 840,000 economically disadvantaged youths. The House June 10 had cleared the bill, 408–8. Originally part of the $5.3 billion jobs bill vetoed by President Ford May 29, the measure was rushed through Congress in four days because of the need of local communities to plan summer work programs. President Ford signed the bill June 16.

Jobs plans overvalued, study finds. A private study issued May 27 found that public employment programs using government funds largely failed to reduce unemployment, produce new services or prepare the jobless for permanent work. The programs did act as a "cash-transfer" mechanism and support the jobless, the study said, but, in the long run, 60%–90% of the federal funds only displaced state and local funds for regular services. The study was done by Alan Fechter of the American Enterprise Institute for Public Policy Research.

Congress votes speeded-up road building. The Senate May 22, by voice vote, approved and sent to the White House a bill designed to create jobs by temporarily relieving states from having to match federal highway assistance funds. The House had approved the measure April 10. President Ford signed it June 4.

Some financially hard-pressed states had complained of being unable to gain use of portions of the $2 billion in impounded highway funds President Ford had ordered released Feb. 12. The federal highway assistance program required the states to put up 30% of the total cost of non-interstate highway construction, with the federal government then supplying the remaining 70%.

Under the bill, states would be able to obtain 100% federal financing for eligible construction projects initiated between Feb. 12 and Sept. 30. The money was to be considered a loan, however, and would have to be repaid by Jan. 1, 1977.

The Administration had opposed the bill, contending that only a few states would have matching fund problems that would be alleviated by the measure.

On signing the measure, the President stated his agreement with the bill's objective to stimulate employment but his opposition to the principle of deferring payment by the states of their shares of project costs. He signed the bill, he said, only because it was a "one-time exception" and it had a "tough provision" requiring payment of the deferred funds as a condition to qualify for future federal highway aid.

Housing bill vetoed. President Ford vetoed a $1.2 billion emergency housing bill June 24 on the grounds that "its cost, ineffectiveness and delayed stimulus" would damage the housing industry and the nation. The bill would have subsidized mortgage interest rates as low as 6% and provided federal loans to unemployed home owners facing foreclosure.

The President announced at the same time his own plan to help speed the housing recovery—release of $2 billion remaining from $7.75 billion authorized in the 1974 housing bill under which the Housing and Urban Development Department (HUD) bought home loans made at below-market interest rates and then sold them at existing market rates. The government's loan rate was pegged to its own cost of borrowing money. HUD Secretary Carla Hills said June 24 the $2 billion program was expected to cost the government $60 million and would finance about 65,000 mortgages at a 7.75% interest rate, compared with the current market rate of slightly less than 9%.

The President also asked Congress to extend the 1974 housing bill another year and to authorize another $7.75 billion for it. As for the jobless home owners, Ford said he would support "a workable plan" to prevent foreclosures and he endorsed a House measure for mortgage-relief loans or a coinsuring of lenders refraining from foreclosing.

Ford contended that his plan to stimulate housing and create jobs would be cheaper and faster than the one he vetoed, which he said would take months to get going, hamper a recovery already under way in housing and cause $2 billion in federal outlays, adding $1 billion to the federal deficit in fiscal 1976.

The veto was deplored June 24 by officials of the housing industry and the AFL-CIO. Supporters of the bill contended that its stimulus to the industry and the economy in general would offset any inflationary impact. They also argued that the HUD program pushed by the President was not very stimulative because the mortgage rates were out of range of middle-income buyers. J. S. Norman Jr., president of the National Association of Home Builders, urged Congress to "rectify the situation" by overriding the veto. "Without a housing recovery to lead the way as it has in the past," he said, "any national economic rebound will be slow and painful." Leon N. Weiner, president of the National Housing Conference, said his membership "deeply" regretted the veto and thought it "somewhat strange" the President waited until he received legislation he opposed before releasing $2 billion in mortgage aid funds.

AFL-CIO President George Meany, addressing a jobs conference in Washington June 24, said the veto "must be overriden." He accused the Ford Administration of a "callous disregard" for the unemployed and the social consequences of sustained high unemployment. "This administration is still fighting inflation with the jobs of workers," Meany said. "It is time the Congress remembered its responsibility to the people who elected them—one in seven of whom are unemployed or underemployed. It is time the President remembered that government by veto means the minority forcing its will on the majority."

Another speaker at the conference was Sen. Hubert H. Humphrey (D, Minn.), who deplored "an unmistakable pattern," that "each recession brings with it an official tolerance of higher unemployment."

The measure had been passed by 253–155 House vote June 5 and 72–24 Senate vote June 11.

Veto sustained in House—The veto was upheld in the House June 25 when a motion to override failed 268–157 (249 D & 19 R vs. 122 R & 35 D). It was 16 short of the two-thirds majority necessary to override.

The failure of the heavily Democratic majority came despite a plea for the bill by House Speaker Carl Albert (D, Okla.), who denounced President Ford's "veto-barricades against the overwhelming majority" of the Congress.

The President opened his news conference that day with a statement hailing the House vote upholding his veto. It demonstrated, he said, "a growing sense of fiscal responsibility in the Congress and a realization by an increasing number of Congressmen that economic recovery need not be bought at the price of unwise legislation and costly inflation."

Jobless aid bill signed. President Ford signed into law June 30 legislation extending the unemployment compensation program through 1975 for a maximum duration of 65 weeks of aid. Without the extension, the program would have reverted July 1 to an aid period of only 52 weeks and 250,000 persons would have been dropped from the lists.

The bill had been passed June 26 by House voice vote and 83–3 Senate vote.

The 65-week maximum of unemployment benefits was to be available in states having a jobless rate exceeding 6% of the workers covered by unemployment insurance. In states having a 5%–6% jobless rate among insured workers, the jobless would be eligible for 52 weeks of benefits, and 39 weeks would be available in states where the jobless trigger was less than 5%. Under the previous law, the extended benefits were available when either the national unemployment rate or a particular state's rate exceeded 4.5% of the work force.

The legislation required those who had received 39 weeks of compensation to apply for state occupational training to be eligible for further benefits. The state was to decide on an individual's need for it.

Special unemployment assistance for some workers, such as domestics and farm workers, outside the coverage of the regular federal-state jobless compensation system, would be expanded from 26 weeks to 39 weeks.

April welfare statistics reported. High unemployment caused the number of families receiving welfare to rise in April, the Department of Health, Education and Welfare reported Aug. 7.

According to HEW, 11.37-million persons from 3.48-million families drew $744.8 million in Aid to Families with Dependent Children (AFDC) benefits during April, the latest month for which statistics were available. The number of recipients represented a two-thirds of one per cent increase over the previous month. AFDC roles had risen 1.4% in January and eight-tenths of one per cent in February and March.

However, HEW said that in 25 states the number of AFDC families with unemployed fathers as heads of household declined in April by nine-tenths of one per cent to a total of 528,000. In the first three months of 1975, the number of AFDC families headed by jobless fathers showed a cumulative increase of 26.3%, HEW said.

Ford wants to cut business red tape. President Ford pledged June 17 to free small business from "the shackles of federal red tape." "We have held no referendum to repeal our economic freedom," he told the National Federation of Independent Business, an organization of small business men, and "Americans have not arrived at a popular consensus for collectivism."

The President spoke of a "direct connection between the spirit of the American Constitution and a competitive, privately oriented economy." He deplored "runaway spending that confines government to no boundary, that undermines individual initiative, that penalizes hard work and excellence, that destroys the balance between the private and public sector of American life."

The federal government should not, he said, become "an instrument of philanthropic collectivism" nor "the big daddy of all citizens." "We must free the business community from regulatory bondage so it can produce."

Cabinet members join in call—Two members of Ford's cabinet echoed the President's call June 17 and urged removal of "the dead hand of government from many areas where it smothers economic incentives and growth." The phrase was that of Treasury Secretary William E. Simon, who appeared, as did Transportation Secretary William T. Coleman, Jr., before the National Coal Association, the industry trade organization, at its annual meeting in Washington. Coleman attacked what he termed stifling federal regulation over transportation. Simon focused on energy. "We must continue to recognize that the chief barriers to all new energy production," Simon said, "lie at our doorstep, right here in Washington, D.C. in the problems created by the Clean Air Act, the moratorium on coal leasing as well as price and supply regulation affecting oil and gas."

No link seen in administered prices & inflation. Albert Rees, chairman of the Council of Wage and Price Stability, said June 17 that a study commissioned by the council uncovered no link between inflation and "administered prices" set by producers in "concentrated" industries. The issue of whether the pricing power of leading companies in industries dominated by a few producers was an independent cause of higher prices had been debated since the 1930s.

According to the study, by Ralph Beals of Amherst College, "wholesale prices in the concentrated industries have risen less rapidly than prices in unconcentrated industries" over the past 20 years. His conclusions were based on an analysis of the Labor Department's wholesale price index.

Beals also concluded that prices in concentrated industries "appear to rise less than competitive prices in [periods of economic] expansions, but have recently fallen less or risen more in recessions."

Action on Energy

President Ford Jan. 23, 1975 fulfilled his promise to try to reduce oil imports by increasing the tariff on them. He also campaigned against Democratic proposals for gasoline rationing. Congress later passed legislation suspending the President's power to raise the oil tariff, but Ford vetoed the measure.

Ford vows gas rationing veto. President Ford said at a televised news conference Jan. 21 that he would veto a mandatory gasoline rationing program if it were passed by Congress. He rejected rationing, which was favored by many Democratic congressmen as a means of conserving fuel, as a short-term, "ineffective" and "inequitable" solution.

To meet the Administration's goal of reducing foreign oil imports by 1 million barrels a day by 1975, Ford said a rationing system would have to limit "each driver to less than nine gallons a week."

"To really curb demand," Ford said, "we would have to embark on a long-range rationing program of more than five years." Moreover, he continued, "rationing provides no stimulus to increase domestic petroleum supply or accelerate alternative energy sources. By concentrating exclusively on gasoline rationing, many other areas for energy conservation are overlooked."

Ford challenged Congress to act quickly on his proposals and to pass them substantially intact. "I will not sit by and watch the nation continue to talk about an energy crisis and do nothing about it," he said. In announcing his own effort to take the "first step toward regaining our energy freedom," Ford said he would use executive authority to raise tariffs on imported oil as a temporary measure until Congress passed legislation setting higher fees.

This step, Ford said, would "set in motion the most important and far-reaching energy conservation program in our nation's history. We must reverse our increasing dependence on imported oil. It seriously threatens our national security and the very existence of our freedom and leadership in the free world."

Ford was asked why the Administration had not included penalties against automobile horsepower and weight among its energy and tax proposals. Responding to a charge by some critics that his was a "made in Detroit" plan designed to "rescue or revive the auto industry," Ford said auto taxes, gas rationing and closure of gas stations on Sunday had been rejected as "little pieces" of a plan. His program was "comprehensive" and "well integrated," Ford said.

White House Press Secretary Ron Nessen Jan. 22 cited Federal Energy Administration estimates that a rationing system would cost $2 billion annually to administer; 15,000–20,000 full time federal workers would be needed to implement the program; and 3,000 offices would be required at the state and local level. In the rush to obtain rationing coupons, Nessen claimed that the number of licensed drivers would rise from 125 million to 140 million, and gasoline purchased legally on the "white market" through the sale of coupons would cost up to $1.25 a gallon.

All of the figures were based on the assumption that gasoline rationing would be the only measure used to attain a 1 million barrel a day reduction in oil imports, a premise most experts considered unrealistic since Congress was also considering a combination of tax, rationing and allocation measures.

According to a Gallup poll published in Newsweek magazine Jan. 20, 55% of those responding favored a nationwide rationing program, compared with 32% who preferred to cut consumption through use of higher gasoline taxes.

New FEA price rules set. The Federal Energy Administration (FEA) announced

Jan. 3 that effective the beginning of the current year it was adopting new price regulations for propane, butane and natural gasoline in order to keep the price of these fuels "as low as possible without affecting dwindling supplies." (Natural gasoline was a liquid extracted from natural gas and blended with products refined from crude oil to produce motor gasoline.)

Among the highlights of the new regulations, as reported by the FEA, was retention of the May 15, 1973 basic price level but with the added stipulation that "sellers use for the purpose of computing current lawful prices" a price of 8.5¢ per gallon for propane, 9¢ for butane and 10¢ for natural gasoline. (After an FEA-authorized price increase for propane in September 1974, under a system which allowed sellers to add production-related costs to the basic price, the gas had been selling for an average price of 14¢–15¢ a gallon.) The new rules would allow "natural gas liquid processors" to add .5¢ a gallon to their prices "to reflect increased non-product costs" including "rents, labor costs, utility rates, and interest charges" incurred "as part of the processing operations." Natural gas "consumed in producing natural gas liquids" could be added to the 1973 basic price. Refiners, gas processors and resellers could apply increased propane costs selectively by charging, for example, a higher price to industrial users than to homeowners. According to the FEA news release, the previous rule had required suppliers to apply increases in the base price for propane "to all classes of purchasers by precisely the same amounts." As "an incentive to construct new facilities," a new rule permitted unspecified higher prices for natural gas liquids (natural gasoline) extracted in gas processing facilities built after January 1975.

Propane overcharge found—An investigation conducted by the FEA showed that rural users of bottled propane gas had been overcharged by about $80 million during the winter of the 1973 Arab oil embargo, it was reported March 17.

An FEA spokesman said the investigation, code-named Project Speculator, had gone on for about nine months. He said the FEA had used threats of legal action to force propane suppliers to roll back prices by nearly $50 million.

The Washington Post March 18 said Project Speculator was generating charges that propane suppliers in farming states of the Midwest had set up dummy corporations among themselves to pass along overcharges to consumers. The newspaper quoted an unnamed FEA source as saying there had been "an inordinate amount of monkeying around with propane prices where suppliers would literally gather around a table, selling bottled gas to each other with everybody taking his historic profit margin." The Post reported that propane was currently selling for 26¢–30¢ a gallon.

Ford OKs higher oil tariffs, rebuffs bids for delay. President Ford signed a proclamation Jan. 23 that was intended to reduce the nation's consumption of foreign oil by making imports more costly. The Ford proclamation provided that tariffs on imported crude oil would rise $1 a month for three months: increasing $1 a barrel on Feb. 1, to $2 on March 1 and to $3 on April 1. (The current levy was 18¢ a barrel.)

Tariffs on finished petroleum products also would be increased, but by varying amounts. According to the White House, the $1 increase in duties would cause the cost of petroleum products to rise an average 1¢ a gallon by March. The ultimate effect of a $3 boost in tariffs would be an increase of about 3.5¢ a gallon, according to the Federal Energy Administration.

Ford defended his order as a "firm" but "fair" way to reduce national dependence on foreign oil. "Each day without action increases the threat to our national security and welfare," he said in a prepared statement.

"We've diddled and dawdled long enough," Ford said at an impromptu press conference after signing the executive order. It was a remark aimed at his critics in Congress, where opposition to higher tariffs was strong and widespread. Ford acknowledged that Congress could nullify the tariff increase by repealing the law which authorized his order, but he warned that such an action would constitute a "backward step." Ford had made a similar charge during his press conference Jan. 21 when asked if he would consider delaying the tariff increase.

Governors of 10 Northeastern states that were heavily dependent on supplies of costly imported oil vehemently opposed his action. They met with Ford just before he signed the proclamation in an unsuccessful effort to dissuade him from authorizing the tariff increase. All of the governors disagreed with Ford's assessment of the inflationary impact of higher import fees. Ford claimed that a rise in tariff's would add only $250 to annual household fuel bills and that electric rates would climb by only 1.5% in New England. According to governors of the six New England states, higher tariffs alone would cost their area $890 million.

Gov. Milton J. Shapp (D, Penn.) said he "told the President I thought his program represented a blueprint for economic disaster, that there would be a shock wave of inflation through the country greater than the one we had when the Arabs lifted their embargo."

Gov. Michael Dukakis (D, Mass.) accused Ford of "holding the Northeast hostage for his program." "I don't think he liked the characterization, but he didn't object when the other governors used terms like 'a lever' or 'leverage' to get your program through [Congress]," Dukakis said.

Gov. Hugh Carey (D, N.Y.) agreed with Dukakis, charging that Ford's strategy was to "coerce Congress into action" on the rest of his energy proposals by imposing higher tariffs. Carey, a former New York congressman and member of the House Ways and Means Committee, claimed that in ordering higher tariffs, Ford "was acting outside the powers granted him by the Trade Expansion Act," which the White House cited as authority for the executive action. Congress "never intended" the legislation to be used for "unilateral actions of this kind," Carey said. "We've suffered in the past from an excessive use of presidential power," he declared.

Ford Jan. 22 had rebuffed a direct appeal for delay from Rep. Al Ullman (D, Ore.), chairman of the House Ways and Means Committee. Ullman asked that action setting higher tariffs be postponed temporarily because the order raised "serious legal questions." Ford's proclamation was issued under a section of the trade law permitting him to raise tariffs when the secretary of the Treasury concluded that certain imports threatened national security. Public hearings usually preceded such a determination, but Secretary William Simon waived them.

Simon testified before the Ways and Means Committee Jan. 23 in defense of the President's action as the committee began consideration of a bill that would prohibit any changes in tariff schedules for 90 days.

Rep. William Green (D, Pa.), chairman of the committee's new subcommittee on international trade, rejected Simon's arguments that a decision was made to authorize higher fees without hearing from opponents of the plan because national security demanded swift action. Green cited the Nixon Administration's use of national security as an excuse for burglaries and their cover-up, saying "this is a most inappropriate time to dispense with public hearings and notice on the ground of national security."

Similar efforts to block increased tariffs were also under way in the Senate where a bill suspending the President's authority to set higher import fees was introduced Jan. 23 by Sens. Edward M. Kennedy (D, Mass.) and Henry M. Jackson (D, Wash.). The legislation already had 52 cosponsors, including four Republicans.

Ford defends tariff action—Ford again took the offensive when he appeared on a nationally televised interview Jan. 23 defending his order raising oil import fees.

Failure to act on the tariff question, Ford said, "would have been a sign of weakness around the world."

In remarks on other aspects of his energy proposals before Congress, Ford said the aim of the plan was to reduce the "percentage of reliance we have or will have on foreign oil." The U.S. currently imported 38% of its total crude oil supplies, according to Ford. Passage of his plan would cause imports to drop to about 10%, the President said.

If Congress rejected his energy program, Ford said he would accept arbitrary allocation of petroleum products as an alternative approach to cut demand

and limit foreign oil imports, but he restated his opposition to fuel rationing as a measure of "last resort."

Court rules oil tariff illegal—The U.S. Court of Appeals ruled Aug. 11 that President Ford exceeded his authority in setting a $2-a-barrel tariff on imported crude oil. The appeals court, in a 2–1 decision overturning an earlier court ruling, declared the fee "cannot stand" and said it would direct the U.S. District Court in Washington to enjoin the government from collecting the tax.

The suit, charging Ford had exceeded the powers granted him under the Trade Expansion Act, was filed by governors of nine states, 10 utilities and Rep. Robert F. Drinan (D, Mass.). A trial judge had rejected the initial challenge Feb. 21 by upholding the tariff.

In finding Ford's action illegal, the court said it recognized "we are overturning an honest attempt by the President to find a solution to a difficult crisis." However, the court added, "this case raises a question about the way the government should operate when responding to crisis."

"The normal checks and balances on each branch of government" could not be suspended by simply invoking national security, as Ford did in imposing the new tax, the court declared. "Our laws were not established merely to be followed only when times are tranquil."

Setting trade and tariff policy was a congressional function that could not be usurped by the president on grounds that the nation faced an "emergency" energy situation, the court stated. "Congress only delegated authority to the President to adjust imports to protect national security through direct mechanisms," such as quotas, the ruling stated.

The states, eight in the Northeastern area and Minnesota, argued that the levy would cause undue economic damage to their regions because they relied heavily on imported oil.

Northeastern states represented in the suit were Connecticut, New York, New Jersey, Massachusetts, Vermont, Pennsylvania, Rhode Island and Maine.

In a speech at Vail, Colo. shortly after the court decision, Ford offered to lift the tariff voluntarily if Congress agreed to end federal price controls on domestic oil. Lifting the import fees, Ford said, would soften the impact of decontrol.

Governors urge energy effort. The nation's governors urged the federal government Feb. 20 to act to revive the economy, aid the unemployed and focus on energy conservation. On the final day of their annual three-day winter meeting, in Washington, the governors declared in a resolution that "a conservation program of massive proportions must be the central focus of our nation's short-range energy management program."

Specifically, it called for tighter standards for more efficient automobiles, enforcement of the 55-mile-an-hour speed limit and more federal aid to public transportation. If other steps were needed after four to six months, the resolution said, a "price mechanism or allocation program could be brought into play."

The resolution was approved 30–1 after a resolution against higher tariffs or taxes to reduce energy use received a 28–12 vote of approval. The vote was largely along party lines, with Democrats for and Republicans against. This resolution would have put the governors on record as disagreeing "with the central thrust of the short-range" Ford Administration program of an oil import duty. The final resolution adopted, however, remained critical of the Administration and Congress, saying "national leadership" was required but "to date we have no such over-all logically integrated effort."

Ford vetoes ban on tariff boost but delays rise. President Ford March 4 vetoed legislation suspending his power to raise the tariff on imported oil. But as a conciliatory gesture, he voluntarily delayed for 60 days the rate increase scheduled to take effect April 1 and rescinded a previous increase he had authorized by administrative action March 1. The $1-a-barrel levy increase which was implemented by executive action Feb. 1 remained in effect.

The White House claimed to have enough votes in the Senate to sustain the veto. However, a test of the issue was avoided when Senate Democratic leaders decided to bury the veto message in the

Senate Finance Committee while efforts were made to reach a compromise with the White House on a mutually acceptable energy program. (There was no deadline on Congressional action to override.)

In another effort to mollify opponents of his energy program, Ford also said he would postpone plans to decontrol the price of "old" domestic oil by administrative action April 1.

Despite the announcement, the Senate Interior Committee March 4 approved a bill giving either house of Congress 30 days to veto any deregulation or price increase for old oil. (Under current law, Congress had five days in which to act.)

The Interior Committee's bill also tried to soften the impact of the $1-a-barrel tariff increases on imported oil that already had taken effect Feb. 1. The legislation would require the Administration to set a price ceiling on "new" domestic oil at its Jan. 31 level in order to prevent new oil, which was not subject to federal price controls, from rising to the new higher price level of imported oil. Imported oil and new U.S. oil both were selling at about $11 a barrel.

The committee also voted to give either chamber 30 days to veto a "tariff import fee quota or other measure" that would in effect set a floor price on oil. Secretary of State Henry Kissinger had proposed establishing a floor price as a safeguard for developers of new domestic oil supplies in case a sharp price drop in imported oil caused other oil prices to decline.

In a compromise of its own, the House leadership decided to postpone a vote to override Ford's veto while his voluntary suspension of the tax increase remained in effect. The House voted March 11 to send the bill suspending the President's authority to raise imported oil tariffs to the Ways and Means Committee; however, the bill could be returned to the House floor at any time for a vote to override.

The bill to suspend (for 90 days) the President's power to raise the tariff on imported oil had been passed by 309–114 House vote Feb. 5 and by 66–28 Senate vote Feb. 19.

Ford delays oil tariff increase. President Ford May 1 postponed a planned $1-a-barrel increase in the tax on imported oil, a move that was seen as a conciliatory gesture toward the Democratic-controlled Congress, which was working on alternative energy-saving approaches to the nation's fuel crisis.

At the same time, however, Ford also directed the Federal Energy Administration (FEA) to develop a plan for phasing out all remaining price controls on domestically-produced oil over a two year period, an action that could provoke a confrontation with the Congressional leadership, which opposed a fast-paced decontrol of U.S. oil.

In announcing the White House action May 1, President Ford's spokesman, FEA Administrator Frank Zarb, said that another 30-day suspension of the May 1 increase would give the House an opportunity to act on energy legislation being drawn up by the Ways and Means Committee. If the House-passed bill met with White House approval and the Senate seemed likely to pass a similar measure, Zarb said Ford might withdraw altogether his plan to impose the second and third tariff increases on imported oil.

Ford originally had proposed that all price controls on oil be lifted April 1. His change to a two-year timetable was seen as a concession to Congress. According to the plan outlined by Zarb, the Administration would free a portion of each oil producer's controlled oil at a rate of about 4% a month, allowing the price to rise slowly to world price levels, currently above $12 a barrel. Zarb contended that decontrol would raise gasoline prices an average 5¢ a gallon.

Ford orders 2d tariff rise. In a nationally televised broadcast May 27, President Ford said he would impose a second $1-a-barrel increase in the tariff on imported oil and set a 60¢-a-barrel fee on imports of refined petroleum products, effective June 1. Ford said he also would send Congress a plan for phasing out price controls on "old" oil.

Ford said he acted because, since February, Congress "has done nothing positive to end our energy dependence."

In addition to its "attempt to prevent the President from doing anything on his own" regarding energy, Ford said, Congress passed an "anti-energy" bill regulating strip mining. That bill, he said, "would reduce domestic coal production instead of increasing it; put thousands of people out of work; needlessly increase the cost of energy to consumers; raise electric bills for many; and compel us to import more foreign oil, not less."

Ford also accused Congress of doing "little or nothing to stimulate production of new energy sources," such as those at the Elk Hills (Calif.) naval petroleum reserve and reserves in Alaska and offshore under the continental shelf. Ford said that "we could save 300,000 barrels a day if only the Congress would allow more electric power plants to substitute American coal for foreign oil. Peaceful atomic power, which we pioneered, is advancing faster abroad than at home."

In discussing the gravity of the energy crisis facing the country, the President emphasized the direct link between energy and unemployment. "Our American economy runs on energy," he said. "No energy, no jobs. It's as simple as that."

The "sudden fourfold increase in foreign oil prices and the 1973 embargo helped to throw us into this recession," Ford said, warning that another embargo could result in another recession. (He also noted that in five years, the nation's fuel bill had skyrocketed from $5 billion to $25 billion annually.)

While Congress continued to "drift, dawdle, and debate" the energy crisis, Ford said, the nation's dependence on foreign oil and its vulnerability to pressure from oil-producing states increased. "In 10 years, if we do nothing," he said, "we will be importing more than half our oil, at prices fixed by others, if they choose to sell to us at all." (The U.S. currently imported 37% of its oil supplies, which totaled an estimated 17 million barrels a day.)

"In two and a half years, we will be twice as vulnerable to a foreign oil embargo as we were two winters ago. Domestic oil production is going down; natural gas production is starting to dwindle and many areas face severe shortages next winter; coal production is still at the level of the 1940s," Ford said.

"This country needs to regain its independence from foreign sources of energy and the sooner the better," Ford declared.

The President's tariff program was designed to discourage energy consumption by making fuel more costly.

The oil industry generally applauded Ford's move. Congressional Democrats, however, were critical of the Administration program and rejected his "do-nothing" charges.

In a rebuttal to Ford's speech, broadcast by CBS immediately following the President's address, Rep. Al Ullman (D, Ore.), chairman of the House Ways and Means Committee, said Ford's action would have "disastrous effects" on inflation and might cause the recession to worsen. Ford was not "going to add any new jobs by raising prices," Ullman declared.

Sen. Henry M. Jackson (D, Wash.), chairman of the Senate Interior Committee, charged that Ford "proposes to do to us in 1975 what the Arab oil cartel did in 1974" in raising prices and spurring inflation.

60¢ oil-products tariff lifted—Federal Energy Administrator Frank Zarb Sept. 22 announced the lifting of the Administration's 60¢-a-barrel import fee on refined petroleum products, retroactive to Sept. 1.

Removal of the tariff on refined products would result in a 1.5¢-a-gallon drop in the price of heating oil, residual fuel, and other refined products, Zarb said. Most of the 2 million–2.5 million barrels of petroleum products imported daily to the U.S. were consumed in the New England and Middle Atlantic states and Florida.

Zarb said the White House acted to lift the tariff because of reports that importers were withholding their products from the market pending a resolution of the price-control debate between the White House and Congress.

"Failure to clarify the situation until Congress acted," Zarb said, "might result in inadequate heating oil stocks through an unusually cold winter."

U.S. oil pricing held illegal. The Temporary Emergency Court of Appeals in Washington ruled, 2–1, Feb. 19, 1975 that the government had acted illegally when it decontrolled "new" crude oil prices in January 1974.

The principal finding of the court was that the Emergency Petroleum Allocation Act of 1973 had required the FEA to set prices for all types of crude oil and that the FEA was therefore in violation of this act when in January 1974 it allowed "new" oil to sell at prices determined by the market.

According to the majority opinion, "While the [Allocation] Act directs that the prices for all categories of crude oil be regulated, it does not specify a method for doing so. Consequently, the FEA has discretion in devising a regulatory scheme, but cannot adopt measures which contravene a statutory mandate.

"It isn't the function of this court to determine what the equitable price is, or should be," the decision said. "We merely hold that the President, through the FEA, by permitting the price of new crude oil to float at free market levels, hasn't struck any balance and, as a result, has failed to satisfy the requirement that prices be set at an equitable level."

Two-tier oil pricing ruled lawful. The Temporary Emergency Court of Appeals July 7 overturned an earlier decision and ruled that the Federal Energy Administration's two-tier system for regulating crude oil prices was lawful.

The court, in a 4–3 decision, rejected a complaint brought by Consumers' Union that the FEA had acted illegally in failing to set ceiling prices for new and released oil.

Oil price controls extended. The system of price controls for "new" and "old" oil expired Aug. 31, 1975. After two temporary extensions, Congress Dec. 17 cleared a compromise bill that provided an immediate rollback of prices of domestic crude oil and an end to oil price controls in 40 months.

President Ford signed the bill Dec. 22 and simultaneously removed the $2-a-barrel tariff on imported oil.

In signing the bill, despite pressure for a veto from the oil industry and conservative Republicans, Ford said "the time had come to end the long debate over national energy policy."

Deploring the legislation Dec. 22, Frank Ikard, president of the American Petroleum Institute, said it would "lead to higher energy costs in the future" and would "increase the nation's vulnerability to a potential embargo."

At a press briefing Dec. 22, Federal Energy Administrator Frank Zarb said the price rollback at the consumer level might not be as much as estimated by Congressional Democrats supporting passage of the bill. They had estimated a reduction of three cents to four cents a gallon at gasoline pumps for motorists as a result of enactment of the bill. Zarb said the maximum reduction possible there was perhaps a penny a gallon and no reduction at all also was a possibility. Despite the mandated price rollback for domestic crude oil, he said, the industry had a backlog of $1.2 billion in cost increases it was legally entitled to pass through to consumers but had not as yet because of competitive considerations. Furthermore, Zarb said, the recent 10% price hike by foreign oil-producing countries had not fully emerged in U.S. retail pricing as yet.

Under the bill, the authority for domestic oil price controls, which expired Dec. 15, would be restored for 40 months. The immediate price reduction required under the bill would cut the average price of crude oil produced in the U.S. from the current level of $8.75 a barrel to $7.66.

After that, the average price would be permitted to rise up to 10% a year to account for inflation and to spur production. If the price rose at the 10% rate annually, the current level of fuel prices would not be regained until mid-1977, well after the 1976 presidential election, observers noted.

Congress retained for itself the power of veto, by a majority vote of either house, of any increase in crude oil prices, after February 1977, that would be in excess of the national rate of inflation.

An exemption at the President's discretion was provided for Alaskan crude oil once it was in production, again subject to Congressional veto.

The bill also contained conservation provisions and others designed to cope with any new Arab oil embargo. The President would be given stand-by power to order rationing or other conservation measures in the event of an embargo, subject to Congressional approval. And a national oil reserve at the billion-barrel level was authorized.

A "maximum efficient rate" of production could be required by the President for oil and natural-gas producers from federally leased onshore and offshore fields.

Energy-conservation targets could be set for voluntary compliance by the 10 industries consuming the most energy.

Grants totaling $150 million would be provided to states drafting conservation plans, covering such things as lighting efficiency and building insulation.

The car industry would be put under statutory requirements for improved gasoline mileage—an average of 18 miles a gallon by 1978, 20 miles a gallon by 1980 and 27.5 miles a gallon by 1985.

Energy consumption labeling would be required for home appliances.

Finally, the oil industry's statistics would be opened to inspection by the General Accounting Office.

An early provision of the legislation for federal loan guarantees for reopening coal mines had been dropped from the bill.

The bill, supported by Zarb, had been passed by 236–160 House vote Dec. 15 and 58–40 Senate vote Dec. 17.

During the long period of debate on the price-control issue, President Ford July 14 had announced a compromise plan to end control of prices of domestic oil gradually over a 30-month period. This proposal was part of his program for letting oil prices rise to discourage consumption. Ford July 14 proposed, for the first time, a ceiling ($13.50 a barrel) on the price of "new" domestic oil, which then was selling for $12.75 a barrel. He also sought a $2-a-barrel excise tax on new oil and a windfall-profits tax on "old" oil to shift some profits back to the consumer.

Congress, however, was moving in the opposite direction. A bill to roll back the price of uncontrolled new domestic oil (to $11.28 a barrel) was passed by 57–40 Senate vote July 16 and 239–172 House vote July 17. Ford vetoed the bill July 21.

Ford's plan for phased decontrol was defeated by 262–167 House vote July 22.

(The consumer affairs advisory committee of the Federal Energy Administration adopted a resolution July 18 opposing Ford's decontrol plan and making the same points as the House Democrats—gradual decontrol would "eventually result in unjustifiably high fuel and other product prices to consumers, windfall profits to the major energy industries and further disruptions to the economy in the form of continued inflation, increased unemployment, etc.")

Two House votes July 23 gave no direction to the path of compromise. The House rejected by a vote of 215–199 a proposal to let the price of oil rise—by a gradual phase-out of controls over the next five years, coupled with a windfall-profits tax. It also rejected by a vote of 215–199 a proposal to reduce the price of oil—by rolling back the price of "new oil" to $7.50 a barrel and letting the price of "old oil," or production below 1972 levels, rise to $7.50 over five years. The average price for domestic oil at the time was about $8.25.

A bill to extend oil price controls for six months was passed by 62–29 Senate vote July 15 and 303–117 House vote July 31. Ford vetoed the measure Sept. 9, and the Senate sustained the veto Sept. 10 when its 61–39 vote to override fell six votes short of the necessary two-thirds majority.

The control system thus expired Aug. 31. A compromise bill to restore controls through Nov. 15 was worked out by the Ford Administration and Congress leaders Sept. 25. The measure was passed by 75–5 Senate vote and 342–16 House vote Sept. 26.

In signing the bill Sept. 29, Ford appealed for "an aroused citizenry" to press Congress to adopt a long-range energy program, one that "encourages Americans to produce our own energy with our own workers from our own resources and at our own prices." "When the price of gasoline goes up at the service station," he said, "I want the American people to know exactly where the blame lies."

In rebuttal, Senate Democratic leader Mike Mansfield (Mont.) said that "it wasn't Congress that put the $2 import tax on oil." Sen. Henry M. Jackson (D, Wash.) said the President "has done nothing but search for scapegoats, whether Congress or the Arabs."

The second temporary extension of oil-price controls (until Dec. 15) was approved by voice votes of both houses and signed by Ford Nov. 14.

Utility costs analyzed. Two Democratic Senators said March 24, 1975 that automatic price increases granted to electric and gas utilities because of increased fuel prices cost consumers about $6.5 billion in 1974. The fuel adjustment increases represented the bulk of the total $9.6 billion rise in utility bills over the year, according to Sens. Edmund S. Muskie (Me.) and Lee Metcalf (Mont.).

The total increase to consumers was 1½ times the size of rate increases granted from 1948 through 1973. The survey, which was based on data from 37 state public service commissions and the District of Columbia, also contrasted the sharp rise in utility bills with an increase in electric power consumption of less than 1% during 1974 and a 4.2% decline in natural gas consumption. Automatic adjustments for higher fuel costs removed most of the incentives for efficient and cost control operations, the Senators charged.

Electricity rates of the nation's 15 largest electric utilities soared 61.3% between June 1973 and December 1974, according to a private utility consulting firm March 24. If these trends continued, National Utility Service Inc. said, U.S. utility rates would be the highest in the world by the end of the decade. Over the 18-month period, only two countries recorded higher rate increases. In Belgium, utilities bills rose 85.4% and in Italy, charges were up 83.3%.

The report called for a redesign of rate structures that would provide consumers with an incentive for savings. Under current rate structures, consumers paid a base price for a certain amount of electricity used and rates were reduced when consumption exceeded that amount. The report stated: "Load factors and time when energy is used must be given more prominent consideration in rate structures. Just as the utility industry requires incentives to invest in plants and equipment to meet future demand, so does the consumer need a stimulus to help maximize the utilization of utility plant facilities and control unnecessary expansion."

The Federal Energy Administration announced March 24 that the agency would fund several experimental rate structures in an effort to redesign the nation's electricity pricing policy. Under the new plan, consumers using electricity during peak load hours would be charged premium rates. Reduced rates would be in effect during off peak times.

Total electricity usage and peak demand had grown at a rate of 7% a year throughout the postwar period, according to the FEA. The aim of the experiment was to reduce the total growth rate to 5% and cut peak demand growth to 4% by encouraging more efficient use of electricity.

The FEA said April 1 that fuel suppliers may have overcharged 72 electrical utilities by millions of dollars during the Arab oil embargo. Since utilities were regulated and allowed to pass on to consumers increases in fuel prices, the alleged price gouging eventually affected homeowners and business persons.

The FEA investigation, which was being conducted in cooperation with the Customs Bureau and the Justice Department, involved charges that suppliers misrepresented relatively low-priced domestic fuel as higher-priced imported fuel in sales to utilities, that unnecessary handling of oil was used to increase prices or that paper sales of fuel were used to raise prices. The price-gouging probe, dubbed Project Escalator, involved investigations of more than 200 of the 407 suppliers of fuel oil to utilities. Similar investigation also had been launched by the FEA to determine whether prices of butane, propane and domestic crude oil had been illegally increased.

The FEA said April 9 that its probe of overcharges to utilities had brought refunds and price reductions totaling $161 million. Another $418 million in planned price increases had been disallowed because of violations of federal pricing rules, the FEA added. Penalties in these cases totaled $898,000, and 12 violations were referred to the Justice Department for possible criminal investigation.

Electricity rates increased an "unprecedented" 30% during 1974, the Environmental Protection Agency reported July 25. An 82.2% rise in the cost of fossil fuels over the year accounted for three-fifths of the annual increase, the agency said.

Anti-pollution measures taken by utilities accounted for no more than 5% of the 1974 increase in rates. Conversion of fuels, from high-sulfur to low-sulfur coal and from coal to oil or coal to gas, represented only half of that percentage gain.

Nonfuel electricity costs were up 16.8% over the year, chiefly because of a rise in interest rates which made borrowing more expensive. Revenues in the electric industry rose $9 billion to total $40 billion in 1974, according to the report.

"Consumers along both the Atlantic and Pacific coasts were the most seriously affected by the higher rates," the EPA said. "New England and the Middle Atlantic regions, which historically have had the highest electric rates, also had the highest rates of increase" in 1974.

Tax breaks for utilities urged. President Ford June 13 endorsed tax proposals of his labor-management committee to stimulate construction of power plants fired by energy other than natural gas or oil. It recommended, among other things, that the investment tax credit for utilities be increased from 10% to 12% for work already in progress, that utilities be allowed a tax deferment for dividends reinvested in new issue common stock, that legislation for an accelerated tax write-off on pollution-control equipment be extended, that the same tax leniency be extended to cover the costs of converting power plants to the use of coal and that environmental restrictions on energy production be stretched out.

Energy reserves seen down. The U.S. Geological Survey, part of the department of the interior, published estimates of the country's energy reserves, cited in the New York Times May 8, which it said were "considerably lower" than those it had released in March 1974.

The agency's study, directed by Vincent E. McKelvey, placed the "undiscovered recoverable resources" of crude oil at 50–127 billion. It set natural gas liquids reserves (natural gasoline) at 11–22 billion barrels and natural gas at 322–655 trillion cubic feet. The March 1974 figures, criticized as being too optimistic, had combined estimates for crude oil and natural gas liquids at 200–400 billion barrels and had pegged natural gas reserves at 2000–4000 cubic feet. Rogers C. B. Morton, secretary of commerce and chairman of the Energy Resources Council, said the new Geological Survey figures were "sobering additional evidence of our need" for "a comprehensive energy program."

(In another study financed partly by the department of interior, the National Research Council of the National Academy of Sciences reported Feb. 11 that the U.S. would run out of oil and natural gas in 25 years. The council's study, which had taken nearly three years to complete, put crude oil reserves at 113 billion barrels and natural gas reserves at no more than 600 trillion cubic feet.)

In related developments, the American Petroleum Institute reported April 1 that despite a 35% increase in crude oil prices in 1974, proven reserves had declined in that year from 35.3 billion barrels to 34.25 billion barrels. It was reported by the American Gas Association the same day that proven reserves of natural gas had dropped in 1974 by about 5%, from 250 trillion to 237.1 trillion cubic feet.

A Feb. 28 FEA news release said domestic crude oil production in 1974 had declined 4.5% below the level for the previous year and that petroleum demand was off 3.8%. FEA Administrator Frank G. Zarb said the figures showed that "1974 domestic energy price increases have resulted in significant energy savings without causing painful shortages."

It was reported March 24 by the Oil and Gas Journal that U.S. crude oil refining capacity had reached 14.8 million barrels a day at the beginning of the year, an increase of 4.4% over the figure for 1974.

Ford, governors discuss gas shortage. President Ford told 16 governors gathered at the White House Aug. 28 that natural gas would be in short supply during the coming winter by 1.3 trillion cubic feet.

As a short-run answer to the problem, governors from the nation's three leading producing states—Texas, Louisiana, and Oklahoma—said they would encourage producers to divert excess supplies to interstate needs, but they warned that deregulation and higher prices promised the only long-range solution to the worsening supply situation.

As a step toward the eventual deregulation of interstate gas prices, most of the governors attending the meeting endorsed a plan drawn up by Oklahoma's Gov. David Boren (D) calling for a five-year suspension of controls on newly-developed gas reserves. Boren said the governors also supported legislation lifting federal price controls for an emergency 180-day period.

The permanent deregulation of natural gas prices was a focal point of the Administration's energy plan.

Pennsylvania Gov. Milton J. Shapp (D) was the only governor who refused to support the temporary decontrol proposal. Shapp called on the White House to investigate whether the current gas shortage was "real or contrived." "The public has been ripped off or thinks it has been ripped off by the energy companies," Shapp said.

The governors of four states—Massachusetts, California, New York, and Illinois—where there was strong consumer opposition to energy price decontrol, did not attend the White House meeting.

Louisiana Gov. Edwin D. Edwards (D) criticized those states and others that also were opposed to offshore exploration of oil and gas reserves. Edwards warned that the coastal industrial states that would "suffer most" from the expected shortage "had better realize there is untapped gas and oil off their Atlantic Coast and it should have been tapped five years ago. We [in Louisiana] have gas because we pay $1.50 and not 52¢ [per 1,000 cubic feet]," the federally regulated price. (The interstate price of gas was raised from 50¢ to 52¢ in January when the Federal Power Commission made its biennial price adjustments. Gas sold in the state in which it was produced was not subject to federal price control, and its price currently was $1 to $2 per 1,000 cubic feet.)

Natural gas price controls eased. The Federal Power Commission ruled Aug. 28 that certain industries could bypass pipeline distributors of their natural gas supplies and buy gas directly from the "field" producers at unregulated prices if industrial gas supplies were curtailed during an expected winter shortage. The ruling only affected industries unable to switch to alternative fuels if their gas supplies were interrupted.

"While this policy will not solve the gas shortage," the FPC said in its 2-1 decision, "direct sales may result in increased producer revenues, which would promote increased exploration for and development of gas supplies."

FPC member William L. Springer dissented from the majority opinion, contending that deregulation was a policy that could be enacted only by Congress.

In another 2-1 decision affecting the price of natural gas, the FPC ruled Aug. 28 that small producers, whose annual output was less than 10 billion cubic feet a year, could charge 30% more than large producers for gas sold across state lines. Small producers accounted for 12% of the nation's annual production.

The aim of the new policy, the FPC said, was to strengthen the competitive position of small producers who faced higher risks than their larger rivals and needed to raise more capital for exploration.

Scaled-down energy targets cited. Two goals of the Administration's program to lessen U.S. dependence on foreign oil supplies were quietly abandoned by the White House, according to two news reports.

The Washington Post reported Sept. 21 that President Ford's goal to produce synthetic fuel from coal and shale by 1985 that was the equivalent of 1 million barrels of oil imported daily had been drastically reduced by the White House Energy Resources Council. The new production target for "synfuel" was 350,000 barrels, according to a report given congressmen by the council.

The staggering cost of the original proposal was given as one reason for scaling down the project. According to current estimates, the more modest synfuel program would cost about $7 billion, compared with more than $20 billion for the larger project.

Other reasons given for reducing the project's scope were environmental hazards associated with the production process, the social upheaval caused by locating large industries in remote Western areas where coal and shale were plentiful, and the shortage of water in these Western regions. (The fuel conversion process required large amounts of water.)

In another indication of scaled-down energy aims, the Journal of Commerce reported Aug. 19 that the Administration no longer considered its 2-million-barrel a day reduction in oil imports a realistic goal for 1977; instead, the Administration sought to reduce imports (currently totaling 7 million barrels a day) by about 1.5 million barrels.

The more modest proposal was dependent upon Congressional approval of several controversial aspects of the Administration's energy plan, such as decontrol, the opening of production at naval oil reserves, and the conversion of oil-burning utilities to coal.

Money, Finance & Banking

$1.1 billion added to money supply. The Federal Reserve took another step toward easing money and credit conditions Jan. 21, 1975, when it announced a cut in reserve requirements—the percentage of checking account deposits that member commercial banks must set aside. The action, the Federal Reserve's second move in three weeks to stimulate the economy as the recession worsened, was expected to free $1.1 billion in bank funds, allowing expanded loan operations at lower interest rates.

Current reserve requirements on all categories of net demand deposits of up to $400 million were reduced .5%, and requirements on deposits of more than $400 million were lowered 1%.

Federal Reserve spokesmen said the easing of reserve requirements was "designed to permit further gradual improvement in bank liquidity," as well as to "facilitate moderate growth" in the nation's money supply. Federal Reserve Chairman Arthur Burns had earlier indicated his uneasiness about the banking industry's financial troubles during a period of high interest rates and low loan demand.

Critics contended that the Federal Reserve's strict monetary policies had contributed to the recession. The Federal Reserve announced Feb. 14 that despite its efforts to increase the supply of cash in circulation plus checking account deposits, the money supply decreased at an annual rate of .6% in the last three months. (The board had voted in mid-December to take action to stimulate a 6%–7% annual rate growth in the money supply.)

Bill curbing Federal Reserve rejected. The House Banking Committee Feb. 20 rejected a bill sponsored by committee chairman Henry S. Reuss (D, Wis.) that would have forced the Federal Reserve Board to lower interest rates.

After rejecting the legislation on a 20–19 vote, the panel approved a "sense of the Congress" resolution, which lacked the force of law, urging the Federal Reserve to change its money management policies in an effort to reduce interest rates and lower unemployment.

The committee also postponed action on a companion measure to require the President to allocate credit to "priority" uses and away from what it termed "inflationary" or "speculative" uses. Credit allocation was a chief legislative goal of the Democratic majority in Congress.

Federal Reserve Chairman Arthur Burns had vehemently opposed the Reuss bill, which in its original form, would have directed the Federal Reserve, a semi-independent agency, to expand the nation's money supply at a rate of 6% a year.

In an unusual evening hearing Feb. 19, Burns told the committee the Federal Reserve's power over long-term interest rates was "very limited," and that any attempt to drive them down could have the "perverse" effect of raising lending rates or lead to an "explosive" expansion of money and credit, further fueling inflation.

If the committee wanted to take action to lower interest rates, Burns said, Congress should cut federal spending and reduce the federal deficit.

Treasury Secretary William E. Simon had testified before the committee Feb. 4 warning that the credit allocation bill would create a "national credit police state" by destroying the flexibility of the nation's monetary system and undermining the Federal Reserve's policy-making independence.

If ordered to allocate credit, Simon warned, the Federal Reserve's "control would be extended to every loan made by every creditor in the country . . . Each and every one of us would find that our financial plans were under the control of the federal government."

In testimony Feb. 25 before the Senate Banking Committee, which also was considering a resolution urging the Federal Reserve to pursue an easier monetary policy, Burns rejected calls for expanding the money supply by 8%–10% over the next six months in an effort to halt the recession quickly.

Money growth plans. In an unprecedented statement made in response to political pressure, Arthur Burns disclosed the Federal Reserve Board's target rates for growth of the money supply over the next year. Burns testified before the Senate Banking Committee May 1 in the first of four annual appearances required by a joint Congressional resolution that made the semiindependent agency's monetary policies subject to legislative scrutiny.

Burns told the committee that the nation's central bank intended to pursue a "moderate" policy of expansion that would result in a 5%–7.5% rate of growth in the money supply during the next 12 months. According to Burns, the money supply (M-1, defined as currency in circulation plus bank-checking account deposits) had expanded at an annual rate of 7% in the 2nd quarter of 1974, 1.6% in the 3rd quarter, 4.6% in the 4th quarter, and 3.5% in the 1st quarter of 1975. (It was reported May 23 that for the three-month period ended May 14, the money supply grew at a 7.2% annual rate.)

Burns' critics in Congress would have preferred that the Federal Reserve adopt a more expansionary policy for the money supply, but he rejected that view, contending that the 5%–7.5% rate of growth was high enough "to finance a vigorous economic recovery." "This is a rather high rate of expansion by historical standards, he said, one that "errs on the side of ease." Burns, who, like Treasury Secretary William E. Simon, emphasized the danger of refueling inflation by stimulating the recessionary economy too vigorously, said a 5%–7.5% rate of growth should not be pursued indefinitely.

"We need to get back to [price] stability in this country, or we will go down the drain the way Great Britain is going now," he said.

In a television interview May 25, Burns urged Congress to "pause" in its efforts to spur the sluggish economy and reduce unemployment. "Sit back for a while," Burns said to the Congress, "and see if the natural forces of economic recovery, along with the stimuli that have been released by Congress and the President and the Federal Reserve, are having the desired effect."

Congress asks eased monetary policy. Congress March 24 completed action on a non-binding resolution calling on the Federal Reserve to promote prosperity by easing its monetary policy. The broadly worded resolution, which did not require the President's signature and, hence, did not have the force of law, also asked for semi-annual appearances of Federal Reserve officials before the House and Senate banking committees.

Adopted by the House March 24 and the Senate March 20, the resolution urged the Federal Reserve Board and the Open Market Committee to "pursue policies in the first half of 1975 so as to encourage lower long-term interest rates and expansion in the monetary and credit aggregates appropriate to facilitating prompt economic recovery and maintain long-run growth of the monetary and credit aggregates commensurate with the economy's long-run potential to increase production, so as to promote effectively the goals of maximum employment, stable prices and moderate long-term interest rates."

Dispute over tight-money policy. In June 1975 the Federal Reserve's Open Market Committee, which makes policy for credit decisions, concluded that the nation's money supply was expanding too rapidly because of the tax rebates, Social Security bonuses and reductions in withholding taxes mandated by Congress.

To counteract what it viewed as an overstimulation of the economy, the committee reaffirmed its earlier decision to restrict the growth of the nation's money supply to an annual rate of 5%–7%. The effect was a sudden tightening of credit, which led to a sharp rise in interest costs.

Federal Reserve Chairman Arthur F. Burns defended the panel's decision in testimony July 24 before the House Banking Committee.

Burns told the committee the Federal Reserve acted to check a temporary "explosion" in the nation's money supply, but he denied that the move marked a deliberate shift toward a restrictive monetary policy. "Although [the Federal Reserve's action] resulted in sharply higher short-term interest rates," he said, "no inference should be drawn that we have embarked on a policy to raise interest rates." (Many members of Congress feared high interest rates would limit business expansion during the recovery and imperil a return to "full" employment.)

Burns noted that the nation's money supply had expanded at an average annual rate of 14.5% in May and June, a rate "larger than we expected and very much larger than we desired. (But the money supply expansion declined as 1975 advanced. The Federal Reserve Board reported Dec. 29 that the money supply had grown at an annual rate of only 1.6% in the three months ended Dec. 17. During the two weeks ended Dec. 17, the money supply dropped by $4 billion to a seasonally adjusted $295.3 billion.)

If the Federal Reserve had not acted to counteract this surge in the money supply, Burns said, "this would have confirmed the fears of the financial and business community that the Fed is unleashing a major new wave of inflation."

Pointing to the sharp rise in consumer prices during June, Burns said "the menace of inflation is still very much with us. Economic recovery is beginning when the rate of inflation, while lower than a year ago, is still well above tolerable levels."

Burns's testimony did not quell Congressional criticism of the Federal Reserve's monetary policies. Members of the Senate Budget Committee, including conservative Republican Henry Bellmon (Okla.), accused the Federal Reserve of "trying to cancel" the effects of the anti-recession tax-cut bill. The committee members questioned whether the Federal Reserve had the right to undercut Congressional efforts to spur the economy.

Congress and the Federal Reserve "are working at cross-purposes," committee chairman Edmund S. Muskie (D, Me.) declared during hearings Sept. 25. "It is time for monetary policy to play a major role in the expansion," he said.

Burns disagreed, saying over-stimulation of the economy could jeopardize the recovery. (Alan Greenspan, chairman of the President's Council of Economic Advisers, voiced similar fears in testimony Sept. 23 before the same committee.)

Burns said he opposed extending the temporary tax-cut provision enacted in March. He also rejected calls for an easier monetary policy that would limit interest rates. Instead, he urged Congress to reduce its spending plans for fiscal 1976, a move, Burns said that would contribute to lower interest rates.

"The massive federal deficit may well cause a further rise in interest rates," Burns said, because of the "enormous demand" placed on the nation's credit markets by the Treasury's need for funds to cover the budget deficit.

Interest rates. A move to lower interest rates continued in early 1975 as the Federal Reserve Jan. 3 reduced its discount rate (the rate commercial member banks paid for short-term funds borrowed from the Federal Reserve System) from 7.75% to 7.25%. The rate continued down—to 6.75% Feb. 4, 6.25% March 7 and 6% May 15.

The lowering of prime interest rates (the minimum rates commercial banks charged their best customers) continued Jan. 10 with a reduction from 10.25% to 10%. Periodic drops were announced thereafter until the rate reached the year's low of 6.75% June 6. Thereafter the rate fluctuated between 7% and 8%.

First National City Bank of New York (Citibank), the nation's second largest commercial bank and the leader in efforts to lower the prime rate, announced Jan. 10 that its minimum interest rate was being cut to 10%. Citibank had raised its rate Jan. 3 from 10% to 10.25%, rejoining most other major banks which had refused to follow Citibank's lead in November 1974 toward the 10% level.

However, in its January action, Citibank was joined by Bank of America, the nation's largest commercial bank, and by Bankers Trust Co. of New York. Morgan Guaranty Trust Co. of New York, the nation's fifth ranked commercial bank, announced Jan. 13 that its prime had been lowered to 9.75% from 10.25%. It was the lowest base lending rate charged by any major bank since April 1974.

The Federal Reserve, whose reduction of its discount rate was designed to induce the commercial banks to lower their rates (the prime rate had hovered at about 10.25%-10.5% between November 1974 and early January 1975), cut its discount rate to 6.75% Feb. 4. The following day Morgan Guarantee cut its prime rate from 9% to 8.75, and Morgan March 5 again led a reduction—to 7.75%.

A new decline in short-term interest rates followed the Treasury Department's announcement May 5 that it would not need to borrow as much money as initially expected to finance the federal deficit. Because April tax receipts had been larger than anticipated, officials said that the government's cash needs through June had been reduced by $5 billion to $9.5 billion. The Treasury's estimated borrowings for the first six months of 1975 were reduced from $41 billion to $36 billion.

The low-point in the prime interest rate during 1975 was reached when the First National City Bank of New York June 6 announced the lowering of its prime interest rate on loans to corporations from 7% to 6.75%. With the quarter-point drop, the prime rate was at its lowest level since April 1973. Citibank's action triggered a move by most other major banks to reduce their minimum interest rate from 7.25% to 7%. Nearly a month later Citibank rejoined the other major banks and announced that its prime rate would be raised to the prevailing rate of 7%.

Citibank's prime rate was increased again to 7.25%, effective July 14, and other major banks quickly began to adopt the new higher rate. Their actions marked the first broad-based increase in the prime since July 1974 when a high of 12% was recorded.

The increases reflected a rise in other short-term money market rates. Citibank's formula for setting its prime was determined by a three-week average of commercial paper rates.

Pressures to raise the prime rate had been triggered by the Federal Reserve's decision to slow the growth of the nation's money supply.

After the Federal Reserve intervened in short-term money markets during the week ended July 2 to tighten credit by raising interest rates, the money supply showed the biggest one-week decline since mid-March.

Another factor influencing the upward trend in the prime rate was a sudden increase in the volume of corporate loans. After months of slack demand, corresponding to a steady decline in the prime rate, business loans made by major New York banks increased $318 million in the week ended July 2. That was the largest one week gain since the week ended Jan. 1, officials said.

Citibank led prime rate raises to 7.5% July 18, to 7.75% Aug. 8 and to 8% Sept. 13. The rate dropped thereafter, with Citibank's rate reaching 7% Nov. 21. None of the other banks followed to the 7% level, and Citibank raised its rate to the prevailing 7.25% Dec. 20.

Housing money. The Department of Housing & Urban Development (HUD) had released $3 billion in November 1974 to finance home mortgage purchases at below-market interest rates, and it released an additional $3 billion Jan. 16, 1975 after the earlier funds were fully committed.

The new money was made available to finance conventional mortgages, as well as those guaranteed by the Federal Housing Administration and insured by the Veterans Administration, for up to $42,000 on single family houses. Most of the money was allocated for newly built houses.

The interest rate on mortgages guaranteed by the Federal Housing Administration and the Veterans Administration was reduced from 9% to 8.5%, Housing and Urban Development Department officials announced Jan. 20. The reduction, the second in two months, reflected a recent downward trend toward lower interest rates and an increasing flow of mortgage money. Rates on conventional mortgages, which were not backed by the government and which comprised the bulk of residential mortgages, currently were about 9.5%.

In two other HUD actions, officials announced Jan. 20 that $900 million was being allocated for a rent subsidy program for the poor and $215 million was being released to finance low interest construction loans for housing projects for the elderly.

In another effort to aid the ailing

housing industry, a two-month moratorium on mortgage foreclosure on government-subsidized low and middle income housing was announced Jan. 14.

The government Feb. 28 then reduced the maximum interest rate from 8.5% to 8% on home loans insured by the Federal Housing Administration or guaranteed by the Veterans Administration. The new rate was the lowest on government-backed home loans since August 1973. The mortgage rate had peaked at 9.5% in 1974. The cut was made possible by "increased flows of funds into savings institutions" and lower mortgage rates on conventional loans not backed by the government, officials said.

But Carla Hills, secretary of housing and urban development, announced April 27 that rates on home mortgages insured by the Federal Housing Administration and guaranteed by the Veterans Administration were being raised from 8% to 8.5%. The action marked the first increase in government-backed mortgages since August 1974 and reversed a three-month downward trend in mortgage rates.

Hills said the increase was needed to bring FHA-VA rates into line with conventional mortgage rates, but spokesmen for the home building industry, currently undergoing a steep and sustained decline, were angered by her action. They noted that savings and loan institutions had reported large inflows of deposits recently.

According to the Wall Street Journal April 28, savings and loan institutions had been slow to resume extensive mortgage lending, which had been curtailed sharply in 1974 when savings outflows had been heavy.

Department officials said that the FHA-VA rates had fallen below yields in the conventional mortgage market and were attracting fewer buyers on the resale mortgage market. To make up the difference between purchase price and loan yield, purchasers of government-backed mortgages had been charging home buyers up to eight discount points of prepaid interest. (A point was 1% of a mortgage's face value.) The large numbers of points charged by lenders discouraged the use of FHA-VA mortgages, HUD officials said. An increased rate could raise the purchaser's yield, thereby making the loans more attractive to investors and making them more accessible to home buyers, they added.

Housing costs soar—The cost of purchasing an average-priced house increased 23% from 1973 to 1974, according to a study prepared by the Library of Congress and released April 28.

Because home buying had suddenly become so costly, the study noted, many middle-class families were priced out of the market. In 1973, the report stated, 21.5% of families had the $19,060 annual income required to make a 10% down payment on a new home with a median price of $37,000. In 1974, however, when the median price of a new home climbed to $41,300, only 15% of families had the $23,300 annual income needed to make a 10% down payment. (The figures were based on an assumption that one-quarter of a family's income was spent on housing.)

New York bank merger averts failure. The financially troubled Security National Bank (Long Island) was bought Jan. 19, 1975 by Chemical Bank (New York), the nation's sixth largest bank, with deposits of $17.8 billion, for $40 million in cash.

The Long Island bank, which operated 95 offices, had assets valued at $1.8 billion and deposits totaling $1.4 billion. It was ranked 55th among the nation's commercial banks.

The merger was quickly approved by government banking regulators after James E. Smith, comptroller of the currency, formally declared Jan. 19 that the bank was in danger of failing unless a takeover were arranged. The merger won immediate approval from the Federal Reserve Board and the New York State superintendent of banks. The Justice Department also gave quick antitrust clearance to the takeover because of the emergency.

Security National had not issued a 1974 earnings report prior to its purchase by Chemical, but its 1974 nine-month net operating revenues had declined 14% over 12 months to $5.8 million. Net operating earnings in 1973 had fallen 34% from the previous year's level. (Security National reported April 23 that its losses during 1974 totaled $38 million after making a $62 million provision for loan losses. The loan loss provision, which was eight times larger than that made in 1973, represented more than 5% of the bank's loan portfolio, estimated at $1.13 billion.)

Chemical Bank chairman Donald C. Platten revealed Jan. 20 that $140 million (12%) of Security National's $1.15 billion loan portfolio had been discounted as bad loans. He also disclosed that on Jan. 7, the date of an evaluation by the comptroller's office, Security National's working capital had declined to $125 million.

Platten tied the loan losses to the national recession and to depressed business conditions on Long Island in particular. He also cited another regional factor in Security National's deteriorating financial situation, linking the earlier failure of Franklin National Bank, also a Long Island based bank with heavy real estate loan commitments, to the steady drain on deposits at Security National as customer confidence ebbed.

(It had earlier been revealed that the number of banks on the government's special surveillance list had increased about 50% over 12 months to about 150 by the end of 1974, its highest level in 12 years. "A few" of those 150 banks were in the "multi-billion deposit category," according to Comptroller Smith.)

If Security National had failed, it would have been the nation's second largest bank failure, exceeded only by Franklin National's collapse and eclipsing the 1973 failure of the U.S. National Bank of San Diego.

Bank failures. There were several bank failures during 1975:

Swope Parkway National Bank, Kansas City's only black-owned bank, with assets of $10.6 million, was declared insolvent Jan. 3 by the Federal Deposit Insurance Corp. (FDIC), but officials said that it would be reopened the next day as the Deposit Insurance National Bank under FDIC receivership. The new bank was being established "in recognition of both the practical and symbolic importance of the Swope Parkway National Bank to [Kansas City's] black community," an FDIC spokesman said.

Ohio banking officials Feb. 14 closed Northern Ohio Bank of Cleveland, a state-chartered bank founded in 1971 with assets listed in 1974 at more than $115 million. The FDIC took receivership and sold the assets for $3.8 million to National City Bank, Cleveland's second largest bank. The FDIC said it had advanced $85 million to National City to facilitate the takeover and would retain about $105 million in Northern Ohio assets, thereby insuring the bank's depositors against losses on accounts up to $40,000. Banking officials said the failed bank's doubtful or uncollectible loans, which sources said totaled more than $10 million, exceeded the bank's $5 million in capital and $2 million loan loss reserves.

Federal and state banking authorities closed the Franklin Bank of Houston and named the FDIC as receiver. The bank cited as reasons for its failure a "deterioration in [its] loan portfolio and a substantial write-off of real estate loans made by prior management."

The FDIC May 9 announced the failure of the Chicopee Bank & Trust Co., a bank with 6,700 depositors and $10.5 million in assets. A Holyoke, Mass. bank, a subsidiary of First National Boston Corp., May 12 paid a $601,000 purchase premium for the failed bank and agreed to assume its liabilities, which were not disclosed. The FDIC said it loaned the Holyoke bank $5 million in cash to facilitate the transfer.

In Arkansas, the FDIC said a purchaser had been found for the insolvent Bank of Chidester, which had been closed July 1 by state authorities. Merchants and Planters Bank of Camden agreed to pay a purchase premium of $155,895 to obtain the Chidester bank, which had $2.3 million in deposits and other liabilities, officials said.

State authorities July 12 closed the State Bank of Clearing, a Chicago bank with listed assets of $81.3 million, because of poor management and losses incurred in real estate investments. The bank was scheduled to reopen July 14 under new ownership and with a new name, Clearing Bank. The Federal Deposit Insurance Corp. loaned the bank's new owners $57 million in cash and temporarily retained assets of about $64 million.

Astro Bank of Houston, a state-chartered bank with $5.2 million in deposits, was closed Oct. 16 by the Texas banking commissioner. The FDIC, which acted as receiver for the failed bank, announced Oct. 23 that another Houston bank, Commonwealth Bank, had assumed Astro's deposit liabilities. No losses were reported for Astro's 1,675 depositors. Commonwealth Bank paid a purchase premium of $210,000 and received a $3.8 million cash advance from the FDIC to facilitate the takeover. (The FDIC retained Astro's assets with a book value of $4.3 million.) Astro's failure was blamed on heavy loan losses.

The American City Bank and Trust Co. of Milwaukee, a federally chartered bank with deposits of $104 million, was declared insolvent Oct. 21 by the comptroller of the currency. The Milwaukee bank failure was the largest since the 1974 collapse of New York's Franklin National Bank. Marine National Exchange Bank, also of Milwaukee, immediately assumed American City's deposit liabilities from the FDIC, which had been named receiver. None of the failed bank's 35,000 depositors was expected to incur losses, the FDIC said. (About $60 million in deposits was not covered by FDIC insurance, limited to $40,000 per account.) The FDIC advanced to marine National $94 million in cash and took over American City's $105 million in book assets. Poor real estate loans and the weakening of the commercial real estate market led to the bank's collapse, according to government sources.

Peoples Bank of the Virgin Islands, the only locally-owned bank in the territory, with 14,500 depositors and $14.5 million in deposits, was declared insolvent Oct. 27. The FDIC, which was appointed receiver, assumed operations of the failed bank, which reopened under the name of Deposit Insurance National Bank of the Virgin Islands.

Bank surveillance plan set—James E. Smith, comptroller of the currency, Aug. 11 announced the establishment of a bank surveillance system to detect financial problems among the U.S.' 4,700 national banks and prevent the recurrence of major bank failures.

Smith's office had been criticized for failing to identify difficulties that led to the collapse of three major banks—U.S. National Bank of San Diego, and Franklin National Bank and Security National Bank, both of Long Island, New York.

Smith said the new computerized early-warning system would detect trouble developing in individual banks and changed situations within the banking industry. Other changes planned included the strengthening of the agency's enforcement and compliance activities, alteration of reporting procedures so that banks would be required to submit quarterly, instead of annual, financial statements, and a restructuring of agency responsibility.

Smith's action followed closely the recommendations made to him by Haskins and Sells, a major accounting firm, which completed a year-long study of the comptroller's office, made at Smith's request, after the failures of U.S. National and Franklin National.

According to the study, the comptroller's office had failed to keep pace with new banking methods, often focused on the wrong banking problems, and had too many informal contacts with bankers. However, the study also contended that despite the need for a fundamental reorganization of the bank regulatory agency, the comptroller's office had "achieved its basic objective of maintaining a sound banking system for the convenience of the public."

Layoffs & Unemployment

Jobless average 8.5% in 1975. With the recession deepening and the number of layoffs mounting in most sectors of the economy, the rate of unemployment in the U.S. rose from a monthly average of 5.6% of the working force in 1974 to 8.5% in 1975.

The year had started with unemployment in January 1975 at a 33-year-high rate of 8.2% (seasonally adjusted), according to the Bureau of Labor Statistics. Unemployment continued at that rate through February, then rose to 8.7% in March, 8.9% in April and the year's high of 9.2% in May, the highest rate since 1941, when unemployment had averaged 9.9% for the year. The rate then declined 8.6% in June, 8.4% in July and August and 8.3% in September. It went up again to 8.6% in October but dropped to 8.3% in November and December.

The number of the unemployed had risen in January to 7,529,000, up 930,000 over the previous month. Total employment declined 640,000 to 84.6 million, marking the fourth straight month the figure had fallen.

Noting that the steep rise in unemployment had begun in the fall of 1974 with drastically reduced automobile sales and resultant industry production cutbacks, Julius Shiskin, commissioner of the Bureau of Labor Statistics (BLS), told the Congressional Joint Economic Committee Feb. 7 that auto industry unemployment had reached 24%. Shiskin added that the recession had become widespread, with 80% of all U.S. industry reporting a decline in the number of jobs for the third month in a row.

According to BLS statistics, the January unemployment rate in the construction industry was 15%, in all manufacturing 10.5%, and in wholesale and retail trade 8.5%.

Data in the government's unemployment index, prepared by the Bureau of Labor Statistics, was based on a sample of 47,000 households, or 1 in every 1,300, throughout the nation. The households were selected from 461 areas of the country designed to reflect urban and rural sections, different types of farming and industrial areas, and the major geographical areas of the country in the same proportion as they occurred in the nation as a whole.

Census Bureau personnel conducted interviews once a month on the job-holding, job-seeking and non-labor force activities of all the civilian household members 16 years of age or older.

The employed category included all full- and part-time employes who worked for pay or profit during the survey work, or who were prevented from working because of illness, vacation, industrial dispute, or other reasons.

Persons without jobs were classified as unemployed if they actively searched for work in the previous four weeks and were available for work. The total unemployment figure represented not only those who had lost their jobs, but also persons who had quit their jobs, experienced workers looking for work after an absence from the labor force, and new workers looking for their first jobs.

Statistics on total unemployment and insured unemployment differed because about 25% of all workers were not covered by jobless benefit programs. Some of the uninsured groups were agricultural workers, domestic service workers, employes of local governments, self-employed workers, unpaid family workers, and workers in religious institutions and nonprofit schools below the college level.

Also not counted as insured unemployed were jobless workers who had exhausted their benefits, had not earned their benefits, or were ineligible to receive benefits.

The unemployment index was adjusted to reflect seasonal variations in the employment situation.

White House Press Secretary Ron Nessen Feb. 7 described President Ford as "concerned" about the steep rise in joblessness. A "close watch" would be kept on the economic situation, Nessen said, and the President "will not hesitate to take further action" if the condition worsened more than expected.

The Labor Department Jan. 6 had increased funding for public service jobs, allocating $787 million to states and localities in an effort to create 100,000 new jobs. The new infusion of funds brought total federal spending on public service jobs to $1.7 billion, enough to provide 300,000 jobs, officials said. By the end of 1974, however, only 78,000 of those jobs had been filled.

In Atlanta Jan. 10, 3,000 persons broke down glass doors at the city's Civic Center Auditorium in a rush to apply for 225 new public service jobs. The job seekers, most of them young blacks, had begun to gather at the site at 3 a.m.

George Meany, the AFL-CIO president, said Feb. 9 that the nation was going into a depression and predicted that unemployment would rise to 10% by July 1975. Meany, appearing on the CBS television program "Face the Nation," repeated the AFL-CIO's recommendations of one million public service jobs, release of $19 billion in impounded U.S. public works funds and forced reduction

U.S. Labor Force, Employment & Unemployment

[Numbers in thousands]

Year	Total noninstitutional population	Total labor force		Civilian labor force						Not in labor force
		Number	Percent of population	Total	Employed			Unemployed		
					Total	Agriculture	Nonagricultural industries	Number	Percent of labor force	
1950	106,645	63,858	59.9	62,208	58,920	7,160	51,760	3,288	5.3	42,787
1955	112,732	68,072	60.4	65,023	62,171	6,449	55,724	2,852	4.4	44,660
1960	119,759	72,142	60.2	69,628	65,778	5,458	60,318	3,852	5.5	47,617
1963	125,154	74,571	59.6	71,833	67,762	4,687	63,076	4,070	5.7	50,583
1964	127,224	75,830	59.6	73,091	69,305	4,523	64,782	3,786	5.2	51,394
1965	129,236	77,178	59.7	74,455	71,088	4,361	66,726	3,366	4.5	52,058
1966	131,180	78,893	60.1	75,770	72,895	3,979	68,915	2,875	3.8	52,288
1967	133,319	80,793	60.6	77,347	74,372	3,844	70,527	2,975	3.8	52,527
1968	135,562	82,272	60.7	78,737	75,920	3,817	72,103	2,817	3.6	53,291
1969	137,841	84,239	61.1	80,733	77,902	3,606	74,296	2,831	3.5	53,602
1970	140,182	85,903	61.3	82,715	78,627	3,462	75,165	4,088	4.9	54,280
1971	142,596	86,929	61.0	84,113	79,120	3,387	75,732	4,993	5.9	55,666
1972	145,775	88,991	61.0	86,542	81,702	3,472	78,230	4,840	5.6	56,785
1973	148,263	91,040	61.4	88,714	84,409	3,452	80,957	4,304	4.9	57,222
1974	150,827	93,240	61.8	91,011	85,936	3,492	82,443	5,076	5.6	57,587
1975	153,449	94,793	61.8	92,613	84,783	3,380	81,403	7,830	8.5	58,655

Table from Bureau of Labor Statistics

of mortgage rates to 6% to revive the sagging housing industry.

Arthur Burns, chairman of the Federal Reserve, took a different view of the nation's economic prospects in testimony before the Joint Economic Committee Feb. 7. Burns said that the current rapid decline in employment was caused by large build-ups of manufacturers' inventories. The inventories were now falling, he said, which might mean that workers would be rehired and the "recession won't last much longer." Burns suggested that the rise in unemployment was also caused by job-searching by the wives and children of unemployed men.

The Labor Department Feb. 21 added 12 new areas to its list of major labor regions with "substantial unemployment," 6% or more. The additions brought the total on the list to 67, 45% of the nation's major labor districts. That was two more than the previous record total registered in October 1961.

Although the unemployment rate continued in February 1975 at 8.2% of the work force, there were other signs that the employment situation was worsening, according to the Labor Department March 7. (All figures were adjusted to reflect seasonal variations.)

Total employment declined by 535,000 persons, a drop that officials termed "extraordinary," to 84 million—an indication that layoffs were continuing. That decline did not cause the unemployment rate to rise because 576,000 persons without jobs stopped their active search for work during the month. Persons who dropped out of the labor force were not included in the number of unemployed persons. Total unemployment in February was 7,484,000 persons, down slightly from January. Every major manufacturing industry reported declining employment during February.

Since September 1974, total employment had dropped by 2.4 million persons. Officials said that was the worst five-month decline since before World War II.

The number of long-term unemployed, those out of work at least 15 weeks, rose by 300,000 persons to total 1.8 million. The average length of time that those who were unemployed in February had been out of work rose from 10.7 weeks to 11.7 weeks. Of those persons without work, 55% were unemployed because they lost their jobs rather than because they left voluntarily. (In prosperous times, the usual rate was about 33%.)

For those with jobs, the average work week and overtime declined during February, but average weekly earnings increased slightly to $157.88.

Although employment rose in April for the first time in seven months, unemployment also rose, as it approached the year's high point. This took place because the labor force grew at a faster rate than did the number of jobs available.

The number of unemployed workers totaled 8,167,000 in April. The total number of persons with jobs was 84.1 million, an increase of about 240,000 over March. The civilian labor force expanded by 433,000 in April to total a seasonally adjusted 92.3 million persons, compared with 91.8 million in March.

Since August 1974, when the unemployment rate was 5.4%, the jobless count had risen by 3.3 million. Layoffs accounted for more than 80% of that number—2.7 million persons had lost their jobs over the nine month period, officials said. "Job loss now accounts for 57% of total joblessness, compared with only 41% last August," a government spokesman said. Between September 1974 and March, employment had declined by 2.6 million.

In one of the encouraging aspects of the jobless report, officials said 43% of all industries registered higher employment in April, compared with 26% in March and a low of 17% in February.

Administration officials remained hopeful that the recession was nearing an end. Alan Greenspan, chairman of the Council of Economic Advisers, told the Joint Economic Committee of Congress May 2 that although the economy "may wobble on the bottom for a while," the "worst does appear to be behind us."

The Labor Department, however, announced May 29 that a record 127 metropolitan areas were classified as have "substantial" levels of unemployment, defined as 6% or more. Only 23 of the nation's 150 major urban areas reported jobless rates, based on April data, below the 6% level.

Unemployment peaked in May at a recorded 9.2% of the nation's labor force.

Monthly Employment & Unemployment

(Seasonally adjusted, in thousands)

Employment status	Annual average		1974	1975											
	1973	1974	Dec.	Jan.	Feb.	Mar.	Apr.	May	June	July	Aug.	Sept.	Oct.	Nov.	Dec.
TOTAL															
Total noninstitutional population	148,263	150,827	152,020	152,230	152,445	152,646	152,840	153,051	153,278	153,585	153,824	154,052	154,256	154,476	154,700
Total labor force	91,040	93,240	94,015	94,284	93,709	94,027	94,457	95,121	94,518	95,102	95,331	95,361	95,607	95,134	95,436
Civilian noninstitutional population	145,936	148,599	149,809	150,037	150,246	150,447	150,645	150,870	151,100	151,399	151,639	151,882	152,092	152,320	152,543
Civilian labor force	88,714	91,011	91,803	92,091	91,511	91,829	92,262	92,940	92,340	92,916	93,146	93,191	93,443	92,979	93,279
Employed	84,409	85,936	85,202	84,562	84,027	83,849	84,086	84,402	84,444	85,078	85,352	85,418	85,441	85,278	85,511
Agriculture	3,452	3,492	3,339	3,383	3,326	3,265	3,238	3,512	3,304	3,450	3,468	3,546	3.422	3,292	3,241
Nonagricultural industries	80,957	82,443	81,863	81,179	80,701	80,584	80,848	80,890	81,140	81,628	81,884	81,872	82,019	81,986	82,270
Unemployed	4,304	5,076	6,601	7,529	7,484	7,980	8,176	8,538	7,896	7,838	7,794	7,773	8,002	7,701	7,768
Unemployment rate	4.9	5.6	7.2	8.2	8.2	8.7	8.9	9.2	8.6	8.4	8.4	8.3	8.6	8.3	8.3
Not in labor force	57,222	57,587	58,006	57,946	58,735	58,618	58,383	57,930	58,760	58,483	58,493	58,691	58,649	59,341	59,264

Duration of Unemployment

(Seasonally adjusted, in thousands)

Period	Annual average		1974	1975											
	1973	1974	Dec.	Jan.	Feb.	Mar.	Apr.	May	June	July	Aug.	Sept.	Oct.	Nov.	Dec.
Less than 5 weeks	2,196	2,567	3,077	3,316	2,914	3,253	2,897	3,134	2,692	2,823	2,676	2,790	3,024	2,641	2,693
5 to 14 weeks	1,296	1,572	2,062	2,663	2,597	2,619	2,695	2,620	2,498	2,120	2,361	2,430	2,388	2,393	2,102
15 weeks and over	812	937	1,319	1,537	1,822	1,991	2,403	2,643	2,887	2,998	2,842	2,856	2,578	2,824	2,919
15 to 26 weeks	475	563	782	914	1,118	1,259	1,452	1,568	1,561	1,604	1,383	1,242	1,185	1,155	1,294
27 weeks and over	337	373	537	623	704	732	951	1,075	1,326	1,394	1,459	1,614	1,393	1,669	1,625
Average (mean) duration, in weeks	10.0	9.7	10.0	10.7	11.7	11.4	12.9	13.4	15.4	15.4	15.7	16.2	15.4	16.8	16.4

Tables from Bureau of Labor Statistics

The number of jobless workers totaled a seasonally adjusted 8,538,000. The 362,-000 increase over April pushed the total number of unemployed workers to its highest level since July 1940. (During the 1940s, however, seasonal adjustments were not made in the index, and unemployed 14- and 15-year olds, currently not included in statistics, were a part of the data.)

Most of the rise in total employment occurred in the farm sector. Layoffs accounted for most of the increase in unemployment: the number of persons who lost their jobs rose 206,000 to 4,863,000; the number of new entrants to the labor force who could not find jobs increased 80,000 to 848,000; those who re-entered the job market and could not obtain work rose 98,000 to 2,114,000.

The average duration of unemployment in May reached 13.4 weeks, the highest level in more than 10 years. The number of persons who were without work for 15 weeks or more rose 240,000 to 2.6 million. The number of unemployed workers who had been seeking jobs for six months or more exceeded one million for the first time since 1958.

Despite the trend toward higher unemployment, Administration officials saw signs of improved economic conditions: total employment in May rose for the fourth consecutive month; the percentage of industries reporting increased unemployment rose for the fourth straight month and the 53.5% rate was the highest since August 1974; the number of initial claims for jobless benefits was below the May 1974 level; and for the third straight month, the factory layoff rate declined and the number of full-time workers forced to accept part-time employment declined.

The Labor Department reported July 3 that its computed rate of unemployment had dropped to 8.6% in June.

Although the June unemployment rate was down from May's record 9.2% level, Julius Shiskin, commissioner of labor statistics, told members of the Joint Economic Committee of Congress, "Don't celebrate until you see the July and August figures." Shiskin explained that unemployment actually was unchanged from May. The drop in the monthly rate, Shiskin said, resulted from a statistical "overcorrection" in the index that was made to factor out the influx of students and graduates in the job market during June.

Shiskin said that the record jobless rate for May probably also was misleading because unemployment had been "overstated" in computing the data. The current jobless rate most likely was about 8.9%, or an average of the May and June figures, according to Shiskin.

The number of "discouraged" workers, those who had given up the search for a job, reached a record 1.2 million persons in the second quarter. Long-term unemployment during June also climbed—the number of persons out of work 15 weeks or longer rose 244,000 to an adjusted 2.9 million persons.

Total employment in July was 85.1 million, up 630,000 from June; 55% of all industries reported gains in employment, compared with 41.6% in June and a low of 16.6% in February.

The number of unemployed persons fell to 7,838,000, the lowest level since February. Long-term unemployment, however, increased in July. The number of persons out of work 15 weeks or longer rose to 3.2% of the labor force, more than triple the year-earlier rate.

Although the jobless rate did not decline, Administration economists were encouraged by two aspects of the report for August: the total number of unemployed persons fell by 44,000 to 7,794,000, and the total number of jobs increased to 85,-352,000, up 274,000 from July and a gain of 1.5 million jobs from the recession low set in March. (The monthly unemployment rate did not fall because the rise in total employment was offset by a 229,-000 increase in the total civilian labor force, which reached 95,331,000 in August.)

Another positive sign of an expanding economy was a decline in long-term unemployment: the number of persons out of work 15 weeks or longer totaled 2.8 million in August. The decline of 160,-000 from July was the first significant drop in extended joblessness since unemployment began to rise in late 1973. However, the department also noted that the number of persons without work 27 weeks or longer continued to rise.

In a separate report published Aug. 29, the Labor Department said that layoffs of manufacturing workers dropped sharply in July to the lowest level in nearly 12 months. The layoff rate declined to 14 per 1,000 workers, down from 20 in June and January's peak of 35 per 1,000 workers.

"Accessions" to manufacturing payrolls, representing new hirings and recalls, rose to 43 per 1,000 workers, up from 36 in June. The accession rate exceeded total separations for the first time in more than a year, officials said.

September's report had both positive and negative aspects. Officials said they were encouraged by a sharp expansion in manufacturing payrolls. The 183,000 increase in factory jobs was the largest monthly gain since December 1970, when a lengthy auto strike ended. The Department of Labor noted, however, that total manufacturing employment for September was 18.43 million, down from 20.1 million the previous September, when the rise in unemployment had not yet accelerated.

Another indication of economic recovery was seen in the department's survey of 172 key industries: 72.1% of these industries reported gains in employment. It was the highest percentage gain since November 1973.

One of the disquieting aspects of the September jobless report was the rise in the number of "hard-core" unemployed, a figure that indicated the depth of the recession. The number of persons out of work at least 27 weeks totaled 1.6 million in September, a post-war high and 20% of the month's jobless total.

The average period of unemployment for jobless workers also increased during September to 16.2 weeks, the highest level since late 1961.

In a separate announcement Oct. 6, the Labor Department reported that of the nation's 150 major labor market areas, a record 135 had "substantial" jobless rates in September.

Although the number of persons holding jobs increased in October, the entire work force expanded at a greater rate; this resulted in a rise in unemployment. Total employment, measured by a survey of 50,000 households, rose 23,000 to 85.4 million persons; the civilian labor force grew by 252,000 to total 93.4 million persons; and the number of unemployed persons rose 229,000 to 8,002,000.

Of the 172 industries surveyed by the Labor Department, 63% reported a rise in employment. Based on this business data, officials reported that nonfarm payroll employment rose for the fourth consecutive month, increasing 220,000 in October to 77.5 million.

The average duration of unemployment showed its first decline since January, falling in October to 15.4 weeks from 16.2 weeks reported the previous month. The number of persons out of work 15 weeks or longer also declined sharply, falling 278,000; however, the number of workers umemployed for less than five weeks rose 234,000.

The unemployment rate declined in November to 8.3% of the labor force, the Labor Department announced Dec. 6. In spite of the monthly decline, Administration economists were not very encouraged by the November report, noting that unemployment had remained at a "virtual plateau" in the 8.3%–8.6% range during a period of emerging economic recovery from recession.

Most of the attention on the November report was focused on employment figures, which provided additional evidence of sluggish economic activity. According to a monthly government survey of 50,000 households, there was a small drop in total employment during November to 85.3 million. This figure had been essentially stable for three months after rising swiftly from March to August.

Another measure of employment, one that was most closely watched by economists, showed a very small decline in total jobs. According to this survey of non-farm employer payrolls (including the government's), employment totaled 77.5 million in November. However, there was no increase in two key components of payroll employment—the number of jobs in manufacturing and construction held steady. These areas of the economy typically suffered the sharpest job loss during a recession, but also the strongest upturn in employment during a recovery.

There was additional evidence in the November report that recovery had not yet taken hold in the job market. The average duration of unemployment was a record high 16.8 weeks.

Highlights of the December report:

■ The number of persons with jobs increased 233,000 to a seasonally adjusted 85.5 million. The civilian labor force expanded 300,000 to 93.3 million persons. The ranks of the unemployed increased 67,000 to 7,768,000.

■ The total number of workers in businesses, in government and in nonprofit establishments grew by 240,000 to 77.8 million persons in December. Since June, payroll employment had expanded 1.5 million, but remained 1 million below the pre-recession peak set in September 1974. Government officials said that 66% of the 172 industries surveyed reported a rise in employment over the month.

■ The December report showed that the average duration of unemployment declined from 16.8 weeks to 16.4 weeks; however the number of persons out of work 15 weeks or more increased slightly.

■ The average factory workweek rose from 39.9 hours in November to 40.3 hours in December. Analyst said the monthly increase was extraordinarily large and indicative of a substantial increase in manufacturing production. Since reaching its recession low, the workweek had gained 1.5 hours but remained .7 hours below the peak set in February 1973.

■ Factory overtime, which had been steady since August at 2.8 hours, rose to 3 hours. Analysts noted that at the beginning of a recovery period, employers tended to increase overtime payments rather than hire new workers. Production, therefore, could increase while unemployment remained steady.

■ Unemployment rates by worker categories: adult women 8%, up from 7.8% in November; adult men 6.5%, down from 6.9%; teenagers 19.9%, up from 18.6%; blue-collar workers 10.3%, down from 11%; heads of household declined to 5.7%.

Auto industry slump. The U.S. automobile industry continued layoffs during 1975 as car sales remained low. Some government and industry officials, however, noted signs of the beginning of a recovery during 1975's closing months.

The year opened with a reported inventory of 1,650,000 cars, a 100-day supply.

Chrysler Corp. announced Jan. 9 that three of its six U.S. car assembly plants and one truck plant would be closed for one week in an effort to cut production while there was a 125-day supply of unsold cars. An estimated 14,800 employes would be idled for the one-week period. Of Chrysler's total blue collar work force of 117,000, 47,500 workers already were laid off indefinitely; 20,000 of 39,000 white collar workers were temporarily without jobs.

General Motors announced cutbacks raising to 93,000 the number of its workers to go on indefinite layoff during January and to 15,505 the number temporarily idled. Ford's announcements disclosed temporary layoffs of 52,525 workers and indefinite layoffs of 32,650 in January.

During the week ending Jan. 29, about 380,000 auto industry employes were unemployed.

In an effort to stimulate sales, the major auto makers, led by Chrysler, began to offer cash rebates to customers who bought specific models of cars.

The rebate campaign proved to be successful in temporarily stimulating sales. During February, new car sales were off only 6% from the year earlier level. However, from Jan. 1 to March 20, new car sales totaled 1.5 million, 12.9% fewer than in the same period of 1974.

An anticipated upturn in sales during the spring failed to materialize, according to reports April 23. Mid-April sales were down 18.4% from the same period of 1974.

The continued slump in sales came at a time when a large number of workers were being recalled for spring production, prompting fears that the industry's backlog of unsold cars would begin to climb again.

The plight of unemployed Chrysler employes, many of whom had been laid off for an extended period, worsened April 11 when the company announced that its Supplemental Unemployment Benefits (SUB) fund had been exhausted because of mass layoffs. Since January 1974, Chrysler had paid $110 million to jobless workers. The money had been paid into the fund by the company for each man-hour worked in order to guarantee that a laid-off worker received 95% of his take-home pay. (The fund was finally replenished in September and Chrysler announced Sept. 22 that weekly payments were resuming.)

All four U.S. auto makers reported sharp profit losses for 1975's first quarter, and three reported deficits.

Chrysler Corp. posted the largest quarterly deficit. In its report May 1, Chrysler said its net loss for the first three months of the year totaled $94.1 million, its worst ever.

Before a last-minute accounting change was made reducing the deficit, Chrysler's loss totaled $116.9 million. The change was made, according to the company, because Ford Motor Co. had instituted a new "flow-through" accounting procedure for investment tax credits that reduced its losses.

Ford announced April 30 that its first quarter net loss, calculated with the new accounting procedure, totaled $10.6 million. Under the old system, its loss would have been $105.8 million. Quarterly revenue declined 6.7% to $5.09 billion. (The first quarter loss was Ford's first since going public in 1956.)

American Motors Corp. posted a $47.8 million loss during its second fiscal quarter, its largest quarterly deficit ever, officials said May 7.

Only GM reported a quarterly profit, but its earnings increase was the smallest in 29 years, officials said April 29. Net income during the first three months totaled $59.2 million, down 51% from the comparable period of 1974.

Auto dealers, as well as assembly workers, were affected by the sales slump. According to a report May 12, the number of U.S. dealers selling American-made cars declined by 213 during the first three months of 1975, the sharpest first quarter drop in 14 years.

New car sales in April were at a 14-year low, according to industry spokesmen May 5. Retail sales for the month totaled 517,637, down 26% from the April 1974 level. During the final third of the month, sales plunged 32% compared with the year-earlier period.

GM's SUB fund was exhausted May 8, and SUB payments to some 55,000 jobless UAW members were suspended. Payouts, however, resumed July 14 after the fund was replenished with regular contributions from GM and the union. However, the fund was quickly exhausted after only seven weeks when a total of $22.6 million was paid in benefits. According to the spokesman, fewer than 35,000 of the estimated 59,000 GM workers currently on indefinite layoff were eligible to receive benefits when payouts resumed. (The remainder had exhausted their benefits earlier or were not eligible for assistance from the fund.) The fund was replenished for a second time, and a resumption of payments was announced by GM Oct. 30.

The Labor Department ruled that 18,000 Chrysler Corp. employes were eligible for special trade-related unemployment benefits because they were either already unemployed or in danger of losing their jobs as a result of increased imports of certain cars and parts from Chrysler's Canadian plants, the Wall Street Journal reported Aug. 4. Such payments were authorized under the 1974 Trade Act. (Aid was denied to 23,000 other Chrysler workers.)

Petitions for the 18,000 workers, filed on their behalf by the United Auto Workers, were based on claims that Chrysler had transferred production from its U.S. plants to its Canadian plants and imported cars from Canada to the U.S. The Canadian plants operated at near-capacity levels while U.S. plants making "like or competitive products," were closed or production was sharply reduced, the workers contended.

The law permitted trade-adjustment assistance when increased imports "contributed importantly" to the absolute decline in sales and production and the total or partial payoff of a significant number of workers at the plants. The Labor Department ruled that average hourly employment at the five affected plants declined 23%-60%, depending on location, from the first nine months of the 1974-model year to the same period of 1975.

Auto industry unemployment still exceeded the national jobless rate despite industry moves to speed the output of new-model cars in anticipation of a broadbased national economic recovery. There were substantial gains in auto employment, however, as 1975 advanced and the recession waned.

On Labor Day, the New York Times reported Sept. 1, 84,275 auto workers—11.8% of the industry's hourly labor force—remained on indefinite layoff. Although higher than the 8.4% national jobless rate, the figures marked an improvement over the industry's peak unemployment rate set during the week of Feb. 3 when 38.5% of all production workers were idle. A recession-high 274,-380 auto workers had been without jobs at that time, according to the Times.

Total employment at the three major car makers—General Motors Corp., Ford Motor Co., and Chrysler Corp.—had declined 178,600 from the peak set in 1973 when production was at a record high level.

The number of GM workers on indefinite layoff peaked at 137,500 at the end of February, officials said. GM currently listed 59,000 workers on indefinite layoff.

Ford's indefinite layoffs peaked at 34,-000 during the week of Feb. 3; currently 13,700 workers were laid off indefinitely.

Chrysler Corp., the auto maker hardest hit by the industry-wide drop in sales, reported a decline in indefinite layoffs from the Feb. 3 peak of 51,500 to 10,100 at the end of August.

American Motors Corp., which emphasized small car production and had been least affected by the impact of the energy crisis on car sales, reported that layoffs peaked at 2,000 in January, and currently numbered only 475.

In October 1975, new-car sales totaled 888,000, up 17% above the depressed level of October 1974. (In September 1975, new-car sales had been 3.9% below the September 1975 level.)

Analysts cautioned that improvement in the October figures was a sign only of an upturn for the hard-pressed auto industry, rather than an indication of booming sales. They noted that sales for the month remained 9% below the October 1973 level, when car purchases fell because of concern over the Arab oil embargo, and were 20% below the record 1972 period.

One aspect of the October report, however, was encouraging to Detroit auto makers—demand for domestic-built cars strengthened while the market weakened for foreign-made autos. Sales of U.S.-built cars totaled 773,623 units, up 23% from the previous year. The percentage gain was attributed to introduction in October of the new 1976 model cars.

Sales of foreign-made autos declined an estimated 11% from the year-earlier pace, the first time since January that foreign-car sales had failed to show a month-to-month rise. Because of the poor monthly showing, foreign-made autos took only 13% of the total market in October, down sharply from the 20%–22% shares reported in recent months.

The U.S. auto industry reported Dec. 23 that 6.72 million cars were produced during 1975, down 8% from the year-earlier level and off 30.4% from the 1973 production year. The production figure for 1975 was the lowest since 1970 when 6.55 million cars were built.

Washington job rallies. An estimated 10,000 unemployed auto workers attended a job rally in Washington Feb. 5, 1975. Sponsored by the United Automobile Workers union and held in the National Guard Armory, the rally was punctuated by cries of "We want jobs." "We do not want politics as usual," UAW President Leonard Woodcock declared, "The country needs action." Woodcock assailed the Ford Administration and what he termed its "planned recession for five long years."

Other speakers at the rally were Sens. Edward M. Kennedy (D, Mass.), Walter F. Mondale (D, Minn.), Harrison A. Williams Jr. (D, N.J.), and Reps. Bella S. Abzug (D, N.Y.), Ray J. Madden (D, Ind.) and Henry S. Reuss (D, Wis.).

Woodcock told reporters Feb. 3 that a massive labor rally might be held in Washington, one of 200,000–250,000 persons, "if by the spring we're not getting positive action out of the government."

Some 60,000 union members took part in a job rally in Washington April 26. Sponsored by the AFL-CIO's Industrial Union Department, the rally consisted of marches and a mass gathering at Robert F. Kennedy Stadium. The latter, however, was disrupted and ended when several thousand of the demonstrators swarmed in front of the speakers' stand demanding "jobs now" and shouted down speakers.

The scheduled speakers, in addition to union leaders, included Sens. Hubert H. Humphrey (D, Minn.) and Richard S. Schweiker (R, Pa.) and Reps. Bella S. Abzug (D, N.Y.) and Barbara C. Jordan (D, Tex.).

The largest delegation of union members, 25,000, came from the New York and New Jersey area.

AFL-CIO President George Meany opposed the event and did not attend.

Ford talks jobs in Maine. President Ford told a labor audience in Augusta, Me. Aug. 30 that he would do "everything in my power to generate new jobs" and that there was no level of unemployment that was acceptable to his Administration.

"We must maintain the social fabric of America," Ford cautioned. "All of us—labor, management and government—must work together if we are to achieve long-term economic health."

The President also cautioned that "stopgap" federal spending programs, "conceived in panic and, perhaps, to some extent, in partisanship," were not the answer.

Sen. Edmund S. Muskie (D, Me.) rebutted the President in a speech later Aug. 30 before the same group, a labor union rally sponsored by the state AFL-CIO. "The President is said to have a policy," Muskie said in deploring the Administration's economic policies. "Well, he sure does. His policy is high prices for you." Congress was said "to have no policy," he continued, "but it does. That policy is holding the line."

Prices Continue to Rise

Indexes at record levels. The consumer price index rose from a record monthly average of 147.7% of the 1967 level in 1974 to 161.2% in 1975. The average percentage increase, however, declined from the "double-digit" 11% of 1974 to 9.1% in 1975. The wholesale price index rose from a record 160.1% of the 1967 average in 1974 to 174.9% in 1975. The 9.2% gain in 1975 compared with gains of 18.9% in 1975 and 13.1% in 1973.

The consumer price index rose a seasonally adjusted 1.2% in July, or 14.4% at an adjusted annual rate, to 162.3% of the 1967 base average. Over a 12-month period, consumer prices had climbed 9.7%.

The large monthly increase, the biggest since September 1974, reflected sharply higher prices paid for food, fuel, and used cars.

Overall food prices were up 1.7% during July. That was the largest increase since August 1974. Grocery prices, paced by higher costs for vegetables, poultry, and meat, rose 1.9%, or 22.8% at an annual rate. (The price index for poultry, pork, and beef had climbed nearly 20% since April.) Restaurant charges increased .5%.

Among nonfood items, gasoline and motor oil prices rose 3.3% from June, reflecting the added costs of the second $1-a-barrel tariff increase imposed by President Ford.

With consumer prices rising at a faster pace than wages, the average worker experienced an actual decline in "real" spendable earnings, according to the Labor Department. Real pay for July fell .5%. That was the sixth decline in seven months and meant that real earnings were .3% below the July 1974 level.

The index's rise moderated in August, when the increase was only .2%, the smallest monthly increase since August 1972.

The August report, which was favorable compared with inflation statistics for June and July, reflected a halt in the rapid food-price spiral of previous months. The index's food component showed no gain during August: the cost of fresh fruits and vegetables declined an adjusted 2.9% after climbing 5.6% in July; the overall price of meat, poultry and fish rose an adjusted 1.5% after spurting 3.5% in July; and beef prices registered their first decline in five months, although pork prices soared.

(According to the New York Times Sept. 21, hog prices in the Midwest were a record $63.25 for 100 pounds, nearly double the year-earlier price. There was little hope for a reduction in retail pork prices, analysts said, because the nation's hog population was at its lowest point in more than 20 years and farmers planned to make further cuts in the population. With corn prices high [about $3 a bushel], "it's more advantageous to hold hog numbers level and enjoy less risk and labor by selling more grain instead of feeding it," a farm economist said.)

By fall, however, food prices were on the way up again, and the consumer price index for all items rose by .7% (seasonally adjusted) in October.

The volatile food price index was the chief cause of the large monthly rise in overall consumer prices, officials said. Grocery prices were up an adjusted 1.5% over the month, reflecting recent price increases for farm products.

Nonfood consumer prices increased an adjusted .3%. Contributing to the increase was a 1.8% price rise for fuel oil and coal, and a .9% rise in gasoline and motor oil prices.

For the 12 months ended in December 1975, consumer food prices rose 6.5%, compared with a 12.2% rise during 1974.

The wholesale price index had declined each month during December 1974 and January, February and March 1975. The drop of 2.2% since November 1974 was the biggest four-month decline since 1951. Despite the index' turndown, wholesale prices in March 1975 were 12.5% higher than in March 1974.

The decline ended in April, when the wholesale price index rose 1.5% (seasonally adjusted) to 172.1% of the 1967 average. The rise in April was due almost entirely to increased prices of farm goods and processed foods and feeds. The index continued to rise in May, for the same reason, but it dropped again in June before heading up again in July, August, September and October. There was a small decline in November, and the index then rose in 1975's final month to 178.7% of the 1967 average.

Food marketing prices rise 9% in 1975—Food marketing spreads—the difference between farm and retail prices—increased 9% in 1975 over the previous year, when price spreads climbed 20%, the Agriculture Department reported Feb. 11, 1976.

Officials added, however, that although the rise in price spreads moderated during the 2nd quarter of 1975 from the first period's record high levels, margins "moved sharply higher in the last half of the year."

Officials attributed the erratic price pattern and subsequent pickup in marketing spreads to "inflationary pressures in the economy" on the cost of packaging, transportation, energy, labor and other factors involved in the marketing of food.

The department published a comparison of cost increases for these items over a two-year period. Energy costs, which rose 46% in 1974, were up 17% in 1975; packaging, up 23% in 1974 and 15% in 1975; rail shipping, up 16% in 1974 and 13% in 1975; and hourly labor, up 9% in 1974 and 10% in 1975.

Consumers absorbed much of the widening market spreads, which increased 8% from September to December 1975, officials said. During that four-month period when price spreads increased sharply, the cost to consumers of a typical "market basket" of farm-produced foods rose 1.5%, and the return to farmers declined 7%.

Profit margins for food manufacturing firms also rose in 1975 as farm prices declined. According to the Federal Trade Commission, their average profit margin was 3.2% of sales during the first nine months of 1975, compared with 2.9% for the same period of 1974.

The after-tax profits of 14 leading food chains (excluding A&P, which reported large losses), increased from 1972's low level of .77¢ per dollar of sales to .89¢ per dollar of sales in 1974. Profits would have been sharply higher (1.1¢ per dollar of sales) if three of the 14 firms had not switched to LIFO inventory accounting to eliminate the distorting effects of inflation.

FCC approves AT&T rate hike. The Federal Communications Commission Feb. 27, 1975 approved a $365 million rate increase for American Telephone & Telegraph Co.

AT&T had sought a $717 million increase.

ICC OKs rail freight rate rise. The Interstate Commerce Commission (ICC) March 25 reversed an earlier decision and gave the nation's railroads permission to increase freight rates up to 7%. In announcing its approval of the rate increase, which was expected to cost shippers an additional $449 million a year, the ICC said the railroads "are in need of additional revenue from their interstate freight rates and charges to offset recently incurred operating costs and to provide an improved level of earnings."

In rejecting the request for higher rates Jan. 30, the ICC had said an increase would "result in rates and charges that would be unjust and unreasonable and otherwise unlawful." Since that date, the Rock Island railroad had declared bank-

Consumer & Wholesale Price Indexes 1951–75

[1967 = 100]

Year	Consumer prices						Wholesale prices					
	All items		Commodities		Services		All commodities		Farm products, processed foods and feeds		Industrial commodities	
	Index	Percent change	Index	Percent change	Index	Percent change	Index	Percent change	Index	Percent change	Index	Percent change
1951	77.8	7.9	85.9	9.0	61.8	5.3	91.1	11.4	106.9	13.8	86.1	10.4
1952	79.5	2.2	87.0	1.3	64.5	4.4	88.6	−2.7	102.7	−3.9	84.1	−2.3
1953	80.1	.8	86.7	−.3	67.3	4.3	87.4	−1.4	96.0	−6.5	84.8	.8
1954	80.5	.5	85.9	−.9	69.5	3.3	87.6	.2	95.7	−.3	85.0	.2
1955	80.2	−.4	85.1	−.9	70.9	2.0	87.8	.2	91.2	−4.7	86.9	2.2
1956	81.4	1.5	85.9	.9	72.7	2.5	90.7	3.3	90.6	−.7	90.8	4.5
1957	84.3	3.6	88.6	3.1	75.6	4.0	93.3	2.9	93.7	3.4	93.3	2.8
1958	86.6	2.7	90.6	2.3	78.5	3.8	94.6	1.4	98.1	4.7	93.6	.3
1959	87.3	.8	90.7	.1	80.8	2.9	94.8	.2	93.5	−4.7	95.3	1.8
1960	88.7	1.6	91.5	.9	83.5	3.3	94.9	.1	93.7	.2	95.3	0
1961	89.6	1.0	92.0	.5	85.2	2.0	94.5	−.4	93.7	0	94.8	−.5
1962	90.6	1.1	92.8	.9	86.8	1.9	94.8	.3	94.7	1.1	94.8	0
1963	91.7	1.2	93.6	.9	88.5	2.0	94.5	−.3	93.8	−1.0	94.7	−.1
1964	92.9	1.3	94.6	1.1	90.2	1.9	94.7	.2	93.2	−.6	95.2	.5
1965	94.5	1.7	95.7	1.2	92.2	2.2	96.6	2.0	97.1	4.2	96.4	1.3
1966	97.2	2.9	98.2	2.6	95.8	3.9	99.8	3.3	103.5	6.6	98.5	2.2
1967	100.0	2.9	100.0	1.8	100.0	4.4	100.0	.2	100.0	−3.4	100.0	1.5
1968	104.2	4.2	103.7	3.7	105.2	5.2	102.5	2.5	102.4	2.4	102.5	2.5
1969	109.8	5.4	108.4	4.5	112.5	6.9	106.5	3.9	108.0	5.5	106.0	3.4
1970	116.3	5.9	113.5	4.7	121.6	8.1	110.4	3.7	111.7	3.4	110.0	3.8
1971	121.3	4.3	117.4	3.4	128.4	5.6	113.9	3.2	113.8	2.0	114.0	3.6
1972	125.3	3.3	120.9	3.0	133.3	3.8	119.1	4.6	122.4	7.6	117.9	3.4
1973	133.1	6.2	129.9	7.4	139.1	4.4	134.7	13.1	159.1	30.0	125.9	6.8
1974	147.7	11.0	145.5	12.0	152.1	9.3	160.1	18.9	177.4	11.5	153.8	22.2
1975	161.2	9.1	158.4	8.9	166.6	9.5	174.9	9.2	184.2	3.8	171.5	11.5

Table from Bureau of Labor Statistics

ruptcy and the ICC had held hearings on deteriorating passenger conditions on Amtrak's trains.

In its decision, the ICC also ruled that the products of some key depressed industries were exempt from the rate increase. Included were motor vehicles and parts, lumber and other building materials, sugar beets and material shipped for recycling. Restrictions also were placed on shipping increases for iron and steel scrap and certain processed foods.

2d freight rate rise—The ICC June 5 approved 1975's second rail-freight rate increase, a 5% rise starting June 20. The roads had filed for the increase, because of higher labor costs, April 28, one day after putting into effect the 7% increase granted in March.

The effective date of the 7% increase had been delayed several weeks because of action by the Chessie System, Inc. The Chessie originally had refused to join in seeking the 7% boost, then later conditioned its participation on inclusion of coal exports, which had been excluded by the ICC from the rate rise. The ICC dropped the exclusion. Other lines asked for delay in the rate hike to avoid having a higher rate than the Chessie, whose participation in the increase had been pushed back to April 27.

The Chessie's stand was influenced by its lawsuit against the ICC protesting the agency's right to require spending 70% of a 1974 rate increase on maintenance or delayed capital improvements. The Chessie won its point April 23 when a U.S. Court of Appeals' panel in Richmond, Va. held that the ICC could not order a railroad how to spend its revenue.

The 5% increase for June 20 would be applied across the board, with no exclusions, and without conditions set on its use by the railroads. Chessie announced May 6 it was joining the bid because of the "depressed conditions announced by many of the railroads in the East," although it was concerned about the impact of the rate rise on car hauling.

Amtrak fares rise—Amtrak announced fare increases June 2. The hikes, effective July 1, applied to first-class and coach fares on trips in the Northeast Corridor, to first-class fares on trains to the West coast and to commuter fares between Harrisburg, Pa., Philadelphia and New York.

'No-frill' air fare approved. The Civil Aeronautics Board March 28, 1975 approved National Airlines' "no-frill" fare proposal that would reduce the cost of air travel for many passengers by up to 35%. Four other airlines—Eastern, American, Delta and Continental—won CAB approval April 9 to implement the bargain fare on the 32 routes proposed by National.

The no-frill plan authorized by the CAB offered fare discounts to passengers willing to forego the free meals, drinks and other amenities offered on regular flights. Passengers also would be required to purchase tickets seven days before departure and pay a $10 or 10% (whichever was higher) fee if the reservation were canceled or changed. The cut-rate flights would be available only Monday through Thursday. The offer would be withdrawn during July and August and certain holiday periods when air travel was heavy.

In some cases, such as on the New York-Miami route, the new austerity fare would be lower than the cost of bus or train travel. The no-frill fare would be $61 one way, compared with $63.05 for the bus and $72 for Amtrak.

The agency's 3-2 decision in favor of the radically different fare came as the industry faced a financial dilemma—how to pay for soaring fuel costs while simultaneously dealing with the sharpest drop in air travel since World War II.

In its previous efforts at revitalizing the financially distressed industry, the CAB had emphasized a pricing policy that favored steep fare increases to offset fuel costs. However, as inflation and recession worsened, passenger traffic had declined. Approval of the no-frill fare and reductions in other tariff rates marked a reversal of this two-year trend toward higher air-travel costs and new efforts for spurring passenger traffic.

In a decision announced March 27, the CAB restored the cut-rate youth fare on trans-Atlantic flights effective April 1. The New York-London youth fare during June, July and August would be $465. The youth fare had been terminated in 1973 after other groups charged that the special discount was discriminatory.

In reviving the youth fare, the CAB also approved a discount for all travelers under

Consumer Price Index: U.S. City Monthly Averages

(Seasonally adjusted, 1967 = 100 unless otherwise indicated)

General summary	Annual average 1975	1974	1975											
		Dec.	Jan.	Feb.	Mar.	Apr.	May	June	July	Aug.	Sept.	Oct.	Nov.	Dec.
All items	161.2	155.4	156.1	157.2	157.8	158.6	159.3	160.6	162.3	162.8	163.6	164.6	165.6	166.3
All items (1957–59=100)	187.5	180.8	181.6	182.8	183.6	184.4	185.2	186.8	188.8	189.4	190.3	191.4	192.6	193.4
Food	175.4	169.7	170.9	171.6	171.3	171.2	171.8	174.4	178.6	178.1	177.8	179.0	179.8	180.7
Food at home	175.8	170.3	171.4	172.0	171.4	171.0	171.6	174.9	179.9	179.0	178.2	179.3	180.0	180.9
Food away from home	174.3	167.6	169.0	170.5	171.3	172.2	172.8	173.1	174.2	175.3	176.5	178.0	179.2	180.0
Housing	166.8	159.9	161.3	162.8	163.6	164.7	165.3	166.4	167.1	167.7	168.9	169.8	171.3	172.2
Rent	137.3	133.7	134.5	135.1	135.5	135.9	136.4	136.9	137.3	138.0	138.4	139.3	139.9	140.6
Homeownership	181.7	174.0	175.6	177.3	178.2	179.4	180.1	181.4	182.3	182.8	183.9	184.8	186.8	187.8
Apparel and upkeep	142.3	141.9	139.4	140.2	140.9	141.3	141.8	141.4	141.1	142.3	143.5	144.6	145.5	145.2
Transportation	150.6	143.5	143.2	143.5	144.8	146.2	147.4	149.8	152.6	153.6	155.4	156.1	157.4	157.6
Health and recreation	153.5	147.5	148.9	150.2	151.1	152.1	152.6	153.2	154.0	154.6	155.4	156.3	156.5	157.5
Medical care	168.6	159.0	161.0	163.0	164.6	165.8	166.8	168.1	169.8	170.9	172.2	173.5	173.3	174.7
Special groups														
All items less shelter	159.1	153.5	154.1	155.0	155.6	156.3	157.0	158.4	160.3	160.8	161.6	162.6	163.4	164.1
All items less food	157.1	151.3	151.9	153.0	153.9	154.9	155.6	156.6	157.6	158.3	159.5	160.4	161.5	162.1
All items less medical care	160.9	155.3	156.0	156.9	157.5	158.2	158.9	160.3	162.0	162.4	163.2	164.1	165.2	165.8
Appliances (including radio and TV)	118.4	115.2	116.0	116.4	116.9	117.2	117.6	117.9	118.3	118.7	119.6	120.2	120.9	120.8
Commodities	158.4	153.0	153.4	154.4	155.0	155.7	156.5	157.9	160.1	160.4	160.8	161.7	162.2	162.7
Nondurables	163.2	158.3	158.7	159.6	159.7	160.1	160.8	162.4	165.0	165.2	165.4	166.4	167.1	167.6
Durables	145.5	138.8	139.3	140.3	142.1	143.6	144.8	145.8	146.9	147.5	148.2	148.9	149.2	149.3
Services	166.6	160.1	161.3	162.6	163.2	164.1	164.5	165.7	166.6	167.4	169.1	170.1	172.0	173.1
Commodities less food	149.1	143.9	143.9	144.9	146.0	147.2	148.1	148.9	149.9	150.7	151.4	152.2	152.6	152.8
Nondurables less food	151.7	147.7	147.2	148.2	148.8	149.8	150.5	151.2	152.2	153.0	153.8	154.6	155.1	155.4
Apparel commodities	141.2	141.6	138.6	139.2	139.9	140.3	140.8	140.3	139.8	141.1	142.3	143.5	144.4	143.9
Apparel commodities less footwear	140.6	141.5	137.9	138.5	139.1	139.5	140.1	139.6	139.1	140.6	141.9	143.1	144.1	143.6
Nondurables less food and apparel	157.9	151.3	152.3	153.6	154.2	155.4	156.3	157.7	159.5	160.1	160.7	161.3	161.5	162.2
Household durables	140.3	136.0	136.8	137.3	138.3	139.4	140.0	140.3	140.6	141.0	141.7	142.3	142.9	143.0
Housefurnishings	144.4	140.0	140.3	141.4	142.4	143.6	144.0	144.6	144.4	144.6	145.9	146.6	147.4	147.5
Services less rent	171.9	164.8	166.2	167.5	168.3	169.2	169.6	170.9	171.9	172.7	174.6	175.7	177.7	179.0
Household services less rent	184.7	177.5	179.0	180.4	180.8	181.7	182.1	183.9	184.8	185.6	187.0	188.2	190.7	192.0
Transportation services	152.7	146.0	146.5	147.2	148.3	149.5	149.6	150.4	151.1	151.9	156.1	157.0	161.7	163.2
Medical care services	179.1	168.5	170.7	172.9	174.7	175.9	177.0	178.4	180.4	181.7	183.2	184.6	184.2	185.8
Other services	152.1	147.7	148.8	149.7	150.1	150.6	151.0	151.4	152.0	152.4	153.8	154.4	155.2	155.7

Table from Bureau of Labor Statistics

an "early bird" plan for passengers making down payments on reservations 60 days in advance of departure. The June, July and August early-bird fare, New York-London, would be $399.

The trans-Atlantic fare package had been submitted to the CAB by the International Air Transport Association. Although the new fares generally were slightly lower than those that had been in effect since November 1974, they remained about 10% higher than fares in effect during most of 1974.

Caribbean route fares increased—The CAB Feb. 25 approved fare increases of 4%-8% on most routes linking the U.S. with Caribbean points and Central and South America. Soaring fuel costs justified the increases, the CAB said.

Low-cost charter rules accepted—CAB adopted new charter-flight rule revisions Aug. 8 that represented a major departure from the board's policy. Effective Sept. 13, the action would provide air travelers with low-cost, ground-and-air charter packages which, according to the CAB, "expand greatly the availability of low-cost air transportation to the public."

Reaction to the changes was mixed, with charter lines solidly behind the program, and scheduled lines generally against it.

The new tour-charter packages would in many cases, according to the CAB, be less expensive than those of regularly scheduled air travel alone. As examples of possible price comparisons, the CAB listed a round trip "tourist" fare of $176 between New York City and Orlando, Florida, as compared with an estimated one-stop tour-charter price of $108, including hotel. Between Washington, D.C., and Paris the lowest discount fare was $353 as compared to an estimated $360 that would include ground charges for six nights.

According to the Washington Post, liberalization of charter rules represented a sharp departure in policy for the CAB, which for years had imposed regulations to keep low-cost charters from draining passenger traffic from scheduled carriers.

Airlines raise cargo rates—Claiming "continuing worldwide inflationary pressures," the 112 member airlines of the International Air Transport Association (IATA) agreed July 11 to hike cargo rates an average of 5% to 8% world-wide.

The rate change, effective Sept. 1 for Atlantic routes and Oct. 1 for all others, was the first increase since early 1974.

CAB OKs 3% air-fare rise. The Civil Aeronautics Board Nov. 7 approved a 3% fare increase for domestic flights, effective Nov. 15. The CAB earlier had rejected airlines' proposals that domestic fares be raised 3.5%-5%, contending that the increased revenues would provide carriers with "excessive return on revenue."

The 3% increase granted in November was the first approved by the CAB since a 4% temporary rise in domestic fares was permitted in October 1974 to offset soaring fuel costs. The CAB had extended the 4% increase June 13 and made it permanent Sept. 30.

Four airlines, angered by the CAB's denial of the proposed 3.5%-5% increase in June, August and September, took the agency to court Oct. 19. American Airlines, Delta Air Lines, Eastern Airlines and Trans World Airlines charged in U.S. District Court in Washington that the CAB had improperly altered its ground rules for establishing domestic-fare levels.

The Wall Street Journal reported Nov. 10, that the CAB's new chairman, John E. Robson, had stated in a speech that proposed fare increases would be rejected if rises in regular fares were intended to offset losses from discount-fare promotions.

The airline industry's trade group, the Air Transport Association had been pushing for higher fares to offset jet-fuel prices, which it claimed Aug. 4 had added $255 million to U.S. airlines' operating expenses in the first half of 1975 as compared to the first half of 1974.

The airline industry received support from the Ford Administration Aug. 19 in its quest to pass on higher jet-fuel costs. The Administration urged the CAB to make it easier for airlines to raise their fares.

In a petition to the CAB filed by the Transportation Dept., the Federal Energy Administration, and the Council on Wage and Price Stability, the Administration had estimated an increase of 3% in fares and cargo rates.

Bus fares up. The Interstate Commerce Commission (ICC) said June 2, 1975 that it had approved a 10% increase in passenger fares and package express rates for interstate bus travel that went into effect May 30.

Aluminum rises delayed. Aluminum producers agreed July 3, 1975 to delay previously announced price increases for 30 days after the Council on Wage and Price Stability requested the postponement to consider whether the price increases were justified during the current period of slack demand.

Complying with the request from Council Chairman Albert Rees were Aluminum Co. of America (Alcoa), the world's largest producer, and Reynolds Metals Co. Kaiser Aluminum and Chemical Corp., a unit of Kaiser Industries Corp., said at first it would not meet the government's appeal but agreed later when Alcoa announced compliance.

Alcan Aluminum Corp., a unit of Alcan Aluminium Ltd. of Canada, the world's second largest producer, July 3 announced a price increase in primary aluminum ingot from 39¢ a pound to 41¢, saying no request for a delay had been received from the council.

Kaiser, the third-ranking aluminum producer, was the first to announce price hikes, saying June 25 that product costs would be raised an average 2.7¢ a pound. Alcoa later announced a 2.3¢-a-pound average increase and other firms quickly followed suit.

At a press conference July 3, Rees said he feared that price increases by aluminum producers would trigger a rash of price hikes in other concentrated industries, such as steel and automobiles.

"If such industries make a decision to increase prices at the first stirrings of recovery, I am concerned that such actions could blunt the recovery that is in progress," Rees said.

The council, which lacked authority to order a price rollback, had asked for production and pricing information from Alcoa, Reynolds, Kaiser, and four other domestic producers in January, questioning why the industry was cutting production instead of prices in a period when demand was light. A spokesman for Alcoa said July 3 that the information justifying those practices had been submitted to the council. Alcoa had laid off 1,000 employes at its smelting plants and currently was operating at 74% of its total capacity, he added. (Anaconda Aluminum planned cutbacks to reduce its operating rate to 71% of capacity, according to the New York Times July 4.)

At hearings held July 21–22 by the Council on Wage & Price Stability, aluminum producers defended their plans to raise prices and warned that a second increase might be required later in the year.

A Kaiser Aluminum official argued July 21 that the company's announced increase, averaging 2.7%, was "fully cost-justified" by higher prices paid for raw material, labor and fuel. An Alcoa official echoed this view July 22, noting that since mid-1970, the price of bauxite had climbed 119%, the cost of fuel and power had increased 95%, and the price of aluminum ingot had risen 41%.

Kaiser also contended that its planned increase was "non-inflationary" and that the impact on consumers would be minimal. The price of refrigerators would rise 25¢ as a result of the price hike and automobiles would cost $1.85 more, he said.

Unless producers were able to improve profits and attract investors to finance needed expansion, the Kaiser spokesman said, the U.S. faced a severe shortage of aluminum. The industry needed $6 billion to meet an estimated increase in demand of 2 million tons by 1980, he said. Alcoa supported this viewpoint, saying that as the market strengthened, "we'll have to move prices upward again."

However, under questioning by council chairman Albert Rees, Kaiser conceded it planned no new capital-investment programs for at least the next two years, even with the anticipated increase. Rees also questioned the need for a price increase when the industry was operating at 75% of capacity, sales were down 46% over the year, and production was being stockpiled.

Rees said July 31 the council would seek no further delay for the price increases, despite its misgivings about the impact on consumer prices, because the aluminum companies' "rise in costs had been well documented."

Steel industry raises prices. U.S. Steel Corp., the nation's largest steel producer, announced Aug. 8 it would raise prices on a broad range of items an average 3.8% by Oct. 1. The No. 2-ranked steel maker, Bethlehem Steel Corp., said Aug. 13 it would match its rival's price increases.

These actions by the nation's dominant steel producers set the pricing pattern for the industry. Two smaller firms, Armco Steel Corp. and Wheeling-Pittsburgh Steel Corp., earlier had announced 9% price increases for flat-rolled products, the industry's largest trade volume group comprising 41% of annual shipments.

U.S. Steel and Bethlehem, which together controlled 30% of the flat-rolled product market, held their increases for the line to 5.7%, an average $17 a ton, forcing Armco and Wheeling-Pittsburgh, the nation's fifth and ninth largest steel makers, to scale back their price increases. Other steel producers, which had delayed their pricing decisions until U.S. Steel acted, subsequently set similar price boosts.

U.S. Steel's pricing package was more comprehensive than those announced by Armco and Wheeling-Pittsburgh, and according to the Wall Street Journal Aug. 11, would result in higher total revenues than a single 9% hike in the price of flat-rolled items.

According to U.S. Steel, prices for 20%–25% of its product line were unchanged; rail costs were raised 10%; the price of certain pipes was hiked 9%; prices for cold-rolled sheet products, another high volume line, were raised about 7%; the cost of reinforcing bars was reduced 4%–9% to counter what U.S. Steel termed the dumping of imported items by European steel makers.

The Council on Wage and Price Stability, which had asked the major steel makers to "exercise restraint" after the Armco and Wheeling-Pittsburgh price decisions were announced, was apparently not displeased with the U.S. Steel action. "The important thing is that U.S. Steel has verified what most people thought—that this [9% increase] wasn't justified by the market," a council spokesman said. "We didn't think the market could take a price hike of that magnitude. We thought it would meet resistance. We thought it would hurt the recovery if it went through," he added.

Other analysts expressed concern about the immediate impact of higher steel prices on consumer products, particularly autos and appliances, whose manufacturers relied heavily on flat-rolled steel products. (Auto makers, trying to limit their price increases for the 1976 model year after a disastrous 1975 sales year, reportedly exerted strong pressure on the major steel producers to hold the line on their price boosts and threatened to cancel orders from Armco and Wheeling-Pittsburgh if the 9% increase were implemented.)

According to the Journal Aug. 11, a 3% rise in overall steel prices would add another .1% to the government's wholesale price index, which already indicated a resurgence of double-digit inflation.

Analysts also feared the effect of industry-wide steel price increases on the nation's long-term economic recovery. An auto official said the steel industry's action would produce a "halo effect," giving "everyone an excuse they wouldn't otherwise have to recover other price increases."

"It's a pretty dispiriting development to find ourselves coming out of the worst recession in 40 years and everyone rushing to raise prices," a Pittsburgh banker told the Journal. "There's no hope for a recovery in a meaningful sense without reasonable price stability," he said.

U.S. Steel argued that by delaying the effective dates of its most significant increases until October, it was acting "to encourage the economic recovery currently underway." Like the aluminum industry, which had resisted government jaw-boning efforts and announced price increases recently, the steel industry cited rising costs as justification for its latest price increases.

Auto prices raised. In the face of higher costs, lower sales and declining profits, automobile makers during the second half of 1975 announced raises in the prices of 1976-model cars.

General Motors Aug. 13 announced a 4.4% increase in the average base price of its 1976 models. The actual cost to consumers was said to be significantly higher because of less-visible price increases.

By camouflaging certain price boosts, the auto industry hoped to soften the impact of higher prices and offset consumer resistance to the new models. Prices for 1975-model cars had been raised about 8%–9%, an increase that contributed to the sharp reduction in sales over the year.

Contributing to the hidden costs of GM's new models were a 6% hike in the cost of popular optional equipment, the elimination of some standard items, and a reduction in dealers' profit margins, which was expected to make discounts negotiated with car buyers more difficult to win.

According to GM, the cost of producing a car climbed $375 over the year. At the same time, officials said, GM's profit margin was slashed by a steep decline in sales. In a statement announcing the 1976 price increases, chairman Thomas A. Murphy said GM decided not to try to recoup all its costs through price increases in order not to "dampen the returning demand in the marketplace."

GM Aug. 26 announced a 7.3% average rise in the base price of its 1976-model trucks.

American Motors Corp. Aug. 1 had announced a $200 average (5.8%) increase in prices of its 1976 models.

Ford Motor Co. announced Sept. 11 that it was increasing the average base price of its 1976 models by $78, or 1.8%. But actual costs would be much higher because much heretofore standard equipment was being made optional and would require additional payment.

An average $136 in standard equipment was stripped from the typical Ford model, officials said. According to GM, standard equipment worth $6 was eliminated from its typical new model.

Both auto makers also raised the price of optional equipment—Ford by 3.2% and GM by 6%. The total changes meant that consumers would pay about $247 (4.7%) more than in the previous year for Ford's new model with average equipment, and about $268, or 4.7% more, for GM's 1976 car with average equipment.

AMC revised its prices Sept. 23 to match the base-price increases of its larger competitors.

AMC's revised base-price increase averaged $154, or 4.4%. However, hidden costs also were built into the total price of a new car: optional equipment prices were raised an average 5%; dealer preparation charges, which heretofore had been included in the base prices, were not reflected in the new sticker price; and dealers' markups were reduced on high-volume small cars and increased on the less popular intermediate-size cars.

The Chrysler Corp. said Oct. 2 that its base prices would be increased an average $122, or 2.8%. However, the actual cost of a new car equipped with the same items as in the previous model year would rise by an average $178, or 4.4%, over 1975 because of hidden price increases. Among the changes in Chrysler pricing: certain previously standard equipment was made optional; the prices of some optional equipment were raised; dealers' markups were reduced; and transportation costs were increased.

Additional price increases were announced by the auto makers in December.

'76 car-price rises called 'restrained'—Price increases for 1976 model cars were "considerably less" than the auto industry's projected costs for those models, according to a study published Nov. 11 by the Council on Wage and Price Stability.

The council noted that although the cost of producing an average 1976 passenger car with average optional equipment was $388 higher than for a similar 1975 model, wholesale prices of 1976 cars rose an average of only $222 over the year.

Based on these figures, the council concluded that the "automobile industry has shown considerably more restraint in its 1976 price increases than it did in the 1975 model year."

According to the council, the industry's production costs for the 1975 model year were $630 higher than in 1974. Auto makers attempted to recover 90% of the higher costs through sharp increases in price, but the strategy backfired when consumers refused to buy the higher-priced 1975 models. Sales plunged and the industry recovered far less than its 90% target.

In 1976, the council noted, the industry set a 57% recovery target, hoping that a rise in sales would compensate for the relatively small hike in wholesale prices.

The study of car prices was undertaken, the council said, because car price increases had a strong impact on consumer prices in general. The council added, however, that the study also was intended to clear up "apparent" public confusion about actual price increases for 1976 model cars. The confusion stemmed in part, the council said, from the industry's decision to minimize dollar increases in the well-publicized base price by eliminating certain standard equipment and making optional equipment more costly on 1976 models.

Auto costs rise 14%—Inflation and higher gasoline prices contributed to a 14% rise in the cost of driving the family car during the past 12-month period, according to figures released Sept. 7 by the Hertz Corp.'s car-leasing division.

Gasoline, which had cost an average 35¢ a gallon in mid-1973, currently cost about 57.5¢; depreciation, the difference between a car's purchase price and its trade-in value, rose an average 2¢ a mile over a 12-month span; interest costs, insurance, license fees, parts service and repairs also increased.

Cost of higher education rises. The cost of a four-year college education rose 8% in the 1974–75 school year, Business Week magazine said in its Aug. 4 issue. The average cost of tuition, fees, room and board at private institutions was put at $3,432 annually; for state residents at public institutions, the cost was $1,587.

Data gathered by the Life Insurance Marketing & Research Association included the following colleges and their current yearly costs:

	Undergraduate enrollment	Tuition, fees, room & board	Additional for out-of-staters
Alabama U.	12,805	$1,729	$595
Amherst	1,340	$5,150	—
Antioch	1,725	$4,741	—
Bennington	595	$6,280	—
Brown	5,100	$5,772	—
Columbia	2,800	$5,573	—
Cornell U.	11,300	$5,425	—
City University of N.Y.	12,600	$116*	$1,200
Harvard	4,600	$5,930	—
Jackson State	4,925	$1,377	$600
Johns Hopkins	2,100	$5,100	—
Louisiana State	19,000	$1,104	$730
Maryland U.	24,100	$1,828	$1,848
Massachusetts U.	18,500	$1,980	$600
M.I.T.	4,200	$6,045	—
Michigan U.	30,085	$2,205	$1,800
New York U.	6,550	$5,200	—
N. Carolina State	12,080	$1,799	$1,546
Notre Dame	6,750	$4,290	—
Ohio State	38,000	$2,130	$1,050
Penn State	42,000	$2,199	$1,200
Princeton	4,300	$5,575	—
Rutgers	12,990	$2,140	$585
Sarah Lawrence	775	$6,290	—
S. Carolina U.	13,900	$1,904	$710
Texas U.	31,000	$1,684	$1,080
U.C.L.A.	19,475	$2,125	$1,500
Wisconsin U.	22,900	$1,825	$1,445
Yale	4,950	$5,920	—

*No housing

Postal rates increased. A postal-rate rise went into effect Dec. 31, 1975 after a lower court injunction against it was lifted Dec. 29 by the U.S. Court of Appeals for the District of Columbia.

A last-minute plea from the bulk-mailing industry to block the increase was denied by Chief Justice Warren E. Burger Dec. 30.

The increases included a raise in the first-class rate that brought the cost of mailing a letter up from 10¢ to 13¢ for the first ounce.

Wages Rise

Wages, like prices, continued to rise throughout 1975. Gross average weekly earnings of private, nonfarm workers rose from $159.43 in December 1974 to about $170.82 in December 1975. "Real" earnings (in terms of "constant," 1967 dollars), however, went up during this period from $102.59 to only about $102.78. The purchasing power of the average private nonfarm worker's higher weekly earnings in 1975 was actually less than the purchasing power of his 1974 earnings.

Major collective bargaining settlements reached during 1975 generally provided for larger wage increases than agreements negotiated during 1974, according to preliminary Bureau of Labor Statistics estimates. The wage settlements reached in 1975 averaged about 10.2% for the contract's first year and about 7.8% a year over the life of the contract. Wage and benefit settlements averaged about 11.2% during the first year and about 8% annually for the life of the contract.

Wage & Benefit Settlements in Major Collective Bargaining Units

(In percent)

Sector and measure	Annual average						Quarterly average					
	1970	1971	1972	1973	1974	1975p	1974		1975p			
							III	IV	I	II	III	IV
Wage and benefit settlements, all industries:												
First-year settlements	13.1	13.1	8.5	7.1	10.7	11.2	11.9	14.6	13.0	9.3	11.4	14.2
Annual rate over life of contract	9.1	8.8	7.4	6.1	7.8	8.0	8.0	8.7	7.5	7.7	8.6	8.8
Wage rate settlements, all industries:												
First-year settlements	11.9	11.6	7.3	5.8	9.8	10.2	11.2	10.3	12.5	9.8	10.0	11.5
Annual rate over life of contract	8.9	8.1	6.4	5.1	7.3	7.8	7.7	7.2	7.7	8.3	7.9	8.1
Manufacturing:												
First-year settlements	8.1	10.9	6.6	5.9	8.7	9.9	10.2	9.0	11.6	10.9	8.8	9.8
Annual rate over life of contract	6.0	7.3	5.6	4.9	6.1	8.1	7.1	5.9	8.5	8.6	7.7	7.2
Nonmanufacturing (excluding construction):												
First-year settlements	14.2	12.2	8.2	6.0	10.2	12.0	10.2	11.1	13.7	12.2	11.7	12.4
Annual rate over life of contract	10.2	8.6	7.3	5.4	7.2	7.9	6.6	7.9	7.6	8.0	8.2	8.2
Construction:												
First-year settlements	17.6	12.6	6.9	5.0	11.0	8.0	15.1	12.9	4.5	8.5	8.0	10.4
Annual rate over life of contract	14.9	10.8	6.0	5.1	9.6	7.4	11.7	10.1	4.1	8.1	7.4	10.1

Effective Wage Adjustments Going Into Effect in Major Collective Bargaining Units

Sector and measure	Average annual changes						Average quarterly changes						
	1970	1971	1972	1973	1974	1975 p	1974			1975p			
							II	III	IV	I	II	III	IV
Total effective wage rate adjustment, all industries	8.8	9.2	6.6	7.0	9.4	8.6	3.0	3.4	1.6	1.7	2.1	3.3	1.5
Change resulting from—													
Current settlement	5.1	4.3	1.7	3.0	4.8	2.7	1.6	2.0	.8	.6	.7	.7	.5
Prior settlement	3.1	4.2	4.2	2.7	2.6	3.7	.9	.9	.3	.6	1.1	1.5	.5
Escalator provision	.6	.7	.7	1.3	1.9	2.2	.5	.5	.5	.4	.3	1.0	.4
Manufacturing	7.1	8.0	5.6	7.3	10.3	8.4	3.5	3.0	2.0	1.8	2.1	2.8	1.6
Nonmanufacturing	10.5	10.3	7.4	6.7	8.6	8.8	2.5	3.7	1.2	1.6	2.2	3.6	1.4

NOTE: Because of rounding and compounding, the sums of individual items may not equal totals

pPreliminary

Tables from Bureau of Labor Statistics

White collar salaries outpaced by inflation. Average salaries paid white-collar employes in private industry increased a record 9% in the 12 months ended March 31, 1975 but failed to keep pace with consumer prices, up 10.3% over the same period, the Labor Department announced July 9.

The annual increase, which followed a 6.4% gain made in the 1973–74 period, was the largest since records were first compiled in 1961. For clerical jobs, increases averaged 9.6%; for professional, administrative and technical occupations, salaries rose 8.3%.

Pacts reached with 4 rail unions. Negotiators for the nation's railroads and four major rail unions reported agreement Jan. 22, 1975 on three-year contracts calling for a 41% increase in wages (24%) and benefits (17%). The industry bargaining group was the National Railway Labor Conference. The unions involved, all AFL-CIO, were the United Transportation Union, the Brotherhood of Maintenance of Way Employes, the Brotherhood of Railroad Signalmen and the Sheet Metal Workers International Association.

The wage provisions would provide increases of 10% retroactive to Jan. 1, 5% in October, 3% in April 1976 and 4% in July 1977. In addition, four cost-of-living increments were due on Jan. 1 and July 1 of 1976 and 1977 (1¢-an-hour for each increase of .4% in the government's consumer price index for the first three increments, lowering to a .3% trigger for the last increment, up to an overall 68¢ maximum rise).

The contracts also would provide a 10th paid holiday and industry payment of a premium increase of $23 a month on current health and welfare coverage. A dental insurance plan was to be adopted by March 1976.

The pacts covered about 45% of the nation's railroad employes.

Clerks win raise—A nationwide rail strike was avoided July 18 when an agreement was reached in the contract dispute between the nation's railroads and the AFL-CIO Brotherhood of Railway Clerks.

The settlement incorporated under a three-year contract the 41% wage-and-benefit increase set in the pattern settlements already approved by seven other rail unions. The union also won a provision beyond the pattern for a cost-of-living increment due Jan. 1, 1978, the day after the new contract would expire.

The agreement was sudden. The union strike deadline, when selective job action was anticipated against major railroads if no agreement were reached, had been 12:01 a.m. July 28, and negotiations had collapsed July 17. The accord came in an unscheduled bargaining session called by W. J. Usery Jr., chief federal mediator.

The 27 general chairmen of the union, which represented 117,000 rail workers, unanimously ratified terms of the new contract July 22. Dennis, saying the average wage of his unionist would rise from $11,818.08 a year to $16,582.99 by Jan. 1, 1978, called the new pact "the best in the history of the American railroad industry."

Last unions settle—Negotiators for the nation's railroads and four shopcraft unions reached agreement on a new three-year contract Dec. 4. The pact, covering 70,000 workers, was similar to the package agreement accepted previously by other unions representing 85% of the industry's organized employes. It contained a 41% improvement in wages and benefits.

The shopcraft unions, the last rail union to settle, insisted on some work-rule changes unique to their jobs, which involved maintenance, repair and rebuilding of rail equipment. The issue was resolved with more specific language on job assignments and on arrangements for outside subcontracting by the carriers. The contract also provided an extra three-cent-an-hour wage increment, effective in 1978, for certain workers who claimed wage-inequities.

The accord averted a nationwide rail strike threatened for Dec. 4.

The shopcraft unions, all AFL-CIO, were the International Brotherhood of Boilermakers, the International Brotherhood of Electrical Workers, the International Brotherhood of Firemen and Oilers, and the Brotherhood of Railway Carmen.

Gross & Spendable Weekly Earnings

Year and month	Private nonagricultural workers						Manufacturing workers					
	Gross average weekly earnings		Spendable average weekly earnings				Gross average weekly earnings		Spendable average weekly earnings			
			Worker with no dependents		Worker with 3 dependents				Worker with no dependents		Worker with 3 dependents	
	Current dollars	1967 dollars	Current dollars	1967 dollars	Current dollars	1967 dollars	Current dollars	1967 dollars	Current dollars	1967 dollars	Current dollars	1967 dollars
1960	$80.67	$90.95	$65.59	$73.95	$72.96	$82.25	$89.72	$101.15	$72.57	$81.82	$80.11	$90.32
1961	82.60	92.19	67.08	74.87	74.48	83.13	92.34	103.06	74.60	83.26	82.18	91.72
1962	85.91	94.82	69.56	76.78	76.99	84.98	96.56	106.58	77.86	85.94	85.53	94.40
1963	88.46	96.47	71.05	77.48	78.56	85.67	99.63	108.65	79.82	87.04	87.58	95.51
1964	91.33	98.31	75.04	80.78	82.57	88.88	102.97	110.84	84.40	90.85	92.18	99.22
1965	95.06	100.59	78.99	83.59	86.30	91.32	107.53	113.79	89.08	94.26	96.78	102.41
1966	98.82	101.67	81.29	83.63	88.66	91.21	112.34	115.58	91.57	94.21	99.45	102.31
1967	101.84	101.84	83.38	83.38	90.86	90.86	114.90	114.90	93.28	93.28	101.26	101.26
1968	107.73	103.39	86.71	83.21	95.28	91.44	122.51	117.57	97.70	93.76	106.75	102.45
1969	114.61	104.38	90.96	82.84	99.99	91.07	129.51	117.95	101.90	92.81	111.44	101.49
1970	119.46	102.72	95.94	82.49	104.61	89.95	133.73	114.99	106.62	91.68	115.90	99.66
1971	127.28	104.93	103.78	85.56	112.41	92.67	142.44	117.43	114.97	94.78	124.24	102.42
1972	136.16	108.67	111.65	89.11	121.09	96.64	154.69	123.46	125.32	100.02	135.56	108.19
1973	145.43	109.26	117.54	88.31	127.41	95.73	166.06	124.76	132.29	99.39	143.20	107.59
1974	154.45	104.57	124.14	84.05	134.37	90.97	176.40	119.43	139.90	94.72	151.25	102.40
1975: January	157.08	100.63	125.99	80.71	136.40	87.38	180.73	115.78	143.09	91.67	154.63	99.06
February	157.79	100.38	126.49	80.46	136.94	87.11	180.18	114.62	142.68	90.76	154.20	98.09
March	158.06	100.16	126.68	80.28	137.15	86.91	182.66	115.75	144.51	91.58	156.13	98.94
April	159.22	100.39	127.49	80.38	138.05	87.04	184.00	116.02	145.50	91.74	157.18	99.10
May	160.38	100.68	131.25	82.39	145.37	91.26	185.25	116.29	148.38	93.15	164.12	103.03
June	163.71	101.94	133.60	83.19	147.97	92.14	188.81	117.57	150.81	93.90	166.75	103.83
July	164.89	101.60	134.43	82.83	148.89	91.74	188.55	116.17	150.63	92.81	166.56	102.62
August	166.90	102.52	135.84	83.44	150.47	92.43	191.35	117.54	152.55	93.70	168.62	103.57
September	168.43	102.95	136.88	83.67	151.65	92.70	196.58	120.16	156.36	95.57	172.48	105.43
October	168.69	102.48	137.06	83.27	151.85	92.25	195.51	118.78	155.56	94.51	171.69	104.31
November	169.42	102.31	137.56	83.07	152.41	92.04	197.69	119.38	157.18	94.92	173.30	104.65
December[p]	170.82	102.72	138.52	83.30	153.48	92.29	204.00	122.67	161.85	97.32	177.95	107.01

[p]Preliminary Table from Bureau of Labor Statistics

West Coast dock pact. Negotiators for the International Longshoremen's and Warehousemen's Union and the Pacific Maritime Association, representing West Coast shippers, announced agreement Feb. 10, 1975 to extend their contract, due to expire June 30, until July 1, 1977 with increased wages and benefits.

The wage guaranteed for workers displaced by mechanization or idled by industry slowdowns would rise from its current level of $200 a week to $234 on March 1, $250 in 1976 and $270 in 1977.

The contract covered 12,000 workers. Negotiations were initiated earlier than usual because of the union's concern about inflation and the possibility of a wage-price freeze from Congress.

Boston dock wage guaranteed—Dock workers on strike for a higher guaranteed annual wage closed the port of Boston during June. The strike began May 31 and ended with votes of ratification June 28–29 for a guarantee of 1,500 hours of pay per year, even if the hours were not worked. With the current wage of $6.80 an hour, this amounted to a guaranteed annual income of $10,200. The 600 dock workers involved were members of the AFL-CIO International Longshoremen's Association (three locals) and the AFL-CIO Brotherhood of Railway, Airline and Steamship Clerks (one local).

Machinists ratify TWA pact. The AFL-CIO International Association of Machinists (IAM) announced March 14 ratification of a 26-month contract with Trans World Airlines that would increase hourly wages more than 19%. The pact, covering 12,000 mechanics, ramp-service and other employes, was retroactive to Sept. 1, 1973, when the previous contract expired. The retroactive pay increases of the new pact, which would expire Oct. 31, totaled $21.7 million.

Base pay for top-rated mechanics would rise from the $6.60 an hour under the previous contract to $7.77 an hour on May 1. That included a 10¢-an-hour cost of living (COL) increment. An additional COL increment—1¢ an hour for each rise of .3 in the consumer price index (up to a maximum of 10¢ an hour a year)—was payable Sept. 1.

Retirement benefits were improved, from $8 monthly for each year of service to a $10.50–$15.00 range according to pay grade. Dental and major medical benefits were boosted 35%, severance pay was increased and an additional paid floating holiday was authorized.

TWU, Pan Am agree on 2-year pacts—The AFL-CIO Transport Workers Union announced ratification Sept. 25 of new two-year contracts with Pan American World Airways. The pacts, covering 10,200 employes, called for raises for top-rated mechanics of about 18%, from the current $7.96 an hour to $9.36 by October, 1977. Monthly pay of flight attendants would go to $1,117 from the current $973.

Raise ends McDonnell Douglas strike. Members of the AFL-CIO International Association of Machinists May 11, 1975 ratified a three-year contract ending a 13-week strike at McDonnell Douglas Corp.'s plant in St. Louis.

The agreement, covering 11,500 workers, would provide a 31¢-an-hour wage rise the first year. A 78¢-an-hour increase already being paid under a cost-of-living clause was folded into the base wage rate, making the first-year increase in the base $1.09. A 3% wage increase would be paid in both the second and third years of the contract.

The strike had begun Feb. 10. A strike at the same time by 7,000 machinists at McDonnell Douglas facilities in California and at Cape Canaveral, Fla. was resolved earlier on similar terms. A ratification vote was taken April 12; he workers returned to work April 15.

Similar terms had been accepted by 11,000 members of the United Auto Workers at McDonnell Douglas' Long Beach, Calif. facility in February.

Mechanics strike United Air Lines. A 16-day strike against United Air Lines ended Dec. 21 with ratification of a new three-year contract to provide wage increases averaging 28% for the 16,800 employes involved. They were members of the AFL-CIO International Association of Machinists. In addition to mechanics, the union represented ramp-service and storage employes, food-service employes and flight dispatchers.

The strike, which began Dec. 6, grounded United, the nation's largest airline. United normally carried 90,000 passengers on an average day, or nearly a fourth of all the nation's air passengers.

Employes covered by the pact were to receive a 5% wage hike retroactive to Nov. 1. Subsequent hikes would follow every six months, beginning on July 1, 1976 and running to 1978. These boosts were 4.7%, 2.8%, 4.3%, 3.4% and 2.2%.

In addition, the employes were to get two cost-of-living increases of 12¢ an hour each on Nov. 1 of 1976 and 1977, based on the assumption of an annual rise in the consumer price index of at least 3.6%.

The pay boosts would bring the base pay scale for mechanics to $10 an hour in mid-1978 (from $7.84 an hour), for ramp-service and storage workers to $8.22 an hour (from $6.40), for cooks to $8.12 an hour (from $6.33), for porters to $5.39 an hour (from $4.13).

Pennsylvania strike ends. The first statewide strike in Pennsylvania's history ended July 19 when 12,000 welfare and unemployment workers ratified a contract for wage increases of 12% over two years. The terms were similar to those accepted earlier by 75,000 other state employes.

Northwest Airlines pilots' pact. An agreement between Northwest Airlines and the AFL-CIO Air Line Pilots Association was reached at 2:00 a.m. July 19, the deadline set for a walkout by the line's 1,550 pilots. The average increase in the new contract was estimated at 34% in wages and benefits over three years.

Postal pact set, strike averted. Negotiators for the Postal Service and four unions representing 600,000 employes reached agreement on a new contract July 21.

Although the threat of a strike was diminished by the agreement, which was to be submitted to the union membership for ratification, the possibility of an increase in postal rates was "quite certain," according to Postmaster General Benjamin F. Bailar. (The postal rate increase took effect at the end of year.)

Postal workers were forbidden to strike, as were other federal employes, but wildcat action had been threatened by several major locals, such as in New York, Philadelphia and Chicago.

Wages and retention of a no-layoffs clause were key issues in the bargaining.

The contract was to provide increases in the hourly wage that would amount to $1,500 on an annual basis by the end of the contract. The first increase, due upon ratification, would be worth $400 a year. The second, due in March 1976, would be equal to $250 a year, as would the third, due in October 1976. The fourth, worth $600 a year, was due in July 1977. The pre-pact average wage was about $13,500 a year at top scale.

The workers also were to receive cost-of-living adjustments each May and November of the contract, based on the previous contract provision of one cent an hour for each .4-point rise in the consumer price index.

The no-layoffs clause was retained but the Postal Service would be permitted under the new pact to hire temporary employes for up to 180 days instead of 89 days as under the previous contract. Such employes, unprotected by the no-layoff clause, would be limited to no more than 10% of the workers at a location.

Another issue involved the Service's experimental use of a computer to plot mail-delivery routes, which the union feared could lead to job reduction through attrition. Under the new agreement, the Service would be permitted to test new work or time standards and the union could take them to grievance and arbitration proceedings before they could be imposed.

The Service's share of the cost of certain health benefits was increased under the new contract to 75%, up from 65%.

The unions involved, in addition to the NALC, representing 193,000 workers, included the AFL-CIO American Postal Workers Union, 318,000 workers; the AFL-CIO Laborers International Union, 40,000 members of its mail handlers division; the unaffiliated National Rural Letter Carriers Association, 50,000 workers.

City workers strike. Strikes by city employes broke out in several places in July.

City policemen in Albuquerque, N.M. went on a 10-day strike despite a court order to return to work. They reacted to that by resigning. The settlement, voted July 22, included reinstatement for the 350 strikers, and an 8% pay rise.

In Cleveland, some 3,600 of the city's 7,400 nonuniformed workers went on strike for seven days before accepting a new 30-month contract July 27.

San Francisco police-fire strike. Mayor Joseph L. Alioto invoked emergency powers Aug. 21 to impose a wage settlement and end a strike by the city's police and firemen. The strikers accepted the settlement, which included the 13% pay raise they sought, but it was rejected by the city's legislature, an 11-member board of supervisors, which had offered a 6.5% increase.

The strike by the 1,935-member police force began Aug. 18 despite Alioto's threat to dismiss officers failing to report for work. It continued despite a state court's temporary restraining order against it and a later order that the pickets be disarmed. Although in civilian dress, some of the picketing policemen wore their weapons.

The pressure for settlement increased when the city's 1,781 firemen joined the strike Aug. 20, a move that threatened to close the city's airport, which received firefighting coverage from the city.

Another complication, the threat of a strike by 1,900 transit workers, set for Aug. 22, dissolved Aug. 20 when a 6.9% pay hike was accepted for settlement.

Alioto, who was attempting to mediate between the board and the unionized police and fire unions, announced a settlement Aug. 21 for the 13% pay hike, effective Oct. 15. It would raise starting pay for policemen and firemen from $16,044 to $18,816. Part of the settlement was that no reprisals would be permitted against the strikers.

The board unanimously rejected the settlement, but Alioto immediately invoked emergency powers under the city's Charter and imposed the settlement as law in the interest of public safety.

Alioto spoke of meeting some of the costs of the settlement through further city economies and through an increase of 6¢ to 7¢ in the property tax rate (currently $12.75 for each $1,000 of assessed valuation).

Teachers strike, seek higher pay. The reopening of schools in September was marked by a rash of teachers' strikes. Teachers in 12 states were on strike by the first week of September. The action affected at least 961,000 elementary and high school pupils, according to United Press International count. Of the total, 530,000 were in Chicago, where 27,700 teachers walked out Sept. 3.

The issues largely were wages, class size and contract retractions. In Chicago, teachers were seeking a cost-of-living pay increase, a reduction in class size and improved fringe benefits. The board's budget did not contain funds for a pay raise and called for elimination of 1,525 teaching positions.

Strikes also were affecting 40,000 other Illinois schoolchildren; 140,000 pupils in Pennsylvania; 80,000 in Rhode Island; 47,000 in Michigan; 41,000 in New York; 24,000 in California; 16,800 in Montana; 15,000 in Massachusetts; 14,200 in Delaware; 8,000 in New Jersey; and 5,500 in Ohio. A strike in Indiana at Marion ended after a day when the teachers agreed to a 7% pay rise Sept. 4. It involved 400 teachers and 11,000 pupils.

A National Education Association spokesman Sept. 6 said that teacher contracts in 2,300 of the country's 16,000 school districts remained unsettled.

New York City teachers also went on strike Sept. 9, the second day of the new term. The strike, by members of the AFL-CIO United Federation of Teachers, effectively halted the education of 1.1 million public schoolchildren. Only 1,300 of the 60,000 teachers in the system reported for work, and many of the 37,129 pupils who went to school were sent home that day. The union had called the strike on charges that contract provisions on class size had been violated and conditions in general were chaotic on opening day. But the union's contract expired at midnight Sept. 8 and negotiations on a new one were stalemated. The major issues were the school board's demands for increased teacher productivity and the union's stand against yielding benefits and working conditions negotiated in previous contracts. The strike was settled Sept. 16 under an agreement that included a $300 cost-of-living adjustment and "longevity" increments of $1,500 annually for those with more than 15 years' service and of $750 for those with 10–15 years.

Teachers in Boston's public schools ended an illegal six-day-old strike Sept. 30

after their union and the Boston School Committee reached agreement on a new, one-year contract providing for a 6% raise, job security and money for teaching materials.

A six-week strike by Wilmington, Del. teachers was settled Oct. 10 with agreement on a three-year pact providing an 18% pay rise in three equal steps.

In New York state, a 28-day strike by teachers in Nyack ended Nov. 24 with ratification of a two-year pact increasing the base salary, which was $10,550, to $11,000 the first year and to $11,800 the second year. The walkout, which affected 3,700 students and began Oct. 14, involved penalties for defiance of the state's Taylor Law forbidding strikes by public employes.

10-year labor pact for N.Y. printers. Representatives of the New York Typographical Union No. 6 and the city's commercial printing shops reached agreement Oct. 27 on a 10-year contract with major job security and automation provisions.

The contract would guarantee full day-scale pay for all current employes of the union in the shops, some 4,400 (including about 700 currently working less than full time) in 400 shops. The current day rate was $344.44 per five-day week. However, the firms could hire computer typists—employing a typewriter-like keyboard rather than a linotype to set copy—at wages lower than the journeyman's scale.

The pact would provide annual wage increases of 3% plus cost-of-living increments to be determined quarterly and to equal the percentage increase in the cost of living.

The work week, currently 34½ hours for the day shift and 32½ for the "lobster," or early morning, shift (current wage $375.44), would be shortened by two hours by 1984.

On automation, the contract would permit use of any form available. Manning requirements under the previous contract would be eliminated, and the shops could establish starting times that overlapped the current definitions of day, night and "lobster" turns. Retirement would be mandatory at age 68 as of Jan. 2, 1977. The contract also provided a $10,000 bonus for those over 60 who chose to retire by July 5, 1976.

The shipyard, which employed a total of 17,500 persons, was the nation's largest nuclear submarine manufacturer. At the time of the strike, the yard was working on $2 billion worth of orders from the U.S. Navy.

Long shipyard strike ends. A five-month strike by 10,000 shipbuilders at the Electric Boat division of General Dynamics Corp. in Groton, Conn. ended Dec. 1. The return to work, 154 days after the strike began July 1, followed ratification of a settlement reached by negotiators Nov. 20.

The new 43-month contract called for a cumulative wage increase of 41% over the life of the pact, beginning with an immediate raise of 13% to an average wage of $5.10 an hour. The old rate of $4.51 an hour would rise over the 43-month period to $6.64, counting cost-of-living increases plus increases in the basic rate.

Job issues also were involved in the dispute, with the union concerned about maintenance of craft boundaries. Some 11 unions in all went on strike, amalgamated under the Metal Trades Council banner.

Other Developments

Record '75 bankruptcy petitions. Bankruptcy petitions filed in fiscal 1975 totaled a record high 254,484, according to Commerce Clearing House Oct. 15. The figure marked a 34.3% increase over fiscal 1974 and far exceeded the previous record set in 1967 when 208,329 petitions were filed.

With 262,283 bankruptcy cases pending at the end of June, the case load also was at a record level. (It was more than 60,000 above the previous peak set in 1971.) The number of cases closed during 1975 totaled 192,792, up 14,615 from 1974.

Individuals filed 88.2% of all bankruptcy petitions entered with the courts during the year, but the number of business filings totaled 30,130, an all-time high and an increase of 20,746 over 1974. (Business filings were made by all who engaged in trade, including farmers and professionals.) The proportion of business bankruptcies to total filings rose to 11.8%—the largest percentage since 1968.

As usual, most bankruptcies, 253,198, were voluntary. California, with nearly 50,000 cases pending, led the state-by-state listing. Other states with bankruptcies exceeding 13,000 were Ohio, New York, Illinois, and Alabama.

(Merger activity during 1975 also was lower than in 1974, according to a merger consulting firm Oct. 8. W. T. Grimm & Co. reported that during the first nine months of the year, mergers totaled 1,732, down 25% from the same period of 1974. The sharpest decline occurred in the 1st quarter when merger activity was off 34% over a 12-month period; falloffs of 21% and 19% were reported in the 2nd and 3rd quarters.)

Postal deficit reported. A record $989 million deficit in fiscal 1975 for the Postal Service was reported by Postmaster General Benjamin Bailar to a Congressional hearing Dec. 10. The deficit amounted to more than a penny on each piece of mail carried (89.27 billion pieces, or 419 for each U.S. resident).

The record deficit, more than double the previous year's deficit of $438 million, was attributed largely to inflation and a .9% decline in total mail volume.

An even larger deficit was forecast for fiscal 1976—$1.4 billion, a rise from the $1 billion deficit previously forecast by the service.

Bailar said the anticipated deficit for the current 1976 fiscal year took into consideration a postal rate increase scheduled for Dec. 28, which would hike first-class mail to 13¢ for the first ounce from 10¢.

The Dec. 28 rate boost, announced Oct. 2, would be effected on a temporary basis while the Postal Rate Commission considered permanent rate rises, averaging 26%, proposed by the service on Sept. 18. The temporary and permanent rates were identical except for postcards, where the temporary rate, 9¢ each, could not be raised to the proposed permanent rate, 10¢, because of a prohibition against raising rates on a temporary basis more than one-third of the current rate, which was 7¢.

A temporary increase was permitted under law when the commission did not act within 90 days on the service's request for new permanent rates.

Recovery Uncertain

Recession's End Questioned

By mid-1975 many Ford Administration leaders were reporting indications that the recession had ended and that the nation was on its way to economic recovery. Some sources, both in and out of the Administration, were more pessimistic, however, and warned of serious threats to recovery.

Greenspan sees recession ending. Alan Greenspan, chairman of the President's Council of Economic Advisers, said in a televised interview June 22, "The recession for all practical purposes is over." On the basis of "pretty conclusive" evidence, Greenspan said, he had concluded that the "recessionary forces are pretty well spent and the next phase of economic activity is pretty well on the upside."

Greenspan warned, however, that large federal deficits and an "overexpansion of the money supply" were "dangerous potential forces" that could "up-end this recovery."

While voicing optimism that the recession had begun to bottom out, Greenspan cautioned that the unemployment rate would not show improvement until the fall.

Administration sees recovery underway. Administration officials were buoyed by several economic reports indicating, they said, that the recession had ended.

A visible upturn in industrial production in June, reversing an eight-month decline, was a sign that "we are in the early stages of a recovery," James Pate, assistant secretary of commerce, said July 15.

Pate was further encouraged July 17 by the Gross National Product report for the second quarter, when total economic output fell only .3%. The slight decline indicated the economy was "at the bottom and is beginning to go up," according to White House Press Secretary Ron Nessen. Commerce Secretary Rogers C. B. Morton also termed the GNP figures "heartening because they indicate that the recession has finally hit bottom."

However, Administration optimism about the nation's economic prospects was tempered July 22 by the report that consumer prices had risen .8% in June, double the May rate of inflation.

Although it was "not anticipated we would get rises of this sort every month," Nessen said, the monthly increase should be regarded as a "warning" that the fight against inflation was not over yet.

Treasury Secretary William E. Simon echoed that view. "The upturn shows that inflationary pressures remain a serious and continuing problem," Simon said.

Alan Greenspan, chairman of the President's Council of Economic Advisers, told a Congressional committee July 23 that business recovery was "ahead of schedule." Pointing to a drastic cutback in inventories, Greenspan said he expected a "somewhat stronger pickup in production and employment in the second half than we had generally anticipated."

Greenspan testified before the Joint Economic Committee. He conceded that the recent increases in the price of grain, triggered by Soviet purchases, might cause the wholesale price index to surge temporarily in July.

In testimony July 24, Albert Rees, chairman of the Council on Wage and Price Stability, identified another Administration-supported policy that could contribute to inflation—the decontrol of old oil prices. Rees said the President's plan to lift controls on old oil could add 1.4% points to the consumer price index.

However, Rees saw a greater threat to price stability in rising industrial prices. List prices of finished-industrial products had not declined during the current recession, unlike in previous periods of economic slump, "and they are beginning to rise very early in the recovery," he said.

Recovery reported in peril. The new Congressional Budget Office June 30 submitted its first detailed forecast of the economy and clashed with Administration economists on several key policies and projections.

The report warned that higher fuel prices, resulting from President Ford's imposition of a $2-a-barrel increase in the tax on foreign oil, his plan to decontrol old oil prices, and an anticipated $2.25-a-barrel increase in the cost of imported oil, would add 2.4% to the inflation rate and .6% to the jobless rate by the end of 1976. The fuel price increases, expected to cost consumers and business $40 billion, "threaten both to rekindle inflation and to slow down the recovery," the report said.

In another position that was contrary to the Administration's stand, the budget office favored an extension of the 1975 tax cut and the enactment of additional tax reductions coming to a total of $15 million. "Prices wouldn't be affected very much" and the unemployment rate would drop .3% if these stimulative actions were taken, according to the report.

On the other hand, a refusal to extend current tax cuts could reduce the nation's total output of goods and services by about $8 billion and add .1% to the jobless rolls by the end of 1976.

The budget office differed with the Administration on the issue of federal budget deficits. Treasury Secretary William E. Simon and others had warned that large-scale federal borrowing to finance the deficits would "crowd out" private investors in the nation's money market. According to the study, budget deficits, instead, would stimulate business activity and create a "crowding-in" effect as businesses improved and expanded their capacity.

AFL-CIO warns of 'deeper recession.' The AFL-CIO executive council warned July 30 that there was a "very real danger of a deeper, more serious recession in the near future" from the combination of a "vulnerable" economy and misguided Ford Administration policies. It criticized in particular revival of a tight-money policy, the large grain sale to the Soviet Union and attempts to raise oil prices. These could cause a new round of inflation, the council cautioned. It also deplored the "failure" of the Administration to spur recoveries in housing, unemployment and consumer confidence.

After the council meeting, in Chicago, AFL-CIO President George Meany attacked President Ford as an "ultraconservative" who "believes if you keep the corporations and the banking interests healthy, that enough will trickle down that the people at the bottom of the economic ladder will get some of the crumbs."

Policies Proposed & Assessed

Ford proposes tax aid for business. President Ford Aug. 25, 1975 proposed to revive the economy by providing tax incentives to business, ending federal regulatory procedures that abetted anti-competitive practices and vigorously enforcing antitrust laws. He advocated the policy in an address in Chicago before the American Hardware Manufacturers Association.

The tax incentives, such as ending double taxation of dividends, he said, would spur new investment which in turn would expand production and create jobs. The tax aid was necessary because industry's ability to accumulate investment capital was "declining," he said, and the new investment was vital to avoid production problems as the economy emerged from recession.

Referring to those who would prefer to expand social welfare programs rather than aid business, Ford said, "Let us expand the size of our economic pie rather than simply redistributing the pieces of a much smaller pie."

The President promised the manufacturers he would "get the federal government out of your business, out of your lives, out of your pockets and out of your hair." He would "cut big government down to size," he told them. "You don't need a lot of bureaucrats looking over your shoulder and telling you how to run your life or your business. Let's take the shackles off American businessmen."

His point was that the unwanted regulatory steps sometimes permitted businesses "to fix prices and divide markets under the regulatory cloak." "Too often the government walks with industry along the road to monopoly," he said, but "this is not—and never will be—an administration of special interests. This is an administration of the public interest."

The pursuit of antitrust enforcement was a related point. "Regulatory reform and antitrust actions go hand-in-hand," Ford said, "with incentives to spark capital investment to create new jobs and new competition. This is what I firmly believe is needed to revive the American economic dream."

He also pledged action in "areas that antitrust laws do not now touch," such as industry rate bureaus and self-regulatory agencies—transportation rate bureaus, shipping conferences, stock exchanges and professional associations, which, he said, "now seem to operate in a congenial cost-plus environment" because government decided "they need not or cannot compete."

Labor scores Administration policies. Organized labor denounced Ford Administration economic policies Aug. 29–31 and urged jobs programs and tax cuts to avoid further economic woes.

In a Labor Day message released Aug. 29, AFL-CIO President George Meany said Administration policies had brought the country to "the edge of another economic calamity." As contributing factors, he cited continuing high interest rates, Soviet grain purchases and the resultant impact on food prices, higher fuel prices, continued depression in the housing industry, the many presidential vetoes of congressional programs and low consumer confidence.

Urging the President and Congress to take remedial action, Meany offered the labor movement's own program. It included another year of individual income tax cuts, implementation of homebuilding incentives, public works and public service job programs, reduced interest rates, aid for high-unemployment areas, railroad rehabilitation, tax reform, an energy policy to stop uncontrolled fuel price rises and regulation of exports that escalated domestic inflation.

In a press interview released for publication Aug. 31, Meany expanded on these and other themes. Among his comments:

■ "Why should we let the Soviet Union manipulate our grain market to our detriment? . . . What right have they got to come in and deal with . . . these greedy, profit-hungry grain operators, to deal with them and play with our market and get our food resources at a cheap price and then cause the American housewife to pay?"

■ President Ford was a "nice guy" but espoused the "outmoded" economic theory that the way to help employment was to cut business taxes, and the President also had a "fetish" that the budget deficit could not go beyond a certain level. But if the deficit were $100 billion and helped bring the jobless rate down by 4%, Meany said, "this would wipe out $64 billion of that $100 billion deficit right away because that would be what you'd get back from people going to work."

Other labor leaders also denounced Ford Administration economic policies in Labor Day remarks.

Leonard Woodcock, president of the United Automobile Workers, said Aug. 30: "Thirteen months and some 35 vetoes after taking office, President Ford has yet to answer the pleas of ordinary citizens for leadership out of the morass of inflation and unemployment."

Appearing on the NBC-TV "Meet the Press" program Aug. 31, Woodcock said Ford's policies to combat unemployment, recession and inflation added up "to absolutely zero." He described Ford's economic leadership as "Herbert Hoover revived."

I.W. Abel, president of the AFL-CIO United Steelworkers of America, who also was on the program, said "the Administration shows no inclination of taking constructive steps" to meet the country's economic problems. One thing that could be done, Abel suggested, was for the government to "get on with assisting all our communities in slum clearance and building of homes for low-cost housing."

Ford pledges needed action. President Ford held a press conference in his office Sept. 16, 1975.

Should the national economy need any more stimulant, Ford said, he would recommend continuation of the 1975 tax cuts. On the other hand, he went on, "If we find that the economy is continuing to come out of the recession, as it is, and there is no danger of added inflationary problems, we would probably not recommend a continuation of the tax cut." In any event, he expected to make a decision on the matter within "a reasonably short time."

The President reasserted his "firm opposition" to wage and price controls. He noted that he had not "had any recommendation from any organization" for an "incomes policy" of any kind.

Burns asks policy reassessment. Declaring conventional economic thinking "inadequate and out of date," Federal Reserve Chairman Arthur F. Burns proposed sweeping "structural" reforms for the economy that he said were intended to reverse the "inflationary bias" built into current policies. The speech was delivered at the University of Georgia Sept. 19.

Among his proposals:

- The government should become the employer of last resort by offering employment in public works projects "to anyone who is willing to work." The pay should be "somewhat below the federal minimum wage," Burns said, so that workers would be encouraged to seek jobs elsewhere.

To pay for the program, Burns urged a "sharp reduction in the scope of unemployment insurance and other governmental programs to alleviate income loss." Jobless benefits, which currently extended up to 65 weeks, were so "generous," Burns said, "that they may be blunting incentives to work." He called for a cutback in the payment period to about 13 weeks.

- Congress should renounce any "intention to return to mandatory [wage and price] controls," and consider instead, a "modest form" of voluntary wage-price restraints. The program would rely on "quiet government intervention, public hearings, and the mobilization of public opinion."

Burns denounced the inflexibility of wages and prices during a period of weak demand. This was a "new pattern of wage and price behavior," he said, with wages and prices always going up, even during a recession, and never coming down.

- Timetables for achieving environmental and job-safety goals should be "stretched out" because of their "dampening effect" on business. The tax structure should be overhauled to provide incentives for business expansion and increased productivity. Antitrust laws should be "reassessed" and enforcement should be improved.

"I totally reject the argument of those who keep urging faster creation of money and still larger governmental deficits," Burns said. He blamed the underlying inflationary trends in the U.S. on government spending and the "changing character of our economic institutions," which, he said, stressed more generous pay, "more holidays, longer vacations, and more coffee breaks."

Inflation "endangered our economic and political system based on freedom," Burns said. He also lashed out at "Western governments" that failed to fight inflation with the same intensity they devoted to the fight against recession.

Ford proposes tax cut. President Ford Oct. 6, 1975 recommended permanent reductions in current federal tax rates coupled with a reduction in federal spending.

In a televised speech from the White House, Ford emphasized that the tax and spending reductions "must be tied together in one package. It would be dangerous and irresponsible to adopt one without the other."

The President proposed that the $17 billion in tax reductions enacted in March be made permanent with some changes, and he proposed enactment of an additional $11 billion in tax cuts for 1976.

This would make a $28 billion tax reduction from the permanent tax rates established in 1972.

He proposed to reduce federal spending by the same amount, $28 billion, to a total of $395 billion for the next fiscal year, ending Oct. 1, 1977. Ford said the $28 billion represented a reduction from "what we will spend if we just stand still and let the train run over us." The growth of spending, which he described as "horrendous," could "easily jump to more than $420 billion" next year without a single new federal program.

The President pointed out that the proposed reduction in taxes and spending was almost on "a dollar-for-dollar" basis. "For every dollar that we return to the American taxpayer," he stressed, "we must also cut our projected spending by the same amount."

The overall goal was to balance the budget. "I want these actions to be a first step—and they are a crucial first step," Ford said, "toward balancing the federal budget within three years."

Individual taxpayers were to receive three-quarters of the proposed permanent tax reductions, Ford said, and "the chief benefits will be concentrated where they belong: among working people."

Ford's proposal would increase the personal income tax exemption from $750 to $1,000, make the standard deduction for single taxpayers a flat $1,800 and for married couples $2,500, and would lower basic personal income rates.

As an example, the President said a typical family of four earning $14,000 a year "would get a permanent tax cut of $412—a 27% reduction." The reduction quoted was from the 1972–1974 tax rates, before the 1975 temporary reduction. In tables issued by the White House Oct. 6, a family of four earning $5,000 a year would have a $98 reduction from the 1972–74 tax rates, but no reduction from tax rates currently in effect. A family of four earning $50,000 a year would be getting a $510 reduction from the 1974 rate, a $390 reduction from the current rate.

The other quarter of the proposed tax was for business. A 2% reduction in corporate tax rates was proposed, from a 48% maximum to 46%, and the increased temporary investment tax credit would be made permanent. This would raise the credit from 7% to 10% for most businesses and from 4% to 10% for utilities. The President also planned a special tax relief program for electric utilities.

"If we allow politics as usual to prevail in the Congress," Ford cautioned, "there will be a temptation to overwhelmingly approve the tax cuts and do nothing on the spending cuts. That must not happen. I will go forward with the tax cuts that I am proposing only if there is a clear, affirmative decision" by Congress to hold federal spending to $395 billion. He would "not hesitate to veto any legislation . . . which violates the spirit of that understanding," he said.

The President did not specify how the spending cuts would be applied, except to say they "cannot be isolated to one area, such as social programs, nor can we completely insulate any area such as defense." He said he wanted to work with Congress "to insure that those who deserve the help of our nation continue receiving that help—the elderly, the poor and the men and women who have borne our nation's arms." "Also, I will not permit reductions in our military budget that would jeopardize our national security," he said.

In his visits across the country, Ford said, he found many people "believe that what the government puts in your front pocket, it slips out of your back pocket through taxes and inflation. They are figuring out that they are not getting their money's worth from their taxes. They believe that the politics of federal spending has become too much of a shell game. And I must say that I agree with them.

"America's greatness was not built by taxing people to their limits but by letting our people exercise their freedom and their ingenuity to their limits. Freedom and prosperity go hand in hand. . . . Only by releasing the full energies of our people—only by getting the government off your back and out of your pocket—will we achieve our goals of stable prices and more jobs."

'Neutral' impact on economy—Alan Greenspan, chairman of the Council of Economic Advisers, said Oct. 6 that the President's program would have an essentially "neutral" impact on the economy in terms of promoting an upturn.

Prior to the President's proposals, Labor Secretary John T. Dunlop was the only member of his cabinet to take a firm public stand in favor of continuing the anti-recession tax reductions enacted in March. An economist, Dunlop noted Sept. 30 that the reductions for individuals would have to be increased, rather than just extended, or taxpayers would experience an increase in their withholding rates in the new year because the current temporary reduction was concentrated into eight months.

Congressional views on tax policy—Rep. Al Ullman (D, Ore.), chairman of the House Ways and Means Committee, said Oct. 6 he favored a simple extension of the current tax reductions adjusted to avoid withholding increases. The President's proposals could be analyzed after that, he said, but he added that he considered the proposals a "mirage." "There is no way we can enact a tax based on a spending ceiling," he said.

The Democratic majority of the Joint Economic Committee, in the panel's mid-year report released Oct. 1, advocated an additional tax reduction of $8 billion to $10 billion in 1976. as well as extension of the 1975 law. If present policies were continued, it said, there was "little prospect" that the current "strong recovery path will be sustained in 1976."

The panel's Republican minority said "a reasonable case can be made for a simple extension" of the current tax reductions and it warned against any further reductions. The majority report also called for a new emergency public jobs program, a special "counter-cyclical revenue sharing" effort, more growth in money supply than projected by the Federal Reserve authorities and an "active, voluntary price-incomes policy."

Labor presses attack. Ford Administration economic policies came under insistent attack at the convention of the AFL-CIO in San Francisco Oct. 2–7.

George Meany, 81, re-elected to his 11th term as AFL-CIO president Oct. 6, led the attack, which was joined by the federation's executive council and four potential Democratic presidential contenders.

In his opening address Oct. 2, Meany charged that no amount of "economic gobbledy-gook" from the White House could hide the fact that the country was in the throes of the "worst economic crisis since the 1930s." Calling for new national leadership, Meany said there was no sign that President Ford would take action to put the nation back to work or to counteract the program for "permanent stagnation" pursued by Arthur F. Burns, chairman of the Federal Reserve Board.

In a preliminary report to the convention Sept. 29, Meany warned that the seeds for another recession, "deeper and more serious than today's," had been sown, that "unemployment remains far too high and production far too low to sustain economic growth."

The executive council's economic report issued Sept. 30 deplored "the most dangerous mess in 40 years" and said only "an anemic pick-up" could be expected because of the policies of Ford and Burns and inaction by Congress.

The council called for extension of the individual tax reductions enacted for 1975 and government action on housing, energy and public works and public service jobs programs. It also urged lower interest rates, tax revision and help for state and local governments in high unemployment areas.

The convention heard the four Democrats Oct. 6. Two of them, Sens. Henry M. Jackson (Wash.) and Lloyd M. Bentsen Jr. (Tex.), were announced candidates for the presidential nomination. Jackson told the delegates the Ford Administration did not "give a damn about working people" and it was "taking much better care of Red Square than of Times Square," a reference to the Soviet Union and New York City. Bentsen said there was nothing basically wrong with the American economic system but it had been "mismanaged" for seven years.

Another of the Democrats, Sen. Birch Bayh (Ind.), was expected to announce his candidacy for the nomination. He attributed a state of national despair to the failure of national leadership for seven years.

The fourth Democrat, Sen. Hubert H. Humphrey (Minn.), spoke for 47 minutes about the need for an administration that was "determined to get America moving again," not one that was "content to rock it to sleep."

An economic resolution adopted by the convention Oct. 3 called for a 35-hour workweek, a $3-an-hour minimum wage (it was $2.10) and action by Congress to stabilize state and local budgets during recessions by provision of "countercyclical assistance."

Treasury borrowing needs raised again. The Treasury Department disclosed Sept. 10 that it would need to borrow $44–$47 billion throughout the second half of 1975 to finance the federal budget deficit. The financing plan was the third announced by government officials. The initial borrowing target had been set at $37 billion; a second projection put the government's cash needs at $41 billion.

The borrowing plan was revised for the third time, officials said, because of higher-than-anticipated federal spending, the expected loss of revenue from the lifting of import fees on foreign oil and petroleum products, and a desire for a larger year-end cash balance as a cushion against contingencies.

According to the Wall Street Journal Sept. 30, government borrowing for fiscal 1976, which began July 1, was expected to exceed $80 billion, compared with $51 billion in fiscal 1975 and $3 billion in fiscal 1974. At the start of fiscal 1976, the Journal reported, the accumulated federal deficit totaled $544 billion, up 68% in 10 years. The interest on that debt alone currently cost the government $36 billion a year, making debt service the third most expensive government activity after social welfare programs and national defense.

Treasury Secretary William E. Simon warned Congress Sept. 29 that "unprecedented" government borrowing was draining funds from housing and business investments, and thereby weakening the economic recovery.

Early in 1975, Simon had warned that the federal government's massive borrowing needs were "crowding out" other borrowers, such as corporations, local governments and home buyers, whose competing credit needs could not be met in the nation's capital markets.

According to the Journal, "no crowding-out occurred in the 1st half of calendar 1975 because the recession sharply reduced business and consumer borrowing and left the Treasury ample elbow room in the credit markets."

However, the Journal said, with recovery underway and federal borrowing needs continuing to expand, financial analysts in and out of government were warning of new strains in the credit markets. They pointed to the recent cancellation of $700 million of corporate bonds and other debt issues; rising interest rates affected by the Federal Reserve's anti-inflation policies; the drop in inflow of savings deposits, used to finance mortgage loans, as investors purchased higher-yielding Treasury securities; and the recent turmoil in the municipal bond market caused by New York City's near-default and continued heavy borrowing by local governments.

Treasury officials asked Congress Sept. 29 for unlimited authority to issue securities with maturities of up to 10 years. By lessening reliance on short-term bills, the government hoped to reduce the upward pressure on short-term interest rates, ease its debt-financing pressures, and halt the outflow of funds from savings institutions by redirecting investors to these short-term investments.

James Needham, chairman of the New York Stock Exchange, told Congress Sept. 17 that his earlier warning that the U.S. faced a $650 billion capital shortage by 1985 might be "conservative." Unless investment tax laws were changed to simulate the flow of equity capital, Needham said, corporations would be unable to raise about $70 billion of the $250 billion in equity financing needed by 1985.

Needham challenged the conclusions of a Brookings Institution study, which saw no threat of a capital crisis if the federal deficit were held at $60 billion for the remainder of the decade. Data from the Office of Management and Budget, Needham said, showed a projected minimum federal deficit of $165 billion by 1980.

Administration frees housing funds. The Ford Administration announced Oct. 17 that it would release $264.1 million in funds intended by Congress to help families of moderate means buy homes.

Carla Hills, secretary of housing and urban development, said the Administration would release the funds, beginning in 1976, over a two-year period to subsidize mortgages on 250,000 new and rehabilitated dwellings for families earning between $9,000 and $11,000 a year. Families qualifying for the HUD program, Hills said, would be able to obtain mortgages of $21,600 to $28,800 at a subsidized interest rate of 5%. (The interest rate for other government-backed mortgages was currently about 9%.)

Hills said that she had recommended reactivation of the program and that her decision had been an "economic" one. She conceded, however, that a General Accounting Office lawsuit seeking release of the funds "obviously was a factor" in President Ford's decision to begin the program again.

The GAO suit had stemmed from President Ford's refusal to spend congressionally appropriated funds for the HUD home ownership subsidy program, which the Nixon Administration had suspended in 1973 as too costly and unworkable.

Hills said that the new program would be restructured to avoid past problems, among them a foreclosure rate exceeding 10%. Thousands of homes had been abandoned after low-income buyers left them because of their inability to keep up with maintenance costs. By gearing the program to a higher income group than before and requiring participants to make at least 3%-down payments ($1,500 to $2,000), Hills said, HUD would be able to "decrease the chances of abandonment." (Under the previous program, home buyers with annual incomes of between $5,000 and $7,000 were able to obtain 1% subsidized mortgages and make down payments as small as $200.)

Homes owned by poor called unrealistic. HUD Secretary Hills said in a speech before the Washington Press Club Sept. 12 that "home ownership for the poor is probably an unrealistic goal in today's economy."

Past government programs to make homes available to the poor did not work, she asserted, because the poor were not prepared to deal with problems associated with owning homes. "When the plumbing backs up, when the heating acts up . . . these people do not have the wherewithal to deal with these problems," Hills said.

Food stamp cutback urged. President Ford sent Congress Oct. 20 a plan that would limit participation in the food-stamp program, generally, to persons whose incomes were below the poverty level. The Administration presented the plan as one that would save taxpayers $1.2 billion a year and remove 3.4 million persons from the program, which currently cost the government $6 billion a year and served 18.8 million persons.

The numerous deductions, currently permitted in the program to bring a family's income down to eligibility at the poverty level, would be eliminated under the Ford plan. Instead, a $100-a-month deduction would be permitted per household, or $125 if a person over 60 years old was in the family. For a family of four, where the poverty level was calculated by the government at $5,050 annual income, the total income it could have under the Ford plan and still qualify for food stamps was $6,250 or $6,550, after adding on the only monthly deductions allowed.

The Ford plan would figure family income, in determining eligibility, on the basis of the average income during the 90 days prior to application for food stamps. Currently, income was figured on the basis of a family's estimate of earnings in the coming month.

A uniform charge was proposed for the food stamps—30% of net income after the standard $100 or $125 monthly deduction. The charge currently varied with a family's income.

The Administration also proposed to tighten eligibility of students and strikers for the program. Students would have to show that their parents were not claiming them as dependents on income-tax returns. The strikers would have to give proof that they looked for other employment before receiving the stamps.

Panel contradicts Ford on economy. A study by the staff of the Joint Economic Committee of Congress, reported Dec. 21, said that implementation of President Ford's budget and tax proposals would lead to economic stagnation in 1977. The study said that in order not to restrain economic recovery, the government would have to effect a combination of spending increases and tax reductions totaling $12 billion.

Ford and the committee staff agreed that spending of approximately $420 billion would be necessary to maintain government services at their 1976 level.

But Ford had said he would submit a $395 billion budget to Congress in January, 1976. The committee study said Ford's proposed cuts would push unemployment up to 9% in 1977 and recommended expenditures of $420 billion to keep the economy on its current course.

Contrary to the Administration's assertions that spending was out of control, the staff report maintained that if no new policies were adopted, there would be substantial surpluses in the federal budget by 1981.

The study also predicted that measures taken to reduce unemployment would create less inflation, rather than more, as the Administration had been arguing. Rapid increase in output, it said, would engender efficiencies which would lower unit production costs and stop prices from rising so fast.

Legislative Action

President Ford and Congress were in frequent disagreement during the second half of 1975 on the desirability of specific spending and other economic legislation and on the effects such bills would have on the fragile economic recovery.

Health bill enacted over veto. A $2 billion health bill was enacted into law by Congress July 29 over a presidential veto. It was the first time in many attempts in 1975 that Congress had overridden a veto.

The bill authorized $2 billion in fiscal 1976–78 for the programs—$1.42 billion in fiscal 1976–77 for formula grants to the states for public health services programs, family planning programs, community mental health centers, migrant health centers, community health centers in rural and inner-city areas. Another $553 million was authorized in fiscal 1976–78 for training programs for nurses; $30 million was authorized in fiscal 1976 for the National Health Service Corps.

The bill was passed by voice votes of the Senate July 14 and House July 16.

President Ford vetoed it July 26 because he considered the appropriations levels "excessive" and its program conception "unsound." The levels were "far in excess of the amounts we can afford," he said.

The Senate met later July 26 to consider a motion to override the veto, which carried, 67–15, 12 more than the two-thirds majority required.

The vote in the House, taken July 29, was 384–43, 99 votes over the requirement.

Congress overrides school aid veto. A $7.9 billion education appropriations bill became law Sept. 10 when the Senate voted to override President Ford's veto. The vote was 88–12, or 21 more than the required two-thirds majority.

The House had voted to override the veto by a 379–41 vote Sept. 9, which was 99 more than the two-thirds majority needed.

The President had vetoed the bill on fiscal grounds, saying it exceeded his budget requests. But supporters of the legislation said it provided $400 million less than set by Congress in its budgetary guide and only $225 million, or 3.6%, more than the previous year's budget. This was well below the current inflation rate of 8%, they pointed out.

Much of the money in the bill was appropriated for fiscal periods beyond fiscal 1976, which had started July 1. This included $464,683,000 for the three-month transition period between fiscal 1976 and fiscal 1977.

School lunch veto overridden. A bill funding school lunch and other child nutrition programs was enacted into law by Congress Oct. 7 over President Ford's veto.

The President had vetoed the bill Oct. 3 on the grounds it exceeded his budget requests by $1.2 billion, was inflationary and would expand benefits to "non-needy" pupils. Ford said Congress could extend current programs or enact his block grant proposal but added, "we should not expand some subsidies to families with incomes above the poverty level."

The margin to override the veto was substantial in both houses Oct. 7. The House vote was 397–18, or 120 more than the two-thirds majority needed. In the Senate the vote was 79–13, or 17 more than the required two-thirds. Even the Republican leaders of both houses—Sen. Hugh Scott (Pa.) and Rep. John J. Rhodes (Ariz.)—voted to override.

U.S. pay hike limited to 5%. The House Oct. 1, by a 278–123 vote, defeated a resolution disapproving a proposal by President Ford to limit pay increases to 5% for Congress, top government officials and 3.5-million other federal employes.

The Senate Sept. 18 had acted similarly, voting, 53–39, to reject a resolution to disapprove Ford's pay proposal.

Ford had urged the 5% increase as an alternative to an 8.66% increase recommended by the Advisory Committee on Federal Pay that was supposed to go into effect Oct. 1. Had the President not acted or had either house of Congress approved a resolution vetoing Ford's proposal, the 8.66% raise would automatically have become effective Oct. 1.

In proposing the 5% ceiling Aug. 29, Ford said his plan would cost $2 billion, $1.6 billion less than the 8.66% raise would have cost. Ford, who stressed the need to fight against continued inflation, said, "The size of the proposed pay raise must be temporarily restrained for the good of the nation."

Those affected by the pay-increase limitation were members of Congress, members of the federal judiciary, high-level political appointees and career officials, 1.3-million white collar federal workers and 2.1-million military personnel, whose salaries were tied to civilian pay levels.

The 8.66% proposal by the Advisory Committee on Federal Pay, an impartial, nongovernment panel, was based on a study by the Bureau of Labor Statistics of salaries paid for comparable jobs in private industry.

Congress rescinds $47.5 million. Congress Oct. 2 completed action on a bill rescinding a $47.5-million helium fund in the Bureau of Mines. Proponents of the rescission had said that the bureau did not need the money because it already had almost 40 billion feet of helium in storage and its authority to purchase more of the gas had been terminated in 1973.

However, Congress refused to rescind another $141 million in appropriations, as requested by President Ford. Among the rescissions not granted were: $90 million for a scenic highway along the Mississippi River, $25.7 million in contract authority for the Forest Service to expand forest trails and roads, $8.7 million for a federal law enforcement training center and $7 million for services for handicapped children under the Head Start program.

Debt ceiling raised. President Ford Nov. 14, 1975 signed into law legislation raising the temporary ceiling on the national debt by $18 billion to $595 billion through March 15, 1976. Had Congress failed to raise the limit, it would have reverted to its permanent level of $400 billion Nov. 15, and the Treasury Department would have been unable to borrow further.

While Senate took only three minutes to pass the bill by voice vote Nov. 13, the House shortly before adopted the measure by the narrow margin of 213–198.

House Republicans had threatened to vote solidly against the bill unless the Democratic majority permitted a vote on an amendment setting a spending limit of $395 billion for fiscal 1977. President Ford, who had yet to send to Congress his budget proposal for fiscal 1977, had threatened to veto any tax-cut bill unless a spending ceiling were approved.

As a result of the Republicans' position, the House leadership, which opposed the amendment as extraneous, made a last-minute appeal to Democratic members to support the bill. Speaker Carl Albert (D, Okla.) said it was "unbelievable that a President . . . would put any limitations and conditions on the lifting of the debt limit at the time it is about to expire." Rep. Al Ullman, chairman of the House Ways and Means Committee, warned that defeat of the bill would leave the federal government in "a desperate fiscal situation" and unable to pay its bills.

On the final vote, 13 Republicans joined 200 Democrats to support the legislation, while 76 Democrats and 122 Republicans voted against it.

The House Oct. 29 had rejected, 217–198, a bill that would have raised the temporary debt ceiling by $20 billion to $597 billion through March 31.

Tax cuts extended in compromise. Congress Dec. 19 passed compromise legislation extending antirecession tax cuts for the first six months of 1976. The bill, identical to a measure vetoed by President Ford Dec. 17 except for a nonbinding provision limiting government spending, was approved by the House, 372–10, and by the Senate on a voice vote. The $8.4 billion tax cut measure was signed by Ford Dec. 23.

Action on the compromise bill followed by one day the House's failure to override the President's veto of a tax-cut-extension measure that did not set, as Ford had demanded, a $395 billion ceiling on government spending for fiscal 1977. The House vote Dec. 18 to override was 265–157, 17 votes short of the two-thirds majority needed.

According to published reports, the compromise bill was the product of negotiations initiated by Sen. Russell Long (D, La.), chairman of the Senate Finance Committee, who, along with other members of Congress and the President, was concerned that a stalemate over the measure would result in the expiration of the 1975 tax cut Dec. 31.

Working with Sen. William Roth (R, Del.), a senior member of the Finance Committee, and Reps. Barber Conable (R, N.Y.) and Joe Waggoner (D, La.), Long was able to obtain a compromise amendment to the bill acceptable to Ford and Congressional Democrats.

The compromise provision, later rewritten somewhat by the House Democratic leadership, stated that Congress was determined to continue the tax cut and "to control spending levels in order to reduce the national deficit."

If "economic conditions warranted" extending the tax cut past June 30, 1976, the amendment said, Congress would agree to provide "for reductions in the level of spending in the fiscal year 1977 . . . equal to any additional reduction in taxes (from the 1974 tax rate levels)" for fiscal 1977. However, the amendment also stated that Congress was not to be precluded from passing a budget resolution "containing a higher or lower expenditure figure if Congress concludes that this is warranted by economic conditions or unforeseen circumstances."

The President, in a statement on his veto Dec. 17, reiterated his claim that Congressional failure to link the tax cut to a budgetary spending ceiling for fiscal 1977 would bring the risk of a "new round of double digit inflation" that would "invisibly tax every dollar" earned by taxpayers at "a much higher figure than any relief the bill" offered.

However, Ford added that his veto did not mean that taxes would have to go up Jan. 1, 1976 when the current tax cut expired. Congress need only approve a tax cut extension for 1976 "coupled with a clear commitment to cut the growth of federal spending," he said.

The legislation, as passed, extended, with some adjustments, tax cuts enacted in March. Over the six months covered by the bill, individuals would pay about $7.4 billion less in taxes and businesses nearly $1 billion less than they would have without the legislation. The bill's specific provisions represented a compromise between the versions originally passed in the House and Senate.

Labor-HEW funds veto overridden. President Ford Dec. 19, 1975 vetoed an appropriation for the departments of Labor and of Health, Education and Welfare. The funds included $36,073,748,318 for fiscal 1976 and $8,953,070,000 for the three-month transition period—July 1–Sept. 30, 1976—between fiscal 1976 and fiscal 1977.

The veto was overridden by 310–110 House vote Jan. 27, 1976 and by 70–24 Senate vote Jan. 28.

Ford's veto, his 42nd since assuming office, was cast because the appropriation, he said, was "a classic example of unchecked spending." He said it exceeded his budget plans by nearly $1 billion and would add $382 million to the fiscal 1976 deficit and increase permanent federal employment rolls by 8,000 workers. "This bill is, therefore, inconsistent with fiscal discipline and with effective restraint on the growth of government," he said.

The veto was deplored Dec. 19 by Sen. Warren G. Magnuson (D, Wash.), chairman of the Senate Appropriations Committee. He said it was "another example of President Ford's failure to cooperate with Congress and to provide real leadership for the American people."

Sen. Edward W. Brooke (R, Mass.) also expressed disappointment Dec. 19 with the veto. The President's budget estimates were unrealistically low, he said, and Congress "had no choice" but to raise them.

The bill had been cleared by Congress

Dec. 8 by a voice vote in the Senate. The final vote in the House was 321–91 Dec. 4.

The appropriations covered social programs—public service jobs, welfare and health programs. None of the funding was for education programs, which was covered in separate legislation.

The appropriations included $3,484,-408,000 for the Labor department and $31,592,976,318 for HEW. The latter included $3,904,971,000 for health programs, where much of the increase over the Administration budget requests was lodged, and $15,003,950,000 for public assistance.

Revised rail aid bill passed. Both houses of Congress, having rescinded their approval of a railroad aid bill in its original form, voted Jan. 28, 1976 for a second conference report on the bill that scaled down the funding authorization to $6.1 billion. The House vote was 353–62, the Senate vote was 58–26.

The President signed the bill Feb. 5.

Congress had originally cleared the bill Dec. 19, 1975, but had not sent it on to the White House because President Ford had announced that the authorizations were excessive and that he would veto it. House and Senate staff members met with administration figures from Jan. 2 to Jan. 23 to work out an acceptable compromise.

The main administration objection to the bill was overcome when Congressional representatives agreed to reduce the authorization for improving rail passenger service between Washington, D.C. and Boston from $2.4 billion to $1.846 billion. Subsidies to keep commuter and light-density branch lines in operation were also cut back from $525 million to $495 million in the bill's final form.

The original bill's authorization of loans of $2.1 billion to Conrail and $1.6 billion to other railroads were kept in the final form. Provisions reforming and restricting the Interstate Commerce Commission's regulation of rail traffic were also carried over from the original bill.

Ford said the financial aid and deregulation would provide the tools to make reorganization of the bankrupt Penn Central Transportation Co. and other northeastern carriers a "success." "It may be," he added, that the reorganization "can be successful only as part of a further restructuring of the rail industry through private-sector initiatives." The remark was interpreted as a reference to the possibility of further restructure by sale of Penn Central and the other northeastern lines to solvent railroads elsewhere, in the event the new northeast system, known as Conrail, failed to turn a profit.

Public works bill vetoed. President Ford vetoed a $6.1 million public works employment bill Feb. 13 as "little more than an election year pork barrel."

He said that the bill "would do little to create jobs for the unemployed" and that the most effective way to create new jobs was "to pursue balanced economic policies that encourage the growth of the private sector without risking a new round of inflation."

In his argument against the bill, Ford said it would create only 250,000 jobs at most, instead of the 600,000 to 800,000 jobs advertised for it, and almost none of them immediately when they were needed but in late 1977 and early 1978. He said the cost of producing the jobs would be "intolerably high, perhaps in excess of $25,000 per job."

He found some merit in the bill's "counter-cyclical" provisions, or revenue-sharing grants to states and cities to areas of high unemployment, but he criticized the section for tying the aid to the spending levels of the state and local governments, which he thought would encourage waste.

The Senate had approved the bill Dec. 17, 1975, and the House passed it by 321–80 vote Jan. 29, 1975 only hours after Ford had said he would veto it if it won Congressional approval.

Ford's veto was sustained Feb. 19 when the Senate voted, 63–35, to override but failed by three votes to achieve the two-thirds majority needed to override a veto. The Feb. 19 House vote to override, 319–98, was 41 votes more than the needed margin.

Statistics of Late 1975

'Real' GNP growth moderated. "Real" gross national product, defined as the market value of the nation's output of goods and services adjusted for inflation, expanded at an annual rate of 4.9% during the 4th quarter of 1975, compared with 12% in the 3rd quarter, the Commerce Department said in a revised report Feb. 19, 1976. (All figures were adjusted for seasonal variation.)

Although the increase was the 3rd consecutive quarterly gain reported since the economy bottomed out in the 1st quarter of 1975, real GNP for all of 1975 was down 2% from 1974, when output declined 1.8%.

Inflation during the 4th quarter of 1975, measured according to the GNP price deflator, increased at an annual rate of 6.8%, down from the 3rd quarter's rate of 7.1%. For the year, inflation measured 8.7%, compared with 9.7% in 1974.

The unadjusted GNP increased by $44 billion, or 12% at an annual rate, to a seasonally adjusted annual rate of $1.573 trillion. In comparison, the unadjusted GNP rose $67.9 billion, or 19.9%, from the 2nd to the 3rd quarter.

The real GNP increased $14.4 billion to $1.216 trillion at an adjusted annual rate. compared with a $133.4 billion gain in the previous period.

Leading indicators up .4%. The government's composite index of leading economic indicators rose .4% in December 1975 to 102.5% of the 1967 average, regaining the level reached earlier in September 1975, the Commerce Department announced Jan. 28, 1976.

The index was regarded by many analysts as a key barometer of the economy because the 12 components measured in the index were said to "lead," or foretell, economic activity.

According to an Administration economist, the figures for the 4th quarter of 1975 reflected "a moderation in the economy's recovery in October and November following [a] strong initial upsurge" that took the index from the 1975 low of 91% (of the 1967 average) in February to the year's high of 102.7% (revised) in August. The December upturn indicated "a resumption in the pace [of recovery] in late 1975 that will probably continue in 1976," the spokesman said.

Five of the 11 indicators available for inclusion in the preliminary December report showed increases from November. A strong gain in the average workweek had the most favorable impact on the index; also showing gains were the layoff rate, new orders, net business formation, and change in total liquid assets.

The indicator having the greatest negative impact on the index was the money supply, which declined .35%; also moving unfavorably were contracts and orders for plant and equipment, building permits, stock prices, change in sensitive prices, and the percentage of companies reporting slower deliveries.

The composite index was a revised one that had been in use only since May.

Use of the old index was discontinued because many of the 12 leading indicators were not adjusted for price changes and failed to reflect distortions in the economy generated by inflation. When these higher prices were reflected in the index as positive signs of economic health, rather than as evidence of an inflationary spiral, the index failed to function as a reliable forecast of economic trends.

Officials noted the differences between the new and old index, which was recalculated back to 1948 using the new list of indicators. Under the old formula, the economy gave no sign of decline until August 1974, long after the November 1973 date that was generally accepted as the start of the current recession.

The new index, however, pointed to a downturn that began in July 1973. The slump continued, with a brief interruption in February and March 1974, until the index hit a low of 90.6 in February 1975 (with 1967 as the base of 100). There was improvement registered in March when the index was at 91.5 and with the record April increase, the index rose to 95.4. Despite this gain, however, the index remained 25% below the June 1973 peak of 126.6. The index rose to 95.9 in May, 99.3 in June, 101.7 in July and 102.7 in August. It then declined to 102.6 in September and to 102.1 in October and November.

Industrial output up. Production in U.S. factories, mines and utilities increased about .9% during December 1975 to about 118.3% of the 1967 average, according to Federal Reserve statistics made public March 16, 1976.

The index's December level was about 8% higher than in its April low but about 9% below the September 1974 pace, officials said. During the 12 months of 1975, U.S. industrial output rose nearly 1%; on a quarterly basis, production during the 4th period was 2.9% higher than in the 3rd quarter of 1975.

Production had declined monthly for nine months before a turnaround started in June. Each succeeding month of 1975 thereafter showed an output gain.

4th-quarter profits at near-record high, full-year decline posted. After-tax corporate profits in the 4th quarter of 1975 increased $1.8 billion from the 3rd quarter to a seasonally adjusted annual rate of $80.6 billion, the second highest level in history, according to the Commerce Department March 19, 1976.

The 4th quarter level was exceeded only by a record $87.4 billion rate posted in the 3rd quarter of 1974.

Officials noted, however, that the 2.3% rise in after-tax earnings over the previous period was small compared with the 3rd quarter's 18.3% profit surge to an adjusted annual rate of $78.8 billion (revised). When compared with the 4th quarter of 1974, after-tax earnings for the final period were down 11.3%.

The advance posted during the final period was the third in a row. However, these quarterly gains were not enough to offset the 20% drop in profits during the 1st quarter of 1975. For the full year, after-tax earnings measured only $71.4 billion, down $8.1 billion, or 10.2%, from the 1974 level. The full-year decline was the first reported since 1970, when profits fell 18.3%.

Since reaching a recession low in the 1st quarter of 1975, profits had rebounded 44%, a gain which exceeded the earnings increase in every post-recession recovery period since 1950. Profits were up 47% in that recovery period.

Pretax profits in the 4th quarter rose $4.3 billion to an adjusted annual rate of $133.8 billion.

Officials said two factors may have contributed to the slowdown in the profit rise during the 4th quarter: smaller sales gains than in the 3rd period and a slimmer rate of worker productivity that failed to keep pace with the rise in profits.

A Wall Street Journal survey of profits announced by 406 major companies showed that their 4th quarter earnings rose 4.4% over the same period of 1974. The survey was published Feb. 3, 1976.

According to the Journal's data, the 4th period was the only quarter of 1975 to show an increase over depressed-year earlier figures. (The year-to-year declines ranged from 21% in the first quarter to 12% in the 3rd quarter.)

Among the 26 categories of firms listed in the Journal survey, seven reported a decline in 4th quarter earnings, compared with the same period of 1974; 18 showed profit gains; no percentage change was listed for another category.

The seven areas reporting a decline in earnings, and the percentage change: five aerospace companies, down 23.5%; 12 chain grocers, down 19.7%; three farm equipment makers, down 61.9%; eight mining and metals companies, down 52.2%; 17 petroleum products firms, down 8.3%; 17 steel producers, down 47%; and 20 banks, down 15.7%.

Categories reporting the largest gains were 12 drug and variety stores, up 292.5%; 13 electrical equipment and electronics firms, up 272.6%; and 10 textile firms, up 115.8%.

Ten airlines, which had shown a combined loss of $14.48 million in the 4th quarter of 1975, reported their deficit widened to $41.67 million in the final period of 1975.

The nation's four auto makers, which released their earnings reports too late for inclusion in the Journal survey, showed varying degrees of recovery in the 4th quarter of 1975.

Chrysler Corp. Feb. 24 reported an operating profit of $34.9 million over the 4th quarter, compared with a loss of $71.1 million in the same period of 1974. (The earnings gains reflected the sale of an unprofitable nonautomotive division.)

For the full year, Chrysler reported a net loss of $259.5 million, compared with a $52.1 million loss a year earlier. (Operating losses incurred by the discontinued division were included in the full-year figure.)

Ford Motor Co. reported the largest percentage gain in earnings from the 4th quarter of 1974 to the last period of 1975. Officials announced Feb. 19 that earnings for the final period totaled $169.9 million, compared with $22.1 million in the same quarter of 1974. For the full year, earnings were $227.5 million, down 37% from 1974, when profits totaled $360.9 million. (The full-year 1975 calculations did not include a one-time tax credit in the 1st quarter.)

General Motors Corp. Feb. 3 reported a 22% rise in earnings during the 4th quarter to $618 million, compared with $508 million a year earlier. For 1975, profits were up 32% to $1.25 billion, from $950 million in 1974.

American Motors Corp. earned $7.5 million in the 1st fiscal quarter, ended Dec. 31, 1975, officials announced Feb. 4. This compared with a $5.6 million profit in the same period of 1974. In its full fiscal year, ended Sept. 31, 1975, AMC lost $27.5 million.

Personal income expanded. Americans' personal income rose .4%, or $5.2 billion, during December 1975 to a seasonally adjusted annual rate of $1.301 trillion, the Commerce Department reported Jan. 19, 1976. For all of 1975, personal income climbed by $91.3 billion, or 7.9%, to $1.246 trillion.

Wages and salaries paid by private industry during December rose $4.1 billion, up .6% from November when payrolls increased $5.8 billion. The monthly increase in factory payrolls was especially strong—wages and salaries climbed $2.9 billion, or 1.3%, nearly triple November's $1 billion increase. Officials said the December gain "resulted from increases in employment, average weekly hours, and average hourly earnings." In 1975, wage and salary disbursements rose 5%, compared with 8.9% in 1974.

Government payrolls were up $900 million during December after rising $1.3 billion in the previous months. Wages and salaries paid by the government throughout 1975 totaled $174.4 billion, up from $160.6 billion in 1974.

Transfer payments, chiefly social security, welfare, unemployment and veterans' payments, increased $1.7 billion in December, compared with $800 million in November. For the year, transfer payments rose 24.6% to $175 billion. In 1974, transfer payments expanded 18.4%.

Farm income fell in December for the third consecutive month, declining $2.5 billion after falling $2.2 billion in November. Farm income for 1975, at $24.6 billion, was down 3.9% from 1974, when farm income had plunged 21%.

Dividend income was off $2.1 billion in December after showing no change from October to November. Dividends totaled $32.8 billion during 1975, up $1.7 billion from 1974.

Consumer confidence falters. The slow recovery in consumer confidence in the economy during the first three quarters of 1975 faltered during the final period, according to the University of Michigan's Survey Research Center. Results of its survey, conducted during October and November, were reported in the Wall Street Journal Dec. 12, 1975.

The center's index on consumer sentiment was at 75.4 during the 4th quarter, near the low point reached during the 1970 recession, but more than 20 higher than the record low reported at the end of 1974. (February 1966–100)

The survey found consumers in an "unusually conservative and skittish mood," according to the center's economist in charge of the poll. Pessimism was especially strong about the nation's long-term outlook—only 11% of those sampled expected "good times" during the next five years, compared with 18% in the 3rd quarter survey. Nearly 75% of those polled in the most recent survey were classified as "savings-minded" compared with 64% in the previous poll.

Five prominent pollsters told the Joint Economic Committee of Congress Oct. 30 that public confidence in the government and in the nation's economic future was at record low levels.

"The public believes that the current respite from the severe difficulties of a year ago is nothing more than the calm before the storm. All the President's statistics and all the President's men cannot put confidence back together again," Peter D. Hart said.

Louis Harris said that his survey, conducted in mid-October, showed that 81% of those polled believed the country was still in a recession and that 56% believed these conditions would persist for another year.

Patrick Caddell said his results showed that consumer confidence was correlated with the perception of inflation, particularly in food prices. Confidence had risen early in the year when the food price spiral slowed, but was now declining with a resumption in food price increase, Caddell said.

Stock market gain in '75. The stock market ended one of its best years with a minor rally Dec. 31, 1975, although the Dow Jones industrial average was unchanged for the day, closing at 852.41.

Throughout 1975, the Dow had added 236.17 points, its largest point gain in history. The 38.3% gain was the third largest on record and the best since 1954 when the Dow rose 44%.

However, most of the year's advances occurred during the first six months of the year when the Dow rose 262.72 points and volume was 2.66 billion shares. The market's strength was attributed to an improving economy, the lowering of interest rates and a moderation in 1974's inflationary spiral, according to The New York Times.

Prices generally were strong during the first half of November when investors were optimistic about the prospects of federal aid for New York City. On Nov. 17, the Dow closed up at 856.66, its highest close since mid-July.

A four-day slump followed the announcement that President Ford remained opposed to a federal solution to the city's crisis, but the market rebounded Nov. 25, gaining 9.76 points on news that the New York state legislature was near an accord on a tax package sought by the White House as a precondition for federal assistance.

By Nov. 28, following the President's announcement he would support federal loans for the city, market reaction was mild. The Dow closed up 2.12 points at 860.67.

Prices fell sharply on the New York Stock Exchange during the first week of December, losing a total of 41.87 points, its heaviest weekly loss since September 1974. On Dec. 5, the Dow closed at 818.8, its lowest level since October.

There was lackluster trading during the remainder of the month.

Dow tops 1,000—The Dow Jones industrial average closed above 1,000 March 11, 1976 in trading on the New York Stock Exchange. The index ended the session up 8.03 points at 1003.31, its highest closing level since Jan. 26, 1973.

The Dow had exceeded 1,000 during daily trading March 9 and 10, but retreated before the days' close as traders and investors sold stocks to take profits accruing from the market's 17% advance since the beginning of the year.

The market had been exceptionally strong during the early months of 1976. New records were set for stock prices and trading volume, only to be surpassed in subsequent sessions. The Dow opened the new year Jan. 2 with a 6.30 point gain to close at 858.71.

During the following week, the Dow moved above the 900 mark, its highest level in 26 months, and gained a total of 52.42 points, its second largest weekly gain in history. Volume also was at its second highest level on record—141.94 million shares were traded in the week ended Jan. 9, a mark exceeded only in the week ended Jan. 31, 1975 when 145.68 million shares changed hands. Declining interest rates and government reports of a pickup in economic activity and a slowdown in inflation were major factors in the bullish market.

The Dow was mixed during the following week, closing up Jan. 16 at 929.63. However, trading remained heavy. A record number of shares, 159.6 million, changed hands over the five-day period. Daily turnover was the highest in exchange history Jan. 15 when 38.45 million shares were traded. Daily volume also had exceeded 30 million shares in each of the previous three sessions.

Another new weekly volume record was set Jan. 23 and the Dow passed the 950 mark. A total of 161.68 million shares were traded during the week and the index closed up at 953.95.

The market ended the month on an explosive rally. Turnover Jan. 30 totaled 38.51 million shares, a new daily volume record. Trading for the week totaled 162.23 million shares, another record amount. The Dow gained 21.36 points during the five-day period to close at 975.28, a 27-month high. Over the month, the Dow had gained 122.87 points, a record one-month advance.

The Dow had first approached the 1,000 mark in early 1966 when it reached a high of 995.15 on Feb. 9. However, by Oct. 7, 1966, the index had slipped to 744.32.

The Dow first pierced the 1,000 mark on Nov. 14, 1972 and reached a historic high of 1051.70 on Jan. 11, 1973. In the pullback that followed, the index fell to 577.60 on Dec. 6, 1974 before beginning its current market climb.

The Dow, which measured the movement of stock prices of 30 large industrial companies, was a barometer of trading in the nation's blue-chip stocks. However, for many the index also symbolized "the market," because of the Dow's longevity —it had been in existence since 1896— and the wide press and financial coverage given it.

Analysts noted that two other market indexes were well below their record high levels. Standard and Poor's index of 500 leading stocks closed March 11 18% below its peak, and the New York Stock Exchange's composite index of all listed common stocks finished 16.8% under its record.

State of the Union: 1976 Message

Ford for 'new realism.' President Ford called on Americans Jan. 19, 1976 to adopt "a new realism that is true to the great principles upon which this nation was founded."

His approach, as outlined in his second State of the Union message, delivered before a joint evening session of Congress, was to reduce taxes and federal spending; secure the financial base of the Social Security system; consolidate federal education, health and social-services programs for more flexible application by the state and local governments.

"And in all that we do," Ford said in his address, which was broadcast nationally, "we must be more honest with the American people, promising them no more than we can deliver, and delivering all that we promise."

America was "crossing a threshold" not just because it was the nation's bicentennial "but because we have been tested in adversity," the President said, and "we have taken a new look at what we want to be and what we want our nation to become." He saw America "resurgent" and "moving forward as before toward a more perfect Union where the government serves and the people rule."

The state of the union at the moment, he said, was "better" than a year ago "but still not good enough." A year ago he had reported that the state of the union "was not good."

"We are not only headed in a new direction, a direction which I proposed 12 months ago," he said, "but it turned out to be the right direction." It was the right direction, he continued, because it involved "a full partnership among all branches and all levels of government, private institutions and individual citizens.

"Common sense tells me to stick to that steady course."

Sound economy the first goal—In his outline for the course of government in 1976, Ford focused largely on the economy. "My first objective is to have sound economic growth without inflation," he said. Although inflation was slowing, "we must stop it cold." To do this, "the government must stop spending so much and stop borrowing so much of our money; more money must remain in private hands, where it will do the most good. To hold down the cost of living, we must hold down the cost of government."

His next budget totaled $394.2 billion, Ford said, which was in keeping with his promise to hold the budget down to $395 billion, and its growth rate was less than half the 10% average annual growth rate of the past decade.

On taxes, he proposed to add $10 billion of federal income tax reductions, effective July 1, to the $18 billion in tax cuts enacted in December 1975 for the first six months of 1976.

Ford also proposed:

- A business tax incentive to speed up plant expansion and equipment purchase in areas of high unemployment.
- A change in estate taxes to help preserve the family farm and family-owned small business.
- A tax change to give "moderate income families income benefits if they make long-term investments in common stock in American companies."

Another tax proposal—for a .3% increase in both employer and employe Social Security taxes, effective Jan. 1, 1977—was made because the Social Security trust fund was "headed for trouble" and needed replenishment. Ford said he was recommending in his budget that the full cost of living increases in the Social Security benefits be paid during 1976.

In other areas vital to the economy, the President called for: additional housing assistance for 500,000 moderate and low income families; a loosening of the "shackles" of government regulation; reform in airlines, trucking, railroads and financial institutions to spur competition and bring consumer prices down; strict enforcement of antitrust laws, for the same purposes; enactment of the Administration's still-pending energy proposals.

The latter would, in the President's view: reduce domestic natural gas shortages; allow production from federal petroleum reserves; stimulate conservation, including revitalization of the railroads and expansion of the urban transportation systems; develop more and cleaner energy from coal resources; expedite clean and safe nuclear power production; create a new national energy independence authority to spur energy investment; accelerate development of technology "to capture energy from the sun and the earth for this and future generations."

In other areas, the President called for changes in the administration of funds for health education and social services programs and for an increased anti-crime effort.

He proposed that 16 current federal programs, including Medicaid, be combined into a single $10 billion federal grant. The funds would be divided among the states under a formula providing a larger share of funds to the states having a larger share of low income families.

The President also said he planned to take steps to improve the quality of medical and hospital care for veterans.

He proposed catastrophic health insurance for everybody covered by Medicare and, to finance this, a fee increase for short-term care. He said "nobody after reaching age 65 will have to pay more than $500 a year for covered hospital or nursing home care nor more than $250 for one year's doctors' bills."

Another consolidation of programs was planned for the areas of education, child nutrition and social services. "Flexible" federal dollar grants were envisaged to "do the job better and do it closer to home."

Among statements Ford made in his State-of-the-Union message:

Take the state of our economy.

Last January most things were rapidly getting worse.

This January most things are slowly but surely getting better.

The worst recession since World War II turned around in April. The best cost of living news of the past year is that double-digit inflation of 12 percent or higher was cut almost in half. The worst—unemployment remains far too high.

Today nearly 1.7 million more Americans are working than at the bottom of the recession. At year's end people were again being hired much faster than they were being laid off.

Yet let's be honest. Many Americans have not yet felt these changes in their daily lives. They still see prices going up far too fast, and they still know the fear of unemployment.

We are also a growing nation. We need more and more jobs every year. Today's economy has produced over 85 million jobs for Americans, but we need a lot more jobs, especially for the young.

My first objective is to have sound economic growth without inflation.

We all know from recent experience what runaway inflation does to ruin every other worthy purpose. We are slowing it; we must stop it cold.

For many Americans the way to a healthy noninflationary economy has become increasingly apparent; the Government must stop spending so much and stop borrowing so much of our money; more money must remain in private hands where it will do the most good. To hold down the cost of living, we must hold down the cost of government.

In the past decade, the federal budget has been growing at an average rate of over 10 percent a year. The budget I am submitting Wednesday cuts this rate of growth in half. I have kept my promise to submit a budget for the next fiscal year of $395 billion. In fact, it is $394.2 billion.

By holding down the growth of federal spending, we can afford additional tax cuts and return to the people who pay taxes more decision-making power over their own lives.

Last month I signed legislation to extend the 1975 tax reduction for the first six months of this year. I now propose that effective July 1, 1976, we give our taxpayers a tax cut of approximately $10 billion more than Congress agreed to in December. . . .

My recommendations for a firm restraint on the growth of federal spending and for greater tax reduction are simple and straightforward. For every dollar saved in cutting the growth in the federal budget we can have an added dollar of federal tax reduction.

We can achieve a balanced budget by 1979 if we have the courage and the wisdom to continue to reduce the growth of federal spending.

One test of a healthy economy is a job for every American who wants to work.

Government—our kind of government—cannot create that many jobs. But the federal government can create conditions and incentives for private business and industry to make more and more jobs.

Five out of six jobs in this country are in private business and industry. Common sense tells us this is the place to look for more jobs and to find them faster.

I mean real, rewarding, permanent jobs.

To achieve this we must offer the American people

greater incentives to invest in the future. My tax proposals are a major step in that direction.

To supplement these proposals, I ask that Congress enact changes in Federal tax laws that will speed up plant expansion and the purchase of new equipment. My recommendations will concentrate this job-creation tax incentive in areas where the unemployment rate now runs over 7 percent. Legislation to get this started must be approved at the earliest possible date.

Within the strict budget total that I will recommend for the coming year, I will ask for additional housing assistance for 500,000 families. These programs will expand housing opportunities, spur construction and help to house moderate and low income families.

We had a disappointing year in the housing industry in 1975, but with lower interest rates and available mortgage money, we can have a healthy recovery in 1976. . . .

Taking a longer look at America's future, there can be neither sustaining growth nor more jobs unless we continue to have an assured supply of energy to run our economy. Domestic production of oil and gas is still declining. Our dependence on foreign oil at high prices is still too great, draining jobs and dollars away from our own economy at the rate of $125 per year for every American.

Last month I signed a compromise national energy bill which enacts a part of my comprehensive energy independence program. This legislation was later not the complete answer to energy independence, but still a start in the right direction.

I again urge the Congress to move ahead immediately on the remainder of my energy proposals to make America invulnerable to the foreign oil cartel.

My proposals, as all of you know, would:

¶Reduce domestic natural gas shortages.

¶Allow production from Federal petroleum reserves.

¶Stimulate effective conservation, including revitalization of our railroads and the expansion of our urban transportation systems.

¶Develop more and cleaner energy from our vast coal resources.

¶Expedite clean and safe nuclear power production.

¶Create a new national energy independence authority to stimulate vital energy investment.

¶And accelerate development of technology to capture energy from the sun and the earth for this and future generations. . . .

Our federal Social Security system for people who have worked and contributed to it for all their lives is a vital part of our economic system. Its value is no longer debatable. In my budget for fiscal 1977 I am recommending that the full cost of living increases in the Social Security benefits be paid during the coming year.

But I am concerned about the integrity of our Social Security trust fund that enables people—those retired and those still working who will retire—to count on this source of retirement income. Younger workers watch their deductions rise and wonder if they will be adequately protected in the future.

We must meet this challenge head-on.

Simple arithmetic warns all of us that the Social Security trust fund is headed for trouble. Unless we act soon to make sure the fund takes in as much as it pays out, there will be no security for old or for young.

I must therefore recommend a three-tenths of 1 percent increase in both employer and employee Social Security taxes effective Jan. 1, 1977. This will cost each covered employee less than one extra dollar a week and will insure the integrity of the trust fund.

As we rebuild our economy, we have a continuing responsibility to provide a temporary cushion to the unemployed. At my request the Congress enacted two extensions and two expansions in unemployment insurance, which helped those who were jobless during 1975. These programs will continue in 1976.

In my fiscal year 1977 budget, I am also requesting funds to continue proven job training and employment opportunity programs for millions of other Americans.

Compassion and a sence of community—two of America's greatest strengths through our history—tell us we must take care of our neighbors who cannot take care of themselves. The host of federal programs in this field reflect our generosity as a people.

But everyone realizes that when it comes to welfare, government at all levels is not doing the job well. Too many of our welfare programs are inequitable and invite abuse. Too many of our welfare programs have problems from beginning to end. Worse, we are wasting badly needed resources without reaching many of the truly needy.

Complex welfare programs cannot be reformed overnight. Surely we cannot simply dump welfare into the laps of the 50 states, their local taxpayers or private charities, and just walk away from it. Nor is it the right time for massive and sweeping changes while we are still recovering from the recession.

Nevertheless, there are still plenty of improvements that we can make. I will ask Congress for Presidential authority to tighten up the rules for eligibility and benefits.

Last year I twice sought long-over-due reform of the scandal-riddled food stamp program. This year I say again: Let's give food stamps to those most in need. Let's not give any to those who don't need them. . . .

Democratic rebuttal by Muskie. A Congressional Democratic rebuttal to President Ford's State of the Union message deplored the Administration's "jobless policies" at home and questionable entanglements abroad without public consultation. It was delivered by Sen. Edmund S. Muskie (D, Me.) in a national telecast Jan. 21 during evening time made available by the three major commercial networks and the Public Broadcasting System. Muskie, chairman of the Senate Budget Committee, was chosen to make the rebuttal by Senate Democratic leader Mike Mansfield (Mont.).

Muskie's theme was that an administration "of timid vision" was presenting impractical, out-of-date policies to an American public that had already lost confidence in government. He urged the public to get involved and use its political power in the "election and supervision" of Congress. "Together we are the Union," he said, "and I find the state of that Union very strong indeed."

"We must reject," he said, "those of timid vision or policy who advise us to go back . . . to simpler times now gone forever, to go back on the promises we have made to each other." He said these involved going back on a guarantee to every American for "a decent job and secure retirement" and a commitment to quality education, affordable health care, consumer protection, worker safety, a clean environment.

The President's State of the Union message, he said, "profoundly misunderstands both the realities and the needs" of America. Ford's plans for the economy were "penny-wise and pound-foolish," he said. "Under them, America's factories are producing only three-fourths as many goods as they actually could. That means fewer jobs and higher prices." The taxpayers "pay a staggering price for these jobless policies," he said.

"What the nation needs at this time," Muskie contended, "is leadership that will not jump from one economic panic button to another."

Muskie recommended energy and food policies with an eye to keeping prices reasonable. He proposed "a wage-price council which will make life miserable for any big corporation that raises prices without very good reason and will do so in the name of the President."

For jobs, he advocated the public service jobs program as the best way to produce the most jobs at the lowest cost. He also recommended federal assistance to local communities "for short-term public works projects and to avoid layoffs in local government services."

Another recommendation was for improved government efficiency, such as in processing medical and pension services and in avoiding defense contract overruns.

In appealing for participation in the political process, Muskie said the politicians should be put "to a stringent test." Were they "men of their word?" If they promised more, did they talk about cost? If they proposed economy, did they talk about the services to be cut? Did they offer "specific proposals or simply slogans?" Those were the test questions, he suggested.

Fiscal 1977 Budget

$394.2 billion budgets with $43 billion deficit. President Ford Jan. 21, 1976 submitted to Congress a $394.2 billion budget for fiscal 1977. Revenues were estimated at $351.3 billion, the deficit at about $43 billion.

The growth rate of the total outlay was 5.5%, about half the average growth rate for the past 10 years. About half that increase came from defense, where spending was projected over the $100 billion mark for the first time, or 25.4% of the total federal budget.

Outlays for domestic programs fell below the inflation line of growth. The budget's total of $394.2 billion, in fact, was about $20 billion less than the budget would have reached through built-in growth even without new programs.

The reductions imposed by the President were exacted from Social Security, Medicare, food stamps, housing subsidies, child nutrition and veterans benefits, among other programs.

The President also planned to consolidate 59 existing federal programs into four "block grants" to the states for health, education, child nutrition and social services for the poor, disabled and elderly.

In addition, the President planned to phase out the emergency public service jobs program for the unemployed and extended unemployment benefits as well.

He requested a catastrophic illness insurance program for Medicare coverage and an increase in charges to pay for it. An increase in Social Security taxes was requested to set the program back on an even financial keel.

A new $10 billion tax cut for individuals and corporations was scheduled in the budget for mid-year. Other new tax provisions requested included a credit for middle-income investment in stocks and a credit for firms to expand in high-employment areas.

In his budget message, Ford said that the combination of tax and spending changes he proposed "will set us on a course that not only leads to a balanced budget within three years, but also improves the prospects for the economy to stay on a growth path that we can sustain.

"This is not a policy of the quick fix; it does not hold out the hollow promise that we can wipe out inflation and unemployment overnight. Instead, it is an honest, realistic policy—a policy that says we can steadily reduce inflation and unemployment if we maintain a prudent, balanced approach."

The President said he had provided

"fully for our defense and energy needs" and, in domestic programs, his objective had been "to achieve a balance between all the things we would like to do and those things we can realistically afford to do."

"The American people know that promises that the federal government will do more for them every year have not been kept," he declared. "I make no such promises."

At a briefing Jan. 21, the President said: "We are at a critical point in our history, a point where we can either allow federal spending and federal deficits to mushroom and allow our economic foundations to erode, or on the other hand we can decide to restrain the growth of federal spending and restore the vitality of our private economy."

The budget was predicated on a continuation of the current moderate economic recovery. It foresaw a 6.2% growth in the gross national product for calendar 1976, the growth in "real" terms after adjustment for inflation. A 5.7% rise was expected for 1977. In 1975, there had been a 2% decline.

Inflation, which increased 7% from December 1974 to December 1975, was expected to level off for a 5.9% increase for the next two years. A slight decline was forecast for unemployment, although the rate would remain relatively high—an average of 7.7% for calendar 1976. The longer-range forecast was for the rate to average 6.9% for 1977 and to run above 5% until 1981.

On a "full employment budget" basis—that is, one calculated with receipts and outlays occurring if the economy were operating at full capacity, normally utilizing a 4% unemployment rate—the new Ford budget would swing from a $16 billion deficit in fiscal 1976 to a $3 billion surplus in fiscal 1977.

For the transition period between the end of fiscal 1976 on June 30 and the beginning of fiscal 1977 on Oct. 1, the budget projected outlays of $98 billion and a deficit of $16.1 billion.

Among details of the budget:

Taxes—The budget reflected plans for a $28 billion-a-year permanent tax reduction, about 75% of which would go to individuals, the rest to businesses. Of the $22.2 billion scheduled to take effect in calendar 1976, about $9 billion had been enacted already for the first six months.

For individuals, the personal exemption of $750 would go to $875 for calendar 1976. A $17.50 tax credit would be allowed for each exemption or, as an alternate, a 1% credit on taxable income up to $9,000.

The low-income allowance of $1,700 would go to $1,750 for one person and from $2,100 to $2,300 for a couple. The regular standard deduction would remain at 16% of adjusted gross income, but the maximums would drop to $2,100 (from $2,400) for one and to $2,650 (from $2,800) for couples.

The special "work bonus" for poor families would be retained at 5% of earned income, with a maximum of $200 in cash payments to families not owing any taxes.

For corporations, the basic tax rate for income over $50,000 would drop a point to 47% in calendar 1976. The President requested anew faster amortization for electric utilities and an investment tax credit of 12%.

For calendar 1977, the personal exemption was scheduled to rise to $1,000 and a single standard deduction was planned of $2,500 for couples and of $1,800 for single taxpayers. A reduction in individual income-tax rates also was envisaged but not specified in the budget. The regular 10% business investment tax credit on purchases of machinery and equipment was to be made permanent.

Businesses in areas with unemployment of 7% or more would receive an accelerated depreciation rate for new equipment and plant expansion.

In other special provisions, the President proposed a tax deferral for investment by individuals in stocks or mutual funds, the investment lasting at least seven years. Some limits were planned al-

The Budget Dollar

Where it comes from:

Individual income taxes	39¢
Social insurance receipts	29¢
Corporation income taxes	13¢
Borrowing	11¢
Excise taxes	4¢
Other	4¢

Where it goes:

Benefit payments to individuals	40¢
Military	26¢
Grants to states and localities	15¢
Other federal operations	11¢
Net interest	8¢

though not set as yet, such as a maximum on the amount of taxes deferred and a maximum on personal income level. The proposal was to become effective July 1 with full deduction allowed for calendar 1976.

An estate-tax change for small businessmen and small farmers would permit heirs to defer the initial estate-tax payments for five years, thereafter payable over the next 20 years at 7% annual interest. The qualification was the first $300,000 in value of the estate. The deferral also could be claimed in part for estates up to $600,000 in value.

A .3% increase in the Social Security payroll taxes for both employers and employes was scheduled to become effective Jan. 1, 1977. The new 6.15% rate would make the maximum payment by workers about $1,014.75 a year. Currently, it was $895.05.

A rise in the federal unemployment-insurance tax rate paid by employers also was planned, effective Jan. 1, 1977. The rate would go from .5% to .65% and the wage base upon which it was paid would be increased also from $4,200 to $6,000.

The President repeated his 1975 proposal to eliminate the "double taxation" on income as it was earned by corporations and again as it was received by stockholders in dividends.

Defense—At $100.1 billion, defense spending for fiscal 1977 represented 5.4% of the gross national product. It was $8.9 billion more than the level estimated for fiscal 1976.

In terms of total obligational authority—money authorized by Congress but not all spent for that fiscal year plus funds appropriated in previous years but still unobligated—the defense budget was up $14.4 billion to $112.7 billion. This increase had a "real" growth of $7.2 billion after adjustment for inflation and pay raises. An anticipated $2 billion "real" growth for fiscal 1976 would be the first "real" rise in defense spending in seven years.

The spending boost was directed into

Budget Receipts and Outlays

In millions of dollars

Receipts by Source	1975 actual	1976 estimate	TQ* estimate	1977 estimate
Individual income taxes	122,386	130,822	40,003	153,641
Corporation income taxes	40,621	40,056	8,416	49,461
Social insurance taxes and contributions	86,441	92,571	25,174	115,052
Excise taxes	16,551	16,901	4,371	17,806
Estate and gift taxes	4,611	5,100	1,400	5,800
Customs duties	3,676	3,800	1,000	4,300
Miscellaneous receipts	6,711	8,284	1,530	7,202
Total receipts	**280,997**	**297,534**	**81,894**	**351,262**
Outlays by Function	**1975 actual**	**1976 estimate**	**TQ* estimate**	**1977 estimate**
Military	86,585	92,759	25,028	101,129
International affairs	4,358	5,665	1,334	6,824
General science, space, and technology	3,989	4,311	1,157	4,507
Natural resources, environment, and energy	9,537	11,796	3,289	13,772
Agriculture	1,660	2,875	742	1,729
Commerce and transportation	16,010	17,801	4,819	16,498
Community and regional development	4,431	5,802	1,529	5,532
Education, training, employment, and social services	15,248	18,900	4,403	16,615
Health	27,647	32,137	8,291	34,393
Income security	108,605	128,509	32,742	137,115
Veterans benefits and services	16,597	19,035	4,362	17,196
Law enforcement and justice	2,942	3,402	914	3,426
General government	3,089	3,547	961	3,433
Revenue sharing and general purpose fiscal assistance	7,005	7,169	2,046	7,351
Interest	30,974	34,835	9,769	41,297
Allowances**	....	200	175	2,260
Undistributed offsetting receipts	−14,075	−15,208	−3,589	−18,840
Total outlays	**324,601**	**373,535**	**97,971**	**394,237**
Budget surplus or deficit (−)	**−43,604**	**−76,001**	**−16,077**	**−42,975**

*The period July 1, 1976–Sept. 30, 1976 is a "transitional quarter" resulting from the change in the government's fiscal year. The old fiscal year started July 1. Starting this year fiscal years will begin Oct. 1.

**Includes allowances for civilian agency pay raises and contingencies.

Source: Office of Management and Budget

weaponry, including some major, expensive items such as the B1 bomber and the Trident submarine and its missiles. The budget called for cuts in personnel costs—a reduced Navy Reserve (by 40,000 to a level of 51,000), a cut in the civilian work force (by 26,000 to 1,036,000), a ceiling on pay raises, a cutback in pensions and some closings of bases.

Uniformed strength was to remain at 2.1 million, after adjustments in the individual services. Their strength levels: Navy 544,000 (up 12,000); Air Force 571,000 (down 13,000); Army 790,000 (unchanged).

Their budget levels were: Navy $37.9 billion; Air Force $32.6 billion; Army $27.3 billion.

Space—The $3.7 billion budgeted for the National Aeronautics and Space Administration was up slightly, by $159 million, from the fiscal 1976 figure.

More than half the total was required for the space shuttle, to maintain the target of a launching by 1979. A test-landing in California was planned for 1977 and a space launching for 1979.

The budget also covered initial work on two new scientific satellites, one for solar studies, another for measurement of the earth's magnetic field.

One other project was for NASA to research advanced technology for airplanes.

Projects deferred for lack of funding included the prospective purchase of a third space shuttle, the orbiting of a big telescope and, by 1985, launch of a space probe to Uranus.

Energy—Total outlays for the Energy Research and Development Administration (ERDA) were budgeted at $5.3 billion, up 30% from the fiscal 1976 estimate of $4 billion. Of this, $2.4 billion was slated for research and development.

The proposed outlays for energy research—which spread into other agencies such as the Interior Department and the Nuclear Regulatory Commission as well as ERDA—totaled $2.9 billion for fiscal 1977, up 30% from the fiscal 1976 estimates (and 85% over actual fiscal 1975 spending).

The nuclear component of research and development in the fiscal 1977 budget was $1.4 billion. Nuclear fission projects (such as the liquid-metal, fast-breeder reactor) were budgeted at $709 million and nuclear fusion programs at $304 million, both up 36% over the previous year's funding levels.

A $282 million program was planned for nuclear-fuel projects, such as exploration for uranium and processing for re-use of spent nuclear fuel from power plants. The funding represented a 73% boost from the previous year's level.

Other ERDA budget levels were: $63 million, up from $12 million, for research on ways to safeguard nuclear fuel against theft and for development of a storage facility for radioactive waste materials accumulated from the nuclear power industry; $116 million, up 35%, for solar-energy research; $50 million, up 41%, for geothermal energy projects; $442 million, up 33%, for research into liquefication and gasification of coal and deep-drilling for oil and gas; $91 million, up 65%, for energy conservation techniques for buildings, business and transit.

Outlays for the Nuclear Regulatory Commission were expected to rise $36 million to the $236 million level.

President Ford renewed his request of 1975 for an independent energy authority to provide loans and guarantees and other aid for energy projects. A $100 billion scale of operation was projected, with $10 billion of it slated for fiscal 1977. The only impact on the budget, however, would be a $42 million outlay estimated for fiscal 1977 from operation of the authority, since its investments were to be repaid.

In an apparent concession to Congressional apathy toward the proposal, the President also reiterated a request that, pending establishment of the authority, a loan-guarantee program be authorized by Congress to foster development of synthetic fuels, mainly oil-shale and coal gasification projects. A $2 billion level for the program, administered by ERDA, was projected for fiscal 1976 and a $6 billion level for fiscal 1977.

Funding for an emergency oil-storage program was contained in the budget; at a level of $100 million in funding authority, budget outlays of $36 million were estimated for fiscal 1977. The Administration was planning to tap naval petroleum reserves for sales to finance the program.

The Administration also was planning some 14 lease sales through fiscal 1977 for development of offshore oil and gas sites, including for the first time ones off the coasts of Alaska and Atlantic states. The budget reflected the activity with estimates of $3 billion in receipts for fiscal 1976 and $6 billion in fiscal 1977.

Health—President Ford proposed major revision of the Medicare program of health insurance for the elderly.

Under new "catastrophe" insurance coverage, cash costs to a beneficiary would be limited to $500 a year for hospitals and $250 for doctors. This would result in additional benefits of $538 million a year for the recipients. But another new provision to raise the fee of Medicare coverage would reduce benefits $1.9 billion.

Still another new proposal was to limit fee increases under Medicare to 7% a year for hospitals and to 4% for doctors. The estimated federal savings for this were $909 million in fiscal 1977 and more than twice as much the following year.

As a result of the changes, Medicare outlays were budgeted at $19.6 billion, $2.2 billion more than in fiscal 1976 but $2.2 billion less than they would be without the revision.

A major innovation also was planned in other health areas, where the Administration wanted to provide $10 billion in a "block grant" formulation to the states to replace funds currently channeled into 16 separate programs, including Medicaid, health planning, community health and mental health centers.

This would result in an initial budget increase of $1 billion for Medicaid, but funding of most of the other health programs would decline. The Administration extended a budgetary guarantee for fiscal 1977 against any decrease in these programs. Beyond that, however, a new distribution would be applied to the states under a formula involving the number of poor people, per capita income and "relative tax effort."

The Administration planned to close or transfer to local control eight Public Health Service hospitals. Congressional approval was required for the action.

A $3.1 billion budget item for medical research represented a $212 million increase over the fiscal 1976 amount.

Education—Total outlays of $6.9 billion were proposed, with $3.3 billion to be assigned to the states in a block-grant form from consolidation of 27 separate education aid programs.

The states would be required to allocate three-quarters of the block-grant funding to disadvantaged or handicapped students, and they would be required to hold public hearings on plans for the allocation. But they would no longer be required to provide matching funds and would have more flexibility in disbursing the funds.

The Basic Opportunity Grants program, providing up to $1,400 a year to college students, was budgeted at $1.1 billion, up $50 million over fiscal 1976.

Budget outlays of $438.5 million for the impact-aid school program represented a decline of $219 million from fiscal 1976. The aid, which went to school districts that had many students whose parents were federal employes, would be restricted to reimbursement for children whose parents lived and worked on federal property, such as the military. Currently, two other categories of aid were sanctioned as well, for children whose parents worked for the government but did not live on federal land or whose parents lived in public housing.

Welfare—In another block-grant proposal, the budget called for $2.5 billion for a variety of social services such as day care centers, aid to senior citizens, foster care, homemakers' care and family planning. A 25% state matching requirement was eliminated and the states were given more flexibility in disbursement.

Outlays for aid to families with dependent children were up $100 million to $6 billion. Outlays for the Supplemental Security Income program for the aged, blind and disabled were up $700 million to $5.2 billion.

In both these and other welfare programs, the Administration planned a drive to enforce and review eligibility requirements.

In a fourth block-grant area, President Ford called for consolidation of 15 child nutrition programs into one $2.4 billion budgetary unit.

Income maintenance—The proposed .6% increase in the Social Security payroll tax, effective Jan. 1, 1977, was expected to add $3.3 billion to the trust fund revenues in fiscal 1977. Split between the employer and employe, it would raise the combined rate to 12.3%. Without the increase, the fund would be depleted by the early 1980s, it was estimated, because of the increase in beneficiaries, higher earned benefits and cost-of-living increments. A cost-of-living adjustment due in July was estimated by the Administration at 6.7%, another in July 1977 at 5.9%.

President Ford did not renew his proposal of 1975 for a "cap" of 5% on the cost-of-living raises, which Congress had ignored.

He did suggest several reductions, said to be worth $826 million in fiscal 1977. One of them was to phase out benefits paid to students aged 18 to 22. Other aid was available, the administration pointed out, such as the Basic Opportunity Grants for college students. Other suggestions were to eliminate retroactive payments on initial application for Social Security benefits and to apply an annual instead of a monthly test of outside earnings to reduce benefits.

On a longer-range basis, partly because the Social Security trust fund was facing a dwindling proportion of workers to support the retired, the administration proposed another financing change, to tie initial benefits only to rising wage levels rather than to the combination of wages and prices. The goal was to stabilize at current levels the proportion of a worker's wages to benefits received upon full retirement.

Unemployment aid—Predicated on the Administration's forecast of a 1.6% drop in the unemployment rate from calendar 1976 to 1977, $15.4 billion was budgeted for unemployment compensation in fiscal 1977 (9.6 million recipients), a drop from $18.2 billion in fiscal 1976 (11.5 million recipients).

The budget also reflected the administration's ($1.3 billion) recommendation that Congress let two emergency jobless-benefit extensions expire as scheduled March 31, 1977.

The $15.4 billion for jobless compensation included $5.7 billion to replenish the unemployment insurance trust funds in states that exhausted them (18 states had done so, and 10 to 12 others were expected to do so by June).

The administration wanted a "major study" of the "future direction" of the federal-state unemployment service. Its budget totals were $549 million in fiscal 1976, for 4.2 million job placements and $569 million in fiscal 1977, for 4.4 million placements.

A rapid diminution was scheduled in the budget for public service jobs programs—from $3.2 billion level in fiscal 1976 to $1.6 billion the following year. The President planned to ask for $1.7 billion in a supplemental budget request in fiscal 1976 to maintain the current program at the 330,000 jobs level until Jan. 1, 1977, but he also wanted the funds applied only to areas with over 6.5% unemployment and to jobs paying no more than $7,000 a year.

Other jobs and training programs also were due for budget reductions. The special program to provide summer jobs for youths was put down for $400 million (670,000 jobs), down from $440 million (740,000 jobs) for the summer of 1976 in the current fiscal year. Training programs operated by states and cities were slotted for $2 billion, down from $2.5 billion in fiscal 1976.

Urban development—The Administration proposed $7.2 billion in outlays for the housing and urban development department (HUD). That level of activity was consistent with that of fiscal 1976. Going into fiscal 1977, the department planned more emphasis on community development grants to local governments and on housing subsidies and less emphasis on older programs, such as urban renewal.

On programs to aid housing by purchase of home mortgages made at below-market interest rates, the budget assumed "that there will no longer be a need for these temporary programs . . . as conditions in the mortgage market return to normal." Despite the same assumption in the previous budget, HUD had injected $8 billion into the housing market in 1975 to buy mortgages in an attempt to spur the market.

In HUD's apartment-subsidy program, under which rent aid was provided for low-income families, the Administration projected subsidies for 400,000 units. The department planned to use part of the funding to ease the problem of defaults on government-insured mortgages by apartment projects. The apartment subsidies were to be applied in both fiscal 1976 and 1977 to up to 110,000 units in apartment projects near default or owned by HUD as a result of default.

Transportation—The Transportation Department's outlays were up 5% in the new budget to $12.87 billion ($12.25 billion in fiscal 1976).

Outlays for federally aided road programs were budgeted at $6.72 billion, a 4.6% increase, but the administration wanted to reduce roadbuilding commitments from what it considered an "abnormally high" level in fiscal 1976 from release of frozen funds to spur employment.

Regular mass-transit outlays of $1.2 billion would be at about the same level as in fiscal 1976. Financing from flexible use of the highway trust fund was raised to $385 million, from $65 million in fiscal 1976. On this, the administration was seeking to put a 50% limit on the amount of flexible funds the cities could use for transit operating subsidies. Cities reportedly were applying almost all of such funds to transit deficits.

Outlays for aid to railroads included $151 million, down from $420 million, for freight operations; $70 million, up from $25 million, for branch-line subsidies; $125 million to improve the rail-passenger service between Boston and Washington; and $484 million, a $44 million rise, for Amtrak.

Because of Amtrak's mounting deficit, the budget contained a demand for service reductions "on the least efficient routes."

In a budget area separate from that of the Federal Railroad Administration, the U.S. Railway Association, a government corporation, planned a 29% rise in aid to the Consolidated Rail Corp. (Conrail), the emerging government-chartered system scheduled to take over declining Northeast freight lines. New budget authority for USRA was put at the $1.4 billion level to cover purchase of Conrail securities.

Federal support for aviation would decline slightly to $581.4 million for facilities and equipment and airport improvements. Subsidy payments to the airlines were expected to rise to $80 million in fiscal 1977, from $60.7 million.

Environment—Federal pollution-control programs were to be funded at $4.4 billion for fiscal 1977, up $1.3 billion from the estimated fiscal 1976 activity.

However, the Environmental Protection Agency budget dropped slightly, by $53 million, to $718 million. The water quality improvement program actually declined $59.7 million in the budget priorities. And the administration recommended against any new contract authority for grants to the states for construction of sewage plants. About $6 billion authorized for such projects in 1972 remained uncommitted, the EPA reported.

The administration wanted to phase out federal financing for storm sewers and sewer replacements, which required Congressional action.

It also sought Congressional approval for a six-year extension of deadline for municipal compliance with water quality standards.

More federal funds would be available to states for their efforts to eliminate pollution from drinking water supplies. The budget item was $42.8 million, up $10.6 million.

The federal air pollution control program was budgeted at $143.4 million, down slightly by $2.3 million. Congress was asked again, as in 1975, to postpone deadlines for compliance with air pollution limits.

Federal funding for solid waste control was up slightly to $15.7 million. Noise control funding was down slightly to $10.3 million.

Agriculture—Agriculture Department funds for fiscal 1977 were figured at $10.7 billion. This was $3.4 billion less than in fiscal 1976, but about $1.2 billion of the reduction came from an accounting procedure because many Farmers Home Administration loans made in fiscal 1976 would not be sold to private banks until fiscal 1977.

Another reduction of $1.3 billion occurred in food programs, which were budgeted at $7.1 billion. Reduction of the food-stamp program, proposed in 1975 but not enacted by Congress, accounted for $900 million of the fund scaleback. The change, pegging eligibility to the poverty-level income ($6,550 for a family of four), would drop 3.4 million persons as food stamp beneficiaries.

A proposed consolidation of other food programs, also broached without avail to Congress in 1975, accounted for the other $400 million reduction in food programs. These programs currently supplied cash or food to subsidize school cafeteria operations, summer meals for needy children and supplementary diets for infants and pregnant women. The Administration proposal was to consolidate these 15 programs into one block grant to the states for administration and to limit eligibility to poverty-level families. This was expected to eliminate 10 million children from the school meal program. The Administration also wanted to end the 25¢ subsidy to all school lunches and to eliminate a supplemental milk program.

The department's support payments to farmers totaled $865 million in the new budget, a drop of $646 million attributed largely to less need for short-term export credit because of high world demand for farm commodities.

Lower commodity prices were reflected in the foreign food-aid budget, which was down $193 million to a $1.28 billion total. This was expected to accommodate export of 6.2 million tons of grain.

The department requested a $15 million three-year program against infestation of the cotton boll weevil.

Federal pay & employment—The federal government payroll was projected on the basis of employment of 4.6 million persons by the end of fiscal 1977. This included 1,919,300 civilians, 543,600 Postal Service workers and 2.1 million military personnel on active duty. The total was a reduction of 12,500 from the fiscal 1976 period.

The payroll for direct compensation was $32.3 billion for the civilians ($31.5 billion in fiscal 1976) and $21.7 billion for the military ($21.8 billion in fiscal 1976).

The budget provided for an average pay boost of 4.7%. A 5% ceiling on pay increases was proposed for white-collar employes and a 3.4% boost was expected for the 500,000 blue-collar workers from a proposed revision in setting the pay raises. To offset inequity in any sector, all federal workers were to be guaranteed at least a 3% pay boost in October.

Military and civilian retirement benefits were expected to cost $19 billion, up from $14 billion in fiscal 1976. The administration sought to drop a one-point percentage adjustment added to the regular cost-of-living increment as a catch-up because of delays between increases.

1976 Economic Reports

Moderate recovery pace advocated. President Ford and his economic advisers Jan. 26, 1976 urged a moderate and steady recovery for the economy with a wary eye on the inflation factor.

In his Economic Report to Congress, President Ford said the "underlying fact about our economy is that it is steadily growing healthier." "It will take several years of sound policies to restore sustained, noninflationary growth," he said. "We must restore the strength of the American economy as quickly as we can. But in so doing we cannot ignore the dangers of refueling inflationary forces, because unchecked inflation makes steady growth and full employment impossible."

The President told Congress "another major tax cut will be feasible by 1979" if proper budgetary restraint were exercised. This would be in addition to the $28 billion-a-year tax reduction proposed by the President in his State of the Union Message.

The message on moderation and caution against inflation was the same in the annual report of the Council of Economic Advisers, which accompanied the President's report to Congress. "If we do not commit ourselves to a gradual recovery over a period of years," the council contended, "we may increase economic instability and lose our chance for sustainable growth, which we believe offers the safest and surest route to full employment in future years."

The council's goal was for "a moderate but sustained recovery." "What we need is a durable recovery," it stressed, "not a boom that carries the seeds of the renewed instability in prices, incomes and employment."

The challenge, it said, was "to set the stage for a gradual transition from stimulation, which is still needed in the current year, to a set of policies appropriate for the long run."

As the President did, the council cautioned that "inflation could pose a major threat to the viability of the present recovery." Its forecast was for a 6% increase in prices in 1976.

Council chairman Alan Greenspan, at a news conference Jan. 26, said there was not any evidence at the moment of a "re-ignition of inflationary forces." He identified the area of the greatest danger of such a "re-ignition"—the federal deficit, which the Administration predicted would drop from the $76 billion range in fiscal 1976 to a $43 billion level in fiscal 1977.

The council conceded that even the moderate recovery it advocated would "almost surely" leave the unemployment rate "distressingly high this year." Its prediction was for the rate to average 7.7% in 1976. Currently, it was 8.3%.

For those working, however, the council forecast that wages would rise 8% to 9% in 1976. Again, it cautioned on inflation. If wage gains were higher in the near term, "inflationary pressure could be intensified" and "inflation rates higher than 6% could be built into the economy for some years to come." The council noted that major union contracts covering 4½ million workers expired or were scheduled for reopening in 1976, but it did not expect the wage agreements in major industries to upset its overall wage forecast.

The council estimated that the gross national product, or total output of goods and services, spurred by rising consumer spending and business outlays for plants and equipment, would grow by 6% to 6½% (adjusted for inflation) during 1976. This was predicated on a money-supply growth rate of 6¼%, among other things. The council indicated its consonance with the current monetary policy of the Federal Reserve Board, whose long-term target was a 5% to 7½% growth rate for money supply (total of private demand deposits plus cash in public hands).

Among other data in the council's report:

- Total consumer outlays, which increased 3.9% in 1975, were predicted to rise almost 6% in real terms (adjusted for inflation) in 1976.
- Business outlays for plants and equipment, which declined about 10% in 1975, could ascend 4% or 5% in real terms.
- The ratio of inventories to final sales was "expected to decline a little more in early 1976," with inventories then growing "at about the same rate as final sales" after midyear.
- Housing starts, at a 1.3 million annual pace at the end of 1975, should expand to 1,750,000 units by the end of 1976.

Among excerpts from the council's report:

The U.S. economy is now recovering from the most severe recession in postwar history. Spurred by a lower inflation rate, tax cuts, and increasing employment, significant gains have already been made in the purchasing power of consumers. Production has been rising rapidly since the spring of last year. But because this recovery started from very low levels of resource utilization, unemployment will almost surely remain distressingly high this year even though large gains in employment are expected during 1976.

The social hardships and economic waste associated with the current level of unemployment should not be underestimated. Accordingly, we must seek to lower unemployment as rapidly as is consistent with the need to ensure that the reductions will be lasting. Policies that might speed the decline in unemployment in the short run should not be so expansionary as to lead to increased instability and greater social hardships in the long run.

Thus, policies for 1976 must attempt to sustain the recovery now in progress but at a pace sufficiently moderate to prevent renewed imbalances and a rise in inflation. They must also continue to mitigate the hardships associated with high unemployment. At the same time, our present policies must lay the foundations for a long period of steady growth.

Because we began the present recovery with more slack than in any of the previous postwar cycles, a much longer period of above-average growth will be required for a return to full resource utilization. Even under the best of circumstances the return to full employment cannot realistically be accomplished this year or next. To ensure that we return to high levels of resource utilization—as is our objective—the recovery must therefore be a durable one.

Our best estimate is that real gross national product (GNP) will be 6 to 6½ percent higher in 1976 than in 1975. This growth rate is not a goal. Rather, it is a projected outcome of the forces of recovery that were set in motion in 1975, by stimulative fiscal measures, by a return of consumer and business confidence, and by external economic factors discussed elsewhere in this report. The availability of much umemployed labor and unused plant capacity requires that economic policy should continue to support an economic expansion at growth rates significantly above the long-term growth of capacity output. But our knowledge of the interdependence between real growth and inflation is not sufficiently precise to permit a direct translation from general goals to specific targets.

As a consequence, policies cannot be designed to reach any particular targets with a high degree of confidence. We believe, however, that policies consistent with a moderate but sustained recovery offer a far safer and surer route to full employment than policies which attempt to engineer a very rapid return to full capacity. What we need is a durable recovery—not a boom that carries the seeds of renewed instability in prices, incomes, and employment. . . .

What is called for in our judgment is a steadier course in macroeconomic policies than has been followed in the past. We should set policies broadly consistent with sustainable long-term noninflationary growth and try to limit the size and duration of any policy deviations that promise short-term benefits but risk interfering with our long-run goals.

The severity of the recent recession does call for maintaining stimulative economic policies to accommodate an expansion of real output at a rate above that sustainable in the long run but departures from the policies that are appropriate in the long run should be moderate. If we do not commit ourselves to a gradual recovery over a period of years, we may increase economic instability and lose our chance for sustainable growth, which we believe offers the safest and surest route to full employment in future years.

It is much easier to enunciate the general principle

of stability in policy than to apply it to specific circumstances. The challenge to current monetary and fiscal policy is to set the stage for a gradual transition from stimulation, which is still needed in the current year, to a set of policies appropriate for long-run growth.

The monetary authorities recognize that the present levels of output and employment are still very far from satisfactory. Yet concern with the achievement of greater economic stability in future years suggests that any rate of growth in money which is at the upper limit of the tolerance range announced by the Federal Reserve (7½ percent for MI, 10½ percent for M2), could not be maintained indefinitely if progress toward lower inflation rates is to continue.

The thrust of fiscal policy will also have to change gradually. Fiscal policy became more expansionary when the recession worsened and unemployment mounted in 1974 and in early 1975. Over the near term, these expansionary fiscal policies will be maintained as most of the provisions of the Tax Reduction Act of 1975 have been extended from the end of last year to the middle of this year through the Revenue Adjustment Act of 1975.

The budget which the President has proposed provides for a marked deceleration in the growth of Federal spending, as outlays are to be held to $394 billion in fiscal 1977, which ends in September of next year. Starting in July 1976, taxes are to be cut by about $28 billion relative to what they would be under 1974 law. Because of the recovery, Federal receipts are then expected to grow over three times as fast as outlays between fiscal 1976 and fiscal 1977 causing the deficit to fall by more than $30 billion.

However, the full-employment balance, on a national income accounts basis, will show little change during calendar 1976 from the $6-billion deficit estimated for the second half of last year. In this way of the fiscal policy stimulus will be maintained throughout 1976. It will then be reduced in 1977 because of the proposed increase in Social Security tax rates and the much faster rise in individual income tax receipts than Federal expenditures.

At the present time, with substantial reserves of labor and capacity available, consumption and investment are complements, not substitutes. Indeed, public expenditures in excess of tax receipts are needed to absorb the excess of private saving over private investment demand at current levels of economic activity. In 1977 and beyond, however, private investment and publicly supported consumption will become increasingly competitive.

To avoid inducing a policy and output mix that is incompatible with the requirements of long-term economic growth, fiscal stimulus must be diminished gradually during coming years. Without greater fiscal restraint, the saving flows available for private capital formation might eventually become too small. Furthermore the danger of intensifying inflationary pressures under such conditions would preclude expanding the money supply sufficiently to finance both the Government deficits and the needed improvements and growth in our industrial capacity.

It is this public-versus-private allocation problem to which the President's program tying a $28 billion cut in the growth of Federal outlays to a comparable cut in taxes is addressed. The source of the problem has been the rapid growth in nondefense budget expenditures in recent years. During the 1960's some growth in the share of national resources allocated to the nondefense expenditures of the Federal Government was considered desirable in order to alleviate poverty and to accomplish other important social goals. Further growth in the ratio of public expenditures to total output, however, directly bears on fundamental issues concerning the efficiency of the economy, equity for the working population, and the scope for private decision making in our economy.

Energy Policy

Ford for 'energy independence.' President Ford sent Congress Feb. 26, 1976 a message on energy emphasizing the need to "regain our energy independence." "We must reduce our vulnerability to the economic disruption which a few foreign countries can cause by cutting off our energy supplies or by arbitrarily raising prices," he told Congress.

Among his major proposals was a request for presidential authority, subject to disapproval by Congress, to decide between two competing proposals for delivery of natural gas from Alaska's north slope. The authority for decision currently lay with the Federal Power Commission, subject to judicial review. Under the President's plan, the FPC would be requested to make recommendations on the choice by February 1977.

One of the proposals, from a consortium of U.S. and Canadian companies, was for a 6,280-mile pipeline from Alaska through Canada to points in the western and midwestern U.S. The other proposal, from El Paso Co., was for an 809-mile pipeline from Prudhoe Bay to the southern coast of Alaska. The line generally would parallel that of the Alaskan oil pipeline currently under construction. At the coast terminal, the gas would be liquefied for shipment by tankers to Southern California, where it would be regasified.

The President requested a provision to prohibit legal challenges to the gasline decision, once approved by Congress. The request was made in light of the requisite Canadian cooperation on the gasline, to bar possible delay from protracted litigation after the Canadian decision on a route, if it were made in favor of the Canadian route.

The message reiterated the Administration's proposal for deregulation of new natural gas. The President said the higher prices from removal of price controls would stimulate 25% more production by 1985.

The President announced in his message that he would take administrative action to limit imports of liquefied natural gas to one trillion cubic feet a year by 1985, or about 5% of total U.S. natural gas demand. Although little liquefied natural gas was currently imported, there were proposals to import it from Nigeria and Algeria, and the Administration was said to be wary of getting into a dependent situation to foreign suppliers.

Another major proposal in the message was for a $1 billion authorization for financial assistance to states and localities for coping with problems flowing from development of energy resources on federal lands, such as offshore oil reserves. The proposed grants, loans and loan guarantees would be extended over a 15-year period for roads, schools, water facilities and other community development projects.

The President urged Congress to complete action on legislation to authorize production of oil from the naval petroleum reserves.

In the nuclear field, Ford reaffirmed the Administration's commitment for further development of the breeder-type of nuclear power reactor. The President also requested again legislation to open the uranium enrichment operation to private business.

Financial Plight of Cities & States

A long-growing economic and political problem was reaching crisis proportions by 1975: The cost of ever-expanding city and state services was growing at a rate considerably faster than were city and state revenues. New York City, the nation's municipal giant, had become the glaring example of a metropolis teetering perpetually on the brink of insolvency. And many other cities, while smaller and therefore less conspicuous, were in equally serious straits. President Ford expressed extreme reluctance to come to New York's fiscal rescue. He held that the city's woes were largely of the city's own making and that New York should shoulder the primary burden of improving its economic management and working its way out of its plight. Only if the city itself took needed action, Ford indicated, would he consider federal aid justified.

Mayors warn of cities' plight. A delegation representing the U.S. Conference of Mayors told the Senate Government Operations Subcommittee on Intergovernmental Relations Jan. 30, 1975 that many if not most of the major U.S. cities would soon be forced to reduce services, lay off employes and raise taxes.

"Any federal program to cure the ills of the economy by a reduction in federal taxes without some form of direct assistance to the cities will be offset by increases in local taxes," Moon Landrieu, mayor of New Orleans, testified. "What the hand of the Internal Revenue Service puts into the pocket of the taxpayer, the hand of the local tax collector will take out of his other pocket."

San Francisco Mayor Joseph Alioto, current president of the mayors' conference, said that many current anti-recession economic proposals were aimed at aiding the taxpayer in the $8,000–$14,000 income bracket. However, he said, financially strapped local governments would be forced to raise property taxes, which already fell most heavily on middle income groups.

The mayors urged Congressional passage of a one-shot, $5 billion emergency relief act to help balance city and state government budgets and head off tax increases. It should be in addition to the $16 billion tax cut proposed by President Ford, they said. A survey of 67 cities, the delegation said, had indicated that 42 cities would either raise taxes or reduce services if outside financial aid were not forthcoming.

States, localities hard hit by recession. State and local government officials shared many of the same fiscal problems confronting the Ford Administration: how to provide adequate services to the increased numbers of persons in need, meet labor demands and pay fuel bills when inflationary pressures had raised the cost of government and recession had caused revenues to shrink.

Neither of the options available to officials—increased taxes or reduced spending on services and personnel—was popular with the electorate. Yet, according to an Associated Press survey published March 16, 1975 by the New York

Times, 16 states planned net tax increases for fiscal 1976. Only eight states reported they would reduce taxes.

Another survey of 67 various-sized municipalities conducted by the National League of Cities and published in the Times March 28 indicated that 36 cities planned to postpone capital improvements, 21 reported municipal job layoffs or hiring freezes, 43 said they expected revenue short falls during the year, 28 planned to raise taxes and 23 intended to reduce city services.

Austerity budgets combining increased taxes and reduced services were planned by nine cities, the study stated: Anchorage, Alaska; Inglewood, Calif.; East St. Louis, Ill.; Auburn, Me.; Newark, N.J.; Binghamton, N.Y.; Buffalo, Syracuse and Cleveland.

Local officials' position—Many state and local officials blamed their financial crises on national economic problems beyond their control, such as tight money conditions that made borrowing difficult, and the soaring unemployment rate that caused demands for social services to rise.

National policies for dealing with the recession also were at odds with state and local efforts to deal with the economic slump, these officials said. They noted that one consequence of the recently enacted federal income tax cut was a sharp cutback in federal revenues earmarked for states and localities at a time when these government faced budget deficits.

New York City's problems—New York City's specific financial woes were highlighted April 2 when Standard & Poor's Corp., one of the nation's foremost credit rating agencies, suspended its "A" rating on New York City bonds.

The action was taken, the firm said, because of the possible "inability or unwillingness of the major underwriting banks to continue to purchase the city's notes and bonds." Standard & Poor's had upgraded its ratings on the city's bonds from "BBB" meaning a medium-good investment, to "A" meaning a good investment, only 16 months earlier.

New York City's cash-flow problems were so bad that state officials April 3 loaned the city $400 million, representing an advance on payments of state revenue-sharing funds not due until late June, so that city welfare benefits could be paid. Seeking to restore the city's credibility in financial markets, Mayor Abraham Beame April 1 offered a $12.8 billion "austerity" budget for fiscal 1976, beginning July 1. Despite some draconian economies, including plans to fire nearly 4,000 city workers and close 43 schools, three hospitals, and eight to ten libraries, Beame said the city still faced a $641.5 million deficit.

New York City's planned personnel cutbacks came at a time when the city's unemployment rate for March was 11.5%, a postwar record.

Difficulties elsewhere—Among problems and attempted solutions in other cities and states during 1975:

Newark, N.J. shared many of New York City's problems. Its tax base was declining as industry and middle class residents fled the city. Heavy demands were being placed on city services by the large numbers of poor persons filling the population void. Newark Mayor Kenneth Gibson (D) announced Jan. 16 that 370 city employes would be laid off in an effort to reduce an anticipated deficit of $35.7 million. In a later announcement May 1, Gibson said the public school staff would be cut 20%—1,600 administrators, teachers and workers faced dismissal.

In Connecticut, the General Assembly March 13 raised the state sales tax from 6% to 7%, making it the highest state sales tax in the country. The added revenues would ease a deficit expected to total more than $90 by the end of fiscal 1975, according to the Times March 16. Gov. Ella Grasso (D), who had been thwarted by the legislature in her plan to refuse a pay increase, April 30 returned a portion of her new higher salary to the state.

Residents of Willimantic, Conn. ended a taxpayers' revolt Jan. 16 when voters approved a $2.4 million budget that was 9% smaller than the original proposal. Voters had rejected three other budget proposals, saying they feared the spending requirement would necessitate a higher tax rate.

Willimantic city government had been paralyzed since Dec. 2, 1974 when the first budget had been voted down at public meeting.

Michigan, whose economic health was directly related to conditions in the auto industry, also faced double digit unemployment and a 30% drop in corporate tax revenues. Cutbacks totaling $80 million already had been made in the state's planned expenditures and more reductions were under consideration to reduce the budget imbalance, the Times reported March 16. Gov. William G. Milliken (R) took a 10% cut in salary.

Detroit officials March 30 announced drastic measures designed to bring the 1976 budget into balance. Up to 25% of the city's 23,000 employes were scheduled to be laid off, paring Detroit's payroll by about $96 million. A budget deficit totaling $65–$85 million had been projected. The action was necessary, city officials said, because municipal unions had refused to forego automatic wage raises and accept pay cuts. However, the planned layoff of 10% of Detroit's police officers was averted May 21 when city officials and representatives of the police force reached agreement on a plan calling for all officers to take 14 consecutive working days off without pay between June and the end of 1976. The police also agreed to accept straight-time pay for holiday work.

Cleveland, also affected by the massive auto industry layoffs, faced a $16 million deficit. To meet the fiscal crisis, Mayor Ralph Perk (R) laid off about 1,100 city workers, including police and firemen, reduced garbage collection and closed four fire stations. Voters defeated Perk's proposal to raise the city income tax.

Ford rebuffs N.Y. plea for aid. New York City, which needed $1.5 billion by June 30, 1975 to meet short-term obligations, sought assistance on many fronts for dealing with the city's fiscal crisis, but met rejection from President Ford, Republican leaders of the New York State Legislature, and New York commercial bankers.

President Ford May 14 rejected Mayor Abraham Beame's plea for $1 billion in aid in the form of a federally guaranteed, 90-day emergency loan. Such a loan, Ford said in a letter to Beame, a Democrat, would "provide no real solution" to the city's fiscal plight, "but would merely postpone, for that period, coming to grips with the problem."

Ford conceded that he was "deeply impressed" by the city's immediate cash needs and by Beame's efforts to reduce a projected $641.5 million budget deficit for fiscal 1976, but he said it was "also clear that the city's basic critical financial condition is not new but has been a long time in the making without being squarely faced." "The adoption of sound budget policies would have a substantial and beneficial effect in both short- and long-term credit of the City of New York," Ford said.

The President urged Beame to practice "fiscal responsibility" by curtailing "less essential services and subsidies" and transferring other activities to the state. Contending that the city was living beyond its means, Ford said, "We must stop promising more and more services without knowing how we will cover their costs."

Beame and New York Gov. Hugh Carey (D), who had accompanied the mayor to a White House meeting with Ford May 13 to present the city's aid proposal, reacted angrily to Ford's statement. The President's response showed a "level of arrogance and disregard for New York that rivals the worst days of Richard Nixon and his gang of cutthroats," Carey told a political gathering May 14.

At the root of the issue dividing city and federal officials was disagreement over whether New York City faced a temporary cash-flow squeeze or a longer-range problem involving the city's basic creditworthiness. The Administration's position on bailing out New York City had been indicated May 10 when Treasury Secretary William E. Simon tentatively rejected the city's plea for aid, pending a final determination by Ford. Simon said he had concluded that "not only is the federal government's legal authority to provide financial assistance limited, but also that such assistance would not be appropriate." "The fundamental solution to the city's financial problems does not lie at the federal level," Simon said.

In a further statement May 14, Simon said the city should regard Ford's response as a signal that "it take the extremely difficult political actions" required "to put its fiscal and financial house in order." In the past, Simon declared, New York City had "demonstrated an absence of fiscal responsibility."

Simon voiced fear that granting aid to one city in financial distress would create "extremely dangerous" precedents requiring that the federal government rescue other municipalities facing budget imbalances during the current recession. A federal official asked, "Where does this stop?" the Journal reported May 13. "We'd have Newark (N.J.) and Detroit and 10 or 12 other cities lined up here if we do this for New York," the official said.

The Administration's rebuff to city hopes for assistance spurred talks that New York City might be forced to default on its debt and plunge into insolvency. Simon acknowledged these fears May 16, but said the possible impact of such an action on the national economy would be "negligible." Earlier he had expressed concern about the possible "ripple effects" of a New York State default on the nation's credit market.

Albany leaders reject city plea—City officials heeded Ford's suggestion that they turn to the state legislature for help, but Republican leaders of the State Senate May 15 turned down Mayor Beame's request for a $640 million package of aid and taxes to finance the city's fiscal 1976 budget.

Approval of Beame's proposed aid package would be "totally imprudent and really a severe disservice to the long-range well-being of the city and its people," Senate Majority Leader Warren M. Anderson said.

(The number of persons on the city's welfare rolls passed the 1 million mark, city officials said May 31. One out of every eight New Yorkers were receiving public assistance.)

New York City spared default. New York City was spared from defaulting on $792 million in notes due June 11 when the New York State Legislature approved the creation of a new state agency, the Municipal Assistance Corp., designed to alleviate the city's immediate cash-flow crisis and oversee New York City's long-range borrowing policies.

Passage of the act, coming at dawn June 10, culminated several weeks of political and financial maneuverings aimed at solving the city's complex short-term and long-term fiscal problems.

The new agency's first task was to gradually refinance the city's current short-term indebtedness, totaling $3 billion, that was due for repayment by September. The corporation, dubbed "Big Mac," was empowered to offer long-term bonds to raise money needed to retire the city's short-term notes. As security for the 15-year bonds, investors would be offered the corporation's reserve fund, made up of money from the city's sales and stock transfer taxes. Nearly $1 billion a year would be earmarked for the reserve fund. The state also offered a "moral obligation" guarantee against default on the agency's bonds. Over the long-term, it was hoped that the corporation's management of the city's debt would restore investor confidence in New York's ability to pay its debts. The recent fiscal crisis and constant talk of default had doomed the city's efforts to raise cash through public offerings, thereby severely limiting prospects for an orderly settlement of the city's immediate debts and the eventual reform of the budgetary process.

In return for Big Mac's help in managing its massive debt, New York officials agreed to turn over partial control of city finances to the state agency. The corporation could set a limit on the city's total short-term borrowing, currently estimated at about $6 billion. The city agreed to adopt an improved, state-approved system of accounting over a 10-year period and cease its much-criticized practice of using capital budget funds, intended for construction projects, to pay off its more immediate needs in the city expense budget.

The city was forced to accede to the state plan, developed by an advisory panel created by Gov. Carey, after the panel informed city officials June 4 that the assistance plan was their only option for solving New York's fiscal problems. The banks would not roll over, or extend, $280 million in short-term notes with a maturation date of June 11 unless the state plan were adopted, investment banker Felix Rohatyn, a member of the advisory panel, told city officials.

With passage of the Municipal Assistance Act, however, New York won immediate pledges of aid from the group of 11 banks which had refused to lend the city any more money until its debt management problems were settled and its budgetary process reformed.

Shortly after Gov. Carey signed the bill into law June 10, the banks announced the notes would be rolled over for one year at 8% interest. A $100 million bridge loan for the city also was made available to the new state agency for 90 days at 5.75% interest.

The state also pledged to advance the city another $200 million from its education funds.

States, localities cut services, raise taxes. Financially-pressed state and local governments, caught in a budgetary squeeze between outlays swollen by inflation and revenues reduced by recession, had been forced to cut about $3.3 billion in services, raise taxes by $3.6 billion, and defer $1 billion in capital spending for 1975—bringing the overall impact of the recession on states and localities to about $8 billion. An estimated 140,000 jobs also would be lost in the budget cutbacks, according to a report released June 6 by the Joint Economic Committee of Congress.

The Congressional survey analyzed data from 48 states and 140 local jurisdictions. Committee members expressed concern that the recession's cost at the state and local level "may significantly undermine the strength of a [national] economic recovery" because service cutbacks and tax increases were working at cross purposes with the Administration's budgetary plans to stimulate the economy through a tax cut.

Most of the retrenching efforts, the study noted, were occurring in areas with the greatest need for economic stimulus—industrial areas with the highest unemployment rate.

Highlights of the survey:

- 20 states and 52 local governments had enacted or planned tax increases; four states planed tax reductions totaling $50 million and five localities reported making tax cutbacks.
- 22 states anticipated cuts in services—about 85% of the reductions were planned for the 18 states whose unemployment rates exceeded the national average; 56 localities reported expenditure cutbacks.
- 23 states had adopted complete or partial hiring freezes and job cuts; payroll cutbacks totaling 52,000 jobs were planned or had been enacted in 48 local jurisdictions.

The report found that the 48 continental states had a net surplus of $3.9 billion at the end of June 1975, but that most of this wealth was concentrated in only 21 states.

Thirteen states with above-average per-capita energy output, mainly oil, finished fiscal 1975 with a combined $1.8 billion surplus, 14% smaller than in the previous year. These states were Oklahoma, Texas, Louisiana, West Virginia, Ohio, Utah, Indiana, New Mexico, Alabama, Arkansas, Montana, Wyoming and Tennessee.

Eight farm states had a combined suprlus of $800 million, down 28% from the previous year. They were Iowa, Minnesota, North Dakota, South Dakota, Wisconsin, Kansas, Nebraska and Idaho.

In contrast, the report noted, the 18 states with unemployment rates equal to, or above, the national average recorded a combined surplus for fiscal 1975 of only $400 million, 83% less than the $2.3 billion surplus recorded in fiscal 1974. These states were Oregon, Washington, Delaware, Pennsylvania, Florida, Georgia, North Carolina, South Carolina, Connecticut, Maine, Massachusetts, Rhode Island, Vermont, New Jersey, New York, Michigan, California and Nevada.

The $400 million surplus "is hardly an adequate cushion in present economic circumstances," the report said. These states were in the "worst squeeze they've faced since the 1930s," an economist for the subcommittee said.

Massachusetts authority averts default. The Massachusetts legislature Sept. 10 approved an emergency bill that would prevent the state Housing Finance Agency from defaulting on $106 million of notes maturing Sept. 15, 1975.

Gov. Michael S. Dukakis (D) requested the legislation after the agency was forced to delay completion of a $78.7-million bond offering because it had been able to sell only $14 million in a weak municipal bond market.

In a concurrent sale, the agency also had won commitments from investors only on $31 million of a $70 million note offering.

The new legislation extended the state's full faith and credit to payment of investors' interest and principal on up to $500 million in one-year notes issued by the housing agency.

Ratings for Massachusett's securities had been downgraded recently by the nation's two major credit-rating agencies, Moody's Investors Service and Standard and Poor's.

Standard and Poor's also had downgraded Connecticut's rating May 30 because the state faced a projected budget deficit of $74 million and planned to erase the deficit by short-term borrowing. The action dropped Connecticut from an AAA rating, the agency's highest, to AA, the second highest classification. It was the first time in 26 years since Standard and Poor's had kept municipal financing records that Connecticut had slipped from the highest rating. Connecticut had the second highest per capita income (about $6,500) of any state in the nation.

Simon on possible N.Y. default. Treasury Secretary William E. Simon Sept. 16 declared that the nation's financial markets were "capable of handling a [New York City] default with no more than moderate and relatively short-lived disruption."

In a letter to Sen. Hubert H. Humphrey (D, Minn.), chairman of the Joint Economic Committee of Congress, which was studying New York City's fiscal crisis, Simon said, "We don't believe default would undermine fundamental confidence in restrictive credit policies." Reiterating his opposition to direct federal aid for New York City, Simon said, "There is serious risk that the capital and credit markets would react adversely" if the federal government were to "act to prevent a default."

Simon said that because bankers, brokers and private investers already anticipated a city default and had acted on those expectations, "We would expect only a moderate degree of further [market] adjustments" if default actually occurred. "We don't believe any other issuer [of bonds] would default as a direct consequence of a default by New York City," Simon said.

Simon shifted his position significantly after bankers warned Administration officials that New York State's financial future might be in jeopardy because of its inability to sell issues in the credit markets.

Although he continued to oppose direct federal aid to New York City, Simon said Oct. 4 that the "psychological effects" of continued predictions of default "can make an impact" and could have a "domino effect" on the markets generally.

Herbert Elish, MAC's executive director, was sharply critical of Simon.

Noting chaotic trading conditions and sharp price drops in the municipal bond market, Elish termed Simon's position "extraordinary," the Wall Street Journal reported Oct. 1. According to Elish, the likelihood of the city's financial collapse had made borrowing more difficult and more expensive for many cities and states, even those with excellent credit ratings and few fiscal problems.

The turmoil in the municipal bond market was especially evident Sept. 30, according to the Washington Post. A number of governmental entities, such as the Virginia Public Schools Authority, withdrew offerings rather than pay interest rates they considered excessive.

Because of its proximity to New York, Connecticut's bonds fell in price despite bearing the highest available credit rating. "We have buyers that will not buy anything in the Northeast, period," a dealer from a major municipal bond firm said.

Noting these developments, Felix Rohatyn, MAC's chairman, said Sept. 30, "If the market acts this way without a default, think what it will be like with a default."

Borrowing difficulties facing cities in New York state were especially acute. Buffalo, a financially-troubled upstate city, Oct. 1 was unable to attract any purchasers for a $17.5 million bond anticipation note offering. On another offering of $6.5 million in notes, only one competitive bid was submitted and the city was forced to pay 10.5% interest.

The problem, however, was not confined to New York's deficit-ridden large cities. New Castle, a small town in affluent Westchester County, which adjoined New York City, was unable to sell a $1.5 million note issue, and finally placed the offering with a local bank at

10.7% interest, the New York Times reported Oct. 2.

According to the Journal Oct. 1, New York's credit difficulties also had spread to California, which had been unable to sell about $14 million of a $50 million bond issue, rated AAA, although it boosted the bonds' yield by .2 percentage points.

The impact of New York's problems was also felt in Georgia. Underwriters for a $10 million state bond issue said Sept. 5 they were able to market the bonds only by selling them at a loss. New York's problem "has had an unsettling effect on the entire capital market," a Georgia banker said. "Prices are lower and interest rates are higher."

The Securities Industry Association, regarded as the most influential association of Wall Street firms, also concluded that New York City's financial problems had been a factor "in pushing up the borrowing costs of all major U.S. cities," the Times reported Sept. 4. The group noted that Philadelphia had paid 2 percentage points more in interest than the rate paid on a similar offering by Chelsea, Mass., a much smaller city. Both bonds were A-rated. Detroit also had been penalized, paying 2.5 percentage points more than Johnson City, Tenn. on similar offerings. Both bonds were rated Baa.

A Pittsburgh banker told the Journal Sept. 12: "There has been a substantial pullback from all kinds of municipal credits by individuals and investors who just are concerned about the unknown. I think the New York situation has had a tremendous effect not only on the municipal market but on other markets as well and on the thinking of monetary authorities."

Other bankers concurred in that assessment. The affluent St. Louis suburbs "already are paying more" on their borrowing because of New York's effect on lenders' confidence, a Missouri bank official said.

A dealer in tax-exempt securities told Business Week Oct. 13, "New York is like a disease that is contaminating all issuers. There is total panic in the credit markets. The city has taken the state down with it, and if the state goes, others will follow."

International repercussions seen—Chancellor Helmut Schmidt of West Germany, who was visiting the U.S., Oct. 2 characterized New York City's fiscal crisis as one with "international" implications.

Meeting privately with President Ford, Schmidt, according to the New York Times Oct. 3, warned that a default by New York City would have a "domino effect," striking at other world financial centers, such as Zurich and Frankfurt. Schmidt cited the "enormous impact" of two bank failures in 1974, involving the Herstatt Bank of Cologne and the Franklin National Bank of New York.

Other European bankers and financial analysts expressed similar fears about the wide-spread consequences of a default by New York City, the Times reported Oct. 6.

Ford, Simon oppose federal bail out. President Ford said at a news conference Oct. 9 that he saw no justification "to bail out New York." He was supported in this view by Treasury Secretary Simon.

In testimony Oct. 9 before the Senate Banking Committee, Simon was questioned by Sen. John Tower (R, Tex.), an opponent of aid, as to what would be the "least obnoxious" type of assistance legislation Congress could enact.

Simon replied that: The plan should "not create a new federal bureaucracy" with power to supervise local budgetary affairs; the plan should be "narrow and restricted, administered by the secretary of Treasury," who would have to be satisfied that "a program is in place" to restore budgetary balance; and thirdly, "the financial terms should be so punitive that no other city will be tempted to turn down the same road."

Simon said New York City's financial problems had not been the crucial factor in causing the recent rise in interest rates for municipal bonds—that came about "primarily because of inflation and the growing federal usurpation of the supply of credit in the country" to finance the federal deficit, Simon said.

"New York City's difficulties have been the major factor in the uncertainty" afflicting the municipal bond market and "have intensified investor concern with quality," Simon said. But he added, "New York's financial crisis did not create the other problems besetting the market and an end to that crisis will not make them go away."

Rockefeller urges swift U.S. aid—Vice President Nelson Rockefeller urged Congress Oct. 12 to extend aid to the beleaguered city as soon as city officials indicated their intention to return to a balanced operating budget.

Rockefeller said he believed federal help was necessary to bridge the "difficult period" between adoption of the fiscal reform plan and the "restoration of investor confidence in the city's full financial viability by June 30, 1978."

Rockefeller urged Congress to act quickly to "avoid a catastrophe." "Time is of the essence," he said, "and the resolution of this immediate New York City situation is crucial."

His remarks were delivered at a Columbus Day dinner in New York City. Rockefeller, a former governor of New York, was the first Administration official to publicly support direct federal aid for the city.

Chase Manhattan Bank of New York, whose chairman was David Rockefeller, a brother of the Vice President, had spoken out Sept. 27 "as a corporate citizen" to urge Congress to intervene in the New York City crisis.

"We feel from both a local and national perspective that temporary federal support for New York City is of the highest priority," Dennis Longwell, president of Chase, said in a letter to the Joint Economic Committee of Congress.

"Throughout the country, the capital market for municipal securities is in turmoil. It can safely be assumed that any failure by either New York state or city to meet maturing obligations will further erode the national market for municipal securities and cause vital government programs at the state, county and local level to go unfunded through the nation," the letter said.

Study analyses city's fiscal plight. In an analysis of New York City's fiscal crisis, the Congressional Budget Office concluded that default was a near certainty by December unless additional state or new federal aid were provided to the city.

The "underlying problems facing New York, as well as a number of other large, aging cities, can be dealt with effectively only by the states or by the federal government," the report stated. The study, which was released Oct. 10, had been requested by Rep. Thomas Ashley (D, Ohio), chairman of the House Banking Committee's Subcommittee on Economic Stabilization.

Attempts to force stringent economies on the city in an effort to bring the budget quickly into balance would be self-defeating, according to the report. If drastic manpower cutbacks were made to reduce city expenditures, the report said, about half of the city's current $726 million deficit would be transferred to the federal government because laid-off workers would be unable to pay taxes and would become eligible for unemployment assistance.

If balancing the budget entailed substantial cutbacks in public services and large tax increases, the study said, the exodus of middle- and upper-income persons and industrial establishments would accelerate, and further erode the city's shrinking tax base.

The report suggested that the federal government assume the city's share of welfare benefits and "related services to the poor." "Unless one is willing to

Cities' Expenditures Compared

New York City's expenses are adjusted in the figures compared below to reflect the additional outlays made by the city as a five-county governmental entity. In other localities, many of these expenses are borne by state or county governments. Expenditures noted below for standard city functions are for elementary and secondary education, police, fire, sanitation, parks, highways, general and financial administration.

	Per Capita Expenditures		City Employes per 10,000 Population	
	All present city functions	Standard city functions only	All present city functions	Standard city functions only
New York	$1,224	$435	517.1	242.9
Boston	858	441	378.0	219.2
Chicago	267	383	140.0	208.4
Newark	692	449	391.1	258.2
Los Angeles	242	408	162.2	206.2
Philadelphia	415	395	163.8	255.7
San Francisco	751	488	312.5	224.6
New Orleans	241	260	177.3	217.5
St. Louis	310	360	241.9	214.2
Denver	473	375	237.0	219.3
Baltimore	806	470	434.1	260.1
Detroit	357	396	194.8	202

Source: Congressional Budget Office

consider policies that would redistribute the low-income populations concentrated in central cities among suburban and rural jurisdictions, or policies that would radically equalize incomes, the main alternative left for addressing the cities' problems is to relieve the city of some major portions of its current fiscal responsibility," the study stated.

Because New York City was composed of five counties, the report noted, the city's $12 billion expense budget included payments for services and employes ordinarily borne by county governments. If New York City's expenditures were limited only to those also paid by other cities, the report concluded that their outlays were similar; San Francisco, Baltimore, Newark and Boston actually spent more per capita than New York did when these adjustments were made. The report also noted that Baltimore, Newark and Philadelphia employed more municipal workers per capita than New York.

"With respect to the salaries paid public employes," the study said, "New York is generous but not the most generous of large cities" when New York's high cost of living was taken into account. However, the report added, "what little evidence there is seems to indicate that New York City provides its employes with considerably more in the way of fringe benefits—pensions, health insurance, etc.—than is offered the employes of other large cities."

In analyzing the city's fiscal problems, the report did not exonerate city or state officials or the financial community. "One cannot ignore the city's questionable accounting procedures and loose fiscal management in relation to the current crisis," the study said. "These procedures masked the fact the New York officials were failing to make the difficult choices that were required if the city's expense budget was to be truly balanced, as required by law.

"The fault does not rest with the city alone. Many of the 'gimmicks' which allowed the budget to appear balanced were tolerated or even suggested by state officials and were certainly not secrets to the banking community. These 'gimmicks' produced small deficits which were allowed to accumulate and grow, producing a problem of large and unmanageable proportions."

N.Y. again averts default. New York City Oct. 17, 1975 again barely escaped default when the city's teachers' union reversed an earlier decision and agreed to use $150 million in pension funds to purchase Municipal Assistance Corp. bonds.

The teachers' purchase was essential to completion of a $2.3 billion rescue plan enacted by the state legislature in September.

New York City's near-default provided a foretaste of what actual default might entail. As tension and uncertainty mounted Oct. 17 and it appeared that the city would not meet its expenses for the day, City Controller Harrison J. Goldin directed the sanitation department to halt its scheduled distribution of paychecks. Irving Trust Co. refused to cash city payroll checks drawn on other banks. City officials also obtained a court order outlining the city's payment priorities in the event of default—leading the list were vital public services, followed by city payrolls, followed by payments to holders of city debts.

In a telegram sent to President Ford after default was averted, Gov. Carey said: "New York, by exhausting all of its resources, can meet its obligations until Dec. 1. After then, the welfare of our citizens rests in the hands of the federal government. I seek your cooperation and leadership."

Carey told reporters, "We need not a bail out, not a hand out, but the recognition that we are part of this country, and that we are suffering because of the economic distress in this country."

White House Press Secretary Ron Nessen said later that Ford remained opposed to federal assistance for New York, believing that if officials implemented stringent cost-cutting reforms, the city could regain its fiscal health. "This is not a natural disaster or an act of God," Nessen said. "It is a self-inflicted act by the people who have been running New York."

Ford vows veto. President Ford Oct. 29 vowed to veto any bill passed by Congress that would prevent New York City's default by providing a federal guarantee of funds for the city. Ford's remarks barring a federal "bailout" were delivered in a televised speech at the National Press Club in Washington.

Ford charged that the "so-called solution" to New York City's fiscal crisis offered in various Congressional aid bills was only a "mirage." Its chief beneficiaries would be the politicians and bankers responsible for New York City's financial disarray, Ford said. A bailout would set a dangerous precedent, promising "immediate rewards and eventual rescue for every other city that follows the tragic example of our largest city," he added.

As a "fair and sensible" alternative to the Congressional rescue plans, Ford asked Congress to modify the federal bankruptcy law so that the federal courts would have "sufficient authority to preside over an orderly reorganization of New York's financial affairs, should that become necessary."

Ford said his bankruptcy plan would "provide a breathing space" for the city to make repayment arrangements with its creditors. While this compromise was being worked out in the court, the President said, "essential government functions" could continue. He promised that "in the event of default, the federal government will work with the court to assure that police and fire and other essential services for the protection of life and property in New York are maintained."

The legislation Ford said he would send to Congress would add a Chapter 16 to the federal Bankruptcy Act. As outlined by Ford, the proposed modification in federal law would allow the city, "with state approval," to file a petition with the U.S. District Court in New York under Chapter 16, stating that it was "unable to pay its debts as they mature." The city's petition would be "accompanied by a proposed way to work out an adjustment of its debt with its creditors," Ford said. The legislation also would require that New York City present a "program for placing the fiscal affairs of the city on a sound basis," he added.

The court would be authorized to accept jurisdiction of the case, and issue an automatic stay of creditors' suits, the President said. This injunction, he noted, would prevent the city's remaining operating funds from being tied up in lengthy litigation.

Ford said his proposed changes in the bankruptcy law would provide the city with a short-term source of funds while undergoing fiscal reorganization. The legislation would empower the court to authorize the sale of debt certificates, secured by future city revenue.

Ford discounted warnings by public officials and financial analysts that a default by New York City would be a "catastrophe for the U.S. and perhaps the world." A federal bailout of the city posed a "greater risk," Ford responded, providing a federal blank check that insured no long-run solution to the city's problems.

According to the President, default would not result in "large or long-standing repercussions" in the nation's financial markets, and the municipal bond market in particular. Credit markets, Ford said, "have already made substantial adjustments in anticipation of possible default." He added that New York City's record of "financial mismanagement" was "unique among municipalities throughout the U.S." State and local governments with "clean records of fiscal responsibility" would have no difficulty in borrowing money if New York City defaulted, Ford said.

A federal guarantee, Ford said, would reduce rather than increase "the prospect that the city's budget will ever be balanced." A federal guarantee, he said, would allow New York City officials to "escape responsibility for their past follies" and to "be further excused from making the hard decisions required now to restore the city's fiscal integrity."

The "secondary beneficiaries" of a federal guarantee, according to Ford, would be the "large investors and financial institutions who purchased these securities anticipating a high rate of tax-free return." In short, Ford said, a federal guarantee of funds would "encourage the continuation of 'politics as usual' in New York, which is precisely not the way to solve the problem."

Ford criticized New York City's high wages and pensions paid municipal workers, its tuition-free university system, its city-run hospital system, and welfare administration. According to Ford, New

York City was suffering from an "insidious disease . . . brought on by years and years of higher spending, higher deficits, more inflation, and more borrowing to pay for higher spending, higher deficits, and so on and so on." "Larger and larger doses" of federal aid were not the proper treatment for New York's sickness, Ford said.

There was no "painless cure," he warned. New York city officials "must either increase revenues or cut expenditures or devise some combination that will bring them to a sound financial position." Why, Ford asked, should taxpayers "support advantages in New York that they have not been able to afford for their communities?"

Citing New York City's fiscal plight as a "lesson," Ford warned that the nation could not "go on spending more than we have, providing more benefits and services than we can pay for." "When that day of reckoning comes" for the federal government, Ford said, "who will bail out the United States?"

Gov. Hugh Carey (D) charged that the "Ford formula deliberately unravels every step we've taken to solve our own problems." The proposed bankruptcy law, Carey said, would destroy investor confidence. "Who would risk his funds knowing that the government could avoid repayment simply by slipping into bankruptcy?" Carey asked.

Ford agrees to aid. President Ford Nov. 26, 1975 ended his opposition to federal aid for New York City and asked Congress to approve legislation making up to $2.3 billion in direct federal loans available to the city annually. Ford announced his decision during a nationally televised press conference from the White House.

Ford denied that his support for federal aid to the city marked a reversal of his stand against a federal "bailout." He claimed that state and city officials had changed their position.

Ford contended that only after he "made it clear that New York would have to solve its fundamental financial problems without the help of the federal taxpayers has there been a conce ted effort to put the finances of the city and the state on a sound basis."

Under such pressure, Ford said, state and city officials now were beginning to make the "tough decisions that the facts of the situation require." Proof of this change in attitude, Ford said, and crucial to his support for federal aid, was the recent adoption of a rigorous "self-help" plan by New York leaders.

As outlined by Ford, the plan consisted of "meaningful spending cuts" in the operation of the city; imposition of $200 million in new taxes; a moratorium on redemption of city notes and a reduction in interest payments to city noteholders; a delay in collection of outstanding loans to the city by banks and their acceptance of reduced interest charges; reform of municipal-union pension plans, including members' contributions to their retirement funds; and additional loans to the city from the city pension system.

New York's self-help program had two aims, Ford said: "to provide financing and to bring the city's budget into balance by the fiscal year beginning July 1, 1977."

The President "commended" state and city leaders for their efforts to achieve a balanced budget. Through these actions, Ford said, "New York has bailed itself out."

However, he added, "in the interim," while these steps were being taken to restore the city's fiscal integrity and credibility with investors, New York City would "lack enough funds to cover its day-to-day operating expenses."

Most cities, he explained, paid their daily operating expenses by borrowing funds in anticipation of receiving tax revenues in the spring. Since the credit market currently was closed to New York City, its cash flow problems were intense. Therefore, Ford said, he had decided "it was necessary to give short-term financing on a seasonal basis" to insure the continuation of essential services to city residents.

Ford asked Congress to enact legislation providing New York State with a line of credit through fiscal 1978 so that the city could borrow up to $2.3 billion annually. Under terms of the proposed legislation, the funds would be loaned from July through March, and repaid from April through May.

The aid package included "stringent conditions," Ford said. Repayment of all federal loans outstanding would be required at the end of each year. Ford vowed to terminate the loan program if New York City failed to meet its debt obligations to the federal government.

Ford said the money would be loaned "at a rate no less than" the rate paid by the federal government in borrowing money on the open market. (According to the White House, the government currently paid about 7%.) Ford added that the secretary of the Treasury, who would administer New York's loan program, would have the option to impose an additional 1% interest charge.

For these reasons, Ford contended that the loan program would entail "no cost" to other U.S. taxpayers. He also denied that the loans to New York City were risky, saying the legislation would include a lien providing the federal government with a priority claim against other creditors in the event New York City failed to meet its debt obligations.

Chase Manahattan Bank Chairman David Rockefeller, a spokesman for the major banks which held large amounts of city notes and a strong supporter of federal aid to prevent default, also expressed relief at the President's decision. Ford's action "came in the nick of time. Without it, I think there would inevitably have been a New York bankruptcy," Rockefeller said.

Aid bill passed—The New York aid bill was passed by 213–203 House vote Dec. 2 and 57–30 Senate vote Dec. 6. Ford signed the measure Dec. 9.

Sponsors of the legislation circumvented normal Congressional procedure to speed up passage because New York was expected to default on payment of loans Dec. 11 if the aid were not forthcoming by then.

The bill contained the following provisions:

The Treasury secretary was authorized to make loans to New York City or to an agent authorized by the state to administer the city's financial affairs. No more than a total of $2.3 billion in loans could be outstanding at any one time.

The loans would have to be repaid at the end of each city fiscal year (June 30) at an interest rate one percentage point higher than the prevailing Treasury borrowing rate.

The secretary was authorized to set terms and conditions of repayment and to withhold other federal funds due the city to offset the amount of any unpaid loans.

The secretary was prohibited from making new loans unless all previous loans had been repaid.

The General Accounting Office was authorized to audit the financial records of the city and the state.

Authority to make the loans was to be terminated June 30, 1978.

International Trade & Monetary Problems

U.S. Trade Gains: From Deficit in 1974 to Surplus in 1975

Because of the tremendous increase in the cost of oil imports, the U.S. trade deficit rose during 1974 to a figure exceeded only by the record set in 1972. In 1975, however, the growth of U.S. exports produced a record trade surplus. Using a valuation system adopted in January 1975, the 1974 trade deficit totaled $2.34 billion and the 1975 surplus $11.05 billion.*

'74 trade deficit was 2nd largest. The nation's 1974 trade deficit totaled $3.07 billion—the second worst trade gap in history, according to the Commerce Department Jan. 27, 1975. (Totals based on pre-1975 valuation method.) The deficit, exceeded only by a $6.4 billion gap in 1972, marked a sharp reversal from 1973, when the U.S. had registered a $1.35 billion surplus.

A huge jump in oil import costs accounted for the deficit, officials said. If oil prices had not tripled during 1974, Commerce Secretary Frederick B. Dent said, the U.S. would had shown a $14 billion surplus for the year. Although the volume of petroleum imports declined slightly over the year from 2.31 billion barrels in 1973 to 2.23 billion barrels in 1974, oil costs soared from $7.8 billion to $24.6 billion.

During the year, exports rose 38% to $97.91 billion; however, imports surged 45% to $100.97 billion.

There was a marked deterioration in the trade situation during December, when imports exceeded exports by a seasonally adjusted $606 million. For the month, exports declined 3.7% to $8.73 billion and imports rose 1.7% to $9.34 billion. (The cost of oil imports declined by $229 million during December.)

When calculated to include the cost of freight, insurance and other import charges, the 1974 trade deficit totaled $10.09 billion. According to this accounting system, which was used by most other nations to measure their trade balances, the December deficit totaled an adjusted $1.23 billion.

The International Monetary Fund reported March 9, 1975 that the oil cartel's trade surplus had increased from $22 billion in 1973 to $97 billion in 1974. In 1974, industrialized nations reported a $67 billion trade deficit, compared with a $21 billion deficit in the previous year. The poor and less-developed countries also were hard hit by rising oil prices; their combined trade deficit rose from $12 billion in 1973 to $26 billion in 1974.

Exports by a group of 17 oil-producing nations soared from $43.4 billion in 1973 to $133 billion in 1974 (despite a slight

*The new system had the effect of lowering the valuation of imports by adding to the purchase price only the cost of transporting foods to the exporting ship.

drop in the volume of oil exported). That was the greatest rate of growth recorded by any group of nations, according to the IMF. The group's exports comprised 17% of all world trade in 1974. Since 1967, its trade had expanded 10 times. The countries were Algeria, Bahrain, Brunei, Ecuador, Gabon, Indonesia, Iran, Iraq, Kuwait, Libya, Nigeria, Oman, Qatar, Saudi Arabia, Trinidad and Tobago, United Arab Emirates, and Venezuela.

Because of the new wealth derived from their oil exports, these nations were able to increase their imports 69% from $21.3 billion in 1973 to $36 billion in 1974.

World trade exports as a whole increased 48% from $518 billion in 1973 to $768 billion in 1974; imports rose 44% from $529 billion to $764 billion. (The growth in trade, however, reflected the inflated price of oil and other commodities rather than a real rise in volume.)

The U.S. remained the world's biggest exporter during 1974. West Germany, whose trade expanded 32% to $89 billion in 1974, ranked second and was the only major country to show a trade surplus.

Record '75 trade surplus. The U.S. posted a record $11.05 billion trade surplus during 1975. It was in sharp contrast to the previous year's $2.34 billion deficit and also far higher than the previous record of $7.08 billion set in 1964, according to the Commerce Department Jan. 27, 1976. (Totals based on post-1974 valuation method.)

However, a surge in imports during December caused a sharp decline in the monthly trade surplus, which shrank from $1.11 billion in November to $578.6 million in December. Officials had warned that the nation's trade balance would begin to deteriorate as economic recovery spured a demand for imported goods.

Exports in December were down .9% to an adjusted $9.32 billion; imports climbed 5.4% to $8.75 billion.

For the year, exports rose by nearly $10 billion to $107.19 billion, and imports declined nearly $4 billion to $96.14 billion. (Inflation accounted for a portion of the increase in exports.)

The U.S. reduced its oil imports for the second consecutive year; however, more money was paid for less oil. Imports totaled 2.186 billion barrels of oil, down 2% from the 1974 purchase of 2.231 billion barrels. The cost of imported oil for 1975 totaled $25.197 billion, about $11.52 a barrel, compared with $24.668 billion, or $11.06 a barrel, in 1974.

The Arab oil embargo accounted in part for the 3% decline in oil imports during 1974; the recession was believed to have been partially responsible for the 1975 decline in imports.

In an assessment of the 1975 trade surplus, the Council of Economic Advisers said Jan. 27: "Export volume remained stable during the year despite the recession in most industrial countries. This stability resulted mainly from a rise in agricultural exports, which partly offset a decline in other merchandise exports. Exports of capital goods stabilized at a rather high level, partly because delivery of these goods tends to lag behind the cycle and partly because shipments to oil-producing countries increased."

The council added that an improvement in the price competitiveness of U.S. goods resulting from the depreciation of the dollar's value from 1971–1973 also contributed to the rise in exports.

According to an Administration economist, the yearly surplus softened the impact of the recession in the U.S. "Were it not for the surplus," he said, "the recession probably would have been deeper in the first half of the year and the recovery would not have been as strong in the second half. The unemployment rate probably would have gone higher and reduction in joblessness would have been slower."

Inflation limits U.S. import duties' impact. "Successive rounds of multilateral trade negotiations over the years have generally lowered U.S. rates of duty," but worldwide inflation "had further eroded" the impact of import duties, the U.S. International Trade Commission said July 22, 1975 in a report to President Ford.

The report summarized the "probable effects" of tariff cuts and other trade concessions under negotiation in Geneva.

"Many rates now are so low as to be of minor commercial significance," the report stated. "For many products, the ratio of duty to the product value can now be measured in terms of tenths of per cent."

Trade Reform Act Adopted; Soviets Deny Emigration Deal

U.S. trade bill OKd despite Soviet disavowal. A comprehensive foreign trade bill was passed by the U.S. Congress Dec. 20, 1974 despite Soviet denials that the Kremlin had pledged freer emigration of Jews as a condition for trade benefits.

The Senate passed the bill by a 72–4 vote; the House passed it by a 323–36 vote. President Ford signed the measure Jan. 3, 1975.

In its final version, the bill gave the President the authority to eliminate tariffs of 5% or lower and to reduce by three-fifths tariffs above 5%. The President could negotiate elimination of non-tariff barriers, on an industry-by-industry basis, subject to Congressional approval.

Tariffs could be eliminated on goods from developing nations, with exceptions for Communist countries (but not Rumania and Yugoslavia), any country restricting supplies to the U.S. in a cartel-like operation and countries discriminating against the U.S. on trade or refusing compensation for confiscations. Exemptions also were provided for certain goods, such as shoes, electronics and watches.

The bill called for relief to industries hurt by imports unless the President found it not in the national interest, but Congress could overrule him.

A major provision of the bill would grant trade concessions to the Soviet Union if Soviet emigration curbs were eased, especially against Jews. Other Communist countries also would be permitted the "most favored nation" tariff status. In the case of Czechoslovakia, the status was tied to settlement of World War II claims to U.S. citizens.

Congress left the Soviet provision intact despite Soviet disavowal Dec. 18 of any commitment on its part on the issue.

On signing the bill, Ford said it "demonstrates our deep commitment to an open world economic order and interdependence as essential conditions of mutual economic health."

Saying he would abide by the terms of the act, Ford expressed reservations about its "legislative language that can only be seen as objectionable and discriminatory by other sovereign states."

The President noted Soviet disavowal that "assurances" had been given the U.S. of freer Soviet emigration policies, a condition attached by the bill to the grant of trade concessions that the U.S. was making. Ford said that "many of the act's provisions in this area are complex and may well prove difficult to implement."

The President also objected to a provision that would bar countries in the Organization of Petroleum Exporting Countries from receiving tariff benefits extended to other developing nations. The provision, although primarily aimed at Arab states, also applied to Venezuela and Ecuador and had evoked complaints from Latin America.

Emigration deal claimed—A formal compromise to extend U.S. trade and credit benefits to the U.S.S.R. in return for the assured relaxation of Soviet emigration policies had been detailed in letters exchanged Oct. 18, 1974 by Secretary of State Henry Kissinger and Sen. Henry Jackson (D, Wash.).

In his letter to Jackson, Kissinger wrote that "on the basis of discussions that have been conducted with Soviet representatives . . . we have been assured" that harassment of would-be emigrants would end.

No statement or acknowledgement was issued by Moscow which, according to Administration sources, was anxious to mute the impact of the reported agreement.

In his response, Jackson indicated that 60,000 emigrants annually would be considered a "minimum standard of initial compliance . . . and we understand that the President proposes to use the same benchmark."

(The White House issued a clarifying statement Oct. 21 emphasizing that Washington had received no guarantee of a "specific number" of emigrants, saying that "all of the assurances we have received from the Soviet Union" were enumerated in Kissinger's letter which cited no figure except to note: "It will be our assumption that . . . the rate of emigration from the U.S.S.R. would begin to rise promptly from the 1973 level.")

On the basis of the Congressional-Administration compromise, the trade bill, which was presented to Congress when it returned from recess in November, authorized President Ford to extend most-favored-nation trade status and the credit facilities of the Export-Import Bank to the Soviet Union for 18 months. The power to discontinue the benefits after this period if Soviet compliance were not deemed adequate would be vested in Congress.

(The Administration had opposed the Jackson-Vanik trade bill amendment linking U.S. trade benefits to Soviet emigration policy. In announcing the exchange of letters Oct. 18, Jackson noted "the deep, personal interest" taken by President Ford in reaching the agreement.)

In his letter to Jackson, Kissinger listed the "criteria and practices [which] will henceforth govern emigration from the U.S.S.R.," according to Soviet assurances:

■ "Punitive actions against individuals seeking to emigrate from the U.S.S.R. would be violations of Soviet laws and regulations and will therefore not be permitted by the government of the U.S.S.R." Job dismissal or demotion or other recriminations were thus barred, the letter said.

■ "No unreasonable or unlawful impediments will be placed in the way of persons desiring to make application for emigration."

■ "Applications for emigration will be processed in the order of receipt, including those previously filed, and on a non-discriminatory basis as regards the place of residence, race, religion, national origin and professional status of the applicant."

■ "Hardship cases will be processed sympathetically and expeditiously."

Kissinger also wrote that understandings included in Jackson's letter "will be among the considerations to be applied by the President" in assessing Soviet compliance. Jackson's letter, in addition to specifying the 60,000 benchmark figure, noted other "punitive actions, intimidations or reprisals" which, it was his understanding, would not be permitted by Moscow: the use of punitive conscription, the bringing of criminal actions that suggest a connection with applications to emigrate, the requirement that adult applicants receive parental permission to emigrate; and the abuse of security clearance restrictions that create unreasonable emigration obstacles.

Moscow denies deal—The Soviet Union Dec. 18, 1974 disavowed the agreement on extending U.S. trade benefits in exchange for freer Soviet emigration policy.

The denial, revealed prior to agreement on the bill by a House-Senate conference committee that night, was brushed aside by congressmen as a "face-saving" gesture.

The statement distributed by the official Soviet press agency Tass asserted that "leading circles" in the U.S.S.R. "flatly reject as unacceptable" any attempts to attach conditions to the extension of trade benefits or to otherwise "interfere in the internal affairs" of the Soviet Union.

Accompanying the statement, Tass also circulated a letter, dated Oct. 26, from Soviet Foreign Minister Andrei Gromyko to U.S. Secretary of State Henry Kissinger, in which Gromyko rejected the content of the letter exchange documented by Jackson as presenting "a distorted picture of our position."

In the letter, Gromyko stated that "we resolutely decline" any interpretation or assumption that there would be an increase in emigration from the Soviet Union in the future. The foreign minister alleged that in his talks with Kissinger, "the point was quite the contrary, namely about the present tendency toward a decrease in the number of persons willing to leave the U.S.S.R."

(In testimony before the Senate Finance Committee Dec. 5, Kissinger had said: "I must state flatly that if I were to assert that a formal agreement on emigration exists between our governments, that statement would immediately be repudiated by the Soviet government." He said he could give no "assurance concerning the precise emigration rate that may result," assuming the extension of most-favored-nation status to the Soviet Union.)

Moscow circulated additional repudiations of the alleged understanding Dec. 21–25 in the Communist Party newspaper Pravda and other publications. A Dec. 25

article in the journal Literaturnaya Gazeta charged that reports of Soviet concessions on emigration in return for U.S. trade benefits had been "invented" to give members of Congress a face-saving explanation for not voting against the trade reform bill because such a negative vote might cost them support of U.S. businesses which, on a whole, favored the liberalization of trade with the Soviet Union.

Congress curbs Eximbank credits. A bill putting restrictions on U.S. government credit to the Soviet Union was cleared by Congress Dec. 19, 1974 and was signed by President Ford Jan. 4, 1975. The measure extended the lending authority of the Export-Import Bank for four years at a $25 billion level.

It set a $300 million ceiling on credit to the Soviet Union, which the President could raise if he found it in the national interest, subject to Congressional approval. The bill also barred any Eximbank credit for production, transport or distribution of energy from the Soviet Union. A $40 million ceiling was set on loans or guarantees for exploration of energy in the Soviet Union.

The bill would bring the bank's operation under closer Congressional supervision by subjecting it, beginning in fiscal 1977, to the same budgetary procedures applied to other federal agencies.

The Senate approved the bill Dec. 19 by 71–24 vote. The House had passed it by a 280–96 vote Dec. 18, the same day it emerged from a second Senate-House conference. The first conference report on the bill, which the House adopted by voice vote Nov. 20, had been tabled Dec. 4 by the Senate on an 84–8 vote after two motions to cut off debate failed.

The Senate objected to dilution of its original version by the conference committee, which had dropped many of the Senate restrictions on the Soviet loans.

The bank itself had been operating since June 30 under temporary extensions, the last of which had expired Dec. 1.

Both the Soviet Union and the U.S. State Department expressed displeasure at the adoption of the restrictions.

State Department officials said Soviet Ambassador Anatoly Dobrynin had told Secretary of State Henry Kissinger Dec. 18 that Moscow regarded the credit limitation as a failure of the U.S. to live up to its side of detente. Dobrynin had also reiterated the Kremlin's disavowal of the informal understanding on freer Soviet emigration in exchange for U.S. trade benefits.

A State Department spokesman Dec. 19 characterized the unprecedented credit ceiling as "grossly discriminatory." It was the first time Congress had set a limit on loans involving a single country.

U.S.S.R. cancels 1972 trade pact. The Soviet Union informed the U.S. Jan. 10, 1975 that because of restrictions imposed under recently enacted legislation in Washington, it would not put into force the 1972 Trade Agreement "which had called for an unconditional elimination of discriminatory trade restrictions." Secretary of State Henry Kissinger announced the action Jan. 14.

Although both countries reaffirmed their commitments to the policy of detente, some concern was expressed that Soviet Ambassador to the U.S. Anatoly Dobrynin had been summoned to Moscow for a major review of foreign policy issues, officials in Washington said Jan. 16.

The Soviet Union asserted that it considered both the limitation placed on the amount of Export-Import Bank credit available to it and the Trade Reform Act amendment linking most-favored-nation status to freer Soviet emigration as "contravening both the 1972 Trade Agreement . . . and the principle of noninterference in domestic affairs."

In making the announcement, which followed several days of negotiations with the Kremlin, Kissinger also reaffirmed Washington's commitment to detente and said the Administration would "pursue all available avenues" to improve overall Soviet-U.S. relations, "including efforts to obtain legislation that will permit normal trading relationships."

The nullification of the Trade Agreement, Kissinger explained, meant that the U.S.S.R. would not make any further payment on its Lend-Lease debts beyond 1975; a pledge to repay the World War II loans had been included in the

1972 Trade Agreement. It also meant, more significantly, that the Soviet Union would not receive most-favored-nation trade status and would not be entitled to any further Eximbank loans.

(According to a New York Times report Jan. 15, Kissinger had remarked of the four-year $300 million credit offered the Soviet Union: "That's peanuts." The Eximbank had, in fact, extended $469 billion in credits to the U.S.S.R. in the less than two years since Soviet loan facilities were first activated. These credits were not jeopardized by the agreement's cancellation.)

Kissinger was circumspect in allocating blame for the collapse of the long-awaited trade agreement, but said: "Evidently, the publicity and public debate had much to do with this." This was a reference to the protracted dispute over the trade-emigration link and to the Oct. 18, 1974 announcement by Sen. Henry Jackson (D, Wash.) of a compromise under which Soviet assurances of freer emigration were understood to have been received in exchange for the most-favored-nation trade status.

President Ford, in his State of the Union address Jan. 15, put the blame on Congress: "If our foreign policy is to be successful we cannot rigidly restrict in legislation the ability of the President to act. The conduct of negotiations is ill-suited for such limitations. Legislative restrictions, intended for the best motives and purposes, can have the opposite results, as we have seen most recently in our trade relationship with the Soviet Union."

Sen. Jackson and other congressmen most closely involved in the legislative actions to secure the amendment in question issued a statement Jan. 15 charging Moscow with blame for the collapse of the agreement: "The compromise of Oct. 18, which was freely entered into by all concerned, appears to have lost its appeal to the Soviets only when it became apparent that the Congress would not approve government credits for multibillion dollar development programs in the Soviet Union."

Kremlin denies blame, detente shift—The Soviet Union said in a Jan. 16 statement released by the official news agency Tass that "no changes have or could have taken place in the Soviet policy of detente" as a result of the decision to annul the 1972 Trade Agreement.

The Tass commentary, Moscow's first official response since the Jan. 14 disclosure in Washington, added: "As for trade, it is not a unilateral process. We want and are prepared to trade with the West, but, needless to repeat, only on the basis of full equality and mutual benefits."

"The Soviet people . . . would never make their right to decide their own internal affairs an object of bargaining. It would never occur to them to predicate their normal state-to-state relations with the U.S., say, on abolition of private ownership of the means of production. Why, then, do some American senators . . . think that someone would allow them to instruct the U.S.S.R. in the 'correct way of life'?"

U.S. rulings on Soviet computer deals. The Department of Commerce ruled on several applications by U.S. firms for permission to supply computer systems to the U.S.S.R. Its approval was required on shipment to the Soviet Union of equipment or materials that were deemed strategic.

The department Nov. 18, 1975 rejected the International Business Machine Corp.'s application of November 1973 to supply a computerized reservation system, valued at more than $11 million, to the Soviet travel agency Intourist. The Soviet Union had awarded IBM the contract in March 1973.

An IBM spokesman said the license had been denied because "the U.S. government concluded that the system couldn't be adequately safeguarded from unauthorized use."

IBM had received permission in July to sell a large computer system valued at more than $10 million for the Soviet Union's Kama River truck plant foundry. The equipment included a System 370 Model 158 computer and peripheral units, according to the Wall Street Journal Nov. 19.

The Commerce Department had issued a license in June to Sperry Rand Corp.'s Sperry Univac division authorizing the sale of a $10 million computer-based reservation system to the Soviet Union's airline, Aeroflot. The system included a Univac 1106-II computer with two central processors and related equipment, but was not in a class with the firm's largest computers. Sperry Univac had applied for the license in July 1974, having signed the contract with Moscow during the preceding month, the Journal report said.

Easing of computer export curbs urged—A number of American computer manufacturers Nov. 19 urged the U.S. government to relax restrictions on exports of their products to the Soviet bloc. The corporate executives were attending a government-sponsored symposium on East-West technological trade in Washington.

In a keynote address, Deputy Secretary of State Robert S. Ingersoll stated that of the $3.2 billion worth of trade with Communist countries in 1974, $533 million was in technological products and skills.

Another speaker, William C. Norris, chairman of Control Data Corp., stressed that the U.S. would realize benefits from cooperative ventures with East European computer manufacturers.

Norris had confirmed earlier that his company had orders to supply large computer systems to China and the Soviet Union, the Wall Street Journal reported Oct. 10. In testimony at the New York trial of the Justice Department's civil antitrust suit against IBM, Norris asserted that Peking had ordered a system, valued at $4 million–$5 million, for use in seismic analysis to aid in oil exploration and that Moscow had ordered a $10 million system for a weather-forecasting center. Norris also confirmed that Control Data had proposed to the White House and State Department in September 1973 that it be permitted to undertake a joint project with the U.S.S.R. for the development of an advanced computer. At the trial Norris said: "We suspected that [Moscow] had some theoretical concepts that were superior to ours."

ENERGY

Oil Supply

Sources of U.S. oil imports. The Federal Energy Administration released figures Oct. 23, 1974 showing that Canada and Nigeria had sent the U.S. twice as much crude oil as had all Arab oil producing countries combined during the first eight months of 1974.

Of the 6 million barrels of petroleum products imported to the U.S. on a daily basis, crude oil comprised two-thirds of that total and refined products about one-third.

Canada was the largest single supplier of foreign oil, but its shipments had been decreasing from 35.8% of U.S. imports (883,800 barrels a day) in 1972 to 24.7% in 1974 (896,400 barrels a day).

Nigeria had nearly tripled its exports to the U.S. Shipments were up from 235,800 in 1972 (9.6% of U.S. imports) to 633,800 (17.5%) in 1974. Nigeria replaced Venezuela as the second largest exporter of oil supplies to the U.S.

Iran ranked third in imports received by the U.S., moving up from fifth place in 1972. It more than doubled its exports in that two-year period—from 140,200 barrels (5.7%) to 561,900 (15.5%) in 1974.

Venezuelan exports to the U.S. fell from a daily average of 534,700 barrels in 1973 to 405,100 barrels daily in 1974, a reflection of Venezuela's decision to freeze production as part of its pricing strategy.

Canada to end oil supply to U.S. Canadian Energy Minister Donald Macdonald said Nov. 22, 1974 that Canada would begin Jan. 1, 1975 an eight-year phase-out of oil exports to the U.S. The cut, set forth in a government statement based on a report issued by the National Energy Board (NEB), would reduce exports Jan. 1 to 800,000 barrels a day from the average level of 896,400 barrels of crude purchased by U.S. importers during the first eight months of 1974. (Current shipments were 977,950 barrels a day.)

Macdonald said a further reduction to 650,000 barrels a day would be imposed July 1, 1975 if the oil-producing provinces of Alberta and Saskatchewan concurred. Subsequent annual reductions would reduce exports to 5,000 barrels a day in 1983. The policy contemplated a complete phase-out thereafter.

The mid-1975 export cut would represent a "shut in," or production cut, of 250,000 barrels a day, if the provinces approved. This was the amount of oil the NEB estimated the Sarnia-Montreal pipeline, scheduled to be completed in 1976, would ship to the Eastern Canadian market, which currently depended largely on imported oil.

The proposals issued by the NEB were designed to extend the period of national oil self-sufficiency by almost two years to the end of 1983 by accelerating export reductions. Macdonald said Ottawa had ruled out an immediate and total halt in exports to the U.S., the only country which imported Canadian oil, because "an immediate halt . . . would be disruptive of Canadian-U.S. relations" and would adversely affect northern U.S. refineries and Canadian producers.

The U.S. State Department said Nov. 23 it was "somewhat disappointed" at the Ottawa decision, but admitted that "we have known for more than a year of the likelihood that Canadian oil exports to the U.S. would be phased out around the end of the present decade."

The Canadian National Energy Board Oct. 18 had already set the allowable limit for oil exports to the U.S. at 977,950 barrels a day for November, compared with about one million barrels a day a year ago and 978,575 barrels a day approved for October.

Total Canadian production was estimated at two million barrels a day. Canadian domestic requirements were 1.02 million barrels a day.

Gas price up—Macdonald had announced Sept. 20 that Canada had decided unilaterally to raise the price of natural gas exported to the U.S. by 67%, to $1 per thousand cubic feet, effective Jan. 1, 1975. The export levy on crude oil had been raised in June. As with oil, a two-price—domestic and export—system was set.

Macdonald said the increase would put Canadian gas in a "more equitable" relationship with other energy sources in the U.S. by pricing Canadian exports "in a competitive relationship" to U.S. alternatives.

The move would provide some $330 million in additional revenues from the 1 trillion cubic feet of natural gas which Canada exported annually to the U.S.

U.S.S.R. offers oil for technology. Soviet Oil Minister Valentin Shashin told Sen. Walter Mondale (D, Minn.) Nov. 12, 1974 that the Soviet Union was "ready to repay technical cooperation" in increasing Soviet oil production with "a certain part of the oil extracted."

Shashin noted that two U.S. firms, Union Oil Co. of California and Standard Oil of Indiana, "had shown an interest in this Soviet proposal," but he added that cooperation was also being encouraged with other countries, particularly France, Great Britain and Japan.

In conceding the need for U.S. technology, Shashin said new American methods could raise the extraction rate of some Soviet oil fields from the 10%-15% possible with traditional methods to "50% or even higher."

Libya ends U.S. oil embargo. Libya had lifted its 14-month oil embargo against the U.S. without making an official announcement, the London Times reported Dec. 31, 1974. Libya had been one of two countries that had refused to

U.S. Average Daily Crude Oil Imports

	1974 (Jan.-Aug.)		1973		1972	
	Thousands of barrels	% of U.S. imports	Thousands of barrels	% of U.S. imports	Thousands of barrels	% of U.S. imports
Canada	896.4	24.7	1,094.1	30.8	883.8	35.8
Nigeria	633.8	17.5	410.0	11.6	235.8	9.6
Iran	561.9	15.5	207.5	5.9	140.2	5.7
Venezuela	405.1	11.2	534.7	15.1	450.6	18.2
Saudi Arabia	301.0	8.3	434.2	12.2	201.3	8.2
Indonesia	283.7	7.8	207.3	5.9	156.8	6.4
Algeria	195.7	5.4	127.6	3.6	85.3	3.5
Ecuador	78.7	2.2	57.3	1.6	—	—
Trinidad	78.6	2.2	—	—	34.2	1.4
United Arab Emirates	62.6	1.7	68.2	1.9	32.9	1.3
Angola	47.3	1.3	44.6	1.3	—	—
Others	80.1	2.2	360.9	10.1	247.8	10.4

join the majority of members of the Organization of Petroleum Exporting Countries (OPEC) when it decided March 18 to end the oil ban it had imposed against the U.S. during the 1973 Arab-Israeli war.

Foreign oil companies in Libya said that although they had not been officially informed of the government's action in ending the embargo, the decision would have little bearing on the resumption of shipments. They cited the high cost of Libyan oil, about $12.50 a barrel, $2.50 more than the foreign companies had to pay for Persian Gulf oil. As a result, Libyan production had dropped to about 800,000 barrels a day in 1974 from an average of 2.2 million in 1973.

International Cooperation

International energy group formed. An International Energy Agency (IEA) to pool energy resources by 16 industrial nations in the event of an emergency was formed in Paris, Nov. 15, 1974.

The body, established within the framework of the 24-nation Organization for Economic Cooperation and Development (OECD), was composed of the U.S., Austria, Belgium, Britain, Canada, Denmark, Ireland, Italy, Japan, Luxembourg, the Netherlands, Spain, Sweden, Switzerland, Turkey and West Germany. Twenty-one OECD nations voted to set up the agency, but five of them refused to join. France, initially refusing to join, abstained along with Greece and Finland.

The IEA replaced the 12-nation Energy Coordinating Group (ECG), which had promoted the creation of the new agency and formed its nucleus. The ECG had held its last meeting Nov. 6 in Brussels.

Norway, an ECG member, refused to join the IEA as a full member because it feared giving up its sovereignty over its oil resources.

France, which had boycotted the ECG from the start, also had decided to remain out of the IEA, arguing that the consumer nations should be negotiating with the producer states rather than forming a bloc that would antagonize them.

A key clause in the charter of the IEA was a pledge by members to come to the assistance of other participants whose oil supply was reduced by 7% even if that meant a reduction of consumption by the donor states.

France forms ties with IEA—It was disclosed Dec. 22 that France had agreed to informal ties with the IEA.

A U.S. official who had attended the IEA's meeting in Paris the previous week said the agency's chairman, Viscount Etienne Davignon of Belgium, had been authorized to brief Jean-Pierre Brunet, the French Foreign Ministry's chief economic officer, after each agency meeting.

In another action aimed at closer French-IEA cooperation, President Valery Giscard d'Estaing permitted the agency to be set up within the OECD. He also agreed to observer status for the Executive Commission of the European Economic Community (EEC) with the IEA. France, along with other OECD and EEC members, had the veto power to block cooperative action with other international agencies.

Kissinger urges world cooperation. The formation of the International Energy Agency had been preceded by an appeal by U.S. Secretary of State Henry A. Kissinger Nov. 14 for "collaboration among the consuming nations" to avoid "perpetual crises" over rising oil prices.

Speaking at the University of Chicago, Kissinger urged the nations of North America, Western Europe and Japan to pool their efforts to protect themselves from "the threat of a new oil embargo." He proposed a $25 billion international-lending agency financed by the consumer nations to help industrial states cope with the high cost of oil. This would serve to stabilize the financial system by providing support to banks already burdened by the impact of oil dollar investments, Kissinger explained.

The secretary also proposed: reduction of oil imports of the industrial nations to one-fifth of total energy needs rather than the current one-third of total needs; development of new energy sources, including coal, solar power and uranium; an effort to bring down the price of oil through dialogue between the oil consumers and the oil producers; and creation of a special trust fund to assist developing nations, which had $20 billion in payments deficits.

Simon explains Kissinger plan—U.S. Treasury Secretary William E. Simon Nov. 18 provided details of the recycling plan proposed by Kissinger.

In a New York speech, Simon proposed that the oil facility be associated with the OECD, 24 major industrial nations, rather than the 130-member International Monetary Fund, in which developing and oil producing nations were heavily represented.

Simon said the U.S. contribution to the loan facility would be financed through the Treasury Department's existing $5 billion Exchange Stabilization Fund, which engaged in international lending operations to stabilize the dollar.

(In testimony before the Joint Economic Committee of Congress Nov. 25, Simon said a final decision had not been made about the amount of the U.S. contribution, but he said it was his "preliminary view" that the U.S. would furnish 25%-30%, or about $8 billion, of the total funds needed. Simon also told the committee that if necessary, the U.S. could meet its payments through the purchase of U.S. government securities by oil exporting nations. Operation of the oil facility "would not require inflationary expansion of money and credit," Simon said, or "lead to an increase in the federal government debt.")

Other key elements in the U.S. proposal as outlined by Simon: participation "should be linked with a commitment to cooperate in reducing dependence on oil imports"; members of the mutual loan fund would be asked "to follow responsible adjustment policies and avoid the use of trade restrictive measures"; the oil facility should supplement and not replace ordinary credit channels within the private market or through official groups, such as the IMF; financial support to member countries would be decided on a weighted vote of participants and not be based on a specific criterion, such as oil import costs, but rather on the nation's overall economic condition; "all nations should share the credit risk on the basis of their share of participation."

Jackson proposes special council—U.S. Sen. Henry M. Jackson (D, Wash.) Nov. 11 urged major oil consuming nations to establish a special council of economic and finance ministers, authorized to work for a reduction of oil prices and to protect the international banking system from an unmanageable flow of investments by oil producing nations.

In a London speech before the Pilgrims Society, Jackson said the council's first act must be "to insulate the price of oil produced by consuming nations from the control of the producers' cartel." The Organization of Petroleum Exporting Countries (OPEC) should not be allowed to set worldwide oil prices, Jackson declared. If oil consuming nations which also produced oil, like the U.S., orderd a rollback in their prices, Jackson said, pressure would be brought on OPEC nations to reduce their prices.

In calling for "tough programs" aimed at lowering the price of oil, Jackson opposed the International Monetary Fund plan, favored by many European states, for dealing with the financial crisis caused by higher oil import costs—recycling petrodollars through oil consuming states in the form of loans and investments.

Recycling would make the U.S. "a lender of last resort and we would end up with all the funny money," Jackson said. One task of the new special council, as outlined by Jackson, would be to issue guidelines for petrodollar investments to insure that industrialized nations maintained "continued control" over "their own essential financial infrastructures" and were not overwhelmed by the volume of OPEC investments.

Giscard calls for global oil meeting. French President Valery Giscard d'Estaing, at a press conference Oct. 24, proposed the convocation of a world energy conference early in 1975, to be attended by 10 or 12 nations representing oil-producing countries and industrialized and nonindustrialized oil consumers. The conference, at which Europe should be represented as a single bloc, must give oil producers a guaranteed income by pegging the price of oil to an index, he said.

Giscard d'Estaing reaffirmed that France would not join a U.S.-proposed oil-sharing group of 12 major industrial nations because it believed such a group might lead to "confrontation." However, he pledged to put "no obstacles" in the way of France's European partners' signing.

Ford & Giscard agree on oil parley. President Ford and French President Valery Giscard d'Estaing conferred on the French Caribbean island of Martinique Dec. 15-16 and reached compromise agreements on energy, gold and other issues.

In the joint communique issued Dec. 16, the U.S. agreed to participate in the French-proposed conference of oil producing and exporting nations "at the earliest possible date," with a "preparatory" producer-consumer meeting to be held in March 1975 to work out procedure for the meeting. France agreed to "intensive consultations among consumer countries in order to prepare positions for the conference," a concession to the U.S. demand for a unified front among oil consuming nations. Both leaders stressed the importance of "solidarity" among the oil consumers. They agreed that prior to the preparatory consumer-producer meeting, consumers would strengthen their cooperation on energy conservation and development and on "setting up of a new mechanism of financial solidarity," the last a reference to U.S. Secretary of State Henry Kissinger's proposal for a $25 billion emergency fund to help oil consuming nations hurt by soaring oil costs.

At the end of the talks, Kissinger told newsmen that France would participate in the $25 billion fund, but not within the framework of the new 16-nation International Energy Agency. He added that the U.S. had abandoned its efforts to persuade France to join the group.

Asserting that the oil accord represented a "fair compromise" between the U.S. and French positions, Kissinger said "we should stop talking about Franco-American relations in terms of confrontation and start talking in terms of cooperation."

10-year EEC goals set. Energy ministers of the European Economic Community (EEC) decided Dec. 17, 1974 on joint objectives for energy use by 1985. They agreed to reduce the 10-year growth in their nations' domestic energy consumption from a projected 50% to 35% and to cut dependence on imported energy supplies from the 1973 level of 63% to 40%–50%. The plan called for reducing the share of oil in energy production from 61% to 41%-49% through increased use of nuclear power and natural gas.

Among other actions, the ministers agreed to require oil companies to report twice a year on their energy imports and decided to create a joint fund of nearly $50 million to encourage oil exploration and development in Europe. Britain stressed it would cooperate on a joint energy policy but insisted it would retain full national control of its North Sea oil and natural gas resources.

Ford links food & oil. President Ford, addressing the U.N. General Assembly Sept. 18, 1974, linked the problems of food and oil and challenged oil-producing nations to stop using petroleum as a political and economic weapon.

Ford urged all countries to join in a "global strategy for food and energy" and warned that "failure to cooperate on oil and food and inflation could spell disaster for every nation represented in this room."

Ford told the General Assembly that the U.S. "recognizes the special responsibilities we bear as the world's largest producer of food," but he said "it has not been our policy to use food as a political weapon despite the oil embargo and recent oil price and production decisions." He emphasized that "energy is required to produce food, and food to produce energy."

Ford challenged oil-exporting nations to "define their policies to meet growing needs" without "imposing unacceptable burdens on the international monetary and trade system." He said that by "confronting consumers with production restrictions, artificial pricing and the prospect of ultimate bankruptcy, producers will eventually become the victims of their own actions."

Ford pledged that the U.S. would "not only maintain the amount it spends for food shipments to nations in need, but it will increase this amount this year." He also promised a substantial increase in U.S. assistance to agriculture production programs in poor countries, and U.S. help in the establishment of an international system of food reserves.

He urged all nations to substantially increase food and energy production, and to hold prices at levels that consumers could afford. He noted that world population would double by the year 2000, requiring such production increases if living standards were to improve.

World Oil Prices & Economic Woes

U.S. warns of 'confrontation.' U.S. leaders warned Sept. 23, 1974 that high prices set by the oil-producing nations imperiled the world's economy and could lead to "confrontation" and "a breakdown of world order and safety." The warnings were contained in speeches delivered by President Ford to the opening of the World Energy Conference in Detroit and by Secretary of State Henry A. Kissinger to the United Nations General Assembly.

The hardening of the U.S. stance on the high oil prices prompted an angry reaction from Arab oil producers and predictions from other quarters of a possible military showdown.

In his address, Ford asserted that the U.S. recognized the oil producers' need to develop their own economy, "but exorbitant prices can only distort the world economy, run the risk of a worldwide depression, and threaten the breakdown of world order and safety." "Sovereign nations," Ford added, "cannot allow their policies to be dictated, or their fate decided, by artificial [price] rigging and distortion of the world commodity markets."

Stressing the principle of interdependence among states, Ford said "There is no way in today's world for any nation to benefit at the expense of others—except for the very short term and at a very great risk." With representatives of Arab oil nations in the audience, Ford said "the whole structure of our society rests upon the expectation of abundant fuel at reasonable prices," and that expectation "has now been challenged." The President noted that "throughout history, nations have gone to war over natural advantages, such as water, or food or convenient passages on land or sea." But he pointed out that in this nuclear age "war brings unacceptable risks for all mankind."

Ford's warning against the use of oil as an economic weapon was coupled with an appeal to oil-consuming nations to take these steps to avoid its consequences: expand domestic oil production; "resolve not to misuse their resources"; "fully utilize their own energy resources"; and "join with others in the cooperative efforts to reduce their energy vulnerability."

In response to newsmen's questions prompted by the Ford and Kissinger warnings, U.S. Defense Secretary James R. Schlesinger said Sept. 25 that the U.S. had no intention of seeking military action against oil-producing nations in the Middle East, but instead was seeking a solution to rising prices through "amicable discussions." While the U.S. "regards the problem of oil prices as deterimental to the world economy, we expect to have a solution through negotiations," Schlesinger said. The inflation that was being caused in part by high oil prices, he said, could reduce the military power of the U.S. and the Western alliance.

Kissinger's warning—Kissinger told the U.N. Assembly Sept. 23 that "strains on the fabric and institutions of the world economy," caused largely by artificially high petroleum prices, threatened to "engulf us all in a general depression."

Observers speculated that Kissinger and President Ford were acting in an effort to get oil-consuming nations to cooperate and to separate producing nations from other Third World countries whose economies were suffering because of inflated petroleum prices,

In a gloomy assessment of the world economic situation, Kissinger said "the early warning signs of a major economic crisis are evident." Inflation rates "unprecedented in the past quarter century are sweeping developing and developed nations alike," he declared. "The world's financial institutions are staggering under the most massive and rapid movements of reserves in history. And profound questions have arisen about meeting man's most fundamental needs for energy and food."

In the past, Kissinger noted, "the world has dealt with the economy as if its constant advance were inexorable." Now, he said, "we continue to deal with economic issues on a national, regional or bloc basis at the precise moment that our interdependence is multiplying."

Kissinger noted that the U.S. had launched programs with such oil producing nations as Saudi Arabia and Iran to help them diversify their economies. He implied that if such cooperation failed to ease oil prices, the U.S. might change its policy. "What has gone up by political decision can be reduced by political decision," he said.

Arab and other reaction—Arab anger over the comments by President Ford and Kissinger was expressed Sept. 24 by political leaders, public figures and the press, who accused the U.S. of waging a war of nerves against the Arab countries.

Kuwaiti Petroleum Minister Abdel Rahman al-Atiki said if the U.S. went ahead with plans to form a bloc of oil-consuming nations, a confrontation with the oil producers was inevitable.

An official of the Organization of Petroleum Exporting Countries (OPEC) took issue with Ford's view that oil prices were exorbitant. He said: "Inflation did not begin with the increase in oil prices. It is rather because of inflation that oil prices have had to be adjusted."

A representative of the Arab League said in Cairo Sept. 24 that his organization had read the Kissinger and Ford statements with "great surprise coupled with concern." "If the United States wants cooperation with the Arabs, one would expect different words" from U.S. leaders, he asserted.

Saudi Arabian Oil Minister Sheik Ahmed Zaki al-Yamani said he "heard no threats" in Ford's speech. "What I heard from him was a tone of cooperation rather than confrontation," he said. Yamani warned the U.S. in a later statement of the danger of "economic imperialism" in dealing with friendly oil-producing states.

French Foreign Minister Jean Sauvagnargues said Sept. 24 that U.N. delegates and their governments seemed "apprehensive about the implicit threats" in the Kissinger and Ford statements. He warned against a confrontation between oil producers and consumers, and noted that Western European nations and Japan were reluctant to push toward such a showdown because they, unlike the U.S., were almost totally dependent on oil imports.

Shah Mohammed Reza Pahlevi of Iran reacted to Ford's address by rejecting the President's bid to cut oil prices. He called instead on industrial nations to reduce prices of their exports first. The shah, who was on a week-long visit to Australia as part of an Asian tour, said in a speech in Canberra Sept. 26: "No one can dictate to us. No one can wave a finger at us, because we will wave a finger back." The Iranian leader added: "If the world prices go down, we will go down with oil prices. But if they go up, why should we pay the bill?"

The U.S. State Department reacted to the shah's statement by saying "there is no spirit of confrontation at all." The U.S., the department said, was attempting "to solve a problem which affects all of us, developed and less-developed countries, consumers and producers."

OPEC to raise oil taxes. The Organization of Petroleum Exporting Countries (OPEC) had agreed Sept. 13, at the end of a two-day meeting in Vienna, to raise by 3.5% taxes and royalties paid by foreign oil companies to the oil-producing states. Saudi Arabia was the only OPEC member which did not approve the decision.

The tax on a barrel of oil would rise by 33¢, effective Oct. 1. An OPEC communique said the government price for oil would remain frozen for the last quarter of 1974 but that "as of January 1975, the rate of inflation in the industrialized countries will automatically be taken into account with a view to correcting any future deterioration in the purchasing power of oil revenues."

In imposing the tax increase, the OPEC countries argued that price increases in industrial countries for machinery and food that the oil countries must import required a boost in government revenue from oil.

Saudi delegate Sheik Ahmed Zaki al-Yamani said his country did not oppose the tax increase, but held that it should be coupled with a reduction in the price of oil.

U.S. Federal Energy Administrator John C. Sawhill, commenting on the OPEC action, said Sept. 13 that any tax or price increase by the international oil cartel was "economic blackmail." He said some of the oil firms might absorb the rise, "but they won't absorb all of it."

Saudis raise oil price—Aramco confirmed Sept. 16 that Saudi Arabia had increased the price it charged oil companies for its petroleum by 22¢ a barrel, or 2%. The price change applied to "buyback" oil, petroleum accruing to the Saudi government from its current 60% interest in Aramco which was sold back to the oil companies.

Saudi Oil Minister Yamani explained Sept. 17 that the increase did not conflict with his government's desire to see the price of oil go down generally. He said U.S. oil executives had been informed by Saudi Arabia in June of its decision to boost the price of buyback oil from 93% of posted price to 94.864%, reflecting the government's policy of keeping participation rates at the same level charged by other Persian Gulf producers.

Yamani told newsmen in Washington Oct. 2 that petroleum prices would fall if there were a political solution to the Arab-Israeli conflict. Yamani warned, however, that if the Israelis did not withdraw from occupied Arab territories, "this would produce a war" that would "have a very dangerous effect on prices, as well as on the supply of oil." "Any solution that will stop the fighting," he said, "is in the hands of the American government."

Asked why he was linking a political solution of the Middle East situation with a cut in oil prices, Yamani said, "If you give them [the Arabs] an incentive, they will be on your side."

Arabs defend stance—Representatives of Kuwait and Egypt defended Arab oil policies before the General Assembly and denied they had contributed to world inflation.

Sheik Sabah al-Ahmad al-Jaber, Kuwait's foreign minister, said Sept. 30 that inflation had plagued the industrial nations since the end of World War II, and he attributed it to these nations' "inability to properly manage their domestic affairs." The countries "which are heaping blame on the oil producing countries now," he asserted, "are the ones that started the practice of classifying goods, treating some of them as strategic materials subject to special trade rules."

Sheik Sabah charged that the major oil companies had deliberately frozen oil prices for more than 25 years, while the prices of all basic commodities, manufactured products and services exported by advanced countries were rising. "Raising the price of oil was in essence the correction of an inequitable situation," he asserted.

Egyptian Foreign Minister Ismail Fahmy echoed Sheik Sabah's statement Oct. 1, saying it was "regrettable" to hear it "even claimed that the fragile framework of international economic cooperation would be exposed to danger if the oil producing countries continue their present pricing policies."

Fahmy asserted that the Arabs had used their oil only to secure their "legitimate rights" and had imposed the 1973 embargo only after "warning the countries which assist Israel" in maintaining control over Arab territory.

5 consumer nations meet on oil prices. Foreign ministers and finance ministers of the U.S., Great Britain, West Germany, France and Japan met Sept. 28–29 in Washington to discuss joint efforts that could be undertaken to meet the oil-price crisis.

The meeting was called by U.S. Secretary of State Henry Kissinger because of fears that unless the major industrialized nations acted decisively to coordinate their policies in the face of the threat posed by higher oil prices and a possible cutoff of supplies, Western nations faced bankruptcy or political collapse.

According to an unofficial report Sept. 29, no agreement was reached on how to force down rising oil prices, although it was accepted that a lower price should remain a long-term goal. French Foreign Minister Jean Sauvagnargues said at a news conference that day that France was opposed to an "economic war" between oil producing and oil importing nations.

One of the strategies reportedly discussed at the meeting was a Kissinger proposal that concerted action be taken to reduce oil consumption—a 15% cutback was mentioned, sources said.

IMF 'oil facility.' An "oil facility," proposed in January 1974 by H. Johannes Witteveen, managing director of the International Monetary Fund (IMF), was set up by the IMF Aug. 22 to assist member nations in meeting their greatly increased balance of payments needs, which had been affected by escalating import costs for petroleum and petroleum products.

Seven oil producing nations agreed to lend the IMF the equivalent of $3.4 billion until Dec. 31, 1975. The funds borrowed by the IMF would then be made available to nations hard pressed to meet their international obligations. (Interest paid by the IMF would be at an annual rate of 7%, with repayment of the loans scheduled to be made in eight equal semiannual installments beginning after three years and to be completed not later than seven years after the transfer of currency to the IMF.)

The seven lending nations participating in the oil facility and their contributions (expressed in SDRs and dollars): Abu Dhabi, 100 million SDRs or $120 million; Canada, 257,913,900 SDRs or $300 million in Canadian currency; Iran, 580 million SDRs or $700 million; Kuwait, 400 million SDRs or $480 million; Oman, 20 million SDRs or $24 million; Saudi Arabia, 1 billion SDRs or $1.2 billion; Venezuela, 450 million SDRs or $540 million.

Nigeria had agreed to loan the IMF currencies equivalent to 100 million SDRs (about $122 million) for use in its oil facility, and also had loaned the World Bank $240 million at 8% interest, according to reports Dec. 23.

The Nigerian loan to the World Bank brought its borrowings from oil producing countries during 1974 to $2.8 billion, including a $750 million loan from Saudi Arabia. It was the largest single World Bank borrowing in history, according to the announcement Dec. 17.

By the end of 1974, 33 nations had borrowed a total of 1.716 billion SDRs ($1.792 billion) from the IMF facility.

Interest on the loans, which would be repaid in 16 equal quarterly payments to be completed not less than seven years after the date of the original borrowing, would be 6.875% annually for the first three years, 7% at the beginning of the fourth year and 7.125% beginning in the fifth year.

IMF, World Bank discuss oil-money crisis. The International Monetary Fund (IMF) and the World Bank held their annual joint meeting in Washington Sept. 30–Oct. 4, 1974. The linked problems of oil and money dominated the talks.

A number of proposals were debated dealing with the need to "recycle" the vast amount of money earned by oil exporting countries and the huge sums paid for oil by importing countries, but no conclusive agreements were reached. It was announced Oct. 4 that the IMF would draw up plans for a major new lending operation, administered by the IMF and funded principally by oil-producing nations, to benefit countries that were in financial disarray because of their inability to pay for the needed oil imports.

Participants at the Washington conference were divided over the need for a new recycling mechanism and over the scope of any proposed expansion in the credit program. According to Treasury Undersecretary Jack F. Bennett, the U.S. questioned the need for a larger oil facility. At a news conference Oct. 4, Bennett said the U.S. preferred to deal with the problems of massive transfers of funds by relying on Eurocurrency markets and an increase in investment by oil exporting countries through nonbanking channels. "There is no proof yet" that an official, expanded IMF aid program was needed, Bennett said. The U.S. view remained unchanged, Bennett said, that worldwide economic distortions caused by higher oil prices could be alleviated by a reduction in price.

Although the U.S. appeared unconvinced about the need for a recycling program, most of the participants at the conference appeared to agree on two central points, IMF Managing Director H. Johannes Witteveen reported Oct. 4. "First, it would be neither realistic nor prudent to expect the private short-term money markets—principally the Eurodollar market—to continue playing as large a role in the recycling process as they have in the past. And second, the problem of recycling requires a bigger role for various forms of official financing, with the IMF having a primary responsibility in this field."

President Ford delivered a brief address at the meeting's opening session, urging "solutions which serve broad interests rather than narrow self-serving ones" to deal with "unparalleled disruptions in the supply of the world's major commodities."

Export credit accord—Six major industrialized nations agreed secretly during the IMF meeting to set a 7.5% minimum interest rate on export credits to each other and to oil exporting states. They also agreed that loans would have a duration of no more than three years.

The accord, reached by the U.S., Great Britain, France, West Germany, Italy, and Japan was revealed Oct. 24 during a meeting of European Economic Community finance ministers. The other five members of the EEC reportedly were interested in joining the export credit pact, which had been sought for more than a year by the U.S. The aim of the agreement was to prevent the competitive undercutting of bidding and to bring current export credits—some as low as 6%—into line with the higher interest rates generally prevailing.

2 oil money lending plans adopted. Two aid plans designed to help nations with balance of payments problems pay for oil imports were adopted Jan. 16, 1975 by finance ministers representing the International Monetary Fund's (IMF) Committee of 10 and its new 20-nation interim committee.

In the compromise agreement worked out at the Washington meetings, the Committee of 10, representing major industrial nations, approved a plan proposed by U.S. Secretary of State Henry Kissinger and U.S. Treasury Secretary William E. Simon for a $25 billion mutual aid program. Participation in the two-year "safety net" program would be open to members of the Organization for Economic Cooperation and Development.

At the same time, the IMF's interim committee voted to establish a $6 billion lending operation within the IMF. (The group also agreed to subsidize interest rates for the poorest nations and ease borrowing restrictions from the oil fund.)

The $6 billion program, which was similar to the emergency oil facility established by the IMF in 1974, would be financed by IMF borrowings from oil producing nations. The U.S. had opposed extending a greatly expanded oil facility within the IMF, a plan supported by Denis Healey, Britain's chancellor of the exchequer and others, but in a concession, agreed to establishment of a scaled down version.

The standby fund was intended to function only on a "last resort" basis, spokesmen said. A weighted voting system based on quotas and a two-thirds vote would be required for approval of any loan. However, before the fund could begin lending operations, approval of the program would be needed from parliaments of all participating nations, including the U.S. Congress.

The finance ministers also agreed on changes in several IMF articles. They voted to abolish the official price of gold, which was $42.22 an ounce and agreed to eliminate obligatory payments in gold to the IMF by member nations.

OPEC aid to developing nations. Members of the Organization of Petroleum Exporting Countries (OPEC) gave $8.6 billion in official economic assistance to developing nations during the first nine months of 1974, the International Monetary Fund reported Nov. 19, 1974.

The aid was in addition to the $3.1 billion made available to the IMF's oil facility for use by nations with balance of payments problems, and $1 billion loaned to the World Bank.

Bilateral commitments made by OPEC nations over the nine-month period totaled $6.2 billion. Major donors were Iran ($2.8 billion) and Saudi Arabia ($2.4 billion). Multilateral aid totaled $2.4 billion, with the largest grant ($900 million) earmarked for the Islamic Development Bank.

OPEC creates fund for poor nations—An $800 million fund to provide developing nations with interest-free long-term loans was created by OPEC finance ministers at the conclusion of a three-day conference in Paris Jan. 28, 1976. The amount was trimmed from the original $1 billion pledged at an OPEC conference in Vienna Nov. 17, 1975 when Ecuador and Indonesia announced they could not make any contributions because of domestic financial difficulties.

The Paris meeting rejected an Iranian and Venezuelan proposal to establish a five-year program for the poor nations in favor of operating the $800 million fund for 1976 only. Contributions by individual nations were: Iran, $210 million; Saudi Arabia, $202 million; Venezuela, $112 million; Kuwait, $72 million; Iraq and Libya, $40 million each; United Arab Emirates, $33 million; Algeria, $20 million; Qatar, $18 million; and Gabon, $1 million.

OPEC raises oil prices. The Organization of Petroleum Exporting Countries (OPEC) decided at a meeting in Vienna Dec. 13, 1974 to raise oil prices and adopt a new, uniform pricing system.

Petroleum prices were to be increased about 38¢ a barrel, or almost 4%, Jan. 1, 1975 and were to continue at that level until Oct. 1, 1975. The decision to increase the government revenue per barrel for oil marketed through their foreign companies to a maximum of $10.12 from $9.74 followed a formula that had been adopted by three OPEC members Nov. 10—Saudi Arabia, United Arab Emirates and Qatar.

An official communique indicated that OPEC's action was aimed at further reducing the profits of the major international oil companies.

Under the new pricing system, OPEC for the first time based actual prices on government revenues instead of the posted price, the traditional artificial price upon which tax and royalties were estimated.

U.S. Interior Secretary Rogers C. B. Morton said Dec. 13 that the OPEC price increase would add an additional $4 billion to world oil costs "and further depress economic activity." Morton said "the OPEC government's take has now risen over fivefold since last year—$1.70 then compared to $10.12 now."

The Arab states that acted Nov. 10 had claimed to be aiding consumers.

Saudi Arabia Petroleum Minister Sheik Ahmed Zaki al-Yamani said: "We have taken away some of the excess profits that the companies have been making and we are giving it to the consumers in lower prices."

United Arab Emirates Petroleum Minister Manna Saeed al-Oteiba said: "It is up to the consumer to keep an eye on the companies and prevent them from passing on the higher taxes and royalties through higher prices."

U.S. Military Move Hinted

Bitter controversy flared in early 1975 over U.S. hints that American military force might be used to prevent a cutoff in oil supplies.

Kissinger warns of use of force. Secretary of State Henry A. Kissinger warned that the U.S. might use military force in the Middle East "to prevent the strangulation of the industrialized world" by the Arab oil producers. Kissinger made the statement in an interview with Business Week in the magazine's Jan. 13 issue (made public Jan. 2). It aroused angry world reaction, particularly among Arab oil-producing nations.

Kissinger said the use of force would be "considered only in the gravest emergency." "We should have learned from Vietnam that it is easier to get into a war than to get out of it," he said. "I am not saying that there's no circumstances where we would not use force. But it is one thing to use it in the case of a dispute over [oil] price; it's another where there is some actual strangulation of the industrialized world."

As for possible counteraction by the U.S.S.R., Kissinger said, "Any President who would resort to military action in the Middle East without worrying about the Soviets would have to be reckless. The question is to what extent he would let himself be deterred by it. But you cannot say you would not consider what the Soviets would do."

Kissinger said "the only chance to bring oil prices down immediately would be massive political warfare against countries like Saudi Arabia and Iran to make them risk their political stability and maybe their security if they did not cooperate." He ruled out this action, however, as being too risky since it entailed the possible destruction of those countries' systems and their take-over by extremists, which would defeat the "economic objectives" of the West.

Kissinger reiterated his call for cooperation among the oil-consuming nations of the West to make them "less vulnerable to the threat of embargo and to the danger of financial collapse."

Questioned by newsmen about the interview, Kissinger Jan. 2 restated his belief that the use of U.S. military force in the Middle East was unlikely and that the circumstances that would warrant it were extremely remote. He expressed confidence that "the oil problem would be dealt with by other methods," but, repeating his remarks to Business Week, Kissinger declared that he was not saying "there's no circumstances where we would not use force."

The secretary repeated his assurances to newsmen Jan. 3 and said his statements in the interview reflected the views of President Ford. "I do not make a major statement on foreign policy on which I do not reflect his views," he said.

Ford's press secretary Ron Nessen Jan. 4 confirmed that Kissinger's statement on the possible employment of military action "did reflect the President's views."

Nessen had said Jan. 3 that Ford regarded Kissinger's statement on the possible use of military action "a highly qualified answer on a hypothetical situation involving only the gravest kind of emergency with the industrialized world."

Ford later reaffirmed his support of Kissinger's hint about using force. The President made the statement in an interview in the Jan. 20 issue of Time magazine (made public Jan. 12).

Ford said the key word was "strangulation. If you read his [Kissinger's] answer to a very hypothetical question, he didn't say that force would be used to bring a price change" in oil exported from the Middle East. "His language said he wouldn't rule out force if the free world or industrialized world would be strangled. I would reaffirm my support of that position as he answered that hypothetical question."

Asked to define his definition of the term "strangle," Ford replied "Strangulation, if you translate it into terms of a human being, means that you are just about on your back."

The use of military force in the Middle East as a possible "option" was said to have been discussed by Ford's energy advisers at a meeting Dec. 14–15, 1974 to prepare policy recommendations for the President. A Ford spokesman said Jan. 3 that the President "knew of no plan for military action" discussed at the meeting. However, Ford conceded that such contingency plans might exist in the Defense Department or in other branches of government, the spokesman said.

Arab and other reaction—Iranian Premier Amir Abbas Hoveida warned that the use of force against the oil-producer states by one superpower would result in military intervention by the other superpower and cause "a catastrophe," according to an interview published Jan. 4 in the Egyptian newspaper Al Ahram.

Algerian President Houari Boumedienne said Jan. 6 that "occupation of one Arab state would be regarded as an occupation of the entire Arab world." U.S. military action, he predicted, would destroy the oil fields.

Egypt endorsed Boumedienne's position in a statement released Jan. 7 by Information Minister Ahmed Kamal Abul Magd. President Sadat warned Jan. 9 that the Arabs would blow up their oil wells if the U.S. attempted to take them over by force. Describing Kissinger's remarks as "very regrettable," Sadat said, "We will not need armies, because it is much easier to blow up oil wells than to carry out an invasion."

Kuwait Oil Minister Abdel Rahman Atiki reacted to the Kissinger warning Jan. 4 by telling other Arab oil producers that "any excessive reduction [of oil output] affecting or threatening world interests means placing ourselves in international trouble." A production cutback, he said, could precipitate "a possible war launched against us by the advanced industrial countries."

The Soviet press and television Jan. 6 carried a summary of critical reaction to Kissinger's remarks by newspapers in Asia, Africa and Europe. These comments, the press agency Tass said, showed "that the times of gunboat diplomacy and intimidation are gone."

The Soviet Communist Party newspaper Pravda charged Jan. 7 that "defenders of monopoly interests" in the West were employing "military blackmail" against the Arab oil producers in an effort to bring oil prices into line.

West German government officials and the press expressed anxiety about Kissinger's statement on force, it was reported Jan. 5. A government spokesman said: "I don't see the danger of [industrial] 'strangulation' at the moment. We are not interested in any kind of confrontation with the oil countries, but rather in cooperation. . . ."

North Atlantic Treaty Organization (NATO) Secretary General Joseph Luns said Jan. 12 that any nation "faced with strangulation" was apt "to consider the use of force. That applies to the European countries as well as to the Arabs or to the Soviets."

Consumers Vs. Producers

OPEC to keep prices unchanged. OPEC energy ministers met in Algiers Jan. 24–26, 1975 and decided against any quick change of oil prices.

A communique issued at the end of the discussions also denounced what it termed U.S. threats of force against the Middle East oil fields, declaring that such "threats create confusion and lead to confrontation."

The OPEC ministers agreed to retain prices at their current level for the remainder of 1975 and gradually increase them in 1976 and 1977 on the basis of an inflation index that might be agreed upon with industrial consumers.

Oil users back conservation plan. The 18-nation International Energy Agency of oil consumers met in Paris Feb. 5–7 and tentatively agreed on plans to continue the search for new fuel sources, to reduce their dependence on Arab oil and to eventually force down the price of petroleum. (The IEA was expanded to 18 nations with the inclusion of two new members—Norway and New Zealand.)

The IEA insisted that any meeting with the Organization of Petroleum Exporting Countries be limited to the discussion of the oil problem, despite recent OPEC demands that such a dialogue be held only if all raw materials were taken up.

The Paris conference reacted coolly to an American proposal for a price floor to assure development of non-Arab energy supplies. The proposal, submitted to the Feb. 5 meeting, had been unveiled by Secretary of State Henry A. Kissinger in a speech to the National Press Club in Washington Feb. 3. Calling for a system of floor prices for imported oil sold in the West, Kissinger suggested that the minimum price be considerably lower than the current price ($10–$11 a barrel), but high enough to make it economically feasible for investment in "long-range development of alternative energy sources." The floor-price plan might also encourage oil producers to agree on a long-term, lower-cost arrangement with the oil consumers, the secretary said. The oil producers, he pointed out, would be faced with two choices: "They can accept a significant price reduction now in return for stability over a long period, or they can run the risk of a dramatic break in prices when the program of alternative sources begins to pay off."

Kissinger saw the possibility that once the West began to develop energy sources of its own, the oil producers might reduce their prices to the old levels and make the alternatives non-competitive. "In order to protect the major investments in the industrialized countries that are needed to bring the international oil prices down, we must insure that the price for oil does not fall below a certain level," he said.

Kissinger proposed a five-point program for consumer-producer relations that included exploration of means of investing the oil producers' huge surpluses, ways to help them develop industries in their own countries and, for consumers, assurance of a steady oil supply.

The IEA agreed March 20 to a minimum common price for oil imports as a means of encouraging investment in alternative energy sources.

Under the plan, which the U.S. had proposed, the value of imported oil would be allowed to fluctuate with international market demand. Consuming nations, however, would maintain prices on their domestic markets at a figure to be determined by July 1 through tariffs, quotas or other means. Once a minimum was established, national legislatures would have to approve appropriate measures to maintain the minimum price.

The U.S. had demanded the agreement as a condition for its participation in an April 7 preliminary meeting between consumers and producers. Energy-rich countries like the U.S. and Canada wanted the plan to protect investments in alternative energy sources such as oil shale and coal gasification. They feared attempts by the oil cartel to expand its markets by drastically increasing the supply of oil, thus causing prices to drop and making the development of alternative energy sources not viable. Energy-poor countries, such as Japan, had objected to the plan since it could keep oil prices artifically high. (European sources said the U.S. had a $7.50 to $8.00 per barrel floor price in mind.)

According to IEA chairman Viscount Etienne Davignon, the decision was nearly unanimous, with an abstention by Sweden, which did not yet want to commit itself to a minimum price. Unanimity was thought essential for successful negotiations with producers.

The IEA agreed at a Paris meeting Dec. 19 to propose to member governments that the minimum price for oil be $7 a barrel, $4 below the current market price.

OPEC offers consumers price talks. A three-day summit meeting of the Organization of Petroleum Exporting Countries ended in Algiers March 6, 1975 with an offer to negotiate with industrial consumer nations on the "stabilization" of oil prices on condition that such a conference not be confined to discussion of prices.

The OPEC bid to the consumers was contained in a 14-point charter declaration that also was to serve as the organization's position in its dialogue with the consumers. Among the other principal points of the document:

- Future oil prices must be based on "availability and cost of alternative sources of energy" and the use of oil for such nonenergy purposes as chemical products. The value of petroleum must be protected against inflation and monetary depreciation by linking oil prices to the prices of manufactured goods and services.
- The producers would "insure supplies that will meet the essential requirements of the economies of the developed countries, provided that the consuming countries do not use artificial barriers to distort the normal operations of the laws of supply and demand."
- OPEC was prepared to assure supplies to the industrialized nations to meet their "essential requirements" but would take "effective measures" against any grouping of consumer nations that sought "confrontation."
- The international monetary system must be reformed in order to provide a "substantial increase in the share of developing countries in decision-making, management and participation in the spirit of partnership for international development and on the basis of equality."

The conference failed to endorse Algeria's proposal for a special OPEC fund of $10 billion–$15 billion for aid to developing countries. It proposed instead coordinating grants and loans by funds under control of individual countries or by regional funds.

King Faisal of Saudi Arabia stayed away from the conference, reportedly because of his displeasure with other OPEC countries' refusal to lower prices. He was represented at the talks by Prince Fahd ibn Abdel Aziz, deputy premier and interior minister.

Preparatory oil talks collapse. Oil producer and consumer nations opened preliminary talks in Paris April 7 to map plans for a full-scale world economic conference later in the year but the discussions collapsed April 15.

The stalemate stemmed from demands by the U.S., the European Economic Community and Japan that the international conference be confined to energy and related economic problems, while oil-producing Algeria, Saudi Arabia, Venezuela and Iran, and three non-oil producing countries—Zaire, Brazil and India—insisted that the projected meeting be broadened to include the discussion of raw materials and development aid.

OPEC raises oil price by 10%. The Organization of Petroleum Exporting Countries agreed Sept. 27, 1975, at the end of a four-day meeting in Vienna, to a 10% increase in the price of oil, effective Oct. 1, and to maintain that cost level until June 30, 1976.

The OPEC action rasied the market price of a barrel of oil from $10.46 to $11.51 and was expected to increase the world oil bill by about $10 billion annually. On the basis of 1974 imports, the U.S. was expected to pay an added cost of more than $2 billion for imported oil, Western Europe more than $5 billion, and Japan between $1.7 billion and $2 billion.

The OPEC decision on the 10% price increase represented a compromise that followed several days of sharp wrangling between member nations favoring a considerable higher boost and others advocating a lesser rise. Saudi Arabia sought to continue prices at their current level or to hold any rise to 5%. Iran led a group that at first backed a 28% increase and later scaled down its demands to 15%. The Saudis argued that further increases would slow world economic recovery. The compromise had been worked out by Venezuela, supported by Kuwait, the United Arab Emirates and Algeria. There also was a dispute over the extent of any price freeze once a new level was set, with Saudi Arabia pressing for a freeze that would continue through 1976.

Oil users score price rise—President Ford said Sept. 27 that he regretted the OPEC price increase, "even though it reflects a moderating influence by some oil-producing countries." Nevertheless, it would "have a significant impact," worsening "inflation throughout the world" and hampering "the fragile process of economic recovery," he said.

Secretary of State Henry A. Kissinger described the increase as "a middle-line compromise," higher than the U.S. might have wanted, but "better than it could have been."

Following a special Japanese cabinet meeting Sept. 29 to consider the OPEC action, Deputy Premier Takeo Fukuda said the oil price increase would seriously affect the government's economic recovery program announced Sept. 16. That plan provided for an outlay of $6.7 billion to lift the economy from its 1.8% growth rate in the six months ending Sept. 30 to 6% for the six months ending March 31, 1976. Fukuda said the oil price rise would delay the program and imperil the government's goal of keeping inflation under control.

Indian Petroleum Minister Keshava Deva Malavia said Sept. 27 that the price increase was "bad news" for India. An oil official said the increase would add about $114 million to India's annual expenditure of $1.467 billion on oil imports.

Tanzania's commerce and industries minister, Amir Jamal, Sept. 29 assailed the OPEC increase, asserting that it appeared the oil producers were turning "their backs on the developing countries, particularly the least developed." OPEC's decision, he said, would cost Tanzania an additional $10 million in foreign exchange.

Canada raises price for gas to U.S. The Canadian National Energy Board (NEB) and the U.S. Federal Power Commission March 18, 1975 approved the short-term export sale of up to 55 million cubic feet a day of Canadian natural gas to the U.S. at prices averaging $1.61 to a maximum of $1.91 per 1,000 cubic feet. The gas, purchased from Pan-Alberta Gas, Ltd., would be supplied over 19 months, beginning Oct. 1, to the U.S. Pacific Northwest by the Northwest Pipeline Corp. of Salt Lake City.

NEB officials said the record high prices were granted as an exemption from the $1 per cubic foot border price. The main factor in the higher price was that the contract required Northwest Pipeline to pay for almost complete amortization over the 19-month delivery period of extra pipeline facilities required in Alberta and British Columbia to bring the gas into production.

The Canadian energy minister announced May 5 that the export price of natural gas would rise by 60¢, in two installments during 1975. The border price per 1,000 cubic feet would go up from $1 to $1.40 Aug. 1 and to $1.60 Nov. 1.

The announcement was criticized by the U.S. State Department May 6. The sole foreign importer of Canadian natural gas, the U.S. imported approximately one trillion cubic feet of gas annually from Canada, or about 45% of total Canadian production. The increased export price would cost U.S. purchasers an additional $583 million a year.

Ottawa's decision to implement a two-phase increase was a concession to the U.S., which had strongly opposed the scheduled single-phase increase.

The energy minister, Donald Macdonald, also predicted future increases, saying the export price of Canadian natural gas would be equal to the world market price in two years.

In another announcement made May 5, the National Energy Board disclosed that the export tax on a barrel of crude oil would drop 80¢ effective June 1, lowering the tax to $4.20–$4.70 a barrel, depending on the quality of oil.

In announcing the tax cut, the NEB cited the need to make Canadian oil more competitive in U.S. markets. The U.S. was the only importer of Canadian oil.

The Canadian government announced Nov. 20, however, that it was further reducing its scheduled estimate of oil exports to the U.S. Ottawa cut the 1976 export rate to an average of about 500,000 barrels a day, effective Jan. 1. This was 50,000 barrels below the level previously assigned. The government said all petroleum exports would be phased out by the end of 1981, or two years earlier than had been planned.

According to the revised schedule, the 1976 export rate would be set at 510,000 barrels a day for the first months of the year, but would be gradually reduced to 250,000 barrels a day.

FOOD

International Grain Trade

Massive sales of U.S. grain to the Soviet Union in 1972 had resulted in bitter controversy. Arrangements for the sales had been made quietly after the U.S.S.R. and many other nations had suffered severe crop failures.

Critics charged that the sales depleted U.S. grain reserves, caused higher prices for food in the U.S. and abroad, cheated American farmers of the higher prices they would have charged had they been informed of the U.S.S.R.'s situation, cost the U.S. heavily in subsidy payments and unduly enriched international grain traders.

U.S. government officials defended the sales as providing markets for U.S. farmers, reducing U.S.-Soviet tensions and improving the U.S.' balance of international payments. But since then the U.S. has been wary of making large, secret grain deals with the Soviets.

Problems therefore arose following new grain deals with the U.S.S.R. in the fall of 1974.

U.S. halts grain to U.S.S.R., sets curbs. Officials of two big U.S. grain exporting firms agreed Oct. 5, 1974 to cancel Soviet orders for corn and wheat valued at $500 million after meeting at the White House with President Ford, Treasury Secretary William E. Simon and Agriculture Secretary Earl L. Butz.

In a statement issued later that day, the White House said that at the meeting with representatives of Continental Grain Co. and Cook Industries Inc., Ford had "expressed his strong concern about the potential domestic impact that such sales could have at a time when the U.S. is experiencing a disappointing harvest of feed grains."

Although Butz told reporters that the Soviet shipments had been halted voluntarily by the exporting firms, the White House had indicated its displeasure with the sales Oct. 4 when Simon announced that the shipments were "being held in abeyance" until grain officials could meet with the President the next day. The announcement was made only hours after the Agriculture Department released reports of contracts signed by Continental and Cook to supply the Soviet Union with 2.4 million tons of corn and 1 million tons of wheat.

Although spokesmen for the Agriculture Department denied that Simon's action constituted an "embargo" on grain exports, Simon said he was also issuing a directive from Ford that "all major exporting companies be informed that for the time being he expects no large contracts for grain will be signed in the future without specific prior approval by the White House."

President Ford attempted to defuse the political impact of the new Soviet grain order when a "modified form of control over grain exports" was outlined for the Administration Oct. 7 by Secretary Butz.

Although he described the plan as "voluntary," Butz added, "It's no use kidding ourselves; this is a modified form of controls."

Butz said the voluntary system would apply to exports of wheat, corn, sorghum, soybeans and soybean flour. Exporters would be required to obtain advance approval from the Agriculture Department for sales involving more than 50,000 tons of a particular commodity on a single day "for shipment to any one country of destination" or when cumulative sales of any commodity to a single destination exceeded 100,000 tons in a week. Advance approval was also necessary when changes in export destinations under existing contracts (including the category of "unknown" destinations) affected more than 30,000 tons of one commodity in a single day or over 100,000 tons during a week. However, the criteria for rejecting export orders had not yet been determined, Agriculture Department spokesmen said.

The aim of the voluntary plan, Butz said, was the "freest possible flow of supplies." He attempted to reassure Japan and other nations, which had traditionally relied on U.S. grain exports to supplement their food supplies, that U.S. shipments were not being curtailed by the new program, although he admitted that if the voluntary system failed, mandatory export curbs would have to be imposed.

Continental said Oct. 7 that it had informed the Agriculture Department Sept. 30 that the Soviet Union was making purchase inquiries about corn. After consultation with government officials, Continental said the sale was limited to about 1 million tons (38 million bushels). The Agriculture Department was informed that the deal had been completed Oct. 3. Cook also announced Oct. 7 that it had reported a corn sale totaling 1.4 million tons and a 1 million ton sale of wheat to the department Oct. 4. Notification of the contracts prompted Ford to issue his order Oct. 5 delaying the sales.

At his news conference Oct. 7, Butz accepted some of the blame for the "very embarrassing" cancellation of the Soviet efforts to conclude the grain deal. Butz conceded that he had not been "firm enough" in warning Soviet officials and U.S. exporters that the Administration would not permit repetition of the massive 1972 grain purchases in light of poor 1974 harvests and reduced reserves. "Errors were made on a number of fronts," Butz said.

Butz's handling of the Soviet contracts was criticized by Secretary of State Henry Kissinger at a news conference Oct. 7. He said there was a "strong possibility that we may have misled the Soviet Union as to what we thought we could deliver over a period of time."

White House Press Secretary Ron Nessen said Oct. 7 that the Administration regarded the Soviet Union as a "valuable customer" and that objections to the sale were largely related to the timing of the shipments.

(The New York Times reported Oct. 5 that sources on the Kansas City Board of Trade, a major commodity market, were "puzzled" by the Administration's unexpected decision to halt sales to the Soviet Union. Since July 1, more than 1 million tons of wheat [49 million bushels] had been shipped to China. "Not a word came from Washington about the sale to China, so we're as puzzled as everybody else about why the Russian sale was suddenly halted," the sources said.)

Hearings probe grain sale halt—The Senate Permanent Investigations Subcommittee held hearings Oct. 8 on the aborted grain deal.

Officials of Cook Industries and Continental Grain testified that Agriculture Secretary Butz had been informed of the Soviet intentions Sept. 25 but that he took no actions opposing the sales.

Bernard Steinweg of Continental testified that Butz had specifically approved the sale of 1 million tons of corn Oct. 1, three days before final negotiations were abruptly halted by the Administration. Butz confirmed the account in later testimony, saying he assumed the Soviets would buy no more grain. Butz said he told Continental Oct. 2 not to sell 2 million tons of wheat to the Soviets, and that it was not apparent to him until Oct. 4 that the Soviets intended to purchase up to 6 million tons of grain.

Butz said Soviet Ambassador Anatoly F. Dobrynin had told him Sept. 26 that Soviet grain purchases would be "modest." Dobrynin would not provide actual figures, Butz added.

Subcommittee chairman Henry Jackson (D, Wash.) responded, "If they don't tell us, I don't think they should be allowed into the marketplace."

Grain company officials recounted their talk at the White House Oct. 5 with President Ford and Administration officials. According to Edward W. Cook, Ford "said that there was a political problem with Congress and a political problem with the people, who would be irate at sales to Russia of this magnitude." Steinweg concurred with that account, and Butz admitted that political considerations surrounding the Soviet sale were discussed.

Cook and Steinweg differed on another point, however. Cook testified that he had been told by William D. Eberle, Ford's trade negotiator, that no future sales would be permitted to China, the Soviet Union or members of the Organization of Petroleum Exporting Countries. Because of this warning, Cook said he canceled a 400,000 ton wheat sale to Iran. Steinweg testified that he was not told of any ban, and that Continental had just sold Iran 160,000 tons of wheat.

(It was reported Oct. 14 that barley and oats had been added to the Agriculture Department's list of grain commodities requiring Administration approval before being sold abroad.)

Corn reserves at 26-year low—The Agriculture Department announced Oct. 24 that the nation's corn reserves totaled 481 million bushels on Oct. 1, its lowest level since 1948. Corn stocks were 32% lower than in 1973. The reduction was attributed to heavy domestic and international demand. The figures did not include the 1974 harvest, which had been damaged by drought and frost.

(The International Wheat Council estimated world wheat production, excluding China, to be about 325 million tons in 1974, compared with 342.1 million tons in 1973, it was reported Dec. 19. Bad weather was blamed for the reduced production.)

U.S. allows limited Soviet grain purchases. Treasury Secretary William E. Simon announced Oct. 19 that the Soviet Union would be allowed to purchase up to 1.2 million metric tons of U.S. wheat and 1 million tons of corn, valued at an estimated $380 million, through June 30, 1975. The Soviets had agreed not to make any "further purchases in the U.S. market this crop year," Simon added.

Arrangements for the new grain sale had been negotiated by Simon during a recent trip to Moscow. Under the deal's terms the Soviet Union also agreed that shipments would be made in phased intervals to further minimize the disruptive effects of the purchase on the U.S. market.

Simon's compromise plan also called for both nations to develop a supply and demand data system to facilitate a better matching of their grain capacities and needs.

Grain aid program adopted. The U.S. and other major grain exporting nations agreed Nov. 29, 1974 to supply 7.5 billion tons of new food aid, worth $1.8 billion, over the next eight months to nations threatened with mass starvation; but they failed to agree on how to finance the food shipments. The aid plan was adopted at a conference in Rome called by Addeke H. Boerma, secretary general of the United Nations Food and Agricultural Organization, during the recent World Food Conference.

Of the 7.5 million tons of wheat, coarse grains, rice and corn, 2 million tons were covered in existing food aid programs. Among the needs agreed upon were India, 2.5 million tons; Bangla Desh, 2.3 million tons; and Pakistan, 1.5 million tons.

The grain exporting nations at the meeting included Canada, Australia, Argentina and the nine-nation European Economic Community. Among the grain importers were India, Bangla Desh, Pakistan and Tanzania. The Soviet Union and China, who had attended earlier meetings, were absent.

Earlier, in Rome, Boerma had organized a private meeting Nov. 6 with principal grain producing nations, including the U.S., Soviet Union and China, and major importers, including India, to tackle the problem of short-term food relief. Boerma produced an FAO paper which estimated the grain shortage in South Asia and sub-Sahara Africa, as of

Oct. 15, at 7 million–11 million tons, which at current prices would cost about $2 billion, and in 20 other countries, mainly in Africa, at 1.3 million tons. The neediest countries were India 3.4 million–7.4 million tons; Bangla Desh 1.9 million; Sri Lanka 200,000; Tanzania 500,000; and Pakistan 1 million.

A similar meeting was held Nov. 13, at which the U.S. reportedly questioned the accuracy of the FAO figures, estimating instead that the crop need of the five most threatened nations was 10.5 million tons, of which six million had been met and the rest was "in sight" if financing were found.

President Ford Nov. 15 had rejected a request of the U.S. delegation to the World Food Conference that he announce a doubling of U.S. humanitarian food aid in fiscal 1975 to 2 million tons, valued at $350 million, for nations facing famine.

Announcing the decision in Rome, U.S. Agriculture Secretary Earl Butz, chief of the U.S. delegation, said the increase "would have a bullish effect on the market." He cited budget constraints, tight supplies and pressure on already inflated U.S. consumer food prices.

The Administration decision was in response to a cablegram sent Nov. 8 by the U.S. delegation to Ford. Butz acknowledged signing the cable, but said he was merely passing along the request by three Democratic senators in the delegation. (According to copies of the cable reported in news stories, the proposal appeared to be the sense of the U.S. delegation.) Sen. Mark Hatfield (R, Ore.) had joined the Democrats in persuading Butz to send the cable.

Butz charged that the Democratic senators—Hubert Humphrey (Minn.), Dick Clark (Iowa) and George McGovern (S. D.)—had acted "for partisan political gain" and had embarrassed the U.S. delegation by their pressure. "These things have placed the United States in a position of seeming reluctant to go along with food aid," Butz said. "Nothing could be further from the truth." He noted that the U.S. had given 46% of all food aid to developing nations since 1962.

White House Press Secretary Ron Nessen said Nov. 15 it would be inaccurate to say Ford had "turned down" the request for increased U.S. food aid. He said the U.S. would honor Secretary of State Henry Kissinger's commitment of increased contributions in the current fiscal year.

(The U.S. had budgeted nearly $1 billion for food aid programs in fiscal 1975, of which 20% had been allotted for the neediest nations, with the bulk used as a prop for foreign policy. Only $175 million was for humanitarian assistance, or outright food donations; the major share was distributed in long-term, low-interest loans with which nations could buy U.S. food.)

China & Moscow cancel orders. China canceled contracts to purchase 601,000 tons of U.S. wheat, Cook Industries, Inc. announced Jan. 27, 1975. The shipment accounted for about 60% of the 991,000 tons of U.S. wheat that was to have been sent to China by June 30, 1976.

Peking's cancellation of the wheat order was attributed by diplomatic sources in Washington Jan. 28 to concern over its foreign exchange drain and debts abroad.

A second Chinese cancellation—covering 382,000 tons of wheat, the balance of the U.S. wheat scheduled to be delivered to China in 1975—was announced by the U.S. Agriculture Department Feb. 27.

Within three months Canada's Wheat Board sold China about 42 million bushels of wheat valued at about $175 million, it was reported April 7. The wheat would be shipped monthly from May 1975 through March 1976. As in previous sales, terms of the contract called for payment of 25% cash when each shipment was loaded in western Canada, with the balance plus interest payable in 18 months.

The Soviets had cancelled orders for 3.7 million bushels (100,000 tons) of U.S. wheat and was negotiating for the cancellation of a further 7.5 million bushels ordered in 1974, it was disclosed Jan. 29, 1975.

The cancellations would represent about a third of the remaining Soviet wheat orders from the 1974 crop.

U.S. grain export curbs eased. U.S. Agriculture Secretary Earl Butz announced Jan. 29, 1975 that export curbs on wheat and soybeans would be eased. The restrictions had been set in October 1974.

Butz said the action "returns the export trade in wheat and soybeans virtually to a free basis, following a period in which tight supplies forced us into a program where the possibility of export controls was to a degree implicit." The new regulations doubled to 100,000 tons the quantity of wheat or soybeans that an exporter could sell to any one destination in a single day without government approval and to 200,000 tons the quantity permitted sold to a single destination in a week. Butz noted that U.S. supplies of wheat and soybeans had increased and that it therefore was unnecessary to keep so close a watch on export sales.

However, the 50,000-ton-a-day and 100,000-ton-a-week regulations would be maintained on corn and feed grains until the supply situation became clearer.

Soviets buy grain in world markets. A major purchase of wheat by the Soviet Union from U.S. exporters and from Canada was announced July 16–17, 1975.

The agreements with American companies, disclosed July 16, involved 3.2 million metric tons of wheat, or about 117 million bushels. Cook Industries of Memphis was to supply 2 million metric tons, Cargill, Inc. of Minneapolis 1.2 million tons.

A 2-million-ton sale was first announced by the Agriculture Department without disclosing the name of the company. The department said the sale was a direct commercial deal without government subsidies or credit involved.

Confirmation came from Edward W. Cook, chairman of Cook Industries, who landed July 16 in Memphis on return from Moscow and the negotiations. He said the transaction was conducted "with the full knowledge" of the Agriculture Department and the Ford Administration and "it was personally reported" to the department and the Senate Permanent Investigations subcommittee upon his return that day to the U.S.

Cook revealed that the agreement permitted "shipment from origins other than" the U.S. "While most will probably be shipped from the United States," he said, "it is also highly probable that some will be shipped from other grain-producing countries." Shipments were to begin in the near future and continue for 12 months.

Announcement of the Cargill sale was made by the company that night in Minneapolis. Some of the U.S. winter wheat was to be delivered in the summer of 1976.

Based on the current winter wheat price of $147 a ton on the domestic markets, the Cook Industries sale was estimated to value more than $300 million, Cargill's $190 million.

The Canadian sale—of two million metric tons of high grade wheat for delivery in the fall—was announced by the Canadian Wheat Board July 17.

Reports of the Soviet interest in grain purchases had been circulating. Sources at the U.S. Agriculture Department said July 10 the size of the U.S. sales could total 10 million metric tons. The U.S. wheat crop estimate for 1975, released at the same time, was 59.5 million metric tons, 22% higher than in 1974. The corn crop was expected to be 30% higher than 1974's (reported by Agriculture Department officials Jan. 16 to have been 4.65 billion bushels, down 18% from 1973).

Agriculture Secretary Earl L. Butz, in testimony to the Senate Agriculture Committee July 11, said that 38 million tons of the bumper wheat crop was expected to be available for export. Confirming that U.S. businessmen were in Moscow negotiating a new grain sale, Butz said the U.S. could sell the Soviet Union up to 10 million tons of grain "with a minimal impact on the price of bread here." "I said a minimal impact," he added, "not a zero impact."

Further large Soviet purchases of grain in the world market were disclosed July 21–25.

The second round of sales involved 4.5 million metric tons, or 177 million bushels of corn and 1.1 million metric tons, or 50.5 million bushels of barley from the Continental Grain Co. of New York, which said July 21 there was an option in the arrangement to substitute corn for the barley. Shipment was to be made from October through August 1976. The grain could be obtained from any part of the company's international operations, but a company spokesman said "we're hoping that the corn can largely originate in this country." The transaction was valued by the company at about $640 million at current export rates.

Cook Industries then announced July 22 the sale of another 36.7 million bushels (1 million metric tons) of wheat to Russia. Delivery was to be completed in 1976.

The Australian Wheat Board also announced July 22 a sale of 27.5 million bushels (.75 million metric tons) of wheat to the Soviet Union, with shipment between September and May 1976.

The U.S.S.R. bought more than one million more metric tons (37.3 million bushels) of Canadian durum wheat, the Canadian Wheat Board announced July 24. The wheat, which would be shipped from November to August 1976, had an estimated market value of $226 million. The latest grain sale raised the Russians' total purchases from Canada, the U.S., and Australia to about 13.55 million tons.

According to the International Wheat Council in London, the U.S.S.R. earlier had purchased 12 million tons of grain on the world market, the Washington Post reported July 25.

Soviet gold sales seen as purchase hint—Early indications that the Soviet Union might be preparing for North American grain purchases had been seen in growing Soviet activity in Western currency, Eurodollar and gold markets in order to acquire substantial dollar balances, according to a July 8 report from the British news agency Reuters.

Bankers in Zurich, Reuters said, calculated that Soviet sales of gold in recent weeks could have created a dollar income of up to $100 million weekly.

The dollar's recent strong advance in European foreign exchange centers, posting a rise of up to 3% against the West German mark and the Swiss franc in the past three weeks, had been accompanied by steady demand from one country, believed to be the Soviet Union, the quoted bankers said.

The U.S.S.R. was also believed to have sold as much as 50 tons of gold directly to Middle Eastern buyers, the Journal of Commerce reported July 10, thus circumventing European bullion markets which, under present trading conditions, would have registered sharp price declines with the appearance of such a large amount of gold.

In another development, the Soviet Bank of Foreign Trade had completed a record $250 million medium-term loan in Western Eurocurrency markets, it was reported July 8.

U.S. food price rise foreseen—Arthur Burns, chairman of the Federal Reserve Board, told the Joint Economic Committee of Congress July 29 that "there already has been a significant increase in grain prices" as a result of the Soviet purchases.

Agriculture Department officials, who had said earlier that the Soviet purchases would have a "minimal" impact on consumer food bills, conceded July 27 that "there may be some" increase in retail food prices because of the U.S.-Soviet grain sale.

Since July, when rumors of Soviet entry into the grain market had begun to circulate, the Post reported July 30, the price of wheat futures had climbed 30%, rising about 90¢ to $3 a bushel; corn futures contracts had increased 20%, rising 60¢ to about $2.90; soybean prices were up 25%, from $5 a bushel to $6.25. (Drought conditions in the U.S. corn and soybean growing areas also had contributed to the recent price increases.)

Two major U.S. food producers, General Mills Inc. and International Multifoods Corp., July 30 announced a 1.6¢-a-pound increase in the price of flour paid by supermarkets. The 10% price hike was expected to cost consumers an additional 2¢ a pound. Higher wheat prices, reflecting the recent Russian purchases, necessitated the increase in flour prices, spokesmen said.

(In a related food-price development, the USDA said July 24 that U.S. corn and wheat stocks were at their lowest levels in many years. Corn stocks on July 1 totaled 1.1 billion bushels—the lowest level since 1952, 21% less than in 1974 and 41% less than in 1973. Wheat stocks totaled 319 million bushels—the second lowest level since 1952, 29% above 1974, but 27% below 1973.

EEC blocks Soviet grain purchase. The European Economic Community Aug. 1, 1975 decided to bar the U.S.S.R. from buying large quantities of European wheat until the size of the EEC's 1975 harvest was known. The measures included the suspension of export subsidies on all exports to the Soviet Union and Eastern Europe. Soviet officials had approached trading companies in France and West Germany for the purchase of one million tons of grain.

U.S.S.R. buys more grain. The Canadian Wheat Board announced Aug. 13 the sale of 750,000 long tons (28 million bushels) of No. 3 utility grade wheat, the quality used for feedstock, and 50,000 long tons of feed oats to the Soviet Union.

A spokesman for the Wheat Board said the sale was especially important for Canada because it "cleared the system" of lower quality grain that had accumulated in record amounts because of unfavorable weather conditions. An early fall frost had resulted, the spokesman said, in a greater quantity of feed-quality grain from the 1974 summer crop than the Canadian market could absorb.

The export price of Canadian wheat had risen from $4.15 a bushel (after the first Soviet purchase in July) to $5.07 a bushel Aug. 12.

The Canadian Wheat Board Aug. 2 had banned further export of higher grade wheat following reduced crop estimates due to heat and drought. After completion of the latest Soviet sale, the export ban was extended to feed grade grain, according to the New York Times Aug. 13.

The Wheat Board, however, negotiated the sale to V-O Exportkhleb, the Soviet grain trading agency, of 150,000 long tons (5.6 million bushels) of wheat, 50,000 tons (3.3 million bushels) of oats and 300,000 tons (14 million bushels) of barley, it was reported Oct. 10.

The sale brought total sales by the Wheat Board to the Soviet Union for shipment during the 1975 crop year to 4.3 million tons.

The sale of another 250,000 tons of Australian wheat to the Soviet Union was reported Aug. 19, and the sale of an additional 500,000 tons was announced by the Australian government Oct. 9. (Australia Oct. 10 also announced the sale of one million tons of wheat to Egypt.)

Unions boycott Soviet grain loadings. The sale of U.S. grain to the Soviet Union ran into opposition from organized labor over the impact on consumer prices.

Maritime unions of the AFL-CIO called a boycott Aug. 18 against loading grain shipments to the Soviet Union. "We are not going to load any grain to the Soviet Union," AFL-CIO President George Meany explained, "unless and until a policy is set forth and agreed to that will protect the American consumer and also the American shipping interests."

Aspects of the policy demanded by the unions included government, instead of private, control of any sales to the Soviet Union and assurance that a larger portion of the grain would be carried in American ships.

Meany protested that Soviet purchases from the U.S., amounting to 9.8 million tons of grain since July 1, would "cost the American consumers billions of dollars." He said Americans were "still paying" for the massive grain sales to the Soviet Union negotiated in 1972.

Later Aug. 19 loading crews, members of the AFL-CIO International Longshoremen's Association, stopped work on two ships in the port of Houston thought to be taking on wheat bound for the Soviet Union.

Grain shippers and dealers sought court relief from the labor stoppage, and U.S. Judge James Noel in Galveston granted it Aug. 19, issuing a temporary restraining order against the work stoppage and ordering a return to work on Aug. 20. The longshoremen obeyed the order.

President Ford sought to cool the dispute. During a visit to the Iowa State Fair in Des Moines Aug. 18, he endorsed the Soviet sales, saying they were "in the interest of all Americans—farmers and consumers alike." Farm exports, he said, were "a vital part" of the country's diplomacy. Ford said that he expected "further purchases of grain" by Russia but that American exporters had been asked to hold off on further grain sales until more crop estimates were in and a firmer estimate could be made of the impact of the sales on U.S. prices. The order to exporters had been announced Aug. 11 after the corn crop estimate had been reduced because of a persistent dry spell.

Agriculture Secretary Earl L. Butz, who was in Peoria, Ill. Aug. 19, declared that if the unions were so concerned about high food prices "they should stop some of the featherbedding practices that jack up those very prices."

The President urged all sides Aug. 20 to "cool it a bit." Back in Vail, Colo., his vacation headquarters, he said, "We want to sell more, we will sell more" of the predicted record grain harvest to Soviet and other foreign markets. Meeting with a delegation of grain marketing executives, Ford said, "if we just lower our voices a bit, I think we can solve the problem."

He also telephoned Meany that day to urge him to work with Labor Secretary John T. Dunlop, who, with the Commerce Department, was seeking Soviet cooperation to get a larger share of the grain shipments pledged to American vessels.

The impact of the grain sales on consumer prices was disclosed Aug. 21. Butz said food prices would rise 9% in 1975, with 1.5% of it attributable to the Soviet grain sales. This was an upward revision of the price forecast given two months before, when a 6%–8% increase for 1975 had been predicted. Butz said the revision covered the possibility of further, "reasonable" grain sales to the Soviet Union.

Ford-union accord—The Ford Administration and the unions reached an accord Sept. 9. The union leaders agreed to a one-month suspension of their boycott; the Administration promised to try to negotiate new long-term purchasing and shipping arrangements with the U.S.S.R. and to extend its current one-month moratorium on new grain sales to the Soviets until mid-October.

The agreement came out of a White House meeting between President Ford and Labor Secretary John T. Dunlop and AFL-CIO President George Meany, Thomas W. Gleason, president of the AFL-CIO International Longshoremen's Association, and other union officials.

The President also announced, as part of the agreement, that he was establishing a food committee in his office to coordinate the various government agencies involved in such undertakings. In addition, Secretary of State Henry Kissinger said at a news conference Sept. 9 that a long-term exchange of American grain for Soviet oil was "one of the factors that might be considered" in the grain negotiations.

In a speech in Pittsburgh Sept. 10, before a convention of the labor federation's industrial union department, Meany said "the most important thing" in the accord with the government was that representatives were being sent to Moscow to negotiate "government-to-government."

A negotiating team headed by Undersecretary of State Charles Robinson arrived in Moscow Sept. 11 and Robinson reported Sept. 16 that a long-term agreement on grain purchases was acceptable to the Soviet team, which included Nikolai Patolichev, minister of trade.

Another U.S. team, led by Assistant Secretary of Commerce Robert J. Blackwell, was in Moscow negotiating the shipping rate, and it was reported from Washington sources Sept. 17 that the Soviet Union had agreed to pay $16 a ton to American ships carrying the grain. This was well above the previous rate of $9.50 a ton negotiated in 1972. The break-even point for the American ships reportedly was $12 to $13 a ton.

President Ford met Sept. 15 with William J. Kuhfuss, president of the American Farm Bureau Federation, which had objected to the moratorium the Administration had settled upon further grain sales to the Soviet Union. Kuhfuss was given assurance by Ford that more sales could be made to the Soviet Union of this year's grain crop but the President said the moratorium would not be lifted until a long-term agreement designed to protect domestic food prices was consummated. After the meeting, Kuhfuss denounced the moratorium as caused by labor's "selfish interests."

Earlier, before the accord was reached with labor, Agriculture Secretary Earl L. Butz had said Sept. 4 the moratorium would not be lifted until a settlement was achieved with the unions on the loading boycott.

Meany had spoken out publicly in defense of the boycott and labor's role in foreign policy. In a letter Sept. 2 to the federation's state affiliates, Meany warned against those who were "trying to drive a wedge" between labor and "its traditional allies, America's family farmers." The boycott, he said, was "aimed not at farmers but at government action and inaction that benefits only commodity speculators and the big grain dealers and that rips off the American consumers in the interest of so-called detente. That is what the AFL-CIO opposes, not the farmer."

U.S.-Soviet grain accord. The White House announced Oct. 20, 1975 a five-year agreement with the Soviet Union for Soviet purchase of six to eight million tons of American grain a year. The White House also released a letter of intent, signed that day in Moscow, to conclude an agreement for the U.S. to buy up to 200,000 barrels a day of Russian oil and petroleum products.

The arrangement on grain, to be effective Oct. 1, 1976, was for the U.S. to supply the Russians up to eight million tons a year unless the total U.S. grain crop fell below 225 million tons. The American crop had not fallen below that in the last 15 years; in the worst crop year of the last 15 years, 1974–75, it totaled 226 million tons.

If the Soviet Union wanted to buy more than eight million tons in any year, the pact called for consultation with U.S. representatives before further deals were closed with American firms.

The grain specified in the agreement was wheat and corn, with the purchase of each by the Russians "in approximately equal proportions." The purchase of soybeans or other grains, therefore, such as rye, oats and rice, would be outside the coverage of the agreement and not counted as part of the minimum or maximum amounts.

President Ford hailed the grain agreement as promoting "American economic stability" and representing "a positive step in our relations with the Soviet Union." He estimated that the Soviet commitment for a minimum annual purchase of six million tons would represent $1 billion a year in export earnings for the U.S.

With the announcement of the accord, the President lifted Oct. 20 the two-month moratorium on further U.S. grain sales to the Soviet Union in 1975. The negotiations with the Russians, conducted by Charles W. Robinson, undersecretary of state for economic affairs, called for further consultation if the Soviet Union wanted to buy more than seven million additional tons of grain this year. Soviet purchases just prior to the moratorium amounted to 9.8 million tons. Added to some grain sales arranged even earlier, the total sales volume of U.S. grain to the Soviet Union was 10.3 million tons thus far in 1975.

Agriculture Secretary Earl L. Butz, in speaking of the Soviet pact, said that further Soviet purchase of grain this year could have only a "negligible" effect on U.S. consumer prices. The volume of sale permitted the Russians before consultation would not overextend U.S. capacity, he said, allowing for both domestic needs and commitments to regular export customers.

A "negligible" effect on consumer prices from the five-year agreement was also forecast by William L. Seidman, President Ford's economic counselor.

A study released by the Joint Economic Committee of Congress Oct. 20 estimated that the grain sales to the Soviet Union thus far in 1975 could raise consumer prices 1% and that further sales of grain and soybeans could raise prices another 1.4%.

The U.S. and Soviet negotiators had signed an agreement on a shipping rate Sept. 17. Effective from Sept. 22 through Dec. 31, 1976, it called for the Soviet Union to pay $16 a metric ton to American ships carrying the U.S. grain to Soviet Black Sea ports.

U.S. lifts ban on grain to Poland—President Ford Oct. 10 lifted a U.S. embargo on grain sales to Poland. The lifting of the ban, which had been imposed by the State Department in early September, followed the release by the Department of Agriculture of new estimates showing record U.S. corn and wheat harvests.

The decision extending the temporary grain sales moratorium imposed on the Soviet Union to include Poland reportedly had been reached in early September by the State Department in the hope of putting additional pressure on Moscow to reach agreement with Washington, according to the New York Times Sept. 29. A top State Department official affirmed Sept. 23 that State had unilaterally taken the initiative in asking Poland to defer further grain purchases from the U.S. because Poland was inquiring about larger-than-normal purchases as a result of the U.S.S.R.'s expected harvest shortfall, the New York Journal of Commerce reported.

The State Department action had been vigorously opposed by the Department of Agriculture, which Sept. 29 reached an agreement in principle with Poland on a long-term grain trade pact.

U.S. bargainers Nov. 27 concluded an understanding with Poland under which Warsaw would purchase an average of 2.5 million tons of grain annually for the next five years.

Letters were exchanged in Warsaw by U.S. Secretary of Agriculture Earl Butz and his Polish counterpart Kazimierz Barcikowski.

Under the accord, prices would vary with world market rates over the five-year period, with 1976 sales expected to be worth about $270 million. The U.S. had previously concluded two other long-term grain agreements with Japan and the Soviet Union.

(In a related development, Poland had earlier purchased 60,000 tons of wheat from East Germany and 40,000 tons from Rumania, the Washington Post reported Sept. 27.)

Farm groups protest Soviet pact—Major U.S. farm organizations protested the five-year Soviet pact Oct. 21 as federal intervention in the free-market system.

William Kuhfuss, president of the American Farm Bureau Federation, said "the State Department has used farmers as political pawns in its diplomatic game through its manipulation of the market of agricultural commodities." The long-range Soviet pact, he said, "establishes a dangerous precedent for future political international commodity agreements and constitutes further interference with the market system in world markets."

Oren Lee Staley, president of the National Farmers Organization, said the pact was "outrageous and illegal interference with farm exports, not just for this year but for the next five." Staley said the 1969 Export Administration Act "clearly says that exports of agricultural commodities in excess of domestic requirements can't be prohibited or curtailed unless the President determines it's necessary for major foreign policy or national security reasons."

In a speech in Salina, Kan. Oct. 28, Staley contended that the Soviet grain deal was depressing, not increasing, prices paid U.S. farmers. "This means the farmers of this nation have not only economic problems and large companies to fight," he said, "but now they again have the strength of the U.S. government to keep their prices down and drive them down."

Butz optimistic about U.S. supply—Agriculture Secretary Earl L. Butz told the Senate Foreign Relations Committee Oct. 22 the U.S. could supply the Soviet Union with seven million more tons of grain in 1975 without undue strain. "We can go up to that with our supply situation," he said, adding there was "no question about our ability to do it" without adverse impact on domestic supplies.

In fact, Butz continued, "U.S. farmers should be able to boost output even beyond what is needed for anticipated domestic and foreign demand through 1985." Even the highest projected domestic and foreign demand could be met, he believed, assuming moderate increases in demand and a continued rise in productivity, with only about 32 million more acres than the 330 million harvested acres estimated for 1975.

U.S.S.R. buys more U.S. grain. Three U.S. grain exporters disclosed Oct. 24 they had made further sales to the Soviet Union from the current season's crop. The sales, concluded after the recent signing of the five-year agreement between the two countries on grain purchases, totaled 1.2 million metric tons of corn, equivalent to 47.2 million bushels.

The Oct. 24 sales were by Cook Industries Inc., Memphis (500,000 metric tons, or 19.7 million bushels), Continental Grain Co., New York (400,000 metric tons, or 15.8 million bushels) and Cargill Inc., Minneapolis (300,000 metric tons, or 11.8 million bushels).

The Department of Agriculture Oct. 29 announced the sale of 400,000 more tons of corn to the Soviet Union for delivery during the 1975–76 marketing year. Cook Industries Nov. 6 announced the sale of 1.1 million tons more. The two deals increased to 9.7 million metric tons the total amount of U.S. corn sold to the Soviet Union in 1975.

Ford bars withholding grain. President Ford told the American Farm Bureau Federation Jan. 5, 1976 that he would not withhold American grain exports from the Soviet Union as a diplomatic weapon against Soviet intervention in Angola. Such a "linkage with diplomacy," he said, "would mean disruption and hardship for you, the farmer, a serious increase in tensions between the world's two superpowers and no effect on Angola whatsoever."

Addressing 5,000 Farm Bureau members in convention in St. Louis, Ford reiterated that continuation of the Soviet role in Angola would damage the Soviet's "broader relations" with the U.S. But he said "it is a serious mistake to assume that linking our exports of grain to the situation in Angola would serve any useful purpose whatsoever." "In fact," he continued, "withholding grain would produce no immediate gain in diplomatic leverage. American grain, while important to the U.S.S.R., is not vital to them."

There was not the slightest doubt, he said, that "the Soviets could get along without American grain and ignore our views."

In his speech to the Farm Bureau, Ford explained at length his Administration's embargo on Soviet grain sales in 1975.

He had acted then, Ford told the convention, to stabilize the grain export market and to head off action by Congress to set up a permanent grain export control board that would be having the government "running your business 365 days a year, year in and year out."

Ford also told the farmers he was planning to propose changes in the estate-tax laws to facilitate continued family ownership of small and middle-sized farms and businesses. "I want this done," he said, "so that farms can be handed down from generation to generation without the forced liquidation of family enterprises."

Ford Vetoes Farm-Price Props

President Ford in 1975–76 vetoed various bills designed to keep farm prices up regardless of market conditions.

Farm bill veto. President Ford May 1, 1975 vetoed a farm price support bill as too costly to consumers, taxpayers and farmers. Agriculture Secretary Earl L. Butz, who had told Congress he would recommend a veto on the bill, said May 1 the rejection would be the "first test" of the President's determination to stand fast on his budget. The veto was sustained by the House May 13. Its vote in support of the bill was 245-182 (212 D & 33 R vs. 111 R & 71 D), which was 40 votes short of the two-thirds necessary to override a veto.

A White House statement said the vote proved there was enough concern in both parties "to hold the line" on the budget deficit. Prior to the vote, Rep. John B. Anderson (R, Ill.) told the House the President had assured him he would "certainly see that those [crop] loan rates are increased" before allowing market prices to decline "any considerable extent."

The compromise bill to raise price supports had been approved by Senate voice vote April 17 and 248–166 House vote April 22.

The President had promised Congressional Republican farm leaders at a White House meeting April 14 to give serious consideration to the farm bill produced by Congress. But Butz reiterated his opposition to the legislation. Butz announced April 21, prior to the House vote, that following a veto the Administration would increase support levels administratively. After the veto, Butz said May 1 Ford and he felt "it would be inconsistent to veto the bill on cost grounds and at the same time take action that would increase costs." He said the markets would be watched "and if prices turn down again we should be prepared to take action."

The bill set target prices, at which payments to farmers would be made if market prices fell below them, for cotton at 45¢ a pound, corn at $2.25 a bushel and wheat at $3.10 a bushel. The loan levels, at which federal loans would be made to farmers putting up their crops as collateral, would be 38¢ a pound for cotton, $1.87 a bushel for corn and $2.50 a bushel for wheat.

The support price for milk was set at 80% of parity, with quarterly adjustments.

The Administration estimated that the bill would cost taxpayers $1.2 billion; the conference committee estimate was $210 million.

A four-year farm bill had been enacted in 1973 and the bills in the current session were passed as emergency legislation to protect the farmer and consumer in a period of sharply declining farm income and rising production costs.

Tobacco price supports vetoed. A tobacco price support bill was vetoed by President Ford Sept. 30.

Passed by voice vote in both houses—by the House Sept. 11 and Senate Sept. 15—the bill would have increased the price supports by about 7¢ a pound for flue-cured tobacco and 10¢ a pound for burley, according to the House Agriculture Committee.

Ford objected to the higher prices. They would make the tobacco less competitive on the world market, thus endangering the country's trade position, he said, and the bill would add $157 million to federal spending at a time the government was trying to hold down the deficit.

(The government had said June 3 that that 1975 federal price supports for tobacco were being increased about 12% over the previous year's level. The increases were ordered under a law tying the support rate to changes in a government index of farm costs, reflecting higher wages, interest, taxes and other operating expenses.)

Milk price bill vetoed. A bill to increase federal price supports for milk was vetoed by Ford Jan. 30, 1976 on the ground that it would produce "unnecessarily high consumer prices" and "huge and costly surpluses" of milk. The veto was recommended by Agriculture Secretary Earl L. Butz.

The bill would have increased the statutory minimum support level for manufacturing-type milk—used in making butter and cheese—to 85% of parity, or the "fair" price set to balance cost against income. The statutory minimum currently was 75% of parity, and the support level currently offered by the Agriculture Department was 80% of parity, although the payment was closer to 77%.

Under the bill, support levels would have been revised every three months to accommodate changes in costs.

Supporters of the legislation contended it was necessary to offset declining prices and milk production.

(A similar increase had been vetoed by Ford Jan. 3, 1975.)

Veto upheld by Senate—The milk-support veto was sustained by the Senate Feb. 4 with assists from the Senate Budget Committee and Secretary Butz.

Butz promised to raise the milk support level to a real payment of 80% of parity on April 1. And Budget Committee chairman Edmund Muskie (D, Me.) and Sen. Henry Bellmon (Okla.), the panel's ranking Republican, urged their colleagues to uphold the veto on budgetary grounds. The budget ceiling set by Congress in December would be exceeded by the legislation, they said, since the cost of higher price supports had not been provided for when the ceiling was set.

Meat Protests

Calves slaughtered in protest. Members of the National Farmers Organization in central Wisconsin Oct. 15, 1974 slaughtered more than 650 calves and buried them in trenches to protest high feed costs and low prices received for farm products. Ranchers in Texas, Oklahoma and Colorado planned similar protests to dramatize the price squeeze involved in livestock production.

Although President Ford criticized the action as "shocking and wasteful" in remarks made Oct. 16 and despite a loud outcry from the public, the killings continued.

By Oct. 28, the NFO had arranged the slaughter of about 1,000 animals. Because of adverse public reaction to their protest, the farmers decided to send the meat to hurricane victims in Honduras and unspecified U.S. charities after the Dubuque Packing Co. agreed to absorb the cost of dressing the livestock for shipment.

Ford was in Sioux City, Ia. Oct. 31 to speak for GOP candidates for Congress. "I would not come to Sioux City, the heart of the slaughter livestock industry," he said at an airport rally, "and not say a word about the production of meat."

Ford said he had made three policy decisions that day: he would invoke the meat import law if the level of imports reached or threatened to reach that point, and then would "either impose quotas or ne-

Farm Products & Foods: Wholesale Price Index

(1967-100)

Commodity group	Annual average 1975	1974	1975											
		Dec.	Jan.	Feb.	Mar.	Apr.	May	June	July	Aug.	Sept.	Oct.	Nov.	Dec.
Farm products and processed foods and feeds	184.2	186.5	183.8	179.5	174.9	178.8	181.2	182.3	188.2	189.0	190.4	190.5	186.1	186.0
Farm products	186.7	183.7	179.7	174.6	171.1	177.7	184.5	186.2	193.7	193.2	197.1	197.3	191.7	193.8
Fresh and dried fruits and vegetables	183.7	163.7	174.9	169.0	163.8	183.4	183.1	206.7	208.6	179.6	182.6	183.3	179.0	190.3
Grains	223.9	276.0	255.4	242.8	223.5	218.5	213.0	203.3	219.3	237.8	232.9	227.4	207.9	205.5
Livestock	187.9	159.5	156.0	152.0	155.4	173.5	197.9	202.4	211.3	203.0	209.9	207.8	193.4	191.6
Live poultry	189.8	167.3	173.6	176.7	170.1	168.3	177.6	190.6	219.1	202.4	203.9	210.8	203.7	181.3
Plant and animal fibers	153.1	143.0	138.8	135.4	138.3	137.6	153.1	145.4	152.7	161.1	164.0	164.5	167.0	179.5
Fluid milk	180.2	172.8	172.0	172.1	169.9	167.5	166.6	165.5	168.8	176.0	186.0	197.6	207.9	212.7
Eggs	159.8	181.1	168.7	162.4	166.3	140.0	145.5	137.9	139.7	156.7	174.4	158.4	175.8	192.3
Hay, hayseeds, and oilseeds	200.2	245.8	232.4	211.4	194.9	214.1	200.2	190.3	204.6	213.3	198.4	188.4	177.2	177.4
Other farm products	169.7	175.5	172.4	174.5	170.9	168.0	165.3	165.6	159.9	168.1	169.8	174.9	172.4	174.3
Processed foods and feeds	182.6	188.2	186.4	182.6	177.3	179.4	179.0	179.7	184.6	186.3	186.1	186.2	182.6	181.0
Cereal and bakery products	178.0	181.9	182.3	183.6	181.9	179.1	176.2	174.4	176.7	175.8	177.0	177.6	177.0	174.6
Meats, poultry, and fish	191.0	160.6	165.6	164.6	163.7	174.4	190.7	199.6	209.7	204.5	209.8	210.4	200.8	198.1
Dairy products	155.8	146.7	148.3	148.5	148.6	148.9	149.6	150.5	153.2	156.3	160.8	165.6	168.1	171.3
Processed fruits and vegetables	169.8	170.1	171.2	170.9	169.5	170.8	171.0	170.9	169.4	168.6	168.4	169.3	169.0	168.5
Sugar and confectionery	254.3	401.4	358.2	347.3	303.0	280.1	239.6	217.8	228.4	243.2	219.4	208.3	207.6	199.1
Beverages and beverage materials	162.4	158.2	162.6	162.2	162.2	161.7	161.0	160.4	159.4	161.6	162.5	165.1	165.1	165.4
Animal fats and oils	341.8	426.0	407.8	322.2	303.2	323.0	309.4	277.4	410.4	401.2	409.3	392.9	324.4	220.8
Crude vegetable oils	208.1	286.0	276.4	249.9	227.2	222.6	186.2	182.1	219.8	247.7	195.9	180.5	161.0	148.0
Refined vegetable oils	213.2	266.6	267.1	243.8	226.2	218.7	177.9	175.6	219.4	237.0	211.4	204.6	192.1	184.8
Vegetable oil end products	211.5	246.9	247.2	239.5	231.1	223.1	215.5	206.7	203.8	207.9	197.7	191.1	190.4	184.0
Miscellaneous processed foods	178.4	179.1	181.9	181.2	179.8	180.1	178.9	177.5	176.1	178.0	178.4	177.3	176.2	174.9
Manufactured animal feeds	172.1	194.6	185.6	167.6	159.2	171.3	164.7	169.0	169.4	177.4	177.3	177.5	171.7	174.5

Table from Bureau of Labor Statistics

gotiate voluntary export restraint agreements with foreign suppliers;" he would not change the dairy import quotas "without a thorough review of market conditions and full opportunity for our dairy producers to be heard;" and he said "the Administration is not going to permit foreign dairy producers to compete against American dairymen in the U.S. market with subsidized products." "If the Europeans reinstate their export subsidies of dairy products directed at this market," he said, "I will impose countervailing duties on these products."

As a further step, Ford said, he had asked that an effort be made to increase government purchase of beef for the national school lunch program.

Cattle protests continue. An estimated 100 South Dakota cattle producers carried their protest about low beef prices, high production costs and federal farm policies to Agriculture Secretary Earl L. Butz Dec. 12, 1974 when 45 cattle were driven to the Agriculture Department headquarters in Washington. The caravan had left Bison, S.D. Dec. 6 in an effort to publicize the plight of ranchers with a "cross country beef-in."

In other protests, cattle producers in Washington, Minnesota and New York slaughtered calves rather than pay escalating feed costs. Nearly 300 calves were killed by Minnesota farmers Nov. 4, and 100 dairy cattle were also shot by Utica, N.Y. farmers. In one Washington county, dairy calves were being slaughtered at a rate of 100 a week, it was reported Nov. 19.

U.S. sets retaliatory meat import quota. President Ford imposed a quota system Nov. 16 on importation of beef and pork from Canada, charging that Ottawa had erected "unjustifiable import restrictions" against U.S. products.

Ford contended that the Canadian meat restrictions "violate the commitments of Canada made to the U.S., . . . oppress the commerce of the U.S. and prevent the expansion of trade on a mutually advantageous basis." Secretary of Agriculture Earl Butz said Nov. 18 that Washington was willing to drop its new quotas if Canada eliminated the restrictions on U.S. imports. Canada had acted following a dispute over the use in the U.S. of the growth-stimulating hormone diethylstilbestrol (DES).

The White House set the following 12-month quotas, retroactive to Aug. 12: 17,000 head of cattle; 50,000 head of swine; and 17 million pounds of fresh, chilled, frozen, prepared or preserved beef and veal. These quotas compared with the Canadian quotas of 82,000 head of cattle and 17.9 million pounds of beef and veal.

Beef import compromise announced. A compromise plan for 1975 beef imports was announced by the Agriculture Department Dec. 31, 1974. The plan would limit imports to 1.15 billion pounds, an increase of 85 million pounds from the expected 1974 level of receipts, but voluntary restraint agreements would be negotiated with major exporting nations to keep the volume of imports from exceeding a "trigger level" that would require the government to set a formal import quota of 1.074 billion pounds.

U.S., Canada lift meat import quotas. Canada and the U.S. dropped their mutual restrictive import quotas on livestock and pork Aug. 6, 1975. The U.S. acted in response to what the White House called Canada's lifting of "its unjustifiable restriction on cattle imports from the U.S." Canada had agreed to accept a U.S. certification formula on the use of the hormone DES.

Sugar

Ford sets 1975 quotas. The White House announced Nov. 18, 1974 that President Ford had set a sugar import quota of seven million tons for 1975 and extended the existing tariff schedule beyond Dec. 31, when the current Sugar Act was due to expire.

Both moves were aimed at reducing the domestic price of sugar. According to the Administration, the sugar quota was intentionally set at a high level to permit all the sugar sold by foreign exporters to enter the country.

The current quota on sugar imports

was 6.7 million tons and applied on a country-by-country basis, in contrast to the new executive action, which was non-restrictive.

In his statement announcing that current tariff duties of .625¢ a pound would be extended through 1975, Ford noted that if the action had not been taken, the law would have required a tariff increase to 1.3¢ a pound, with consumers eventually paying the added cost.

In a message directed at consumers and U.S. producers, Ford said "there is no risk we will run out of sugar," but he urged increased production. Until supplies equaled demand and the price dropped, Ford asked consumers to "help ease prices by buying wisely, conserving supplies and consuming less sugar."

Ford also directed the White House Economic Policy Board to monitor the sugar situation on a weekly basis and report signs of speculation on the world market that might aggravate supply conditions.

The Sugar Act, which was enacted in 1934 and amended in 1948, had protected domestic refiners from price fluctuations on the world sugar market and had enabled them to obtain exports at relatively stable prices. However, rising world demand for sugar, coupled with reduced crop production, had caused prices to move up sharply higher on the world market recently.

The price situation in the U.S. was complicated in June when Congress refused a plea by domestic refiners to extend the expiring Sugar Act.

Speculation on the world sugar market also contributed to dramatic price increases. It was reported Nov. 11 that Arab oil producers were investing surplus revenues in sugar. Since January, their purchases were estimated at 3 million–4 million tons, about 20% of all the sugar traded on the world market. Another major factor in the price rises, according to an unidentified United Nations official Nov. 10, was a series of major sugar beet crop failures in the Soviet Union. In 1971, the Soviets had sold 1 million tons of sugar on the world market, but in 1973, they purchased 2.6 million tons, and were reported Nov. 4 to have purchased 400,000 tons from the Philippines. However, the Philippines government announced Nov. 7 that all trading and export of sugar would be halted to determine the extent of damage to cane fields following the sixth typhoon of the season.

Sugar prices hit record levels Nov. 19 on the New York Coffee and Sugar Exchange. Futures contracts for March delivery climbed the 2¢ a pound limit to 63.2¢. The spot price, the actual cost for immediate delivery after sale, was also up to the maximum to 63.5¢.

The two major U.S. refiners Nov. 15 announced their sixth major price increase since Oct. 9, bringing the estimated retail price to about 63¢–65¢ a pound. On Jan. 1, consumers had paid about 18¢ a pound. Both firms said the rising cost of raw sugar necessitated the increase.

Hearings probe sugar price rise. The Council on Wage and Price Stability held hearings Nov. 24–25, 1974 to investigate the sharp rise in sugar prices. Treasury Secretary William E. Simon, President Ford's chief economic spokesman, opened the meeting to restate the Administration's flat opposition to price controls on any commodity, including sugar.

The council heard conflicting testimony on the causes of inflated sugar prices. Consumers groups accused refiners of profiteering and monopolistic practices and said a "gross" miscalculation by the Agriculture Department of expected sugar consumption in the U.S. during 1974 also contributed to the price spiral; refiners blamed the increase on speculation on the world markets; economists noted that world sugar consumption had outpaced sugar production since the 1970–71 crop year, exerting upward pressure on prices; a spokesman for the chief sugar exchange market in the U.S. denied that speculators had forced up prices.

At the close of the hearings, council chairman Albert Rees said he was not satisfied with the answers.

Attention was focused on the role of oil rich nations and the Soviet Union in the sugar market. Simon said a government investigation had uncovered no evidence of a "conspiracy" between the Soviets and the Arabs to hoard sugar and drive up prices. Earle MacHardy, president of the New York Coffee and Sugar Exchange, later testified that Mideast nations had bought substantial amounts of sugar, "which is normal for them and each year reflects their consumption increase."

According to a report prepared by the wage-price council staff, "all sectors of the U.S. sugar industry have in varying degrees reaped large windfall gains" or inventory profits, but the growers had been the chief beneficiaries of high retail prices.

Carol Foreman, who headed the Consumer Federation of America, called for a consumer boycott of sugar products during the first 10 days of December.

She also cited the Agriculture Department's forecast, issued in January, that U.S. sugar consumption would jump from 11.5 million tons in 1973 to 12.5 million tons in 1974. This projection, which proved excessive by a million tons, caused the price of sugar to rise 50% immediately, according to Rep. Dawson Mathis (D, Ga.), a member of the House Agriculture Committee.

Wage-price council figures showed that the price of raw sugar had increased 413% on the world market in the one-year period since November 1973, rising from 9.95¢ a pound to 51¢ a pound.

Three of the nation's largest sugar refiners—Amstar, Sucrest and CPC International—Dec. 2 announced a 7% cut in sugar prices (about 5¢ a pound). It was the first price reduction in 20 months and followed announcements of seven price increases over a five-week period. The last increase, totaling about 12%, was announced Nov. 22 by Amstar, Sucrest and the National Sugar Refining Co. Prices also were dropping on the world market.

Price rise studied. In a limited study, the Federal Trade Commission concluded Aug. 13, 1975 that the rise in sugar prices during 1973–74 was caused by "natural market forces" such as weather conditions and low prices that previously depressed world production.

Officials added, however, that the report was based "solely on publicly available information" and that an "extensive inquiry as to the possibility of collusive activities wasn't made."

"The highly inelastic nature of demand for sugar makes the product vulnerable to very large increases in price in response to relatively small reductions in quantity supplies," the report stated in explaining the sudden price increases.

OTHER INTERNATIONAL ISSUES

Money & Finance

World financial problems discussed. Worsening international financial problems resulting from the destabilizing effects of petrodollars and fears that the worldwide banking structure could collapse because of huge losses registered recently in foreign currency dealings were discussed at two high level meetings. The finance ministers of the U.S., West Germany, France, Great Britain and Japan met secretely Sept. 7–8, 1974 outside Paris. A followup meeting was held Sept. 9–10 in Basel, Switzerland by the Bank for International Settlements for the governors of central banks from Group of 10 nations and Switzerland. (The group of 10 represented the major industrial nations in the International Monetary Fund.)

The Paris meeting was called by French Finance Minister Jean-Pierre Fourcade. Representatives of the Italian government, which had not been invited to the conference, joined the meeting after pressure was exerted to secure participation. The group focused on four areas of international concern: the fight against inflation, international money markets, the price of energy, and support by central banks for banks in difficulties. The group agreed "to put the accent on the basic necessity of fighting inflation without reducing the level of world economic activity and without harming employment."

Spokesmen said the finance ministers also agreed on a multi-level approach to the problem of rechanneling petrodollars into the economies of Western countries by dealing with the issue on national and regional bases and through international organizations. It was also agreed that the six nations should coordinate their handling of payments deficits resulting from sharply higher oil import costs.

Regarding liquidity problems and the

recent collapse of several banks, the group agreed on the need for a better exchange of information and closer supervision of foreign exchange operations.

A remark by U.S. Treasury Secretary William P. Simon summed up the mood of the conference: "We are not optimistic. We are determined."

IMF seeks anti-inflation fight. The International Monetary Fund (IMF) warned Sept. 15, 1974 that "inflation is a worldwide problem that must be dealt with before it gets further out of hand."

"At mid-1974," the IMF said in its annual report, "the world economy was in the throes of a virulent and widespread inflation, a deceleration of economic growth in reaction to the preceding high rate of expansion and a massive disequilibrium in international payments. This situation constitutes perhaps the most complex and serious set of economic problems to confront national governments and the international community since the end of World War II."

According to the IMF, industrial nations bore "the chief responsibility" for curbing inflation, "before it leads to serious and prolonged damage to the world economy." Anti-inflation strategies outlined by the IMF would require that these nations accept the politically distasteful goals of a slower rate of economic growth and a higher rate of unemployment than had been tolerated in the past. The IMF also called for a "cooling off period," during which time industrial nations would engage in "demand management to suppress demand for goods, and thus, ease price pressures" with the aim of absorbing "economic slack gradually rather than quickly." "Income policies" providing direct government control of wages and prices were required in some countries, the IMF added.

The IMF acknowledged that the gravity of the situation required "international cooperation of a quality rarely achieved in the past," but it warned that if "unduly nationalistic policies" were pursued, an "international recession" could result.

Americans authorized to own gold. The 41-year ban on gold ownership by Americans ended Dec. 31, 1974 under legislation signed in August. The price of gold had soared to a record $197.50 an ounce on the London bullion market Dec. 30 in anticipation of heavy sales to Americans the following day. But U.S. gold trading Dec. 31 was slow.

Coupled with the steep rise in gold was a sharp decline in the value of the dollar requiring frequent central bank intervention for support. On Dec. 31, the dollar ended the year valued at 4.4463 French francs, 2.525 Swiss francs, and 2.406 West German marks. The pound was valued at $2.3453.

Gold dealing rules — Federal banking authorities set guidelines Dec. 9 for commercial dealings in gold. The Federal Reserve announced that commercial banks would be allowed to buy, sell and hold gold but they were not permitted to use gold as collateral in seeking a loan from regional Federal Reserve banks or in calculating their reserve requirements (funds set aside to support deposits). Banks legally were allowed to speculate in gold, but officials said it would be "preferable" if banks acted only as agents or on an assignment basis.

Savings banks would be permitted to deal in gold if authorized by state law or charter. Savings and loan associations and their parent companies, regulated by the Federal Home Loan Bank Board, were prohibited from dealing in gold. The 12 district Home Loan banks also were barred from participating in gold transactions.

U.S. gold auction draws little interest—Treasury Secretary William E. Simon announced Dec. 3, 1974 that the U.S. would sell 2 million ounces of its gold reserves at public auction Jan. 6, 1975. But Treasury Department Jan. 6 was able to dispose of only 750,000 ounces at its price of $153 (minimum) or higher. The weighted average price for the gold sold was $165.67.

Bids, which ranged from a low of $1 an ounce to $185 an ounce, were received for 954,800 ounces. Foreign banks and foreign citizens were allowed to submit bids for the U.S. gold; foreign governments were barred from participating in the sale. A West German bank submitted the largest single bid for 402,800 ounces.

The U.S. sale price was far below the

London market price of $172 an ounce Jan. 6 and $170 Jan. 7.

As the price of gold declined, the dollar also weakened in European trading. The central banks of West Germany and Switzerland intervened Jan. 6 and 7 to support the dollar and prevent a rapid rise in the value of their currencies. Despite the aid, the dollar reached a 16-month low of 2.371 marks Jan. 7, when it also slipped against the French franc to 4.3985 francs.

Monetary reform talks collapse. The 20-member interim committee of the International Monetary Fund met in Paris June 10–11, 1975 to continue talks on reform of the world monetary system, but the talks collapsed because of U.S. and French differences on the issues of exchange rates and the role of gold in the monetary network.

Although both countries agreed on ultimate goals related to these issues, there was sharp disagreement on the implementation of the broad objectives for an eventual return to "stable but adjustable" exchange rates and a long-range plan to "write out" gold from the IMF-regulated monetary system.

French Finance Minister Jean-Pierre Fourcade, who did not attend the final session, said there was an "irreconcilable" conflict on exchange rates because the U.S. favored a continuation of the present floating rate system guided generally by market forces, while the French sought a return to fixed parity rates.

The French feared that the continued slide in the dollar's value was giving the U.S. a competitive edge in trade. The French also noted that because of the dollar's recent depreciation, pressure was intensifying for oil-exporting countries to raise their prices in compensation for the eroding purchasing power of their oil revenues.

The French supported a resolution empowering the IMF to assure an eventual return to fixed rates. U.S. opposition to this "surveillance" plan was voiced by Treasury Secretary William E. Simon. "We do not feel that the IMF should have the power to mandate a return to a par value system for a country," Simon said June 11.

On the gold issue, the U.S. favored a minimal role for gold in the monetary dealings, while the French wanted gold retained as a central fixture of a reformed monetary system. The U.S. opposed a French proposal that would allow central banks to buy as well as sell gold on the open market, fearing that widespread use of gold in international transactions would cause the metal to return to its former place of prominence in world monetary dealings. If nations were permitted to accumulate gold stocks through central bank dealings, this would abrogate U.S. efforts to reduce gold's role in the IMF-regulated monetary system, officials said.

The deadlock over the gold question delayed implementation of a plan to sell a portion of the IMF's gold reserves, currently valued on the open market at $25 billion, for the benefit of developing nations. The U.S. favored maximum sales of gold to drive down the selling price; the French wanted a smaller-scale sale so that market prices would remain high.

U.S. Secretary of State Henry Kissinger had offered the aid plan. Finance ministers accepted the concept and agreed that gold would be sold to finance a trust for poorer countries. Another part of the IMF gold reserves would be returned to industrial nations, which had put it up initially as a portion of their share in funding the IMF. The world agency would retain at least half of its current stockpile of 150 million ounces of gold to prevent any nation from unduly influencing the market.

There also was disagreement at the interim committee's meeting over a redistribution of voting-right shares in the IMF. It was generally agreed that voting rights for the group of oil-exporting countries should be increased from 5% to 10%, but there was conflict over the corresponding reduction required in the share of voting rights for industrial countries. To protect its veto right over any of the fund's decisions, the U.S. refused to accept a share that was less than 20%. France would not consider a share that fell below 5%.

In an effort to break the negotiations stalemate, Arthur F. Burns, chairman of the U.S. Federal Reserve Board, June 13 proposed that the scope of monetary reform talks be broadened to include the problem of "dollar overhang"—the buildup of surplus dollars abroad. The overhang issue involved the larger problem of excess liquidity, the accumulation of massive monetary reserves, and was regarded as a major factor in international inflation.

Development in the Americas. The Inter-American Development Bank held an annual assembly in Santo Domingo, the Dominican Republic May 19–21, 1975 with more than 1,000 delegates, observers and guests attending from more than 40 countries in Europe, Asia, Africa and the Americas.

The IDB issued its annual report May 19, noting that it had provided a record $1.11 billion in social and economic development loans to member nations in 1974, 26% more than the 1973 record level. In addition, the bank provided $22 million worth of technical cooperation in 1974, compared with $6.4 million in 1973.

Nevertheless, bank officials said the IDB needed an additional $4 billion in capital to maintain projected lending levels. Ten European countries, Israel and Japan had said in 1974 that they sought membership in the bank and would contribute $745 million to it in the next three years, the IDB report noted.

U.S. Treasury Secretary William Simon announced May 20 that the U.S. was prepared to contribute $1.8 billion to the bank in the same period. "The economic development of Latin America continues to be a high priority of the United States government and we look upon the bank as a major vehicle by which that objective can be realized," Simon said.

(U.S. Assistant Secretary of State William D. Rogers said May 20 that the U.S. would give commodity-by-commodity consideration to easing its import restrictions on primary products from Latin America and the Caribbean. The U.S. Trade Reform Act of 1974, which placed restrictions on a number of products from the area, had caused considerable resentment of the U.S. among Latin American nations.)

U.S. out of development fund. The World Bank's 20-member Development committee voted June 13, 1975 to establish a new lending facility that would make $1 billion in low-cost loans available to developing countries for one year, beginning July 1.

The action was taken on behalf of the 126-member IMF. The U.S., however, declined to participate. Treasury Secretary William E. Simon noted that the Administration had had difficulty obtaining Congressional approval for other contributions to the World Bank's aid programs.

World Bank & Fund confer on currency & gold. The 30th annual joint meeting of the International Monetary Fund and the International Bank for Reconstruction & Development (World Bank) was held in Washington Sept. 1–5, 1975. It was marked by the participants' "willingness to compromise and desire for cooperation," IMF managing director Johannes Witteveen said in his closing remarks.

The expected confrontations between rich and poor nations, industrial countries and members of the Organization of Petroleum-Exporting Countries, and the U.S. and France, failed to materialize.

Compromises were reached on two of the three major issues on the meeting's agenda dealing with the long-awaited reform of the international monetary system. Steps were taken to reduce gold's pivotal role in the monetary network and IMF quotas were adjusted to reflect the new wealth and power of oil-exporting nations. But the major issue facing the assembled finance ministers remained unresolved: it was decided to postpone negotiations on establishing a new exchange-rate system.

The U.S. and France, which represented opposite sides of the "floating v. fixed" exchange-rate issue, both eased their positions during the week-long conference and round of preliminary committee meetings that preceded the formal conference.

The chief U.S. delegate to the talks, Treasury Secretary William E. Simon, indicated the U.S. would not object if nations set fixed exchange rates among themselves, as long as the U.S. remained free to "float" the dollar, allowing its value to be determined by market forces.

French Finance Minister Jean-Pierre Fourcade called for a return to "stable but adjustable parities." This position was in sharp contrast to previously expressed French support for "fixed," or rigidly established, rates. Fourcade said French efforts would be directed toward "narrowing the magnitude of permitted fluctuations."

Two other subjects dominated the week's proceedings—the worldwide recession and the worsening payments deficits facing the non-oil producing developing nations.

Most participants agreed that although a "second-half recovery" was well established in the U.S., few other nations showed signs of emerging from the worldwide recession, the Wall Street Journal reported Sept. 3.

In his opening address Sept. 1, Witteveen urged West Germany, Japan, and the U.S., those nations with the healthiest economies, to make greater efforts at stimulating their domestic economies in order to lead the rest of the world out of recession. West Germany, Japan, and the U.S., Witteveen said, had the most favorable balance of payments situation and the best record of fighting inflation. As the world's major trading nations, their efforts to spur internal recovery would have an enormous impact on the rest of the world.

"It is reasonable, indeed necessary," Witteveen said, "to ask these three countries to conduct their [monetary and fiscal] policies so as to take particular account of the international recession and of the serious constraints felt by many other countries in pursuing an expansionary course."

There was considerable support for Witteveen's views from other participants at the conference.

Despite the pressures, spokesmen for the U.S., Japan, and West Germany resisted pleas that they reflate their economies as a means to end the international recession.

In an address Sept. 2, President Ford rejected the appeals for additional expansionary policies. The U.S. recovery was "well under way," Ford said, but he cautioned that it would be necessary to wait an "uncomfortable" period of time to feel the results of the stimulative action already taken. The path to "noninflationary economic growth will not be easy," Ford said, and he added bluntly, "No country should expect the actions of others to solve its problems."

Treasury Secretary Simon echoed these views Sept. 2. "Some have suggested that in order to help other nations out of recession, the U.S. should embark on much more stimulative fiscal and monetary policies," Simon said. "We respectfully disagree."

His immediate concern, Simon said, was that "we have already done too much" and risked rekindling inflation, a view also expressed by Ford. (Fourcade later gave emphatic support to the U.S. position against the additional expansion of economic activity.)

Finance ministers of West Germany and Japan also rebuffed pleas for reflating their economies. They listed actions already taken to stimulate economic activity and suggested that these policies were sufficient for the time being.

The conference also discussed the specific impact of the recession on less-developed nations, which had incurred huge balance of payments deficits as a combined result of explosive increases in food and oil imports and the general downturn in economic activity.

World Bank President Robert McNamara Sept. 1 urged a vast increase in aid to poorer countries. If the flow of capital to the developing world remained constant (in real terms averaging $49.4 billion annually), McNamara said, the poorest nations would show economic growth rates of only 1.2% by 1980, and middle-income countries would expand by only 2.8%—figures far below the World Bank's 10-year growth targets.

Total capital flow should expand to $71.7 billion a year for the rest of the decade, McNamara said, giving the poorest nations a growth rate of 3.2% and middle-income countries a 3.8% expansion rate.

McNamara's views on financing this expanded aid program were in sharp disagreement with the U.S. position. The U.S. felt OPEC nations should make substantial increases in their donations to the World Bank's "soft-loan" (zero-interest) fund administered by the International Development Association. Mc-

Namara expected the U.S. and other major industrial nations to replenish the fund, because he said, despite the OPEC nations' sudden accumulation of wealth, their reserves were being depleted by inflation, a cutback in oil production, and an intensification of their internal development programs and external aid programs.

(The U.S. voiced the only opposition heard at the meeting to an anticipated increase in oil prices by OPEC nations. Simon said an increase "would seriously jeopardize the balance upon which global economic recovery depends.")

According to Witteveen Aug. 30, the OPEC nations' balance of payments surplus for 1975 was expected to total $45 billion, 25% less than the surplus accumulated in 1974.

The 100 nations of the non-oil producing developing world were expected to run a combined payments deficit of $35 billion for 1975, Witteveen added.

To deal with the worsening payments problem, the conference agreed to expand the IMF's aid program, although implementation of most of the proposals required further negotiations.

The IMF's aid package included:

- A new trust fund, yielding about $1.2 billion annually, to be financed by the sale of gold.
- An expanded "compensatory financing facility" to stabilize poor countries' export earnings (but not an individual country's commodity prices). U.S. Secretary of State Henry Kissinger suggested a $2.5 billion facility in a proposal Sept. 1 to the United Nations.
- Further reliance on the IMF's regular resources, which under a preliminary agreement, would be expanded 32.5%.
- The oil facility established in 1974 giving extra drawing rights to nations with payments difficulties.
- The IMF's new "subsidy account," which would extend borrowing facilities with low interest rates to the very poorest countries.

Gold-sale agreement reached—Members of the IMF's Interim Committee agreed Aug. 31 to dispose of one-third of the fund's total gold holdings, estimated at 150 million ounces. Finance ministers reached agreement to sell 25 million ounces, one-sixth of the IMF's gold reserves, at free market prices and use the profits for IMF loans and other aid to developing nations. Profits from the sale, calculated as the difference between the official price of gold, which was $42.22 an ounce or 35 SDRs, and the current free market price of $150 an ounce, would total $2.7 billion.

The committee also agreed to return another 25 million ounces of gold to the member nations that had originally contributed to the fund. Payment would be made in proportion to their IMF quotas.

A third aspect of the agreement was the decision to abolish gold's official price and eliminate requirements for the use of gold in transactions with the IMF.

Final approval of the agreement was needed from the IMF board of governors and from legislatures of the individual countries.

The decisions of the interim committee dovetailed with an agreement reached Aug. 30 by the Group of Five, representing the U.S., West Germany, Britain, France and Japan, and ratified Aug. 31 by the Committee of 10, made up of the leading industrial powers (which owned most of the world's monetary gold).

The five finance ministers, who were joined at their private meeting by Interim Committee chairman John N. Turner, Canada's Finance Minister, accepted a three point-pact covering a two-year period. They agreed that:

- Free market forces would be allowed to set the price of gold and no action would be taken to fix gold prices.
- Aggregate gold stocks held by the IMF and central banks would be increased; however, as the IMF's reserves were reduced, central banks of the 10 industrial nations would be allowed to add to their holdings through open-market purchases.
- Each nation would make a semiannual report of its gold sales and purchases, and would accept restrictions on gold trading that were adopted by the 10 central bankers at their regular meetings in Basel, Switzerland; at the end of two years, modifications could be made in the accord and any participating nation could withdraw from the pact.

The agreements reached by the two committees represented a significant compromise on the differences that had divided the IMF, and particularly the U.S. and France, for several years.

U.S. Treasury Secretary Simon accepted the agreement because he said it advanced the U.S. position that gold's role in international transactions must be reduced, and eventually eliminated.

France, which favored the retention of gold as a pivotal basis for currency values, joined in the accord because it would be allowed to buy and stockpile gold, and thereby maintain its use in government dealings and own gold as a hedge against inflation.

Vital to the compromise was a concession by the U.S., which dropped its demand that there be a two-year ceiling on an individual government's gold holdings, and accepted the overall limit on the combined reserves of the IMF and the 10 central banks.

Representatives of developing nations protested that the agreement would benefit rich nations more than poorer ones. Phasing out the monetary role of gold would "give rise to a highly arbitrary distribution of new liquidity" and detract from the accepted objective to make SDRs, the IMF's monetary unit, the principal basis of exchange in a reformed world monetary system, they said.

Quotas, voting revised—In its meeting Aug. 31, the Interim Committee agreed to double the IMF quotas and voting rights of members of the Organization of Petroleum Exporting Countries from 5% to 10%. (Quotas established the proportion of contributions to the fund made by individual nations, and "weighted" voting rights were based on these figures.)

Reductions were made in the IMF quotas of other nations, Reuters News Agency reported Sept. 1. The U.S. share was reduced from 22.95% to 21.55% and its voting right was cut to 20%; France's new share was reduced to 4.92%; Britain 7.5%; Italy 3.1%; Canada 3.4%; and Austria .85%.

The committee also voted to increase the necessary veto majority from 80% to 85%, thereby preserving the U.S. veto authority. However, the new arrangement also would permit other groups, such as OPEC or European nations, to command at least 15% of the total votes needed to block IMF action on important issues.

A 32.5% increase in overall quotas also was adopted at the committee meeting. The increase, which would raise the IMF's total resources from $29 billion to $39 billion, would compensate for inflation and permit the IMF's lending ability to keep pace with a growth in world trade.

U.N. adopts economic aid plan. The U.N. General Assembly, at its seventh special session on development and economic cooperation, held in New York Sept. 1–16, 1975, adopted a plan for "redressing the economic imbalances" in the world.

The program represented a compromise between the industrial nations, led by the U.S., and the developing countries. The plan did not call for a new world economic order—a goal often proclaimed by leaders of developing nations—but it did endorse certain concepts to which the U.S. objected, such as "indexing" the prices of raw materials to the prices of exports from the industrial nations.

The program was essentially a set of guidelines for detailed economic negotiations between the industrial and developing nations in the coming decade. Its provisions included establishment of a $10 billion fund to protect poor nations from the extreme fluctuations of world market prices for their raw material exports; easier access by developing countries to the capital markets, science and technology of the advanced nations; a redistribution of global wealth through mechanisms for the automatic transfer of funds to poor nations, including changes in the world monetary system; and changes in the U.N. structure to streamline its socioeconomic agencies and enhance the role of developing countries in the organization.

The plan was adopted unanimously, but the U.S. delegation delivered a long statement of reservations, including objections to the study of "indexing" mechanisms and to the plan's stated goal of official aid grants amounting to .7% of the gross national products of nations by the end of the 1970s.

The program evolved largely from a working paper presented to the session by the U.S. delegation Sept. 8. The paper emphasized a complex series of proposals submitted by the U.S. on the opening day of the conference, but also synthesized a number of proposals by developing nations with which the U.S. disagreed but which it was prepared to support.

The U.S. proposals, elaborated by Secretary of State Henry Kissinger in collaboration with Treasury Secretary William Simon, had been read to the conference Sept. 1 by Daniel P. Moynihan, the chief U.S. delegate. They included the $10 billion fund adopted by the conference as well as preferential trade agreements between advanced and poor nations, transfer of technology to developing countries, an increase in funds available to international lending agencies for development loans, and creation of an international investment trust to mobilize portfolio capital from government and private sources for investment in local enterprises.

Delegates from both the industrial and developing nations felt there was a new spirit of cooperation and compromise in the session, and a new willingness on the part of the U.S. to compromise, according to most press reports.

6-nation summit talks. Leaders of six major industrial nations held an economic summit conference Nov. 15–17, 1975 and concluded with agreement that their "most urgent task" was to assure economic recovery and reduce unemployment. "We will not allow the recovery to falter. We will not accept another outburst of inflation," the leaders said in a joint declaration.

Attending the three-day meeting at the Chateau de Rambouillet, 35 miles west of Paris, were French President Valery Giscard d'Estaing, U.S. President Gerald Ford, British Prime Minister Harold Wilson, West German Chancellor Helmut Schmidt, Japanese Premier Takeo Miki and Italian Premier Aldo Moro. The six nations' finance and foreign ministers also joined the private talks.

The talks were marked by a spirit of compromise and cooperation that extended even to the problem of how to achieve currency stability—a matter of long-standing dispute between the U.S. and France.

It was reported Nov. 17 that French Finance Minister Jean-Pierre Fourcade and U.S. Treasury Secretary William E. Simon had signed an agreement that apparently resolved the dispute. The unpublished agreement, it was reported, set down conditions under which central banks could intervene in currency trading to prevent "erratic" fluctuations in exchange rates, particularly between the generally free-floating U.S. dollar and the controlled float of the European "snake." (The currencies of France, West Germany, Belgium, the Netherlands, Luxembourg, Norway, Sweden and Denmark floated together within certain limited ranges.)

President Ford did not comment on the currency stabilization agreement, but President Giscard d'Estaing said that the U.S.-French dispute now was "settled." The six leaders' joint declaration spoke of a "welcome . . . rapprochement" between the U.S. and France on the monetary issue.

According to most observers, French negotiators had made the most significant compromises in reaching the monetary accord. Fixed parities were "conceivable under other circumstances," but not under current economic conditions, Giscard d'Estaing told reporters. The currency system "needs some flexibility to cushion it against the blows to which it is and will remain exposed," he added.

Differences about the degree of flexibility that was required over the long-range remained a matter for discussion, he said. According to Giscard d'Estaing, reform of the international monetary network should aim for a currency system that was "viscous" rather than "fluid." In a viscous system, he said, "movements take place in a medium that restrains them, and this is what we have achieved with the European snake."

Settlement of the U.S.-French difference over monetary policy had been a chief aim of Giscard d'Estaing, who had first proposed the economic summit talks.

The monetary agreement was the only concrete result of the summit talks. Other matters discussed were reflation, trade and energy policies and relations with developing nations.

President Ford presented a highly optimistic assessment of U.S. economic recovery and restated his opposition to implementing further stimulative measures to spur the economic revival. Chancellor Schmidt supported Ford on the issue of reflation, noting that West Germany was operating with a budget deficit because of the many stimulative actions already undertaken.

The six leaders acknowledged that "pressures were developing for a return to protectionism" because of the worldwide recession, but urged a rejection of the "beggar my neighbor" trade philosophy in which one nation's trade problems were solved at the expense of others.

All of the six leaders renewed their commitments to the Organization for Economic Cooperation and Development's pledge not to adopt restrictive trade policies, including import controls.

The joint declaration spoke of their energy talks only in general terms. The U.S. asked the conference to support its call for a reduction in imported oil prices and a warning against future oil price increases, but Giscard d'Estaing opposed the move, saying too few nations were represented in the summit talks.

Ford also invited investments from the five other industrial nations in U.S. energy projects. In exchange, he offered them a "portion" of the new energy supplies for export to their own consumers.

In the joint declaration, the six leaders spoke of the need for a reduction in imported energy through conservation and the development of alternative supplies. They also called for cooperation between producer and consumer nations.

Inflation in OECD nations reported. The Organization for Economic Cooperation & Development said Nov. 7, 1975 that consumer prices in the OECD's 24 member nations rose 10.4% during the 12-month period ended in September. That was the lowest year-to-year rate of increase since a 10.3% inflation rate was recorded in the December 1972-1973 period.

Consumer prices had increased .4% from July to August, the smallest monthly gain since 1970. However, inflation accelerated in September, when prices rose .7%.

Paris economic cooperation talks. The 27-nation Conference on International Economic Cooperation met in Paris Dec. 16–19, 1975, but ministers of industrial, developing and oil-producing countries failed to reach agreement on establishing guidelines for their four working commissions dealing with energy, finance, development aid and raw materials.

The final communique represented a compromise between the two factions. Spearheading the oil-producers-developing nations group, Algeria had sought a more detailed mandate for the commissions, as it had in the conference's preparatory meeting in October. Algeria insisted that the indexation of oil and raw materials on world inflation should be placed on the agenda when the conference reconvened Jan. 26. The U.S. and the other industrialized states continued to press for more flexible guidelines.

At the opening meeting Dec. 16, Secretary of State Henry Kissinger had reiterated the American view that "the abrupt and arbitrary increase in the price of oil has been a major factor in rates of inflation and unemployment unprecedented since the 1930s." The secretary called for "a lower oil price that would

Inflation Rates for OECD Nations

	Increase from Aug.-Sept.	Increase from Sept. '74-Sept. '75
Canada	.2%	10.7%
United States	.5%	7.8%
Japan	1.9%	10.3%
Australia	.3%*	12.1%
New Zealand	1.2%*	14.8%
France	.8%	10.7%
West Germany	.5%	6.1%
Italy	.8%	13.0%
Great Britain	.9%	26.6%
Belgium	.8%	10.9%
Luxembourg	.8%	10.8%
Netherlands	1.3%	10.4%
Denmark	.8%	8.6%
Ireland	−.3%*	19.0%
Austria	.2%	8.7%
Finland	1.4%	16.5%
Greece	4.0%	13.9%
Iceland	2.5%	51.3%
Norway	1.4%	12.6%
Portugal	—	10.9%†
Spain	1.6%	17.3%
Sweden	.3%	11.1%
Switzerland	.4%	5.4%
Turkey	—	19.1%†
OECD	.7%	10.4%
OECD Europe	.9%	13.3%
OECD European Community	.8%	13.3%

*quarterly change
†latest available figure

Source: OECD

make possible more rapid economic recovery around the globe."

Some oil-producing delegates rejected Kissinger's arguments in speeches to the meeting Dec. 17. Algerian Foreign Minister Abdelaziz Bouteflika described them as "notorious untruths." Iranian Interior Minister Jamshid Amouzegar blamed "the failure of the fiscal and monetary leadership" in the industrialized world, rather than oil price increases, for world inflation and recession.

Conference participants: Industrialized nations—U.S., Canada, Japan, Australia, Spain, Sweden, Switzerland and the European Community; Nonindustrialized states and oil producers—Venezuela, Algeria, Saudi Arabia, Brazil, India, Iran, Zaire, Cameroon, Egypt, Nigeria, Zambia, Argentina, Jamaica, Mexico, Peru, Indonesia, Iraq, Pakistan and Yugoslavia.

'75 financing at record high. The New York Times reported Dec. 29 that 1975 was a record year for credit markets in the U.S. and abroad.

In the U.S., the federal government raised a record $80 billion, corporations a record $43 billion, and local governments a record $30 billion, despite fears of "crowding out," the recession and the crisis in municipal funding caused by New York City's near default.

On the international credit market, volume totaled $18.4 billion, up from $6.8 billion in 1974. Nearly half the amount for 1975 was raised in the Eurobond market, where volume totaled $8.5 billion, compared with $2.1 billion in 1974.

(The Eurobond obligation, denominated in any currency but traded only outside of the currency-issuing country, was marketed mainly in Europe by international syndicates of banks and securities dealers. A Eurodollar obligation, issued on dollars borrowed outside the U.S., was a type of Eurobond.)

Two significant financing developments occurred in late 1975. The World Bank returned to the U.S. market Dec. 10 after a period of heavy borrowing from Japan and the oil-exporting nations. The World Bank sold $750 million of notes and bonds, its largest financing effort in the U.S. to date.

The largest private placement in Wall Street history was completed Nov. 13 when 76 institutional lenders, led by major insurance companies and pension funds, committed themselves to the purchase of $1.75 billion of notes sold by Standard Oil Co. (Ohio) and British Petroleum Co. to finance the Alaskan pipeline. (In a private placement, securities were not traded on the public market.) The financing was arranged by Morgan Stanley & Co.

Financial analysts cited in the Times Dec. 15 said that Eastern European countries had accumulated a debt of $7 billion–$9 billion in the West during 1975, bringing the total Eastern debt with Western nations to approximately $32 billion.

Much of the borrowing, the analysts said, had been made to finance a growing trade deficit with the West, only a small part of it due to Eastern grain purchases. The deficit was instead attributed to "an unanticipated falloff in Eastern European exports as a result of the recession and slow down of demand in Western Europe and the U.S."

Chase Manhattan Bank officials estimated that the 1974 deficit of $5 billion had grown to $12 billion during 1975, with the Soviet Union accounting for almost half the total.

In efforts to finance the Western imports through credit channels, the members of the Council for Mutual Economic Assistance (Comecon) had raised more than $6 billion on the Eurocurrency market. Analysts said international banks had expressed reluctance to make further loans because of the Eastern nations' growing debt.

Monetary reform agreement. Finance ministers of rich and poor nations attending an International Monetary Fund conference in Jamaica reached agreement Jan. 8, 1976 on plans to reform the world currency system and to give additional IMF aid to developing nations.

Acceptance of the proposals by the IMF's Interim Committee of 20, representing industrial and developing nations, ended more than three years of debate over the restructuring of the world monetary system.

The proposed revision of the IMF charter had three basic features:

Floating Rates—"Floating" rates, based on market conditions of supply and demand, won official recognition, but a stable system of exchange remained the IMF's chief objective. "Managed" floats, in which central banks intervened to prevent erratic and disorderly fluctuations in value, were authorized to foster the operation of a flexible, but stable rate system.

However, "dirty" floats, in which central banks intervened to halt an upward or downward trend in currency valuation were barred. Countries were required to "avoid manipulating exchange rates or the international monetary system in order to prevent effective balance-of-payments adjustments or to gain an unfair competitive advantage over other members."

The new rules made a return to fixed exchange rates technically possible, but highly improbable. An 85% majority of the IMF's total voting power was required to authorize a restoration of fixed rates. Since the U.S. held 20% of the fund's total voting power, it could veto this or any other change requiring an 85% majority.

As a concession to the French, who favored fixed parities, the draft proposals would let a nation set a par value for its currency, but not in terms of gold. Parity would be established with the IMF's special drawing right, thus making the SDR the "principal reserve asset of the international monetary system," replacing gold.

If a country desired to set a par value for its currency, concurrence of the IMF would be required. The country also was required to agree to maintain its par value by intervention in the market so that rate fluctuations would be limited to a band of 4.5%, "or by other such margin as the fund may adopt by an 85% majority."

Since flexibility was the hallmark of the new system, the draft proposals allowed a country to change its par value to correct "or prevent the emergence of" fundamental disequilibrium in the currency's value. A country could abandon its par value by notifying the IMF; an 85% majority was required to force a continued adherence to the par value. If a country abandoned the parity despite an 85% vote by the fund for retention, that country would face sanctions, such as loss of credit facilities at the IMF and expulsion from the fund.

There were two fundamental differences between the Jamaica agreements and the Bretton Woods system, according to Edwin H. Yeo, U.S. Treasury undersecretary for monetary affairs, Jan. 9.

The new system recognized that substantial flows of capital across national borders affected the market value of national currencies, Yeo said. As examples, he cited the effect of interest rates in Europe on the dollar—when European rates were high, investors sold dollars and bought European currencies. In contrast, when the Bretton Woods charter was drawn up, international capital markets were smaller and less mobile. Until recently, he added, the balance of trade in goods and services had had a more substantial impact on currency rates than capital flows.

Yeo said another difference between the two systems, drafted more than 30 years apart, was the belief, embodied in the Bretton Woods Agreement, that a strict monetary system would impose stability on exchange rates, regardless of a country's underlying economic condition. Under the Bretton Woods system, nations had been required to set par values for their currencies and defend them, even at great cost, until overwhelming market forces forced a change.

Yeo said the new system would promote currency stability by creating stability in the underlying economic situation.

It became evident that reform of the Bretton Woods system was necessary when the maintenance of fixed rates led to excessively costly support operations by central banks.

Gold sale—With gold no longer the common denominator of the revamped monetary system, its official price of $42.22 an ounce would be abolished.

News of the Jamaica accord sent the price of gold plummeting on the London buillon market Jan. 8 when it lost $2.55 to close at $135.80, a three-month low.

Greater access to IMF loans—The greatest disagreement at the Jamaica talks was generated by the issue of the amount and conditions of new IMF credit facilities to be provided poor nations to overcome balance-of payments problems.

Under current IMF rules, member nations could borrow up to 25% of their quotas in each of four credit facilities, or tranches. There were few borrowing restrictions on the first tranch, but the conditions became gradually more stringent for each of the three other tranches.

The new liberalized credit policy accepted at the Jamaica meeting made no changes in conditions on borrowing but provided a 45% increase in borrowing under each of the four credit categories: a member nation could borrow up to 36.25% of its quota in each category to a total of 145% compared with 100% under existing rules.

(The 45% increase in borrowing rights was only a temporary measure, lasting about two years until a one-third increase in members' quotas, from $36 billion to $48 billion, was completed. The higher quotas would automatically increase members' access to IMF credit.)

During the meeting in Jamaica, finance ministers from developing countries argued strenuously for increased access to IMF loans and an easing of conditions for obtaining the credit.

Industrial nations, led by the U.S., West Germany and the Netherlands, opposed these demands, fearing that too-easy access to the IMF would make the fund a foreign-aid agency.

There was disagreement on another aspect of the IMF's credit policy, i.e., what currencies the IMF should use in making loans. For many years, it was the practice to use the currencies of nations with balance-of-payments surpluses. However, recently, oil exporting nations, with huge surpluses, had refused to allow the use of their currencies in IMF loan transactions.

The U.S. insisted that these currencies be made available, and won its point at Jamaica. The new accord promised that currencies of the oil-producing nations would be made available "within six months." Upon ratification of the new agreement, member nations would be obligated to make their currencies available for use in IMF loans.

Index

A

G

J

K

L

M

U

V

W